WOODEN TITAN

PRESIDENT VON HINDENBURG—1925

HINDENBURG

IN TWENTY YEARS OF
GERMAN HISTORY
1914 - 1934

By John W. Wheeler-Bennett

HAMDEN   ARCHON BOOKS   LONDON

TO

MRS. ANDREW J. GEORGE

WITH GRATEFUL AFFECTION

INTRODUCTION

✠

MY INTENTION to write this book arose originally from a conversation at a dinner-party in Berlin during the fateful summer of 1932, which witnessed the close of the Weimar Period in postwar German history and the ringing up of the curtain on the Prelude to Hitler.

The past days had been full of great happenings. The Chancellor, Dr. Brüning, had resigned together with his Cabinet, and his successor was Herr von Papen, nominally a man of the President's own choice, actually the nominee and puppet of the leaders of the Palace *Camarilla*, General Kurt von Schleicher, the President's own son, Colonel Oskar von Hindenburg, and the Secretary of State, Dr. Meissner.

Later, a decree had been published dissolving the *Reichstag* and fixing July 16 as the date for new elections. The *Reichstag* President, Dr. Löbe, had gone at once to the President to protest against the dissolution of a body which only a few days before had given a vote of confidence to Dr. Brüning's Government, and, alternatively, if there must be new elections, to secure the President's assurances that the liberty of the voter should be guaranteed as heretofore. As a result, an anxiously expectant public was informed that President von Hinderburg had promised full liberty to the electorate and that the elections should be held in the usual manner.

It was this latest event which formed the general topic of conversation at dinner, and the anxiety of many of those present was in great measure relieved by it. If the President had given his word everythng would be all right. At length, however, a very different view was put forward by a retired naval officer, since dead, who had earned great distinction during the war.

"Hindenburg's record is a bad one," he said. "Ludendorff won his battles for him, and he betrayed Ludendorff; the Kaiser made him a Field-Marshal, and he betrayed the Kaiser; the Right elected him in 1925, and he betrayed the Right; the Left elected him in 1932, and he has betrayed the Left. Were I Löbe, I would not put too much faith in Hindenburg's promises."

"And," added someone, "if you remember, there was another Paul von Hindenburg."

The significance of the last remark escaped me, but the officer's statement came as a very definite shock to my beliefs concerning the President. In company, I believe, with most Englishmen, I entertained a strong admiration for the veteran Field-Marshal, regarding him as the almost ideal type of single-minded patriot who had twice emerged from a well-earned retirement to answer his country's call to further service, and having every claim to the title of *Vater des Volkes*, and the more familiar and endearing designation *Der Alte Herr*.

To one holding these views, therefore, the naval officer's strictures sounded little short of blasphemy, and I left that evening with the firm intention of investigating them with the greatest care, for it seemed necessary in the interest of historical truth that they should either be substantiated or disproved.

As a result, then, of researches which have involved, besides consultations of memoirs and official documents, long conversations with those best qualified to know and state the facts of the case, I believe that it is not inadmissible to place upon certain of the principal events in the life of Marshal von Hindenburg the interpretation put on them by the naval officer, more particularly, perhaps, upon those which occurred after his remark was made. But like most generalities of its kind, which are apt to be made by strong individual personalities, it was an over-statement.[1]

Essentially Hindenburg's character shows him to have been a man of service, without ambition, and with no love of pomp and ceremony. He had little regard for reward; he asked simply, throughout the seventy years of his active life, "Where can I serve?" but he did not always consider sufficiently the answer. Once convinced along what line his duty lay—and the ease with which conviction was achieved became progressively greater with advancing years—he would pursue that policy with obstinate stolidity and little discrimination until deflected towards some other path of service.

With a temperament of this nature it was impossible to escape the charges of disloyalty and betrayal, more particularly as the changes of course and conviction became more frequent. But throughout the intricate pattern of inconsistencies which marked the last fifteen years of Hindenburg's life there ran the single thread of service to Germany which had dominated his whole career.

Not the least remarkable part of that career was the legend which suddenly surrounded his name, and the manner of its birth. If ever there was a victim of a legend it was Hindenburg, for, despite himself, he was in time translated from a military sphere, for which he was eminently well fitted by training and tradition, to the political arena, for which he had neither liking, aptitude, nor equipment. His misfortune was the sudden attainment of almost supernatural adoration on the part of the German people, who elevated him to the position of a god and expected from him god-like achievements.

The story of his life is both pitiful and tragic, for no figures in history are more tragic than those who have outlived the faith

[1] It will be remembered, for example, that the German General Elections of July 1932 were held in perfect freedom though the campaign preceding them was marred by much violence.

in their greatness, and Hindenburg must be numbered amongst these. It was not given to him to die before his name had become one for execration by many of his countrymen.

In approaching my subject my greatest difficulty has been one of focus. Hindenburg's personality is an elusive one, or perhaps it is truer to say that it has a "self-protective colouring"; it is continually melting into the background. For the Marshal very rarely dominated the events of his long lifetime. Far more often he was dwarfed by them, and always he played the part of a façade. At no time can it be said that he was a free agent. Forces for good and evil used his name and his legend to promote policies or to facilitate intrigue. Throughout he remained a Wooden Titan, a giant among men, but a dumb giant.

For this reason it has been necessary to consider in rather greater detail than the reader may at first think justified the circumstances and personalities which controlled and influenced Hindenburg throughout his long life. Because of the tendency of the central figure to merge into the background, it is essential to understand fully what the background was, and only by this means is it possible to arrive at even a partially faithful picture. This, then, is what I have tried to do.

For reasons which I am sure will be fully understood it is impossible for me to acknowledge my indebtedness publicly by name to many of those whose recollections have provided so important a part of my material. They themselves know how deeply grateful I am to them.

I can and must, however, express my most sincere gratitude to those whose advice has proved of such great assistance to me, and first amongst these is my friend Professor L. B. Namier, whose searching criticism, inexhaustible patience, and warm encouragement have meant so much both to me and to the book. Among others who have been kind enough either to read the MS. or to give me assistance on certain points are Major-General Sir Neill Malcolm, Major-General Sir Frederick Maurice, and Miss Elizabeth Monroe, and for their invaluable help I offer my most grateful thanks. I am also deeply indebted and very grateful to Major Archibald Church. No list of acknowledgments would be complete without a recognition of my deep obligation to my secretary, Miss Margaret Dunk, upon whom has fallen much of the onus of preparation, and to whom I offer my most appreciative thanks.

Lastly, I would say "Thank you" as sincerely as I can to Mr. Gerald Palmer and to his mother for many weeks of their most kind and generous hospitality at "Prior's Court."

JOHN W. WHEELER-BENNETT

PRIOR'S COURT,
CHIEVELEY, BERKS
Feb., 1936.

BIBLIOGRAPHICAL NOTE

✠

FOR a book of this nature it is neither possible nor politic for the author to acknowledge all his sources of information, and this is especially true when the book deals with the internal politics of Germany. Out of regard for my many friends whose help has been invaluable to me, and to whom my gratitude can never be adequately expressed, I will only say that wherever possible I have supplemented the written word by personal conversations with the authors, and with many whose memories and recollections have not yet been committed to paper.

There already exist a number of biographical works on Marshal von Hindenburg, chief among which are those by Alfred Niemann, Theodore Lessing, Frederick Voigt and Margaret Goldsmith, General Buat, A. M. K. Watson, Thomas Ybarra, Gerhard Schultze-Pfaelzer, Emil Ludwig, Rudolf Olden, and Major Gert von Hindenburg. In the writing of this book I have consulted all of these works, of which only the last three have been published since the Marshal's death, but I have been very much more dependent upon first-hand material.

For Parts I and II I have made use of the memoirs and diaries of Hindenburg himself, Generals Ludendorff, Hoffmann, von Falkenhayn, the younger von Moltke, von François, and von Kluck, Field-Marshal Conrad von Hötzendorf, Colonel Bauer, Grand-Admiral von Tirpitz, the Kaiser, the German Crown

Prince, the Crown Prince of Bavaria, Prince Max of Baden, Herr von Bethmann Hollweg, Dr. Michaelis, the younger Hertling, Herr von Payer, Dr. Erzberger, Count von Valentini, Frau Margarethe Ludendorff, Count Ottokar Czernin, Philip Scheidemann, the younger Ebert, Gustav Noske, Lenin, and Leon Trotsky, and of H. E. Armstrong's *Grey Wolf*.

Invaluable material was found in the publications of the Reichstag Committee of Investigation, *Die Ursachen des deutschen Zusammenbruchs im Jahre 1918*. Translations of the reports of this committee have been prepared and published in English by the Carnegie Endowment for International Peace under the title of *German Official Documents Relating to the World War*, and by Dr. Ralph Haswell Lutz, under the auspices of the Hoover War Library at Stanford University, California, entitled *The Causes of the German Collapse in 1918*. There is also the very valuable study, *The Birth of the German Republic*, by Dr. Arthur Rosenberg, one of the Secretaries of the Committee, and many important documents are to be found in Ludendorff's two volumes on *The General Staff and Its Problems*.

For the war episodes, apart from the information contained in the authorities referred to, I have made use of the *Official History of the Great War*, published under the direction of the Historical Section of the Committee of Imperial Defence, particularly those volumes dealing with the military operations in France and Belgium in 1918; the Reports of General von Kuhl and Colonel Schwertfeger; General Sir Edmund Ironside's exhaustive study of the battle of Tannenberg; Rudolf van Wehrt's *Tannenberg*; and the comprehensive works of the Rt. Hon. Winston Churchill and Professor C. R. M. F. Crutwell, Principal of Hertford College, Oxford.

The account of the events at Spa and in Berlin during October—November 1918 is based upon a study of the memoranda and reports prepared by the principal actors in the drama, including Admiral von Hintze, General Count von Schulenburg, General von Plessen, General Count von Marschall, Count Gonthard, Colonel Niemann, and General Eisenbart-Rothe, together with the official German White Book on the Preliminary History of the Armistice, *Vorgeschichte des Waffenstillstandes*, of which an English translation has been published by the Carnegie Endowment for International Peace. In addition, there is the admirable work of Dr. Maurice Beaumont, *The Fall of the Kaiser*.

Other works which I have found of particular assistance in the preparation of these first two Parts are Karl Tschuppik's *Ludendorff;* Karl Nowak's *The Collapse of Central Europe* and *Chaos;* and Dr. Lutz' *The German Revolution, 1918–1919,* supplemented by his documentary work, *The Fall of the German Empire,* both published under the auspices of the Hoover War Library.

In the preparation of Part III I was confronted with an *embarras de choix mais pas de richesse.* The political literature of the post-war period in Germany is enormous, and, for the most part, inaccurate and partisan. Of first-hand material there is little of great value, for political passions render the memoirs and writings of Grzesinski and Otto Strasser as untrustworthy as those of Göring and Goebbels, and such works as the *Berlin Diaries* and the *White Book* on the events in Germany and Austria in June and July 1934, though they contain much truth, must of necessity be discounted to a great extent by the anonymity of their authors.

I was fortunate, however, in being a fairly constant visitor to Germany during much of this period and in close contact with a number of the leading figures. I have, therefore, drawn largely upon my own records, together with notes and memoranda made at the time.

But there are certain books which were of the greatest assistance, among them Konrad Heiden's *Geschichte des Nationalsozialismus* and *Geburt des dritten Reich,* published in English in one volume as *A History of National Socialism;* Georg Bernhard's *Die deutsche Tragödie;* Arthur Rosenberg's *Geschichte des deutschen Republik;* and, of course, the Stresemann Papers, and the admirable biographical studies of him by Rudolf Olden and Antonina Vallentin. Certain works by English and American authors must be included in this category; for example, *Germany Puts the Clock Back*, by Edgar Mowrer, and *The Fall of the German Republic*, by R. T. Clark; while for accurate studies of the Nazi Revolution itself there is nothing better than Powys Greenwood's *German Revolution*, and *Germany Enters the Third Reich*, by Calvin B. Hoover.

I have also used my own works on Disarmament, Security, and Reparations, viz.: *The Problem of Security, Disarmament and Security Since Locarno, The Pipe Dream of Peace, The Reparation Settlement of 1930*, and *The Wreck of Reparations*.

JOHN W. WHEELER-BENNETT

CONTENTS

ILLUSTRATIONS

✠

WOODEN TITAN

1

TANNENBERG AND PLESS

✠

IT MUST be a rare thing for a man to be virtually reborn twice during his lifetime, so that he experiences three completely different lives, each separated from the other by an interval of several years, and each progressively greater and more important than the last. Yet this is true of Paul von Beneckendorf und von Hindenburg, General-Field-Marshal and twice President of the German *Reich*.

The first of these "lives" dates from his birth in 1847 to his retirement from the Army in 1911; the second begins three years later, when, at the age of 67, he was appointed to the command of the 8th Army and ends with his second retirement in 1919; then, after six years interval, when he was 78, begins the third and last "life," dating from his election to the Presidency in 1925 until his death nine years later.

Born in Posen on October 2, 1847, he was the eldest of three sons in a family which had its origin in the union of two houses, each of which traced its military record back to the thirteenth century, when their ancestors had been Knights of the Teutonic Order. Frederick the Great had bestowed upon the Hindenburgs the two estates of Limbsee and Neudeck in the Neumark of West Prussia in reward for their services in the Silesian War, and although Limbsee had to be sold in the days of retrenchment

3

following the War of Liberation, Neudeck remained the "home" of the family and remained in their possession uninterruptedly until the death of the widow of one of the Marshal's younger brothers some years after the termination of the Great War. As in all ancient families, there was the inevitable skeleton in the cupboard. A certain Major Paul von Hindenburg was court-martialled and shot in 1806 for treacherously surrendering the fortress of Spandau to the French.

Paul von Hindenburg, steeped by family tradition in the history of his country, passed his childhood in the Spartan manner of the Prussian military caste. No weakness was tolerated, and it is recorded that his nurse, who seems to have been a female type of Prussian Grenadier, would at once quell any protest or argument with a roar of "Silence in the ranks." At the age of eleven he joined the Prussian Cadet Corps, of which he himself relates that the discipline was "consciously and purposely rough," and he remained there until 1866, when after a brief period of service as page of honour to the widowed Queen Elizabeth of Prussia, he was commissioned a second-lieutenant in the Third Regiment of Foot Guards.

Too young to take part in the war against Denmark, Hindenburg received his baptism of fire from the Austrians at Soor in the Seven Weeks' War, and at the close of the campaign was decorated with the Order of the Red Eagle for the capture of a battery of guns at Königgrätz, in the course of which he was wounded. Four years later, in the Franco-Prussian War, he won the Iron Cross for bravery in the field and was chosen to represent his regiment at the proclamation of the German Emperor at Versailles.

At the end of the war in 1871 he returned to the ordinary existence of any rising young officer engaged in "military peace work," and during those years even his most enthusiastic biographer, Niemann, is forced to admit that his services "were valuable, though not decisive." He was a part, and a rather insignificant part, of the new German Empire's new army, which was organized and developed during the Wilhelmian era, and through the ranks of which he slowly worked his way, in forty years of staff and regimental duties from captain to lieutenant-general. He was never promoted on account of any outstanding service, but rose in the regular advancement of a conscientious officer, and the number of medals and orders conferred on him by the Emperor was but the minimum amount consistent with his rank.

At length in 1904 he was appointed to the command of the Fourth Army Corps, with headquarters at Magdeburg, and it was in this capacity that he took part in the Imperial manœuvres of 1908. Here, however, he allowed zeal to outrun discretion and committed the fatal mistake of letting the army corps commanded by the Kaiser lose the battle. The All-Highest disliked defeat at the hands of his own generals, even if it was an accident, and when three years later Hindenburg made application to retire at the end of his period of command, there was a strong rumour that it was not unconnected with the unfortunate event of the 1908 manœuvres. He himself emphatically denied it: "My military career had carried me much farther than I had ever dared to hope. There was no prospect of a war, and, as I recognised that it was my duty to make way for younger men, I applied in the year 1911 to be allowed to retire."

There is, however, evidence to show that even before this date Hindenburg had ceased to enjoy the Imperial favour, if, indeed, he had ever enjoyed it. During the discussions which preceded the appointment of Moltke to succeed Schlieffen as Chief of the Imperial General Staff in 1905, Hindenburg's name, in company with others, was put forward, but the Kaiser dismissed him from consideration as a *raisonneur*.

He therefore resigned himself at the age of sixty-four to a life

of well-earned rest and tranquillity in Hanover, and to the congenial occupation of watching and advancing the military career
of his son Oskar, then a second-lieutenant in his father's old
regiment, the *Dritte Garde Regiment zu Fuss*. The name of Hindenburg was unknown to most of his fellow countrymen. He was
just one of the many retired generals retained *à la suite* of their
regiments, and twelve other individuals were listed on the same
page as he in the current issue of the German *Who's Who*.

For four years General von Hindenburg lived a monotonously
pleasant existence in the autumn of his life. He travelled, and,
whilst in Rome, began that collection of pictures of the Madonna
and Child which, with shooting (*der Jagdpassion*), formed his
chief recreations. His health began to fail. Work would have
suited him better; he had always led an active if not an athletic
life, and though he enjoyed freedom from anxiety and responsibility, he was subconsciously irked by inaction. It seemed as if
he might not live to be seventy.

And then suddenly out of the blue summer sky of 1914 there
came the war which galvanized him once more into activity.
The Day for which every German soldier had lived and planned
had arrived at last, and it found him no longer in harness. With
no further information than the man in the street, Hindenburg
gleaned his war news from the newspapers, reading daily of the
German advance upon Paris and of the Russian invasion of East
Prussia. With an envious eye he watched the mobilization at
Hanover proceed without him. The troops marching through the
streets from barracks to train passed him by unrecognized. He
chafed in a fever of inactivity. "I placed myself in the hands of
fate and waited in longing expectation." At last in the late afternoon of August 22 he received a telegram from the Kaiser at
Imperial G.H.Q. at Coblenz asking him if he were ready for
immediate service. Thankfully the General replied "Am ready"
and joyfully set about his preparations. Subsequent telegrams

informed him of his promotion to the rank of Colonel-General and his appointment to the command of the Eighth Army in East Prussia, with General Ludendorff as his Chief of Staff. His second "life" had begun.

· 2 ·

The circumstances which led up to Hindenburg's sudden appointment on August 22, 1914, are of very considerable importance both in relation to his career and to the subsequent events at Tannenberg, upon which the Hindenburg Legend was founded.

The military position in East Prussia at the outbreak of the war was dominated, in so far as Germany was concerned, by the operation of the strategic plan by which the General Staff essayed to meet a war on two fronts. This plan had its origins as far back as 1880, when the great Moltke had had to envisage the possibility of a simultaneous war with France and Russia. For military, political, and psychological reasons Moltke had decided to attack the Russians with the larger force and to take up a defensive attitude against France, being even prepared to retire to a position east of the Rhine.

In time, however, the reasons which influenced Moltke's decisions changed or became modified, and his successor, Count von Waldersee, with recollections of 1812, elaborated two plans according to the season of the year. If war broke out in summer, the main attack was to be in the east; if in winter, in the west.

It was the third of the German Chief of Staff, Count Alfred von Schlieffen, who finally abandoned Moltke's plan and adopted one based on precisely opposite principles. France had by this time become the more dangerous enemy for Germany; hence the rules of strategy demanded that, regardless of the season of the year, the main attack should be in the west. This would be delivered through northern France and Belgium against Paris, whilst there would be a retreat in Alsace-Lorraine before the French armies. In the meantime the east must look after itself until the decisive battle in the west freed sufficient forces for an offensive.

But here Nature had provided a strong measure of protection. The Russian armies, on entering German territory, would inevitably be divided by the Masurian Lakes and could only continue their advance by sending one army to the north and the other to the south of this chain. The German army therefore must be prepared to attack one of these armies, while they were disunited, and defeat it; being ready then to turn upon the other.

Unfortunately for Germany, but providentially for the Allies, the Imperial Chief of Staff at the outbreak of the war, though a Moltke, had none of the great qualities of his uncle, nor indeed of any of his predecessors. A man of weak nerves, a figure of straw, he was the least worthy incumbent of the high military office since its inception by Gneisenau, a hundred years before, but in justice to him it must be said that he had protested energetically against his own appointment, feeling himself in every way unfitted for it. His protests, however, proved vain in the face of the historical mania of Wilhelm II, who was determined that he, too, should have his Moltke.[1] Under the younger Moltke the Schlieffen plan was modified in the west, and the strategic retreat in Alsace-Lorraine abandoned. The provision for defensive measures in the east remained unchanged.

[1] Prince Bülow in his *Memoirs* (vol. ii. pp. 175-176) relates how, one morning in the autumn of 1905, he was riding in the Berlin Hippodrome when he met Count Moltke, who told him with evident distress that the Kaiser had determined to make him Chief of the General Staff in succession to Schlieffen. Moltke seemed terrified at the idea of such a responsible post. "Everything in me dislikes the thought of the appointment," he declared. "I do not lack personal courage but I lack the power of rapid decision; I am too reflective; too scrupulous, or, if you like, too conscientious for such a post. I lack the capacity for risking all on a single throw."

Never was so tragically penetrating a self-analysis so fully justified by subsequent events.

In August 1914, therefore, the eastern front was lightly held by the Eighth Army, numbering some eleven divisions of infantry and one cavalry division, and commanded by Colonel-General Max von Prittwitz und Gaffron,[1] with General Count von Waldersee (the nephew of Schlieffen's predecessor) as Chief of Staff. Opposed to them was a Russian army group commanded by General Jilinsky, consisting of two armies under Generals Rennenkampf and Samsonov, having between them thirty infantry and eight cavalry divisions, which gave them a numerical superiority over the Germans of almost three to one in infantry and of eight to one in cavalry.

Strategic advantage, however, lay with the smaller force, for with their highly efficient system of railways the Germans had a far greater mobility than the Russians and could manœuvre behind the screen of the Masurian Lakes to meet whichever invading army emerged first. It was, however, an essential feature of the Schlieffen plan that whichever Russian army was struck must be defeated and not merely checked, and that the German forces should be able to disengage themselves to meet the second enemy advance.

In accordance with German expectations, the northern army under General Rennenkampf emerged first from the line of the Lakes. It began its advance on August 17 marching due west, in the expectation that Samsonov's southern army, coming up from the southeast, would strike the German right flank two days after Rennenkampf's attack. From the first, however, the Russian timetable was at fault, not only between Rennenkampf and Samsonov, but also between the units of Rennenkampf's own army, where a wide gap was left between the Third and Fourth Army Corps. Discovering this, General von François, in command of the First German Corps, slipped through it and attacked Rennenkampf from the rear; causing widespread confusion and

[1] Who had achieved the uninspiring nickname of *der dicke Soldat*.

panic, he captured 3000 prisoners and withdrew without great loss.

This engagement, known as the battle of Stallupönen, was remarkable as the first of several occasions during the campaign on which François disregarded his orders and acted on his own initiative. This did not necessarily betoken insubordination, for, in the tradition of the great Moltke, corps commanders were left a maximum amount of liberty within the limits of their general task; none the less, supreme importance was attached to discipline.[1]

In this particular case General von François, a man of great independence of thought and of some impetuosity, had always entertained certain mental reservations with regard to the working of the Schlieffen plan. As commander of the East Prussian Army Corps he regarded himself as specially called upon to protect the province, and he was unwilling to see a single East Prussian village given over to the horrors of war. He was of opinion that the task of frontier defence was to act on the offensive, and, by attacking the Russian forces, to keep them off the frontier. He apparently disregarded the fact that, as a result of his action, the whole army might have to move to the support of his corps, and might therefore be obliged to fight on the east side of the Masurian Lakes, thereby foregoing the geographical advantages offered for defensive warfare. The action of Stallupönen, though a success for the First Corps, was an error of judgment on the part of its commander, for while large numbers of prisoners were taken, the Germans also suffered losses in men and material, and more particularly in attacking power, which should have been husbanded against the decisive battle. Moreover no real advantage was gained by delaying Rennenkampf;

---

[1] The military tradition of the Austrian Army was at variance with the German. Here independent non-compliance with orders was rewarded with the highest military decoration, the Order of Maria Theresa, provided that such action met with success.

on the contrary, it was to the German interest that he should advance as rapidly as possible so that they might crush him before the arrival of Samsonov. Nevertheless it was the willingness of General von François to accept responsibility for independent action which, some ten days later, was to play an important part in the German victory of Tannenberg.

After the initial check at Stallupönen, the Russian advance continued, and by August 19 had reached Gömbinnen. The German Commander-in-Chief, Prittwitz, would have retired still further, but again François' impetuous nature prevailed, and on the following morning a general frontal attack was made on the Russian position. On the right and left the German advance was successful, but in the centre Mackensen's Seventeenth Corps failed to reach its objectives and was defeated and rolled back.

The nerves of the army commander and of his Chief of Staff already showed signs of fraying, but in the opinion of the Quartermaster-General, General von Grünert, and of the senior staff officer, Lieutenant-Colonel Hoffmann, the action, despite Mackensen's defeat, was extremely favourable for the continuation of the attack on the 21st, and should in their opinion be fought out. Could they have known how entirely conditions on the Russian side justified their opinion, they might have been even more emphatic; for Rennenkampf's army was on the verge of collapse, and his staff, almost to a man, was urging him to retreat.

On August 20, between six and seven o'clock in the evening, news reached Grünert and Hoffmann that Samsonov's Army had emerged south of the Masurian Lakes and was threatening the German troops opposed to them, namely the Twentieth Corps, which, contrary to the Schlieffen plan, Count von Waldersee had not ordered to take part in the general German retiring movement. The corps commander, however, was not at all disturbed by this development, and reported that he was in a position to

fight a delaying action long enough to allow the battle of Gömbinnen to be brought to a successful finish.

The nervous state of the Army Commander and the Chief of
Staff may be judged by the fact that for a moment the thought
flashed through the minds of both Grünert and Hoffmann as to
whether they should withhold this information from their superiors. Such a thought was, of course, immediately rejected, but
the effect of the news must have justified their worst fears. Prittwitz's nerves, which had never been really under control, now
cracked altogether, and he at once gave orders for the breaking
off of the action at Gömbinnen and, overriding the strong protest
of François, Grünert, and Hoffmann, ordered the general retirement of the Eighth Army behind the Vistula. At the same time,
without informing his staff of what he proposed to do, he telephoned hysterically to Imperial General Headquarters at Coblenz
that he could not even hold the line of the Vistula unless strong
reinforcements were sent to him immediately.

But now a change came over the High Command of the Eighth
Army, and the dominating genius of Lieut.-Col. Hoffmann
became the controlling influence. With quiet tact and authority
the senior staff officer explained to his agitated superiors, who
had no real conception as to how the general retreat was to be
effected, the impossibility of executing their last order *in toto*.
He demonstrated that the withdrawal to the Vistula could not be
carried out without severe fighting. The troops had to be dis-
engaged from contact with Rennenkampf's army, and the left
flank of Samsonov's army must be checked since it was nearer
to the Vistula than the Eighth Army. He suggested a concentration of forces for an attack against Samsonov in order to carry
out the withdrawal.

In face of this cool reasoning Prittwitz and Waldersee regained a little courage, and by half-past nine on the evening of
the 20th Hoffmann, having quelled the panic at headquarters,

was able to issue orders in accordance with his own proposals, namely to disengage from Rennenkampf, leaving a light screen to mask the operation, and to concentrate the Eighth Army at a point from whence a blow could be struck later against either Rennenkampf or Samsonov.

But though his courage had in part returned, Prittwitz had not yet entirely mastered his agitation, for he omitted to acquaint Imperial General Headquarters of his change of plan, leaving them in the belief that the retreat behind the Vistula was in progress. There was in fact no further communication between the Eighth Army and Coblenz until the evening of August 22, when it was announced that a new commander and Chief of Staff were on their way to army headquarters. The orders recalling Prittwitz and Waldersee did not arrive until some few hours later.

· 3 ·

The scene now changes to Coblenz on the evening of August 20, where the Chief of the Imperial Staff, already harassed and ill, listened with dismay to the stricken voice of the Eighth Army Commander in East Prussia entreating reinforcements to enable him to hold the line of the Vistula, behind which he was retiring. Imperial G.H.Q. remained in ignorance of the fact that this unjustifiable panic was almost immediately overcome and that the order for a general retirement was countermanded, but Moltke received the perfectly correct impression that his lieutenant in East Prussia was psychologically a beaten man and that neither he nor his Chief of Staff was in any way fitted to remain in active command.

The question arose who should succeed them, and at once the name of his former Director of Operations, the new hero, Erich Ludendorff, who had recently taken over the command of an infantry brigade and had been decorated by the Emperor with the *Pour le Mérite* cross for capturing, almost single-handed, the citadel of Liége, presented itself to Moltke for Chief of the Staff of the Eighth Army. But whose name should appear as General Commanding? No one very greatly cared who should be the "dear old Excellency" whose business it would be to shield, or reflect, the shining light of Ludendorff's genius, but there had to be someone.

The names of retired army corps commanders were discussed by the circle of junior staff officers, one of whom suggested that a distant cousin of his, Beneckendorff [1] by name, was eligible for the post and had the added advantage of being conveniently at Hanover, on the direct route to the east. Moltke recollected the long record of yeoman service and staff experience, as well as the sturdy bulk of the general. No weak nerves there; and a sure rock against which the "slings and arrows of outrageous fortune" could avail nothing. There ought to be no delay, the Staff suggested; the Emperor's approval should be obtained at once. This was impossible before the following morning, but no objection was raised by Wilhelm II to the suggested appointment, and the decisive message was sent by telegraph, as nobody seemed quite sure whether the thrifty habits of the general had allowed him, at that time, the luxury of a private telephone.

In such deliberations passed the 21st of August, and on the 22nd, at 9 A.M., Ludendorff at Wavre received the news of his appointment, together with the information that his Chief would be General von Beneckendorff und von Hindenburg, though at the moment it was not known if he would accept the command. Personal letters from the Chief of the Imperial General Staff and the Quartermaster-General accompanied the official appointment. "A difficult task is being entrusted to you, one more diffi-

---

[1] It was not until after Tannenberg that the general was known by the single name of "Hindenburg"; hitherto he had been called Beneckendorff and had appeared under the letter B in the Army List and in directories.

cult perhaps than the capture of Liége," wrote Moltke. "I know of no other person whom I trust as implicitly as yourself. Perhaps you may succeed in saving the position in the east. . . . Your energy is such that you may still succeed in averting the worst." And General von Stein added his appeal, "Your place is on the eastern front. . . . The safety of the country demands it."

It is clear then that, from the first, the Imperial High Command relied upon Ludendorff rather than Hindenburg to avert disaster in the east, and, if possible, turn defeat into victory. No such personal messages of confidence accompanied the succession of telegrams which were on their way to Hanover, during the time that Ludendorff was motoring with all speed from Wavre to Coblenz. Hindenburg had been recalled from retirement as a figure-head who would inspire public confidence and act as a foil to Ludendorff's genius, but the Imperial High Command reposed their confidence in the Chief of Staff.

Ludendorff reached Coblenz on August 22 at 6 P.M., and received from Moltke and Stein a résumé of all that had occurred in the east up to the last telephonic conversation with Prittwitz. The new Chief of Staff of the Eighth Army at once began to issue orders direct to the units of the command assuming, with his incomplete knowledge of the final phases of the situation, that the Army Headquarters Staff was out of the picture. He was frankly delighted with his new position and was fully aware that a rare chance was offered to the strategist.

But the point of absorbing interest is that Ludendorff at Coblenz, hundreds of miles away from the theatre of operations, was issuing on the 22nd, orders almost identical with those which Hoffmann had issued on the spot two days earlier, immediately after he had allayed the panic of his superiors. Both Ludendorff and Hoffmann realized, independently, that Samsonov's army was, for the moment, the greater menace and must be dealt with first, and the orders which both of them issued, aimed at the concentration of the Eighth Army to meet this immediate danger. That these two men came to the same conclusions to meet the situation is a signal proof of the high standard of training in the German General Staff, and it is difficult to know to whom to allot the greater share of praise; to Hoffmann, who had to cope not only with the enemy, but with a querulous and incompetent Army Commander and Chief of Staff, or to Ludendorff, who assumed the responsibility for issuing orders without reference to the new Army Commander, whoever he might be—for it was not until eight o'clock in the evening, some time after Ludendorff's final instructions had been despatched, that he learned that Hindenburg had in fact accepted the command of the Eighth Army and that they were to proceed together that night to the east.

On August 23, at 3 A.M., Hindenburg stood, stolid and impassive, upon the station platform at Hanover awaiting the special train which was to take him to his new command. It had taxed even the capacities of a Prussian officer's wife to get him ready in the ten hours at her disposal between the receipt of the first telegram and the moment of his departure. All sorts of intimate details had to be attended to. The general had grown stouter during his retirement, and Frau von Hindenburg had to let out his tunics and breeches here and there. Even now he stood in the blue peace time uniform of a Prussian general and not in the field-grey equipment of the German army at war.[1] But all had been accomplished somehow, and, he stood, his farewells over, waiting on the threshold of his second "life." It was to close five years later, in 1919, in the gloom of Germany's defeat and humiliation, but with Hindenburg's personal

---

[1] General Ludendorff's wife accompanied him on the train from Coblenz as far east as Küstrin, and to her Hindenburg deplored his lack of equipment. It seemed at the moment to be his chief concern. Cf. Margarethe Ludendorff, *My Married Life with Ludendorff*, p. 84.

reputation enhanced a thousandfold and his name a legend throughout Germany.

The special train steamed into the dimly lighted station, just an engine and two coaches; a tall military figure in regulation field-grey alighted and stiffly saluted Hindenburg.

"Major-General Ludendorff, your Excellency, by order of August 21 of the All-Highest's Military Cabinet, appointed Chief of Staff of the Eighth Army."

They exchanged salutes and handshakes and entered the train, which continued on its journey eastward.

In this simple, correct manner was inaugurated that extraordinary relationship between Hindenburg and Ludendorff which was so outstanding a feature of this period of Hindenburg's life. In many ways they were antithetical yet complementary. Hindenburg was modest and retiring, Ludendorff arrogant and egotistical—towards men at any rate. Hindenburg, in his account of the years of their partnership, uses the pronoun "we" throughout, while Ludendorff's memoirs are characterized by the constantly recurring use of "I." Hindenburg was a man of slow but accurate judgment, and he never lost his nerve, while Ludendorff, certainly the more brilliant, and with a swifter grasp of the situation in the final analysis, was prone to moments of panic. In their combination Ludendorff was the arm, and in some cases, not always the happiest, the head also, and Hindenburg often permitted himself to approve suggestions without complete assurance of what he did. Yet he possessed great insight, and his mature and considered judgments often restrained Ludendorff's unstable and less perfectly balanced temper.

Hindenburg himself has described their relations as "those of a happy marriage," but in that marriage Ludendorff was the dominating husband, for he possessed a strong will, the will of a fanatic, which drives straight to its goal, without a thought for those who stand in its way. From the military aspect the combination was vastly effective, but politically it was most unfortunate, for while in the direction of operations their two minds worked in complementary accord, in the political intrigues of the later years Ludendorff made use of his chief's name and position in the most unwarrantable manner.

But in these August days of 1914 this "marriage" was but in the honeymoon stage, and within an hour of their departure from Hanover, Ludendorff had won the complete approval of his chief for the orders he had issued to the Eighth Army from Coblenz and for the plan of campaign which he was already maturing. By the time they reached headquarters at Marienburg on the following afternoon, the most complete sense of mutual confidence prevailed between them.

· 4 ·

Few battles in history have given rise to so many myths as Tannenberg. According to one popular legend, to which Mr. John Buchan (now Lord Tweedsmuir), in his *History of the Great War,* gave considerable publicity in England, Hindenburg had worked out his plans for this battle twenty-five years before, when as a captain he was G.S.O.2 to the First Division. He is said to have explored the country and averted the carrying-out of schemes for draining the lakes and marshes in that district, and now applied his long-cherished plan of driving the Russians into these death-traps of Nature, where thousands died a horrible death of suffocation. Another version describes him as hurrying across Germany in his special train from Hanover to Marienburg, receiving reports at wayside stations and issuing his orders accordingly as he went along.

All these "colourful" stories are mythology; Hindenburg himself disposes of the first legend in a single sentence: "Before this day [August 24] I had never seen the battlefield." And both

Ludendorff and Hoffmann have left it on record—Ludendorff in reply to a direct enquiry from the Spanish military attaché—that Tannenberg was not fought according to a long-conceived and prepared plan. As regards the second fable, the facts already related show how little truth there is in it.

When the new High Command of the Eighth Army reached their headquarters at Marienburg, on the evening of August 23, they found, much to their surprise, that all their orders had been anticipated by Lieut.-Col. Hoffmann and that the disposition of troops was already in progress. They had no fresh instructions to issue: their orders were simply in effect to "carry on." Probably neither Hindenburg nor Ludendorff was entirely delighted at the part played by their senior staff officer in the preliminary preparations for the battle or in its subsequent development. Hoffmann's independent action had, to a certain extent, stolen their thunder, and his name does not occur in the four hundred and fifty pages of Hindenburg's bulky memoirs, while Ludendorff gives him but scant credit for his timely action and forethought, which had unquestionably saved the situation at a most critical moment. Hoffmann, on the other hand, is very much more generous. He makes out the best case possible for Prittwitz, giving him more than his fair share of responsibility for the change of orders on August 20, and is full of praise for his two immediate superiors in their conduct of the battle.

The task before the reconstituted German Eighth Army was clear, and there was no alternative course. Samsonov had not only to be defeated, but annihilated, in order to give them a free hand to complete the defeat of Rennenkampf, before he had time to recover fully from the shock received at Gömbinnen, and before he could move to the support of his colleague. Time, therefore, was the essence of the contract, and in the plan which Hoffmann outlined, and which Ludendorff adopted, this factor was taken fully into account.

It was proposed to leave a weak but well-masked force consisting of a cavalry division and some reserves and militia to
hold Rennenkampf in check, and with the remainder of the
Eighth Army to envelop and destroy Samsonov. The plan was
essentially a bold one, for should Rennenkampf discover the
weakness of the force opposed to him, or should he receive an
appeal for help from Samsonov, he could with ease sweep aside
the German cavalry screen and by forced marches to the south-
west come upon his enemy's rear.

But Hoffmann, in drawing up his plans, counted on one psychological factor, of which he alone at German headquarters was
informed. This knowledge gave him added confidence and relieved him from those agonies of anxiety which attacked his
chiefs. In the years of his retirement in Berlin after the war,
it was one of General Hoffmann's chief delights to retell the story
of his special information.

In the Russo-Japanese War of 1904–5 Hoffmann, then a staff
captain, was attached as an observer to the Japanese armies in
Manchuria, and as such had his first experiences of modern warfare. What, however, proved of supreme value to him was an
incident retold to him by his "opposite number" with the Imperial Russian Armies. In the course of the battle of Liawyang,
during the Mukden campaign, the commander of the Siberian
Cossack Division defending the Yentai coal-mines found himself unable to hold his position and blamed his failure upon the
inactivity and bad leadership of the divisional commander supporting him. In the bitterness of the general defeat the two officers, who had been keen rivals from their days at the Military
Academy, met on the railway platform at Mukden, and reproached each other with acrid recrimination. The dispute became heated, the Siberian Cossack commander knocked the
other down, and the disheartened army was treated to the in-
spiring picture of two major-generals rolling on the ground be-

fore the eyes of their scandalized staffs, who eventually tore them apart. The name of the commander of the Siberian Cossack Division was Samsonov, and that of his rival Rennenkampf.

The Tsar forbade a duel, but the former rivalry had developed into a passion for revenge, and during the next ten years Hoffmann kept himself informed of the progress of the quarrel. His latest information in July 1914 was that the two remained unreconciled, and when he knew that they were opposed to him, he felt sure that Samsonov would now be paid out for that box on the ears ten years before. Hoffmann, as he told the story, would add with a chuckle, sipping from his inevitable tumbler of neat cognac, that, "if the battle of Waterloo was won on the playing-fields of Eton, the battle of Tannenberg was lost on the railway platform at Mukden."

Thus the boldness of the German scheme was tempered with an inner knowledge of the personalities of the Russian commanding officers, and while this does not detract from the excellence of the conception, it at least explains how Hoffmann was enabled to maintain his cool judgment at a moment when Ludendorff, and even, in some degree, Hindenburg, fell a prey to nervous anxiety.

Two other factors favoured the German plans. In the pocketbook of a dead Russian staff officer had been found notes on the general movements of both Rennenkampf's and Samsonov's armies, evidently made at Jilinsky's Army Group Headquarters, and this valuable information showed the General Staff of the Eighth Army how far their opponents had departed from the scheduled time-table. Added to this was the almost incredible fact that the headquarters staffs of Jilinsky, Rennenkampf, and Samsonov communicated with each other by wireless messages sent out *en clair* so that the operators at German Headquarters could keep in close touch with every move of the enemy.

August 24 and 25 were devoted by the Germans to final preparations and dispositions of troops for a decisive struggle. The plan of operations was simple in conception but difficult of execution. The right and left wings were strengthened at the expense of the centre, which, lightly held, was the bait held out to Samsonov to tempt him to attack. By the evening of the 25th all was in order for the morrow, and Hindenburg was able to say to his staff, "Gentlemen, our preparations are so well in hand that we can sleep soundly to-night."

The drama upon which the curtain rose on August 26 was not in one self-contained act but in a number of detached scenes. The stage, which stretched over more than sixty miles of East Prussian territory, covered ground which prevented the formation of a continuous battle-line. The battle called, therefore, for individual initiative on the part of the various corps commanders and is particularly remarkable for the success of these independent actions.

Samsonov fell headlong into the temptingly baited trap and launched a terrible assault against the weak German centre. But the position was held by the Twentieth Corps composed of troops drawn from the very district in which they fought, Allenstein men fighting for the defence of their own homesteads, and though the line writhed and shook beneath the weight of successive Russian onslaughts, it did not break. Meanwhile François on the right and Mackensen and Bülow on the left were driving forward against the Russian flanks. Towards evening the German centre abandoned its defensive tactics and took the offensive, making contact with François and enveloping Samsonov's main body in such a manner that it had no alternative but to retire eastwards.

But though the battle progressed favourably, at general headquarters the joy of success was overshadowed by anxiety as to the movements of Rennenkampf. Ludendorff was showing signs of nervous exhaustion, the joy of victory was utterly spoilt for him by the burden of anxiety. Even the stolid Hindenburg felt the strain. "Is it surprising," he asks, "that misgivings filled many a heart? that firm resolution began to yield to vacillation, and that doubts crept in where a clear vision had hitherto prevailed?" At G.H.Q. only Hoffmann, sure in his inner knowledge and confident in his own belief, maintained his equanimity and observed, perhaps even with a tinge of secret enjoyment, the mental discomfiture of his chiefs.

But as the day wore on it seemed that even the worst anxieties might be fulfilled. The German wireless operators reported to the High Command message after message from Samsonov, who, realizing the magnitude of the disaster that was about to overwhelm him, was filling the air with his demands, prayers, and entreaties to Rennenkampf to come to his assistance. But the Russian First Army was skirmishing outside Königsberg. That ten-year-old box on the ear still tingled. Rennenkampf did not move.

Suddenly, however, during the evening of the 26th, the moment of supreme crisis occurred at German Headquarters. It was announced that a strong force of Russian cavalry was in movement to the south and threatening François, and at the same moment it was reported by an air-scout that one of Rennenkampf's corps was in motion to the rear of Mackensen's enveloping force on the left. At this decisive moment Ludendorff's nerves gave way completely, and he wanted to recall François, and call off the operation closing the ring around Samsonov. Hindenburg rose magnificently to the crisis, his courage and composure were unshaken, and supported by Hoffmann, who now contributed his knowledge of the existing relations between Samsonov and Rennenkampf, and Lieutenant-Colonel Hell, Chief of Staff of the Twentieth Corps, he refused to be stampeded into hasty and panicky action. "We overcame the inward crisis," are his own words on the subject, "and adhered to our original intention, turning in full strength to effect its realization by attack."

In the handling of this crisis lies Hindenburg's real claim to fame at Tannenberg. Unlike Prittwitz, he was undeterred by impending danger, and his more phlegmatic nature was of greater value than Ludendorff's more temperamental genius. Had the Chief of Staff been allowed his way, Samsonov's army would have escaped, even though shattered and decimated, into the forests of Poland. By refusing to allow plans, which had been carefully considered and adopted, to be hastily changed or abandoned, Hindenburg ensured the encirclement of Samsonov and rendered certain his complete destruction. Moreover, overwhelming justification of the wisdom of Hindenburg's action was provided next morning when it was shown that the advance of Rennenkampf's corps was but the figment of the airman's over-excited imagination, and that François' independence of mind rendered him more than capable of taking measures for his own safety.

The battle continued with great fierceness throughout August 27, 28, and 29, but the final issue was never again in doubt. In every way the German generalship and staff work was superior to the Russian, who were "out-thought" on all points. But the Russian army fought with great gallantry, and, indeed, had the quality of leadership been equal to the fighting quality of the troops, the result of the battles in East Prussia might have been very different. For Samsonov, deserted by his colleague, fought with the fury of despair to break from the enveloping movement which, inexorable as the march of time, was slowly but surely compassing his destruction. Again and again he drove like a bull against the ring, but to no purpose. On the evening of the 29th Mackensen on the left and François on the right joined hands and the encircling movement was complete. Fresh Russian forces attempted on the following day to break the circle from outside, but without success, and hour by hour the ring of fire around the Russian masses, crowded closely together, swaying this way and that, milling against each other, and ceasing to have any military formation, became closer and narrower.

By evening all was over and the Russian forces had sustained what General Sir Edmund Ironside has described as "the greatest defeat suffered by any of the combatants during the war." The dead, lying in heaps and swaths, numbered over 100,000; the number of prisoners taken was no less. Three whole army corps had been destroyed, and the small body of troops that remained outside the German circle was in panic-stricken flight towards the frontier.

As the German search parties scoured the field they found amongst a mound of dead the body of a white-haired general officer, a bullet wound in his head, a revolver in his hand. In the last moment of overwhelming disaster Samsonov had taken the only course which to him seemed compatible with honour.

But for the weary and victorious Eighth Army there was no repose, no respite to enjoy its victory. Rennenkampf, now reinforced with new corps from Finland and Siberia, still hung like a menacing cloud in the north. There were signs that he had begun to realize the enormity of his conduct in not supporting Samsonov, and to be appalled at the colossal dimensions of the defeat to Russian arms which his desertion had caused. That feud between the Russian army commanders had already cost the Tsar 200,000 men in killed and prisoners and was to be the cause of the destruction of many thousand more. Had Rennenkampf's resolution been as great as his resources, he could have attacked the Eighth Army while it lay at the moment of its greatest weakness, exhausted and crowded together on the battlefield of Tannenberg, but he allowed the Germans a whole week to disentangle their units, to rest and bring up reinforcements, and to concentrate afresh and mature a plan whereby to destroy him.

In the preparation of this plan Ludendorff and Hoffmann cooperated closely, Hoffmann being "proud that some of my ideas have been included." Rennenkampf, with fresh reserves approaching and a number of new divisions already up, was in a strong defensive position between the Masurian Lakes and the Kurische Haff which did not allow of an encircling movement as at Tannenberg. It was therefore proposed to make a frontal assault upon this position with four corps, whilst the two corps of François and Mackensen pushed through the lake region on the Russian left and attacked his rear.

The action known as the first battle of the Masurian Lakes began on September 8, and, while the German assault met with little success, the flanking movement made good progress. The same was true of the following day. Rennenkampf repulsed the attack in his front, but François and Mackensen had moved still further round his left wing. Rennenkampf's nerve now failed him; terrified at the possibility of being caught in a similar trap to Samsonov's, he relinquished the advantage afforded him by his numerical superiority and his strong position and ordered a general retreat. Beginning on September 10, this movement continued until the 14th, by which time it had degenerated into a rout, with the German artillery blowing great gaps in the tightly packed masses before them. By the 18th Rennenkampf's army was once more on Russian soil, having lost 145,000 men in casualties and prisoners. It had been in East Prussia just twenty-eight days.

· 5 ·

Two questions now present themselves. What was Hindenburg's part in the victory of Tannenberg, and was he or someone else responsible for that victory?

In the preliminary preparations for the battle he had no part at all. Here the credit must be divided between Hoffmann and Ludendorff, for the almost identical orders which they issued were given on August 20 and 22 respectively, that is to say, before Hindenburg's appointment to the command of the Eighth Army became operative. In the immediate disposition of the troops for battle he also bore no part. Here Hoffmann suggested and Ludendorff endorsed a certain plan of campaign, the orders for the execution of which were later signed by Hindenburg. "I realized that one of my principal tasks was, as far as possible, to give free scope to the intellectual powers, the almost superhuman capacity for work and untiring resolution of my Chief of Staff, and if necessary to clear the way for him," wrote Hindenburg of Ludendorff at this moment; and Ludendorff has left the complementary statement, "General von Hindenburg had always agreed to my suggestions and gladly accepted the responsibility of consenting to them."

Hindenburg's greatest contribution to the victory lies in his never-failing capacity and willingness to accept responsibility, a feature of his character which became less apparent in his later life. It was Hindenburg who had accepted the prepared plans of Ludendorff and Hoffmann; it was Hindenburg who had signed the battle orders; it was Hindenburg who, at the critical moment, on the evening of August 26, refused to be stampeded by Ludendorff's nervous brain-storm; it was upon Hindenburg that the final responsibility for success or failure rested; and it was he who signed the telegraphic report to the Emperor announcing the tremendous news of victory.

And in effect was this not exactly the function which he had been sent to fulfil? In making the original appointments on August 22, Moltke had counted upon Ludendorff for genius and upon Hindenburg for character. It was impossible to risk a repetition of the Prittwitz-Waldersee régime in which the Chief of Staff and the Army Commander had lost their heads at the moment of great crisis. Hindenburg had been sent to East Prussia as a symbol and a foil. In these capacities he justified to the full the judgment of those who selected him for the position. He was the solid rock upon which the edifice of the High Command was built, but apart from this very important function he had little or no part in the actual victory.

The Emperor was suitably grateful in his rewards. Hindenburg received the Order *Pour le Mérite* and Ludendorff the Iron Cross, which, he is at pains to point out, had not at that time dwindled in value as it did later in the war. Hoffmann too received the Iron Cross, and writes in his diary that he never expected to receive this finest of all military decorations by sitting at the end of a telephone-line. "However," he adds, "I realize that there must be someone who keeps his nerve, and by brute determination and the will to victory overcomes difficulties, panics and such like nonsense." Not for nothing had Hoffmann seen Prittwitz, Waldersee, and Ludendorff wilt beneath the burden of anxiety.

Hoffmann's part in the victory is indeed one of the most important, for his cool courage and calm determination had been a pillar of strength to both the Prittwitz-Waldersee and the Hindenburg-Ludendorff combinations. It was he indeed who gave the battle its historic name. While dictating the final report for Hindenburg's signature, Ludendorff had dated it from Frögenau. Hoffmann suggested that instead the despatch should be headed from the little village of Tannenberg, which had formed the focal point of the line held by the Twentieth Corps against the earlier attacks of Samsonov, and which is sacred to every Prussian; for it is the site of the battle where five centuries before the marshaled chivalry of the Order of Teutonic Knights, in which had fought a Beneckendorff and a Hindenburg, had been annihilated almost to a man by an advancing host of the Lithuanians and Slavs. Now the memory of that terrible defeat had been wiped out, and a Slav host had gone down to destruction before a Teutonic force commanded by a descendant of the Teutonic

Knights. The historic answer was complete, but it was Hoffmann, a Hessian, who thought of it.

As Hoffmann himself points out, the final success was in great measure due to a succession of most important events resulting, not from the orders of the High Command, but from the individual initiative of the subordinate leaders. Of these the most salient example is that of General von François. At a point which was decisive for the brilliant success of the battle he indisputably did a great service in putting off the attack until he had in position all his fighting troops, and more especially his artillery. If he had advanced a day earlier against the prepared Russian position, as the High Command wanted him to do, when his troops had been only partly concentrated, and without extensive artillery preparations, the all-important flanking movement on the right would almost certainly have met with failure. Fortunate, too, in their results were the actions taken by François and Mackensen to make contact and thereby complete the encirclement of the Russians, and of great importance was Mackensen's independent decision to swing his force round at Allenstein, and thereby cut off the enemy to the east.

It is easier to say who lost the battle than who won it. The inferior generalship of the Russian armies, the incredible conduct of Rennenkampf in placing personal revenge before national honour, the criminal carelessness of the headquarters staff in sending out their wireless communications *en clair*, and the failure of both generals to utilize their numerical superiority and the strength of their position, all render the magnitude of the German victory more comprehensible.

The truth is to be found more nearly than anywhere else in Hoffmann's own analysis that whereas the battle of Tannenberg had been lost in the railway station of Mukden, responsibility for the German victory was not due to any one individual.

· 6 ·

The people of Germany in the late summer of 1914 had no such difficulty in determining the victor of Tannenberg. They gave their verdict with no uncertain voice and the hero of their choice was the man henceforth called Hindenburg. There is scarcely a parallel in history for so meteoric a rise from obscurity to idolization. Within a week his name had become a household word. Yet so little had he been known before that people had no clear idea of what he looked like.[1] Such few photographs of him as existed rose to a premium, and an army of press photographers was despatched to the east for more recent pictures. Most of them returned empty-handed, but the square head, the heavy face, and upturned moustaches were soon to be seen in every home in Germany. The legend of Tannenberg had grown overnight and it increased to prodigious proportions after the battle of the Masurian Lakes and the final freeing of East Prussia. *Hoch Hindenburg!* resounded in every *Bier-halle* and *Weinstube* throughout the country. In Hanover, where he had lived for three years in obscurity, people asked each other in the streets who he was, but the city placed his name at the head of its honour roll of citizens. The township of Zabrze, in Silesia, went further and changed its name to Hindenburg. Field postmen, with unerring instinct, began to deliver to his headquarters the correspondence addressed to "The Most Popular Man in Germany," while shopkeepers vied in stocking "Hindenburg" cigars, boots, and ties, and restaurants called their choicest dishes after him.

[1] So unfamiliar was the face of their army commander to his own troops that when, after the battle of the Masurian Lakes, he was returning to his headquarters at Insterburg after a day's hunting, Hindenburg's car was stopped in the market-place where preparations were being made for a service of thanksgiving and he was forced to make a *détour*. Those who were about to celebrate deliverance from the Russian occupation had not recognized their deliverer!

With the approach of winter it was rumoured that he was unwell, and he was deluged with letters advising this and that treatment and cure. Country housewives sent him the prescriptions of
nostrums which had been in their families for generations and
pharmacies informed him that he had been placed on their free-
lists for life. During the first Christmas of the war he received
over six hundred gifts of wine, tobacco, and pipes alone, in addition to thousands of other presents. Old ladies sent him go-
loshes, and young ones pillows stuffed with their own hair.

He was taken to the warm heart of his people and became
affectionately known as *"Unser Hindenburg."* At once there
sprang up about his life a crop of anecdotes, the majority of
them false, and many of them hoary with years. Amongst these
was the remark attributed to every great captain in history who
fought a winter campaign, from Hannibal downwards: "Every
day I walk two hours against the wind so that I may have some
idea of what my soldiers are suffering." To the end of his life
he was the victim of the ingenious inventor of "good stories," the
tone of which became progressively more bitter.

Amongst this welter of hysterical adulation one man remained
unmoved and unimpressed. Hindenburg himself was never deceived by the legend of his own greatness. He at least knew the
truth of Tannenberg, and knew also the worth of public adoration. "Remember," he admonished his friends who crowded
about him with congratulations, "if Tannenberg had not gone
well for us, there would have been a name cursed by all Germans through eternity: the name of Hindenburg."

But he could not fight against his destiny, and official quarters
were quick to take advantage of his popularity to distract public attention from the position in the west, though they were well
aware that the success of Tannenberg was of minor importance
beside the failure of the Marne.

For the campaign in France and Belgium had failed signally.

Paris was safe and the race to the sea had been abandoned. Moltke, *"le général malgré lui,"* had proved unequal to the task of conducting a campaign on a grand scale. He had neither the resolution nor the moral courage to withstand the anxiety of waiting, nor the military judgment to pierce the fog of uncertainty which besets all modern commanders. In modifying the Schlieffen Plan in the south he had violated his predecessor's cardinal principle ever repeated till his death, "See that the right wing is strong." For, abandoning the plan of a strategic retirement in Alsace-Lorraine, Moltke had reinforced his left at the expense of his right. That wing, the key-point in Schlieffen's plan, was not sufficiently strong to perform its task, and gradually a gap opened between the advancing armies of Kluck and Bülow.

By September 4—at the time when in East Prussia the Eighth Army, having annihilated Samsonov, was turning northward to destroy Rennenkampf—Moltke, who had sat for days at Imperial Headquarters wrapped in nervous depression and gloomy reflections,[1] realized that by reinforcing the Lorraine front and endeavouring to break through between Toul and Epinal, he had so weakened his right wing that the enveloping movement from the north, the fundamental idea upon which Schlieffen had based the battle in the west, could not succeed. Unwell, unhappy, and completely lacking in self-confidence, Moltke lost his head and despatched one of his staff officers, Lieut.-Col. Hentsch, to Bülow and Kluck, with authority, if he saw fit to do so, to give verbal orders to retreat. This in fact he did, overruling their protests, and in that moment there vanished Germany's hope of a rapid war of conquest.

In relation to the situation in the west therefore, the German

---

[1] "Physically, Moltke is a wreck," wrote Grand-Admiral von Tirpitz from Luxemburg at this time; "it is such a mistake not to send him home as a heart and kidney patient, which as a matter of fact he is."

victory in the east was of very secondary importance. In the brain of the great Schlieffen, whose death in 1912, from a septic varicose ulcer, was the greatest blow that the German military machine sustained, the eastern theatre of war was subordinate in importance to the west. The Russian armies were to be destroyed, not in the hope of securing an early peace, but in order to leave the German forces free to fight and win the decisive battle in France and Belgium. After a false start, the eastern part of the Schlieffen Plan had been accomplished, but its success was very greatly robbed of its value by the fact that in the west the High Command had failed to fight and win a decisive battle.

Moltke's failure had lost for Germany her chance of winning the war, for from the autumn of 1914 the Western Front became an outer bastion of a besieged fortress from whence troops issued from time to time to repel attack or to effect a sortie. The serious hope of breaking through had vanished, and though the war might continue for years, it could only be a question of holding out and not of achieving victory.

It is uncertain whether the German High Command realized fully at that moment the grave importance of the failure of the Marne. They were, however, concerned with finding some method of diverting popular interest from failure to success, and for this purpose the sudden rise of Hindenburg as a national idol was most opportune. Every possible official means was taken to stimulate and foster the enthusiasm, and the victories on the East Prussian front were invested with a halo wholly disproportionate to their importance. The Emperor was prevailed upon to write a laudatory letter to the new hero, universities were encouraged to confer honorary degrees upon him, and municipalities their honorary citizenships.

The effect was all that could be desired. Public confidence rallied and optimism was regained. Hindenburg became not only a hero, but a living symbol of embattled Germany, a star to which his country now could look with hope and certainty to guide them through war to victory.

· 7 ·

But it required more even than the glorification of Hindenburg in the east, to restore the confidence of German arms in the west. By September 12 it had become evident to all that Moltke's mental and physical state rendered it impossible for him to continue a moment longer in the vitally important position of Chief of the General Staff,[1] and once again and for the last time, the Kaiser made use of his unfettered authority in the selection of a successor. His choice fell upon the Prussian Minister for War, Lieut.-Gen. Erich von Falkenhayn, who received his appointment on September 14, and, at his own request, retained his position in the Prussian Cabinet.

The change in the High Command, which was made purely on the grounds of the most urgent necessity and was mainly directed towards restoring the confidence of the headquarters staff and the army and corps commanders, was cloaked in the greatest secrecy. Moltke still remained at headquarters in an anomalous position, and as late as October 10 the Kaiser at a banquet at G.H.Q. at Charleville publicly toasted his success![2] And, though

[1] The German Crown Prince recalls his alarm and surprise at Moltke's sudden appearance at his headquarters on this date, "completely broken down and literally struggling to suppress his tears. According to his impressions, the entire German army had been defeated and was being rapidly and unceasingly rolled back" (*Memoirs*, p. 169).

[2] A tragic picture of the fallen general at this period has been left by the Crown Prince. "It was in the headquarters at Charleville; he had already been removed from his command; I found him aged by years; he was poring over maps in a little room in the prefecture—a bent and broken man . . . later he sank into a morbid search after the reasons for his evil fate, and tried to discover exonerations and justifications for his failure, losing himself in all kinds of barren mysticism. In the end he died at Berlin of a broken heart." (*Memoirs*, p. 172.)

This is not, however, an entirely fair picture of General von Moltke, for he was not only physically ill but spiritually distressed. He was convinced almost from the beginning that a successful issue of the war was impossible for Germany. Ever

his name was gradually allowed to drop out of circulation, it was not till November 3 that the appointment of General von Falkenhayn was made public. Army *communiqués* ceased for a while, and throughout the war the German nation was never told the truth of the crisis at headquarters; even leading members of the *Reichstag* only learnt much later, indirectly and incompletely, of what really happened on the Western Front in September 1914.

The new Chief of the General Staff, a native of West Prussia, a comparatively young man and of considerable personal charm, had one great advantage over his predecessor in that he was at least physically fit for the task. But though his conduct of the Rumanian campaign of 1916 showed him to be capable of fulfilling the position of an army commander with distinction, he was as unequal as Moltke to the supreme responsibility. Indeed, though the German army of 1914 had staff officers of the very highest ability, as, for example, Gröner, Seeckt, Willisen, and Hoffmann, these men rarely came into decisive power because, lacking seniority, their abilities remained hidden. For two long years the supreme military direction of the German armies remained in inept hands, and when, in the summer of 1916, the great military genius of Ludendorff finally took over the command, all hope of attaining a military victory had passed away.

What might not have happened had the Kaiser appointed the military combination of Hindenburg, Ludendorff, and Hoffmann to the Supreme Command in September 1914? The controlling brains of the combination, Ludendorff and Hoffmann, were essentially Schlieffen men, and in the opinion of some of the best

---

before his eyes was that fateful session of the Prussian Cabinet on August 3 at which Bethmann Hollweg had declared that the participation of Great Britain in the war had now become inevitable, a statement which brought a cry from Admiral von Tirpitz of "All is then lost!" At hearing this exclamation from one who had done more than any other to promote conflict between England and Germany, the last hope of victory vanished for the Chief of the General Staff, and he at once became a prey to the deepest depression and despair.

military authorities in Germany, the Schlieffen Plan was still capable of operation after the failure of the Marne. Hoffmann believed it and declared himself in favour of transferring ten army corps from the left to the right wing and of making, with these united forces, a renewed attack, even if, as a necessary condition, large parts of Alsace and Lorraine must pass temporarily into French hands. Gröner, according to Ludendorff, actually made a similar suggestion to Falkenhayn and had worked out, in his capacity of Director of Field Railways, a plan for the transport north of six army corps, but his proposal was rejected.[1] Falkenhayn, as a matter of fact, did eventually transfer the greater part of the Sixth and Seventh Armies from his right wing, but his movement coincided with Joffre's strengthening of his southern flank, prolonging the French line to the northward. Thus in succession the German corps arriving from the south found themselves confronted at each point with a similar concentration of troops opposite them, and Falkenhayn finally abandoned the Schlieffen Plan in favour of the capture of Antwerp and a great drive against the Channel Ports. It is, however, a matter of interesting speculation as to what the genius of Ludendorff, the fortitude of Hindenburg, supported by the technical expert knowledge of Gröner and Hoffmann, might have accomplished at this juncture.

The appointment of Falkenhayn marked the close of the first

---

[1] It is possible that Ludendorff may not have entirely understood the full meaning of Gröner's proposal which was of a more audacious nature than he suggests. It appeared to Gröner that the transfer of troops from the left to the right would take too long and was too cumbersome an operation in view of the fact that there was no adequate French Railway line available for the purpose. He, therefore, proposed that the cavalry divisions on the extreme right, of which Major von Willisen was Chief of Staff, should be retained in their positions at Kemmel; that the new divisions, then being formed in Germany, should be brought straight to the west to strengthen the German right and that troops should be withdrawn from the left in Alsace-Lorraine to reinforce the Eastern Front. These operations would take full advantage of the excellently organized system of the German strategic railways and their execution would, therefore, have been possible within a very brief space of time.

phase of the war, during which the Central Powers had achieved a brilliant success in East Prussia and had sustained two outstanding defeats on the Marne and around Lemberg, where the Austro-Hungarian army had lost more than 200,000 men. In addition the initiative had passed into the hands of the Allies.

Falkenhayn hoped by his drive against the Channel Ports to liquidate the position in the west, but in the meantime urgent and immediate assistance had to be sent to Germany's eastern ally. Clearly, no troops could be spared from the west and help must therefore come from the wearied but victorious troops of Hindenburg.

The advancing Russian armies, after their success at Lemberg, threatened both the Austrian forces in Galicia and the German province of Silesia, and as early as September 14, the day of Falkenhayn's appointment, Hindenburg had received orders to operate in Silesia in support of the Austrians. It had originally been intended to form a new Ninth Army under General von Schubert, with Ludendorff as Chief of Staff, to carry out these operations, but in deference to representations from all parties concerned the Kaiser appointed Hindenburg to the command of both the Eighth and Ninth Armies, and thus the combination, which Mr. Winston Churchill has designated by the symbol HL, but which might well be expanded to HLH to include Hoffmann, remained unsevered.

The position now confronting the combination HLH was of equal seriousness and danger to that before Tannenberg, with the additional disadvantages that the German veterans had been but slightly reinforced whereas the Russian armies were fresh, and their High Command, now under the personal direction of the Grand Duke Nicholas, had learned much from the previous campaign and was no longer hampered by petty jealousies. The Grand Duke had drawn up one and a quarter million men so disposed that they could either make an advance into Germany or meet an impending German attack.

To oppose this host there were the Ninth and part of the Eighth Armies, some eighteen divisions, concentrated in Silesia, together with Dankl's First Austrian Army on the right, leaving the remainder of the Eighth Army for the defence of East Prussia. The object of the main force was to seize and hold all the crossings of the Vistula from the confluence of the San to Warsaw, and thus protected, to strike at Warsaw itself. With this end in view Mackensen and Dankl began their advance on September 28.

The plans of each headquarters staff were disclosed to the other in the true tradition of military melodrama. On September 30 a pocket-book taken from a dead German officer revealed to the Grand Duke the significant fact that only two German corps remained in East Prussia, thereby confirming reports already received of the concentration of troops to the southward, and justifying the belief that the advance which had begun on September 28 was being made by a German army closely in touch with the Austrian left wing.

A few days later (October 9) an order found on a Russian corpse revealed to German Headquarters the magnitude of the plan opposed to them. "It appeared that we had four Russian armies to cope with," writes Hindenburg, "that is, about sixty divisions to eighteen of ours. . . . The enemy's superiority was increased by the fact that, as a result of the previous fighting in East Prussia and France, as well as the long and exhausting marches of more than 200 miles over indescribable roads, our troops had been reduced to scarcely half establishment and in some cases even to a quarter of their original strength. And these weak units of ours were to meet fresh arrivals at full strength . . . the Siberian Corps, the *élite* of the Tsar's Empire! The enemy's intention was to hold us fast along the Vistula while a

decisive attack from Warsaw was to spell our ruin. It was unquestionably a great plan of the Grand Duke Nicholas Nicho-
laievitch, indeed the greatest I had known, and in my view it
remained his greatest until he was transferred to the Cauca-
sus. . . ." [1]

Stout hearts indeed and all the resources of iron will and cool
audacity were required in the face of these odds to continue an
advance which even at the first had not been assured of success.
There are few episodes in German military history which show
a more generous effort to relieve an ally or a more accurate
estimation of German military superiority over an enemy. It was
in every sense a "sporting" operation but not a foolhardy one.
Every precaution had been taken for a speedy retreat in the
event of failure. Bridges and tunnels were mined at the same
time that they were repaired, and the whole of the communications of the advancing army were so organized as to make the
swiftest retreat possible. No episode in the war on the Eastern
Front illustrated more clearly the superb combination of Ludendorff's strategy and Hoffmann's technical efficiency, surmounted
by the growing legend and prestige of Hindenburg.

By October 6 the German advance had reached the Vistula
over almost impassable roads. The immediate strategic effect
was enormous, for the Russians broke up their front in Galicia
and raised the siege of the fortress of Przemyśl. The Austrians
were able to advance to the San without finding any noteworthy
resistance. But at the Vistula two new factors came into play.
The Germans met with fierce and heroic resistance from the Cau-
casian corps whose gun trails were actually in the river but who
could not be dislodged, while to the right the Austrians, who
were to attack the Russian left flank, proved so weak in striking

[1] Ludendorff, too, usually so chary of eulogy, expresses the opinion that this
plan disclosed the Grand Duke as *"einen ganze General."*

power that they did not succeed in forcing the crossing of the San.

Thus held on the river front, a German frontal attack was impossible, but by the 12th Mackensen on the left was within a dozen miles of Warsaw and was holding an important railway junction almost inside the perimeter of the city. Now, however, the Grand Duke launched four armies on the German centre and for three days a terrific battle ensued in which the German divisions opposed in their turn the passage of the Vistula, hoping in vain that their Austrian allies on the right would create a diversion.

Gradually Russian preponderance of numbers became irresistible and at German headquarters at Radom there was the greatest anxiety. "It was indeed the hardest time of the campaign in my experience," writes Hoffmann. "Ludendorff and I stand and support each other and the chief says 'God be with us, I can do no more!' " Hindenburg admits frankly the doubts which mingled with his resolution. Further advance was impossible, yet "what would the Homeland say when our retreat approached its frontiers? Was it remarkable that terror reigned in Silesia? Its inhabitants would think of how the Russians had laid waste East Prussia, of robbing and looting, the deportation of non-combatants and other horrors. Fertile Silesia, with its highly developed coal mines and great industrial areas, both as vital to our military operations as daily bread itself. It is not an easy thing to say in war, 'I am going to evacuate this region!' You must be an economist as well as a soldier. Ordinary human feelings also assert themselves. It is often these last which are hardest to overcome."

It is easy enough to appreciate the feelings of Hindenburg at this juncture. It was his first taste of failure as a commanding general. Hitherto victory, even though after hard-fought battles, had been his, and now there was no alternative but to retreat and accept the inevitable. He had undoubtedly hoped at the outset, with the assistance of the Austrians, to inflict some real defeat upon the Russians and may indeed have been slightly puzzled why this had not come about. "The worst of matters here," writes Hoffmann in his diary at this moment, "is that Hindenburg simply cannot understand why we do not win another victory like that in East Prussia."

But a moment arrived when flesh and blood could stand no more, and on October 17 the order was given for a general retreat. This movement, carried out through the sleet and slush of a Polish autumn, where Napoleon's "fourth element"—mud— was predominant, was executed with the same amazing skill which marked the advance. Marching sixty miles in six days and with more than one stubborn rear-guard action, the Ninth Army had by the end of October returned to its original position, but less 40,000 men; while the Russian forces, flushed with success, were once more advancing towards Silesia.

It was clear that not a moment must be lost if the great Silesian industrial areas were to be saved from invasion, yet it was impossible to meet the Russian hordes in the present position and with depleted forces. An element of surprise must be introduced and reinforcements solicited from the west.

At a Headquarters Conference at Chenstokhova, on November 3, the new plan took form in the brains of Ludendorff and Hoffmann, and, in imparting it to the staff, Hindenburg indicated its nature by a gesture of his left hand, pointing to the north. All present understood and agreed. The Ninth Army, now facing north-east from Posen to Cracow, must be reunited with the Eighth and re-formed, facing south-east from Posen to Thorn, and an attack made against Lodz to draw the Russians from their present objectives.

By a miracle of railway transport this movement was carried out with the greatest speed and secrecy. Within a week (by November 10) the transfer was completed and the German army multiplied by two was deployed on a new 70-mile front, while the Russians remained completely ignorant of its departure, or of the fact that its place had been taken by General Böhm-Ermolli's Second Austrian Army.

German general headquarters were established in the castle of Posen, where, writes Ludendorff, "we got into the habit of sitting together for a time after dinner at a round table on which stood an aspidistra, the gift of H.M. our Kaiserin, a true German woman."

· 8 ·

The plans for the projected German counter-offensive on the Thorn-Posen line required two factors for complete success, unity of command in the east and adequate reinforcements. When, therefore, Ludendorff in the last week of October was summoned to Supreme Headquarters at Mezières to confer with Falkenhayn, he put these two points very forcibly to the Chief of the General Staff, sparing him nothing of the very serious position in which the Eighth and Ninth Armies were placed in the face of the Russian numerical superiority.

This meeting between Ludendorff and Falkenhayn is of very considerable importance, for it marked the first direct personal contact between the Western and Eastern theatres of war, and the first skirmish in that long campaign between Falkenhayn and HLH which ended two years later in Falkenhayn's resignation. Ludendorff learned now the truth of what had happened in the west in September; Falkenhayn heard, and it is certain that Ludendorff's story lost nothing in the telling, of the prodigious feats accomplished in the east with limited forces, and what might yet be done with adequate reinforcements. Ludendorff and Hoffmann felt sure that with two or three fresh corps they could drive the Russians back from East Prussia and Silesia, capture Warsaw, and inflict a really crushing defeat, comparable to those of Tannenberg and the Lakes, upon the Tsar's armies.

Falkenhayn, though sensible of the requirements of the Eastern Front, had his own plans. His ambitions to take the Channel Ports had dwindled first to the capture of Ypres and Armentières, and finally to Ypres. But Ypres he must have, its capture had become an obsession both with him and with the Kaiser. Once Ypres had fallen, three or four corps should be transported to the east, but until then all he could spare was two cavalry divisions and with these the Eastern Command must do what it could. All Ludendorff's appeals were vain, and he left with the impression that Falkenhayn was deliberately starving the Eastern Front and failed to appreciate the opportunities for decisive victory which were there presented. He left Imperial Headquarters in a spirit of dissatisfaction which he imparted to his colleagues at Posen. Nor was this spirit dispelled by a visit from Falkenhayn's Chief of Operations and *alter ego*, Colonel von Tappen, whom, says Hoffmann, "I implored, almost on my knees, to persuade the Chief of the General Staff to put at our disposal, besides the promised reinforcements, at least two more army corps." The refusal was again definite.

In its second object, however, the mission of Ludendorff to Mezières was more successful. On November 1 the Kaiser appointed Hindenburg Commander-in-Chief in the East, having under him all German forces from the Baltic to the Austrian frontier, with Ludendorff as his Chief of Staff, and Hoffmann as senior Staff Officer. Thus HLH were translated intact to a higher sphere of action.

The operation which opened on November 11 in East Prussia was carried out by the slightly reinforced Eighth and Ninth Armies, and resulted in the battle of Lodz, which Hindenburg himself described as "exceeding in ferocity all the battles which had previously been fought on the Eastern Front." In the course of it a quarter of a million Germans were pitted against over half a million Russians. At one moment the Germans only just failed to surround and capture 150,000 Russians, at another the Russians actually surrounded but failed to hold 60,000 Germans. The battle lasted with varying intensity till December 6, when the fortress of Lodz surrendered and the Russians finally retreated.

All Russian hopes of an advance into Silesia had been effectively frustrated, but the Germans, as the reinforcements from the west arrived by driblets, had been unable to inflict a decisive defeat. The colossal mass which they had tried to roll back only retired a short stretch and then stood still in immmobility. The energies of both armies flagged, worn out by defeats, fighting, and the vileness of the swampy country; the frost was becoming more and more severe, with icy winds, and the temperature at night fell to within ten degrees (F.) of zero. The approach of winter laid its paralysing hand on the activity of German and Russian alike.

· 9 ·

Though the results of the campaigns in Poland and East Prussia in the autumn and winter of 1914 may have failed to satisfy the High Command in the east, they convinced the German people of the titanic qualities of Hindenburg. What if he had retreated from before Warsaw? Had he not had four Russian armies against him and had he not, by the master stroke at Lodz, saved Silesia from the spoiling hand of the invader? Fresh laurels adorned him, new and more ecstatic enthusiasm greeted the mention of his name, and the Kaiser promoted him to the rank of Field-Marshal.

HINDENBURG WITH WOUNDED MEN ON HIS 70TH BIRTHDAY, OCTOBER 2, 1917

To a great extent this confidence in the Hindenburg-Ludendorff combination (Hoffmann's part in the triumvirate was not appreciated until much later) was shared in high quarters at Berlin; more especially when the achievements in the east were compared with the failures in the west. For Falkenhayn's ambition to capture Ypres had been finally shattered on the afternoon of November 11, when the Prussian Guard had been first held and then hurled back upon the Menin Road. Twelve Allied divisions, seven British and five French, had withstood the onslaught of twenty-two German divisions converging upon the Ypres salient, and when night fell and the line remained intact, Falkenhayn was forced to recognize that his campaign for the salient must now end, and end in very costly failure.

It was inevitable that the commanders and their achievements should be contrasted by soldiers, sailors, and politicians, and that such a comparison should be invidious to Falkenhayn. Grand-Admiral von Tirpitz was writing in his diary: "Great leaders have not arisen among us, except in the east," and he was shortly to make an entry of almost lyrical appeal: "O blessed Hindenburg, help us soon, we are in sore need of it."

With the general adoption of trench warfare, both in the east and west, after the battles of Lodz and Ypres, both sides were exhausted, the fronts became stationary and there occurred a lull for stock-taking and the formation of new plans. Within the German camp divisions of opinion at once began to appear. All hope of achieving Schlieffen's ambition of a swift war and a swift peace had now vanished, and as a result political necessity began increasingly to predominate over military actions. Here again were dissensions, for not only were there rival military schools of thought but opposing political theses also. In the first years of the war, Germany suffered to a marked degree from the absence of an agreed policy for the conduct of war and peace. Surrounded on all sides by an increasing number of enemies, she was unable to make up her mind which to crush first and her hands were tied still further by the fact that for Allies she had little more than a collection of corpses, in some of which decomposition had already set in.

In the political, as in the military, counsels of the Kaiser, there were the eastern and the western schools. The Chancellor, Bethmann Hollweg, never ceased to hope that by conciliating England it might be possible to detach her from the Allies and to reach a separate peace agreement with her. He therefore opposed strenuously the adoption of unrestricted U-boat warfare and advocated an aggressive policy on the Eastern Front. As against this view there was that of Tirpitz, and to some extent of Falkenhayn, who regarded England as the arch-enemy of the Fatherland. "Our most dangerous enemy," wrote the Chief of the General Staff, "is not in the east, but England, with whom the conspiracy against Germany stands and falls."

In the military sphere the issue was more clear-cut and more technical. It was clear that an outstanding German victory must be achieved by the spring; much, very much, depended on it, and most important of all the attitude of Italy and the Balkan States, which had hitherto remained neutral. The point at issue was: should this victory be won in the east or the west?

It was now that the German Supreme Command began to reap the fruits of their zealous fostering of the Hindenburg legend after Tannenberg. Then they had been only too thankful that the failure of the Marne should be glossed over by the East Prussian victories, and accordingly the name of Hindenburg had been exalted to the skies. Now this same glittering galaxy of military pundits discovered that they had created a new factor which rapidly threatened to escape their control. Hindenburg and Ludendorff attended conferences at Imperial General Headquarters with the air of men who have done things and have more to achieve. Moreover, they commanded an army whose victories had imbued it with a feeling of unquestioned superiority over the enemy, a conviction shared by the oldest *Landsturm* man with the youngest recruit.

As against this record of success in the east, the High Command in the west could only point to the collapse of Moltke, the failure of the Marne, the retreat to the Aisne, and the defeat of the Prussian Guard before Ypres. How near they had been to victory on a number of occasions and how thin a line had prevented their advance along the Menin Road, they could not know, but the fact remained that though they had won territory they had not achieved victory.

It is true that, in the west, Germany had been confronted by troops and military organizations of the highest order, the flower of the armies of France and Britain, while in the east, the Russian armies, though numerically superior, were badly equipped, weak in artillery, and in most cases poorly led. Nevertheless it was unassailably true that victories and large numbers of prisoners had graced German arms in the east, whereas failures and heavy losses were their portion in the west.

Hindenburg and Ludendorff therefore felt fully justified in urging the Supreme Command "to let them go on winning the war." They believed, and in this they had the full support of the Chief of the Austrian General Staff, Field-Marshal Conrad von Hötzendorf, that it was both possible and imperative to drive Russia out of the war by means of a decisive victory. A great effort must be made in the spring with every available corps; and if it were not made, the war might be speedily lost by the desertion to the Allies of the Balkan neutrals and by the conclusion of a separate peace by Austria. The Dual Monarchy must be bolstered up, Serbia crushed, Italy kept neutral, Greece, Bulgaria, and Rumania brought in on the side of the Central Powers, and Turkey supported in her *Jehad* against Britain. Such was the thesis advanced by HLH.

Falkenhayn, however, was completely and utterly opposed to this theory. To him the assumption that a final decision could be obtained in the east was unfounded and "based upon sophisms." He did not believe, and subsequent events proved him right, that the Western Allies would give way if Russia were beaten. "No decision in the east," he wrote subsequently, "even though it was as thorough as was possible to imagine, could spare us from fighting to a conclusion in the west."

As early as January 1915, the Chief of the General Staff had assumed an attitude of mind which was fundamentally defeatist. He was no longer fighting for victory, but for escape. No more than an indemnity could be exacted from Russia and France. But he was convinced that if Germany must go on fighting, her best chance of success lay in the west. To this end he evolved the principle of "limited offensives," which should injure and weaken the enemy more than they would weaken and injure the Germans, and he was preparing to make the first of these against the northern sections of the Anglo-French lines in late January or early February.

Herein lay the deep-seated cause of the struggle between HLH and Falkenhayn. They still believed in the possibility of victory, he did not. They regarded his policy of "limited offensives" as dissipating the man-power of Germany in isolated efforts without achieving lasting results; he viewed their hopes of achieving a decision in the east as military sophistry. Moreover, he, as Chief of the General Staff, was their superior and was in control of the German army machine and of five-sixths of its strength.

But Hindenburg and Ludendorff, too, had powerful allies. The Chancellor and the Foreign Office supported them, and Conrad von Hötzendorf posted from Vienna to Berlin to emphasize his view that "complete success in the Eastern theatre is still, as hitherto, decisive for the general situation and extremely urgent." Falkenhayn was adamant. He would send no fresh troops to the east, he needed the four new corps then being raised for his attacks in the west. He even refused to countenance the sending of divisions south from Hindenburg's command to the support of the Austrians.

Conrad returned to his headquarters at Teschen and ordered the preparation for an offensive in Galicia to forestall a Russian attack upon him and the entry of Italy into the war on the side of the Allies. He telegraphed for aid both to Falkenhayn and Hindenburg. Falkenhayn refused on behalf of both.

HLH then performed their first act of defiance and independence. They informed Falkenhayn that they were in complete accord with Conrad's views, and that, without the consent of the Chief of the General Staff, they had promised to send several divisions to the support of the Austrians.

This was open war, and both sides appealed to the Kaiser, as All-Highest War Lord, for a decision. The Imperial position had changed considerably in the last few months. In September 1914, without taking advice or counsel with anyone, the Kaiser had appointed Falkenhayn to succeed Moltke, and none had even attempted to influence his decision. Now in January 1915, he was faced with the predicament of supporting the leader of his own Imperial choice against the acclaimed idols of the people, who had unquestionably committed an act of insubordination. To dismiss or even reprimand Hindenburg and Ludendorff had by January 1915 become an impossibility; all Germany would have supported them even against the Emperor, and the Emperor knew it. On January 8 he gave his approval for Conrad's Carpathian operations and for the despatch of German troops for their support.

But Falkenhayn also had his moment of victory. Though forced to concede on the major issue, he made a determined effort to break up the sinister combination of HLH, which had so flagrantly flouted his authority. Ludendorff had supported Conrad in his demand for German divisions for the Galician offensive; Ludendorff then should share in the command of the divisions, and forthwith Falkenhayn persuaded the Kaiser to appoint Ludendorff as Chief of Staff to the new *Südarmee*, which was being formed under the command of Linsingen to co-operate with Conrad. The appointment was accompanied by a flattering expression of the Kaiser's deep confidence in Ludendorff's military ability, but its true meaning was plain for all to see.

It may be imagined with what feelings Hindenburg received the news of Ludendorff's transfer to Galicia. For the past five months, ever since that strangely correct meeting on the station platform at Hanover, the two men had been practically inseparable, and Hindenburg's self had been, to a very large degree, absorbed into the more dominating personality of Ludendorff. Tannenberg, the Lakes, the advance to Warsaw, the dismal retreat to Silesia, and the bitter struggle around Lodz, had welded the two together into an irrefragable union, and though Ludendorff could have operated without Hindenburg, it is very certain that Hindenburg could not have functioned without Ludendorff. Not even Hoffmann could take his place.

Faced therefore with this danger of spiritual disruption, Hindenburg was moved to take independent action of a drastic nature. Once more ignoring Falkenhayn, he petitioned the Emperor direct on two scores; first, that the four new corps in process of formation should be employed in a decisive blow in East Prussia, and secondly, that Ludendorff might be returned to him.

The employment of these [corps] in the east [he wrote] is a necessity. With them it will not be difficult quickly to inflict on the enemy in East Prussia a decisive and annihilating blow and at last to free entirely that sorely afflicted province and to push on thence with our whole force. . . . I regard this operation, with the employment in the east of the newly raised forces, as decisive for the outcome of the whole war; whereas their employment in the west will only lead to a strengthening of our defence, or—as at Ypres—to a costly and not very promising frontal push. Our army in the west ought to be able to hold well-constructed positions sited in successive lines and to maintain itself without being reinforced by the new corps until decisive success in the east has been attained.

Here, in a concise form, was the kernel of the military philosophy of HLH. A period of vigilant quiescence in the west until the annihilation of the Russian armies had been accomplished, and possibly an armistice signed, and then a smashing offensive against the Anglo-French positions. It was this strategy which Hindenburg and Ludendorff employed in 1917–18, but by that time it was too late.

Hindenburg's request for reunion with Ludendorff was impassioned and deeply significant, for it betrayed the degree to which he had already become dependent upon the other. Despite the restraint of the language, there is something pitiful, something almost of fear, underlying the appeal.

Your Imperial and Royal Majesty has been graciously pleased to command that General Ludendorff should, as Chief of the Staff, be transferred from me to the Southern Army. . . . During the days of Tannenberg and the Masurian Lakes, during the operations against Ivangorod and Warsaw, and in the advance from the Wreschen-Thorn line, I have grown into close union with my Chief of Staff; he has become to me a true helper and friend, irreplaceable by any other, one on whom I bestow my fullest confidence. Your Majesty knows from the history of the war how important so happy a relationship is for the course of affairs and the well-being of the troops. To that is to be added that his new and so much smaller sphere of action does not do justice to the General's comprehensive ability and great capacity. . . . On all these grounds I venture most respectfully to beg that my war-comrade may graciously be restored to me so soon as the operations in the south are under way. It is no personal ambition which leads me to lay this petition at the feet of your Imperial and Royal Majesty. That be far from me! Your Majesty has overwhelmed me with favours beyond my deserts, and after the war is ended I shall retire again into the background with a thankful and joyful heart. Far rather do I believe that I am fulfilling a duty in expressing with all submission this request.

Falkenhayn, in personal interviews with Conrad, Linsingen, and Ludendorff at Breslau on January 10, and with Hindenburg, Ludendorff, and Hoffmann two days later at Posen, sought to impose his views. The leaders of the Eastern School refused absolutely to make any concession to him and stood upon their appeal to Caesar; and they added their voices to that of the Chancellor in Berlin, urging that Falkenhayn should be dismissed. In this they were unsuccessful, but on all other heads Wilhelm II once more bowed before the storm. The offensive in East Prussia was approved, and Ludendorff was reunited with his old chief. Falkenhayn had "with a heavy heart to make up his mind to employ in the east the young corps which were the only available reserves at the time," and, moreover, had to surrender the Prussian Ministry of War to General Wild von Hohenborn. That, having sustained this damaging blow to his prestige, he continued as Imperial Chief of the General Staff for a further eighteen months is surprising, for his authority never entirely recovered from the rebuff, and though in the conflict between himself and HLH, he now and then scored a success, the ultimate issue was hardly ever in doubt.

· 10 ·

Hindenburg, Ludendorff, and Hoffmann were in the dangerous position of having got all they wanted and having given definite hopes of a decisive victory. They had now to prove the truth of their convictions, the whole thesis of the easterners was at stake.

The plan of campaign was on a gigantic scale and envisaged

an offensive on the right and left flanks of the Grand Duke's position; in East Prussia by the Eighth, Ninth, and Tenth German Armies, and in the south by the Austro-Hungarian forces supported by Linsingen's *Südarmee*. The whole Russian army was to be caught between the pincers. In the north it was hoped to repeat the Cannae manœuvre of the previous September, and to encircle and annihilate the opposing Russian forces.

In effect neither of these ambitions was realized. The operations against both wings of the Russian front did not come up to the far-reaching expectations expressed in Hindenburg's letter to the Kaiser. In the south the Austrian attack was stopped almost at once by a Russian counter-offensive, and only Linsingen's army was able to make progress; while in the north, though the winter battle of the Masurian Lakes, which opened on February 7 and raged until the end of March, resulted in the eventual destruction of the Tenth Russian Army in the forest of Augustovo, with the capture of a large amount of artillery and many thousands of prisoners, it was found impossible to exploit and follow up this success. The failure occurred partly on account of the rigour of the climate and the consequent tax upon the endurance of the troops, and partly because of the endless stream of reinforcements which arrived to fill the gaps made by the Russian casualties.

Both Hindenburg and Ludendorff admit frankly that the operations had failed to achieve the decisive result for which they had hoped. "In spite of the great tactical success . . . we failed strategically," wrote the Marshal. But in the country at large and in the estimation of many leaders in Berlin, their laurels, and especially those of Hindenburg, were not only untarnished but re-gilded. It was at this moment that Grand-Admiral von Tirpitz was advocating a plan, to which he even succeeded in enlisting the support of the Kaiserin and the Crown Prince; the Emperor was to dismiss Bethmann Hollweg and Falkenhayn, and then to go temporarily into retirement, having called Hindenburg to the position of Dictator, a rôle which would combine the offices of Chancellor and of Commander-in-Chief on land and sea. This course alone, the Admiral believed, could save Germany, and more especially was he anxious to get rid of the immediate Imperial entourage, the heads of the Emperor's Civil, Military, and Naval Cabinets, known to their many enemies as "the Hydra."

But Falkenhayn's star was temporarily in the ascendant, and it was to him now that the ears of the Emperor and "the Hydra" were inclined. Hoffmann at this moment was noting in his diary: "Falkenhayn is the evil genius of our Fatherland, and, unfortunately, he has the Kaiser in his pocket. Now we must depend upon ourselves."

Having successfully defeated the French offensive in Champagne during the months of February and March, 1915, Falkenhayn had allowed himself to be momentarily wooed from his western "orthodoxy" by the sheer necessity of events. The Russian armies had by no means been exhausted by the winter offensive, nor were they fundamentally discouraged by the defeat of the Second Masurian Battle. They were counterattacking fiercely along the German front, and in Galicia they had all but stormed the Carpathian barrier. The fertile plains of Hungary lay open to invasion once this great natural defence was passed, and Conrad von Hötzendorf was calling again, this time more imperatively than ever, for assistance from his ally.

Of the great figures which passed across the Central European stage during the years of war, that of Conrad von Hötzendorf is among the most tragic. Perhaps the ablest of all the strategists produced by the Central Powers, his brilliant conceptions were for ever doomed to failure by reason of the quality of the material with which he sought to carry them into effect. The Austro-Hungarian army, through lack of homogeneity, through faulty and obsolete organization, and through corruption at home, was never a weapon worthy of the genius of its Chief of Staff, whose great ability was fully appreciated by his German colleagues. "The ideas of the Chief of the Austrian General Staff were good, they were all good. . . . The misfortune of that man of genius was that he had not the proper instrument by which he could transform his ideas into facts. The troops failed." So wrote Hoffmann, the most penetrating of critics on the Eastern Front.

In face of the grim pressure of events, Falkenhayn reluctantly abandoned his dreams of an offensive in the west and turned his thoughts eastward. Here for the moment must be the centre of military activity, but he would direct operations himself; HLH had had a free hand and had failed, such new operations as might be undertaken must be the fruit of the labours of the Chief of the General Staff.

For this reason Imperial General Headquarters were transferred from Mezières to the Silesian castle of the Prince of Pless, where the Chief of the General Staff, adhering to his conviction that the enveloping tactics of the Schlieffen school, as practised by Hindenburg and Ludendorff, had not been justified by success, began to develop a new stratagem with the more direct objective of a "break-through" of the Russian lines between Gorlice and Tarnov, just north of the Carpathians.

In reality this was merely a reversion to a proposal which had been outlined to Falkenhayn by Conrad von Hötzendorf at their conference in December 1914 at the Hotel Adlon, but in his book Falkenhayn is silent as to the author of the idea.

Here indeed was irony for Hindenburg, Ludendorff, and Hoffmann. At last there had occurred that for which they had so incessantly asked, the transfer of the centre of activity from west to east; at last the interest of Imperial General Headquarters was centred on the destruction of the Russians; at last heavy reinforcements were being brought eastward. But all this was Dead Sea fruit. The command of the Eastern Front, which they had grown to regard as their own personal preserve, automatically reverted to Imperial General Headquarters at Pless. The sacred teachings of Schlieffen were to be abandoned for a new doctrine of a frontal assault, and even this was not to be under their direction. A new army of German and Austro-Hungarian divisions, commanded by Mackensen, with Seeckt as Chief of Staff, was entrusted with the "break-through" at Gorlice, in which the armies under the control of the Commander-in-Chief in the East played but a secondary part. "My Headquarters," wrote Hindenburg, "was only an indirect participant in the great operation which began at Gorlice. Our first duty, within the framework of this mighty enterprise, was to tie down strong enemy forces."

This duty was discharged by means of a gas attack (the first to be executed in the east) delivered along the front of the Ninth Army, by means of an advance on Suvalki, and by a cavalry raid into Courland and Northern Lithuania. Thus covered, the operation of the "break-through" at Gorlice, which began on May 2, was a great success, a success which amazed and perhaps chagrined the disciples of Schlieffen.[1] But although the Russian front was rolled back, yielding provinces and cities, till almost the whole of Galicia was cleared of the invader and even Warsaw was threatened, there was no overwhelming defeat and no great increase in booty; by June the operations were approaching a deadlock

---

[1] Count Ottokar Czernin, the late Austro-Hungarian Foreign Minister, in a defence of his policy before the Vienna Parliament immediately after the war (December 11, 1918), declared his belief that at one point only in the history of the war, namely, after the battle of Gorlice, "with the Russian army in flight and the Russian fortresses falling like houses of cards," was it possible to have secured a peace based on "a policy of renunciation." The Russians, he believed, were prepared for it, but the German military party refused to consider the possibility (*In the World War*, p. 329).

and HLH were quick to take advantage of the position to propose a return to their theory of enveloping tactics.

A super-Tannenberg was envisaged, an outflanking movement designed cut off the Russian centre, which still projected
in a salient westwards beyond Warsaw; an operation which, beginning east and south against Kovno, would open up the road
to Vilna, and cut off the Russian retreat. "Perhaps for the last
time," records Hoffmann, "we had the opportunity of inflicting
a decisive blow upon the Russian army."

So confident were the headquarters of the Commander-in-
Chief in the East that this plan would be accepted by the High
Command, that preparations for the Kovno offensive were
pushed forward with enthusiasm and were well advanced when,
on July 1, the Marshal and Ludendorff were summoned to a
conference with the Emperor and Falkenhayn at Posen.

With high expectations they left their headquarters at Lötzen,
Ludendorff arranging to telephone to Hoffmann immediately
after the audience, so that the final orders might be issued without delay. Hour after hour Hoffmann waited in his office. The
audience had been timed for the early morning. Noon passed
and no telephone message came. Hoffmann was as near to
nervous anxiety as he ever permitted himself to approach. At
last, late in the afternoon, the tensely savage voice of Ludendorff
ordered him to stop everything and to abandon all preparations.
Falkenhayn had won another trick.

At Posen, Falkenhayn, elated at the success of the Gorlice
venture and faithful as ever to his strategy of limited aims,
had declined to consider the proposed offensive "into the blue,"
and advocated a repetition of a frontal attack in the shape of
a second "break-through" on the line of the Narev. Both sides
appealed to the Emperor, but times had changed since the previous January and its vital decisions, and the Emperor had
come under other influences. By this time he had gone over

wholly to Falkenhayn and Tappen, and for this there is the
evidence of both Colonel Bauer, and of Hoffmann. Bauer, who
was present at the Posen discussions, declares that Wilhelm II
was "wholly under the influence of Falkenhayn and Tappen"
and records a brief episode in confirmation. Ludendorff advanced the argument in defence of his plan that the proposed
attack would meet with no more than feeble resistance, where-
upon Tappen remarked sarcastically: "These people only want
to attack where there is no one to oppose them." Under the influence of such advice the Emperor vetoed the plans of HLH,
and approved the "break-through" on the Narev, to be made by
the forces of Gallwitz and Scholtz, withdrawn for the purpose
from the authority of the Commander-in-Chief in the East. When
Hindenburg and Ludendorff left Posen the breach with Falkenhayn was complete.

· 11 ·

In the constant bickering that now took place between Imperial General Headquarters and the Commander-in-Chief in
the East, it is doubtful whether such a degree of bitterness
would have been attained had not the Marshal allowed himself
to be so greatly influenced by his two lieutenants. For Hindenburg's character was too phlegmatic and his temperament too
sluggish for strong passion. Nor was he of a jealous nature. It
mattered little to him that he, a Field-Marshal with fifty years
of service, should act under Falkenhayn, a man far younger
both in years and in rank. To Hindenburg his Supreme War
Lord was the Emperor, to whom he regarded himself as directly
responsible, and his sense of personal loyalty to his sovereign
would inevitably have led him to accept without demur the Imperial decision, even though in his heart he might have disagreed
with it.

But if Tappen incited Falkenhayn against Hindenburg, Ludendorff and Hoffmann inflamed the Marshal against the Chief of the General Staff. After Ludendorff's return from Posen to Lötzen, Hoffmann describes the evening which they spent together, "both of us cursing G.H.Q. for interfering with our plans and ordering us to do something which we all thought impracticable"; these two now bent all their energies towards fanning the flames of the quarrel. For to them the blow was of double import. Not only were they convinced that their plan alone could lead to victory, but in rejecting it General Headquarters had flouted and insulted the sacred doctrines of Schlieffen, which they regarded as the God-given tables of the law.

Day by day the quarrel grew in bitterness and with an almost diabolical glee Hoffmann recorded its progress. More and more frequently there appear in his diary entries such as "on both sides there is much drafting of offensive telegrams," or "Ludendorff has sent an offensive telegram and to-day, of course, got an even more offensive reply." The Marshal became increasingly deeply involved. "The quarrel between Falkenhayn and Hindenburg is developing. The Field-Marshal is at last telling him the truth"; and—in a burst of triumph—"We forced the Field-Marshal to the point of resignation—he refused, until Ludendorff threatened to resign also . . . as a result we have had two slimy telegrams from G.H.Q."

Falkenhayn and Tappen were not behind in pettiness and triviality. They frequently pursued a pin-pricking policy towards HLH, rejecting their proposals, imposing small humiliations, and answering their offensive communications in kind and with interest.

There is little to choose between the parties in this discreditable episode. Both sides appear to have lost at this time all sense of wider vision, and, though both could claim that their contentions were actuated by a deep-seated devotion to the Fatherland and that their sole care was the destruction of the enemy, it seems to have occurred to neither that a policy of mutual distrust and recrimination between two great military departments in time of war was not calculated to secure victory over the enemy or confidence at home.

These events provide an early and important example of the degree to which Hindenburg allowed himself to be dominated by his surrounding influences. It was his chief and most vital failing, and became increasingly apparent in the years to come. So essential a part of his life does it become that it is impossible to conceive of the Marshal as standing alone. Throughout he appears as one of a constellation, outshone in brilliance by the surrounding stars, yet giving his name to the whole. In the east his satellites were Ludendorff and Hoffmann; in the west, Ludendorff alone. During the first Presidency he was dominated by Meissner, a self-effacing satellite; in the second, by the Palace *Camarilla*. The Wooden Titan remained the "cover" for the quarrels of Ludendorff and Hoffmann with G.H.Q., for the later political ventures of Ludendorff, and for the tortuous intrigues of Schleicher, Papen, and his own son, Oskar. Many things were committed in his name of which he never approved and more of which he never knew. In the early days his "legend" covered him as it were with a buckler, but in time that, too, grew dimmer and faded.

· 12 ·

In the meantime the war on the Eastern Front continued. The "break-through" of Gallwitz, which began on July 13, was successful in its primary objective, and by the 17th he had reached the Narev. Under the pressure of the German and Austro-Hungarian armies, breaking in on every front, the Rus-

sians gradually began to give way at all points and to withdraw slowly before the menace of envelopment. Warsaw fell
on August 5, Kovno was stormed on the 17th, the great fortress
of Novo-Georgievsk capitulated two days later. Again Falkenhayn seemed to have achieved success, but again the Grand
Duke evaded annihilation. The German pursuit began to lose
its force in incessant frontal attacks and HLH returned once
more to their earlier plans of encirclement. By pressing forward beyond Kovno and Vilna they hoped to force the Russian
centre against the Pripet Marshes and cut their communications
with the interior of the country. Once more, however, they were
doomed to disappointment. Falkenhayn insisted upon a straight-
forward pursuit. "A pursuit," comments Hindenburg, "in which
the pursuer gets more exhausted than the pursued."

Under the walls of Novo-Georgievsk, after the surrender on
August 19, Hindenburg and Ludendorff encountered Falkenhayn in the presence of the Emperor. The meeting was courteous but cool. Said the Chief of the General Staff to Ludendorff: "Now are you at last convinced that my operation was
right?" "On the contrary," was the icy reply. The Emperor
made some non-committal remarks and distributed decorations.

The dreams of a super-Tannenberg, the last opportunity of
inflicting a crushing defeat upon the Russian armies, had
vanished. Only the month of September remained before the
summer weather broke, and that period was too short to carry
out the great enveloping movement which Ludendorff had envisaged in July. But the strategy of Falkenhayn's "limited offensive" had in the end yielded no real and lasting results. The
superficial success of the eastern campaign had obscured the
fact that in its essence it was a frustrated plan, and this despite
the fact that in a year Russia had lost in killed, wounded, and
prisoners over two million men, and guns and stores approxi-
mately equivalent to what she possessed at the outbreak of the

war. In the removal of the Grand Duke Nicholas from the supreme command, an event which followed the defeats of the summer, she also lost her ablest military leader. Nevertheless, the Russian army, depleted and weakened though it was, still remained a functioning military machine, capable of being re-equipped and reinforced, and of returning to the attack. A further German offensive was out of the question: it was time for the army to get ready for the winter.

In addition, the summer campaign had failed in its chief political objectives. Despite the success of Gorlice in May, it had been found impossible to hold Italy to her neutrality. She had declared war on Austria on May 23.

The headquarters of the Commander-in-Chief in the East were moved from Lötzen to Kovno, and here Hindenburg celebrated the fiftieth anniversary of his entry into the Prussian Army. "With thanks in my heart to God and my Emperor and King, who glorified the day with a gracious message, I looked back on half a century which I had spent in war and peace in the service of Throne and Fatherland." He was to spend nearly twenty years more in the service of his country, but at their close he would not be able to look back with so clear a conscience as at Kovno.

· 13 ·

In the period which followed (October 1915–August 1916), the quarrel between the Commander-in-Chief in the East and the Chief of the General Staff reached its fiercest heat. The summer campaign of 1915 had marked the high-water mark of Falkenhayn's success and from thence his star waned gradually to eclipse. The reputation of Hindenburg and Ludendorff on the contrary grew steadily greater until it became impossible to exclude them any longer from the Supreme Command.

But this was not achieved without a bitter struggle. Falkenhayn, satisfied that he had put the Russians out of the reckoning for a considerable period, shook himself free from the heresies of the eastern school, and returned to meet the speedily maturing Allied offensive in the west. In addition, it was found necessary to support Austria still further by an attack on Serbia and to give encouragement to Germany's latest ally, Bulgaria, who had joined the Central Powers on September 6 and was menaced by the Allied forces at Salonika. For all these activities German troops were required to stiffen those of Germany's allies and Falkenhayn began to withdraw divisions from the Eastern Front.

Dominated by Ludendorff and Hoffmann, Hindenburg resisted with all his force this policy of denuding the Eastern Front, fighting tooth and nail for each division. The correspondence with Falkenhayn disclosed a hostility of almost unparalleled intensity between a regional commander and a Chief of the General Staff, and it reached its height when, on October 6, 1915, Hindenburg refused point-blank to make further transfers of troops, and in a formal protest to the Supreme Command challenged Falkenhayn's conduct of the whole campaign:

I have always taken the general situation into consideration by relinquishing as many troops as I could . . . and I have also sent off without delay any divisions which could be spared. The fact that the further relinquishment of divisions is now meeting with difficulties, is due to the plan of campaign pursued in the summer, which was unable to strike a deadly blow at the Russians, in spite of the favourable circumstances and my urgent entreaties. I am not blind to the difficulties of the general military situation which have ensued, and if the Russian attacks are beaten off really decisively, I shall relinquish further divisions as soon as it seems possible for me to do so. . . . But I cannot bind myself to a definite time. A premature relinquishment would give rise to a crisis, such as is now being experienced, to my regret, on the Western Front, and in certain circumstances it would mean a catastrophe for the Army Group, as any retiring movement of my troops, which are but weak in comparison with the enemy, must lead to very great harm being done to the formations, owing to the unfavourable condition of the terrain. I request that my views should be represented to His Majesty.

"With all the consideration due to the person of the Commander-in-Chief in the East whose name was associated by the German people with the victory of Tannenberg," writes Falkenhayn, "it was impossible to allow these remarks to pass without a definite reply."

He, therefore, responded to Hindenburg's strictures with vigour and in the same critical spirit:

Much as I regret that Your Excellency should without any cause consider the present moment [1] suited for explanations of events of the past, which are, therefore, unimportant at the moment, I should not trouble to refute your statements, if they concerned only me personally.

But as it concerns a criticism of orders issued by G.H.Q., which, as is well known, have in all important cases met with the previous consent of His Majesty, I am unhappily compelled to do so.

Whether Your Excellency agrees with the views of G.H.Q. does not matter, once a decision has been made by His Majesty. In this case every portion of our forces has to adapt itself unconditionally to G.H.Q.

Thereafter followed a spirited refutation of Hindenburg's criticism of the campaign conducted by G.H.Q. in the east and a caustic commentary on the Marshal's own operations. Falkenhayn continued:

In spite of my attitude to your operations, I did not propose to His Majesty to interfere, but even supported them in every way; the reason for this is to be found in my respect for the convictions of another person so long as they keep within the necessary limits, and do not threaten

[1] The French offensive in Champagne was at its height and the offensive against Serbia had just begun.

to harm operations as a whole; and because it is impossible to gauge with mathematical precision the issue of any operations which are carried out with the energy usual in such cases.

I will report to His Majesty the scruples which Your Excellency raises against the withdrawal of the two divisions. I must refuse to bring the remaining points of your telegram to the knowledge of the Emperor, because they only concern consideration of past events, about which, therefore, I do not intend in any case to approach the Supreme War Lord in these grave days.

Once again the Emperor was called upon to decide between the views of his bickering generals and for the last time he decided in favour of Falkenhayn; his decision was to the effect that the divisions must be relinquished to G.H.Q. as ordered. For the rest Falkenhayn's reply fulfilled its purpose. Hindenburg acquiesced in it despite the protests of Ludendorff and Hoffmann, and mature consideration led him to admit that Falkenhayn might have been right throughout. "In judging the plans of our High Command," he wrote years later, "we must not lose sight of the whole military situation. We ourselves then saw only a part of the picture. The question whether we should have made other plans and acted otherwise if we had known the whole political and military situation must be left open." In any case there was now a pause of several months in the dispute with G.H.Q., and it was not until the situation again became acute, in the summer of 1916, that the Eastern Command renewed its efforts to influence the conduct of the war.

The time had come to decide on the plans to be pursued in the coming year, and once again a conflict of plans occurred. HLH urged, as usual, the crushing of Russia before undertaking an extensive operation in the west. Their new plan favoured a movement against the Russian left wing, with the added political element of forcing Rumania to declare herself. Conrad von Hötzendorf, on the other hand, desired a campaign in

Italy. Falkenhayn rejected both plans in favour of an idea of his own.

In an exhaustive report submitted to the Emperor at Christmas, he surveyed the whole field of operations in detail and gave his reasons for arriving at the conclusion that the most suitable point for the next assault against the Allies was Verdun.

The French lines at that point are barely twelve miles distant from the German railway communications. Verdun is, therefore, the most powerful *point d'appui* for an attempt, with a relatively small expenditure of effort, to make the whole German front in France and Belgium untenable . . . [on the other hand] within our reach behind the French sector of the Western Front there are objectives for the retention of which the French General Staff would be compelled to throw in every man they have. If they do so the forces of France will bleed to death—as there can be no question of a voluntary withdrawal—whether we reach our goal or not. . . . For an operation limited to a narrow front Germany will not be compelled to spend herself so completely that all other fronts are practically drained. . . . She is perfectly free to accelerate or draw out her offensive, to intensify or break it off from time to time as suits her purpose.

Here, therefore, is the epitome of Falkenhayn's military philosophy of "limited offensives," accompanied politically by a readiness to negotiate. The capture of Verdun would break the heart of France and "England's sword would be knocked out of her hand." London and Paris would sue for peace and a settlement might be reached on the basis of the *status quo*. Unfortunately it was precisely at this time that Bethmann Hollweg had sadly reached the conclusion that "after these gigantic events there can be no *status quo*."

Nevertheless, Falkenhayn's proposals received the Imperial approval and on February 21, 1916, the great attack upon Verdun was launched.

In the east, however, the calculations of the Imperial Chief of the General Staff had gone awry. He had reckoned that the moral and material defeats inflicted on the Russians during the summer of 1915 would incapacitate them for some considerable period of time, but he had seriously underestimated the Slav capacity for recuperation and resilience. With the Tsar in personal command of his European armies and Alexeiev as Chief of Staff, the Russian forces were reorganized and re-equipped with thousands of rifles and guns which had been brought from England and America, via Japan. A new group of armies under General Ewart was concentrated on a narrow strip of the German front between the Narev and Lake Vishniev, where it was proposed to break through the denuded line and force a road to Kovno. With the depleted forces at his disposal, Hindenburg was able to oppose only 66 German battalions to 400 Russian. He had no reserves.

The offensive opened on March 19. It was the first time that HLH had been engaged in a defensive battle, and they were only able to meet the Russian attacks by withdrawing troops from the points in the line where danger seemed least and concentrating them at those where the pressure was most severe. They were forced to give ground, but so resolutely did they fight off thrust after thrust that the line remained unbroken and by March 28 the Russian offensive had been brought to a standstill. From then until the summer a quiet period intervened in the east. The Russians were preparing for their next onslaught and the Austrians were engaged in an offensive on the Italian front. Meanwhile, the German forces waited in anxious anticipation of what might follow.

That which was to follow came with appalling suddenness. On June 4, a new Russian army under Brussilov fell upon the Austrian front, breaking through at Lutsk, capturing an entire army of 250,000 men, together with all its guns and equipment and advancing some thirty-seven miles. In a month he had taken a further 100,000 prisoners and had cleared an area two hundred miles wide and in places sixty miles deep.

From this moment dated Falkenhayn's eclipse, for he was held powerless in the west and could do nothing. The operations around Verdun, though they had inflicted ghastly losses on the French, had cost the Germans almost as dearly. Moreover, they had failed in their two initial objectives. The French bled, but they did not bleed to death. Verdun did not fall and the Allies were not prevented from launching their own offensive on the Somme at the end of June. Though this attack was a failure, German troops were too occupied elsewhere to organize a counter-offensive. The star of the easterners was coming into the ascendant.

At the beginning of June, Hindenburg and Ludendorff were summoned to Pless to confer with the Emperor on the situation in the east. They declared that the only means of salvation lay in a unified command, but to this the Austrians would not yet agree. Disaster came hard upon the heels of disaster. By the end of July the Russians had captured Czernovitz, and the Italians, against whom Conrad's offensive had to be abandoned, had taken Gorizia. On all fronts the German armies were on the defensive, and hard-pressed. All opposition subsided in the face of such stern necessity, and at a second conference at Pless, on July 27, it was agreed that Hindenburg should take over the command of the whole Eastern Front as far south as Brody, east of Lemberg, with headquarters at Brest-Litovsk.

Opposition to the extension of Hindenburg's sphere of command had not been confined to the Austrians. Falkenhayn resisted most vehemently this increase in the power of his rivals, sensing therein the prelude to his own downfall. But now the Kaiser and "the Hydra" were giving ear to a new sound which, beginning as a murmur among the dead reeds of Falkenhayn's shattered reputation, was now increasing rapidly to the roar of a popular demand. "Falkenhayn must go! Hindenburg to the rescue!"

The party leaders too had become alarmed, and chief amongst them in activity was Dr. Erzberger of the Centre Party, himself closely allied with Tirpitz, Falkenhayn's enemy. Erzberger had become convinced that a change in the Supreme Command was absolutely essential if Germany were to be saved, and to this end he visited the princes of South Germany, the Kings of Bavaria and Württemberg, and the Grand Duke of Baden, to convert them to his views. They agreed with him and consented to his conveying the united expression of their alarm to the Emperor Franz Joseph, with the request that he would interfere. Erzberger went forthwith to Vienna and, having been equally successful there, sought out the Kaiser at Pless and confronted him with an ultimatum. Either Falkenhayn must go or the German princes and the Austrian Emperor would press for the immediate conclusion of peace.

The Emperor, with this clamour in his ears, in the course of the conversations at Pless, which at times became acrimonious, decided in favour of Hindenburg and Ludendorff, and against Falkenhayn, and this so piqued the latter that he did not appear at the Imperial dinner-table. Hopes arose that he was so deeply offended that he might take his departure, but the Chief of the General Staff emerged from his sulks and sought to strengthen his position. He went to Berlin to rally the Chancellor, to Teschen to mobilize the support of Austrian G.H.Q.; he sought to placate HLH by consulting them at every turn. All was in vain; the thumb of popular opinion was turned down; the cry was "Habet!"

Meanwhile at Brest-Litovsk there was discomfort and jubilation. Here the headquarters staff were housed in their special train in far from ideal circumstances. The August sun beat

pitilessly down on the steel roof and made the cramped space
unendurable. There was no room to work, and such as there
was, was encumbered by the big staff-maps. Hoffmann alone
succeeded in making himself comfortable, and the ingenuity
which he displayed in the use of what he called his "salon" was
a source of continuous amazement. Soon, however, on Ludendorff's suggestion, headquarters were moved into the Citadel,
the only habitable place in the city which had not been burned
by the Russians before its evacuation.

But HLH had considerable cause for satisfaction. They were
able to repulse the Russian attacks upon their own front and,
by a judicious stiffening of Austrian troops by German battalions, succeeded in persuading their allies to stand. It was
believed also that the second conference at Pless had seriously
shaken Falkenhayn's position and had strengthened theirs. The
days of their eclipse were over.

Judge then of their alarm, surprise, and indignation when,
by the middle of August 1916, it appeared that the impossible
had happened and Falkenhayn, unsuccessful in enlisting support in any other direction, had re-established his hold over the
Kaiser. Telegrams were received from Pless instructing HLH to
confine their attention to their own front, and the Imperial ear
was deaf to their protests against Falkenhayn's decision to
withdraw further troops from their command. Hindenburg was
in favour of compromise—"He has been repeating since yesterday, 'Yes, what my King commands, that must I do,' " wrote
Hoffmann furiously—but Ludendorff sent off an orderly with
a request to be allowed to resign. It was only in the face of this
rupture of their union that the Marshal could be persuaded to
ask the Emperor for an audience. The request was refused, and
a long despatch was prepared instead. On Hoffmann's earnest
entreaty Ludendorff agreed to postpone his resignation until
after the Imperial reply was received, and when this reply

arrived on August 24, and was found to be graciously plati-
tudinous, he allowed himself to be persuaded to reflect once
more.

This crisis would seem to have affected Hindenburg more
deeply than anything which had gone before. In the previous
disputes with G.H.Q. Hoffmann continuously refers to his
"Olympian calm," but now he records that "the Field-Marshal
is in a state of great excitement." It was the last round, and
Falkenhayn might conceivably have won it had not a further
error in his calculations been revealed at this moment.

Ever since the Russian victory at Lutsk and the penetration
of the Austrian line in June it had become apparent that Rumania would now inevitably throw in her lot with the Allies.
This, indeed, had been one of the secondary objects of Brussilov's offensive and its success was assured. The German General Staff had at once become reconciled to this and had conferred with the General Staffs of Austria-Hungary, Bulgaria,
and Turkey as to what measures should be taken to meet this
new contingency. Falkenhayn, however, had been convinced
that no move would be made by the Rumanians until after the
harvest was in, that is to say, until the autumn. How completely
he had convinced both himself and the Kaiser of this may be
seen from an incident recounted by Colonel Bauer, of the Headquarters Staff.

"On the 27th of August, when I was walking in the castle
grounds at Pless with Freiherr von dem Bussche of the Operations Section, we came upon the Kaiser. He was calm and cheer-
ful, and told us that Rumania would certainly not declare war,
that the reports were favourable, and that in any case the maize
harvest was in progress at the moment. A few moments later
we received news in our office that Rumania had already declared war." [1]

[1] At the same time Italy declared war on Germany.

This incident finally rang Falkenhayn's death-knell. He had lost the confidence not only of the military, naval, and civilian authorities, but even of his own headquarters staff. "I approached General von Plessen," Colonel Bauer continues, "represented to him that the only man who could help us was Ludendorff, and begged him to assist us."

In face of the opposition of the Imperial Government, the party leaders, "the Hydra," and the General Staff, the Emperor once again gave way.

At one o'clock in the afternoon of August 28, 1916, Hindenburg in the citadel of Brest-Litovsk was called to the telephone from Pless by General von Lyncker, the chief of the Emperor's Military Cabinet. The Emperor, he said, required the presence of the Marshal and Ludendorff at Pless immediately. He would give no reason save that "The position is serious," but he added that Falkenhayn knew nothing about the summons and would be informed of it only after their arrival.[1]

To Ludendorff and Hoffmann such a summons could mean only one thing, Falkenhayn had fallen or was at least in the act of toppling. They administered a final "gingering-up" to the Marshal before his departure, lest he might again fall by the way of compromise.

A remarkable example of Hindenburg's simplicity of mind is offered here. Despite the fact that he had struggled for nearly a year against the views of Falkenhayn, and notwithstanding the conviction of his immediate subordinates that in the event of success he himself would succeed to the Chief of the General Staff, the Marshal seems to have had no idea that this summons

[1] This procedure was not, however, adhered to. That same evening Lyncker informed Falkenhayn that the Kaiser had decided to seek independent military advice and had called in Hindenburg and Ludendorff. Falkenhayn was received later by the Kaiser, to whom he protested that he regarded his action as "a sign of mistrust to which he could not submit." He begged leave to resign and this was granted him in a letter signed "Your well-disposed and grateful King. Wilhelm" (Zwehl, *Erich von Falkenhayn*, pp. 212-213).

to Pless betokened his own victory and his translation to a higher sphere. So little did he anticipate a long absence from his own headquarters at Brest-Litovsk that he took only the minimum amount of kit on his journey.

The writer was at first disposed to treat this lack of perception on the part of the Marshal as a *naïveté* to which not much credence need be given, but, on discussing the point with those who had had intimate knowledge of Hindenburg's character, he became convinced that this incident illustrated, *par excellence,* the Marshal's simple nature and lack of ambition. Once the immediate excitement of the dispute with Falkenhayn had passed, Hindenburg relapsed into his natural phlegmatic impassivity and was incapable of connecting the summons to Pless with the defeat of his opponent.

The Marshal and Ludendorff were met at the station on their arrival at Pless, at 10 o'clock next morning, by General von Lyncker, who at once informed them of their appointments as Chief and Second Chief of the General Staff of the Army in the Field. They were greeted at the Schloss by the Kaiser, accompanied by the Kaiserin and the Chancellor, and during a stroll in the garden the appointments were personally confirmed. Ludendorff, though he secured permission to change his title to "First Quartermaster-General," received express assurance that he should have joint responsibility in all decisions and measures that might be taken.

The business of taking over was completed that afternoon and Falkenhayn, who contemplated "only with greater anxiety the certainty that a change in office must inevitably mean a change of system in the conduct of the war," took leave of his successor with a hand-shake and the words "God help you and our Fatherland."

Thus in the space of two days Hindenburg and Ludendorff found themselves in supreme command of the German army, "supreme" in every sense of the word, for from that day the position of the Kaiser as All-Highest War Lord became the merest fiction. Just two years ago they had fought and won Tannenberg, two years of strenuous united work and mighty victories lay behind them, and ahead of them two further years of service in double harness before the disappearance of Ludendorff from the scene.

2

KREUZNACH AND SPA

✠

AUTUMN, 1916. The German armies on the defensive on every front, their allies but little removed from defeat and already showing a tendency to bicker amongst themselves; Rumania added to the ranks of the enemy and capable of putting three-quarters of a million fresh troops into the field; Germany herself apprehensive, beginning to show signs of war-weariness, with a government divided against itself on many vital issues; the sinews of war unorganized and the fundamentals of such organization not understood; army commands in the west in the hands of incapable generals and a general headquarters staff shaken in its confidence in the Supreme Command; above all, a growing shortage of food; such was the heritage to which Hindenburg and Ludendorff succeeded at Pless.

In comparison with the new tasks which faced them, their previous problems in the east seemed almost parochial. Now only did they realize the difficulties under which their predecessor had laboured and which had influenced the decisions they had so strenuously opposed. "I will not hesitate to admit," wrote Hindenburg later, "that it was only now that I fully realized all that the western armies had done hitherto"; and Ludendorff confessed that he had not fully appreciated the danger of transferring troops to the east and that, had he done so, he would not have had the courage to weaken the Western Front.

One ray of sunlight penetrated this murky cloud. Though in the east matters were far from satisfactory, both Hindenburg and Ludendorff knew that in leaving Hoffmann as Chief of Staff to the new Commander-in-Chief, Prince Leopold of Bavaria, they had ensured a continuity of policy and a unity of spirit with themselves, and had provided against a repetition of that deplorable wrangling between the High Command in the east and G.H.Q. which had characterized their own tenure of office. Thus, though physically divided, the combination of HLH still continued to function. Later, divergences of opinion between Hoffmann and Ludendorff marred the smooth working of the triple formula, but for the time being all was well, though there is no doubt that the absence of Hoffmann's expert genius at G.H.Q. was greatly missed. Had it been possible for him to accompany Hindenburg and Ludendorff to the west, that is to say, had HLH remained united in space as well as in spirit, his influence over Ludendorff might well have restrained the First Quartermaster-General from his later political excesses.

Immediate action was necessary to restore confidence both on the Home Front and in the west. In this the Hindenburg Legend played an enormous part. The German people, whose knowledge of the true course of the war was strictly regulated by official propaganda, had, nevertheless, a feeling of hope rekindled on hearing that the victor of Tannenberg had assumed supreme command. With *"der alte Kerl"* at the head, it was worth making new sacrifices for victory, and a touching personal confidence in the Marshal was manifested in a hundred ways. After Tannenberg the popular imagination had been kindled by this figure of granite with its expressionless face and its grave brooding eyes; now the belief of the people was founded upon him. He was regarded as a friend and confidant by thousands who had never seen him, and his headquarters mail became clogged with so great a mass of personal correspondence that the services of a special officer were required to deal with it. People of every class and standing opened their hearts to the Marshal, some sent him verses in his honour, others asked for his patronage in securing positions for themselves or for their children. The clerk of a municipal council sought his help in securing better means of removing refuse, and a German lady from Chile wrote to ask his assistance in connection with the loss of her certificate of baptism. At no time in the history of the German people was a military commander taken so completely into their hearts.

As in 1914, the machinery of official propaganda was called into play to enhance the legend. New and higher honours were heaped upon Hindenburg, and every means was employed to keep his name and prestige before the popular mind. A new battleship was christened *Hindenburg* and his wife was invited to launch it. Parks, squares, and cafés were, under official encouragement, accorded his name. Above all there occurred that crowning episode of the Hindenburg cult, the erection of wooden colossi in his image.

These statues were symbolic. They were huge, crude, and rugged, and recalled the primitive sculptures of an earlier civilization. They were indeed a "throw-back" to the images of Thor and Odin, the Nordic war-gods so dear to an earlier German tradition, and to them were made sacrifices in a truly Nordic spirit, sacrifices not of garlands or of doves but of iron nails hammered into the figure till they stood out "like quills upon the fretful porcupine." The proceeds of the sale of the nails to the faithful who desired the privilege of knocking them in went to the German Red Cross.

Here the underlying streak of paganism in the German character was combined with Christian humanity, the worship of the war-god with alleviation of the ghastly results of such worship. The contrast is sharp; the incongruity almost frightening. The strange problem of German psychology is here displayed, a fierce and pagan sadism mingling in the German character with the Christian spirit of human kindliness.

And if the figures and their cult were significant of the German people as a whole, they were even more symbolic of Hindenburg. A Wooden Titan he had become, and remained so to the end; a figure-head carved upon the prow of the German barque to ward off evil spirits and to bring good fortune; a dumb god to whom prayers might be offered but from whom no word would come. The German people had created for themselves an idol not of clay but of wood, which the dry-rot of intrigue would enter and destroy, leaving but a hollow shell.

· 2 ·

To Hindenburg, and in a lesser degree to Ludendorff, the period immediately succeeding their translation to Pless was one almost of bewilderment. Everything was so very strange and new. The conditions of warfare to which they had been accustomed in the east were of the old-fashioned variety, and the experience gained therein availed them comparatively little in meeting the new tasks with which they were confronted. Their first act was to make a tour of the Western Front, as much for their own education as to enable the various army-group and army commanders to become acquainted with the new High Command. On September 6 a war-council was summoned at Cambrai, the headquarters of the German Crown Prince, and thither Hindenburg and Ludendorff travelled by special train. At every station they received an ovation, the troops crowding the platforms to cheer "our old Hindenburg." As the train pulled into Metz the usual accompaniment of cheering and waving of caps was suddenly stilled by the scream of an alarm siren.

French airmen swooped down over the station and narrowly missed bombing the special train before being driven off.

At Cambrai the Marshal presented field-marshals' batons to the Crown Prince Rupprecht of Bavaria and the Duke Albrecht of Württemberg, both army-group commanders, and received reports from all quarters. He learnt for the first time of the German inferiority in aircraft, artillery, and the supply of ammunition in comparison with the Allies. He saw a steel helmet for the first time and was informed of its proved efficacy in trench warfare. He inspected the battlefield of the Somme with its "lunar landscape" of shell-holes and trenches which for desolation seemed even worse than that of Verdun, and here perhaps for the first time he realized the full horror of modern warfare. He was strangely moved by this discovery, and the impression created remained with him long after.

The extent of the demands which were made on the army in the west was brought before my eyes quite vividly for the first time during this visit to France [he wrote in 1919]. What a thankless task it was for the commanders and troops, on whom pure defence was imposed and who had to renounce the vision of a tangible victory. . . . How many of our brave men have ever known this, the purest of a soldier's joys? They hardly ever saw anything but trenches and shell-holes in and around which they fought with the enemy for weeks and even months. . . . I could now understand how everyone, officers and men alike, longed to get away from such an atmosphere.

Back at Pless by September 8, Hindenburg and Ludendorff arrived at momentous decisions. The war, they were now convinced, must be decided in the west. The eastern solution, so dear to their hearts at Lötzen and Kovno and Brest-Litovsk, was now a thing of the past. A victorious peace was only possible by a defeat of the Anglo-French armies in France and Flanders. To this end the running sore of Verdun must be stopped and the Western Front made secure for defensive warfare until the shortage of men and material had been made good and it was possible once more to assume the offensive. On the other hand, the Rumanians must be eliminated from the start, and this task was entrusted to two mixed armies under Mackensen and Falkenhayn. The absolute necessity of a unified command for the Central Powers was insisted upon, and the conclusion of the negotiations already in progress was hurried forward. Finally, it was imperative to shorten the war, and to this end two madly conflicting methods were advised: the invitation to the United States to mediate and the adoption of unrestricted submarine warfare.

The unification of command was achieved almost at once. The Supreme War Command (*Oberste Kriegsleitung*) was created and exercised by Hindenburg in the name of the Kaiser; the benefits of this system were therefore enjoyed by the Central Powers for eighteen months before the Allies could be persuaded to adopt it. His legend had carried Hindenburg very far. Little more than two years before he had been an unknown general in retirement, now he was in virtual command of some six million men, the armies of Germany, Austria-Hungary, Turkey, and Bulgaria.

But victory could not be conjured in a moment. It was impossible to carry out with sufficient rapidity the operations necessary to liquidate the position at Verdun, and on October 24, 1916 the French attacked to the east of the Meuse. Fort Douaumont, for the capture of which so many German lives had been sacrificed, was abandoned, and the line was only held with the greatest difficulty. In the same month, however, the Allies were forced to break off the battle of the Somme, and a temporary lull supervened along the Western Front.

In the east the Rumanian campaign had been crowned with victory. Mackensen and Falkenhayn, after a series of successes on their respective fronts, joined hands, and on December 3 they entered Bucharest. What remained of the Rumanian army retreated northward; stiffened by Russian reinforcements and French and British equipment, they formed a line on the Sereth which brought their opponents finally to a halt and an armistice was concluded. Ludendorff had directed the campaign from Pless and had enabled Hindenburg to make good his boast to the Kaiser in October: "By the end of the year the Rumanian campaign will have come to a victorious close." It was true, but the success was qualified. The Rumanian army, though defeated had not been annihilated, and, above all, the German pursuit had not been swift enough to prevent the destruction of the oil-fields whose production was so necessary to Germany. Only the vast stores of grain fell into the hands of the Central Powers, but even these were not sufficient to satisfy the clamorous demands of their populations.

There remained the vital question of the supply of war material, with its closely allied problem of labour, and in addition the issue of peace by mediation and of humiliating the Allies by the destruction of their commerce. The handling of these non-military matters disclosed an essential difference in the characters of the two commanders. Hindenburg disliked politics and frankly said so; he realized his own lack of qualifications for dealing with such matters. "It was against my inclination to take any interest in current politics. . . . I had the feeling that the business of diplomacy made unfamiliar demands on us Germans, and even after I was appointed Chief of the General Staff of the Field Army, I never felt either the necessity nor inclination to mix myself up in politics more than was absolutely essential."

Ludendorff had no more aptitude for politics than Hindenburg, but he did not share his chief's disinclination for them. Though he entertained a lively contempt for politicians and regarded the Home Front merely as so much material which

G.H.Q. could fashion as they would, Ludendorff had returned from the Cambrai Conference in September with a strong conviction that his sphere of activities embraced complete control of the civilian situation and of foreign policy. "Not only had I to probe deeply into the inner workings of the war-direction, and get a grasp of both great and small matters that affected the home life of the people, but I had to familiarize myself with great world questions which raised all sorts of problems."

And here became evident the importance of those conditions which Ludendorff had exacted from the Kaiser during their stroll in the castle gardens at Pless on August 28. Not for nothing had Ludendorff refused to accept the title of "Second Chief of the Staff," and insisted upon that of "First Quartermaster-General." For him the word "second" no longer existed with regard to rank, though he still remained only a lieutenant-general; before he would accept his position at all he had made it clear that he must have "joint responsibility in all decisions and measures that might be taken."

In principle this meant that he and the Marshal matured their plans in common, and that Hindenburg then presented them to the Emperor as nominal commander-in-chief; and in military matters this procedure largely obtained. In politics, however, the Marshal stood aloof and Ludendorff acted alone. The Supreme Command, therefore, became an *imperium in imperio*, with the First Quartermaster-General negotiating independently with the Emperor, with the Chancellor, with the Foreign Office, with the party leaders in the *Reichstag*, with industrial magnates and trade-union officials, in fact with everyone who had to be subordinated to the will of G.H.Q.

Gradually a complete dictatorship was built up on the interpretation which Ludendorff put upon the word "responsibility." For example, when the Imperial Chancellor pursued some policy of which Ludendorff disapproved or which he consid-

ered injurious to the conduct of the war, he declared he could
not assume "responsibility" for such action, and asked leave to
resign. But it was the Chancellor who resigned. By exercise of
this method of "persuasion" the First Quartermaster-General
forced everyone from the Kaiser downwards to give way to him.
Sometimes he obtained Hindenburg's approval for his proposals, frequently he made use of his name in negotiation,
always his final argument was, "The Field-Marshal and I will
resign."

In pursuing this policy of "persuasion" Ludendorff was
greatly aided by the fact that during the autumn and early winter of 1916, Hindenburg was in very poor health. The rigours
of the campaigns in the east had made inroads upon even his
iron constitution, and now a kind of low fever attacked him,
so that, whether or not he had wished to do so, he was in no shape
to check the activities of his dominating lieutenant. With his customary disregard of opinion Ludendorff pressed on along his
tortuous way, sure of the moral support of his chief in any crisis
that might arise.

"I grant that I have covered many expressions of opinion on
political matters with my name and responsibility even when
they were only loosely connected with our military situation at
the time," confessed Hindenburg. "In such cases I thrust my
views on no one. But whenever anyone asked what I thought
. . . I saw no reason why I should hold my peace." Too frequently he gave his approval without his opinion being asked,
and in fact, in political affairs his opinion was not always worth
the asking.

· 3 ·

The first issue on which military and political views came
into conflict was in the matter of Poland. In the middle of
August 1916, the governments in Berlin and Vienna had

reached an agreement to create, at some future date, an independent Kingdom of Poland, with an hereditary constitutional
monarchy. This policy had been warmly supported by the Gov-
ernor-General of Warsaw, General von Beseler, and by Ludendorff, both of whom believed that it would be possible to create
a Polish army, which, with a stiffening of German officers, would
be willing to shed its blood in gratitude to its liberators.
"Let us found a Grand Duchy of Poland with a Polish army
under German officers," wrote Ludendorff enthusiastically to
the Foreign Minister, Zimmermann, in July. "Such an army is
bound to come one day, and at the present moment we can make
use of it."

Falkenhayn, however, had been sceptical of such gratitude
(and this view Hindenburg undoubtedly shared) and had protested against the immediate proclamation of the Polish Kingdom. The Emperor had decided in his favour and the plan had
been pigeon-holed, the idea being that it should be kept a secret.
State secrets of this nature are difficult enough to guard in one
capital. In two capitals it is impossible to keep them, especially
if one of these capitals is Vienna, and by September the knowledge that Polish Independence had been agreed upon was common property. Beseler and Ludendorff, who had even worked
out, on the basis of the Polish population, the number of new
divisions they would acquire, overcame Hindenburg's scruples,
urging him to revive the plan and have the official proclamation made as soon as possible.

Now, however, the rôles were reversed. The Supreme Command were in favour of the Polish Kingdom, the Chancellor
was opposed. Bethmann Hollweg had at last determined to effect
a separate peace with Russia and had found the Tsar disposed
to negotiate. Informal preliminary conversations had taken
place at Stockholm between the German industrial magnate,
Stinnes, and Protopopoff, Vice-President of the Duma. The in-

creasingly serious domestic situation within the Empire and the dominant pro-German influence of the Tsaritsa assisted the prospects of peace, and the Tsar had appointed as his Prime Minister Baron Stürmer, a statesman notorious for his desire to negotiate with Germany.

So far had the negotiations progressed by the beginning of November that Lenin, writing in Geneva, was seriously concerned that their success might prevent the outbreak of the Revolution in Russia, and the Entente Governments were equally disquieted at the prospect of Russia's desertion.

But the Chancellor yielded to the demands of the Supreme Command and Germany committed one of the worst political blunders of the war. The Kingdom of Poland was proclaimed on November 5, and with its proclamation vanished all hopes of a separate peace with Russia.

The Supreme Command had got its way but the policy was barren of results. The Poles accepted the gift of independence as nothing more than their due and had no intention of placing their man-power at the disposal of the Central Powers. Indeed they had never given any indication that there was the slightest chance of their doing so. "No army without a government to direct it" was Pilsudski's watchword, and he saw no reason now to place a Polish army under the control of the Supreme Command. The new divisions, so carefully calculated on paper, vanished like a mirage. Snatching at the shadow, Germany had missed the substance.

Though the sudden vacillation of the Chancellor had tipped the scale at the critical moment, the burden of responsibility must lie with Hindenburg and Ludendorff, and no literary afterthought can relieve them of it. Had Ludendorff not been blinded by the purely military desire for new divisions, however doubtful their origin, he must have seen the superior advantage of a separate Russian peace. Had Hindenburg stuck to the sceptical view which he had held of Beseler's original proposals, he might have succeeded in further postponing the proclamation, as Falkenhayn had done before him.

The advantage to Germany would have been incalculable. Peace with Russia at the end of 1916 would have released Hoffmann's army for service in the south and west, and would have given again to Germany the numerical preponderance she had lost. Moreover, the Allied blockade would have been broken and Germany could have secured those essential supplies of food, the lack of which was already beginning to cripple her. A few months of peace in Russia might well have staved off Revolution, and even if it had not, Germany would have avoided the early contact with Bolshevism at Brest-Litovsk which proved so disastrous to her.

By a major political blunder the Supreme Command had failed to eliminate Russia from the ranks of Germany's enemies, but by a blunder of far greater proportions they ensured the adherence to her opponents of the most powerful ally in the world, the United States of America.

· 4 ·

When Hindenburg and Ludendorff came to Pless, one of the more pressing problems which confronted them was that of the effect, both physical and psychological, of the Allied blockade. From the early days of the war the German navy had been eliminated as an active factor. Save for the gallant actions off Coronel and the Falkland Islands, the less gallant shelling of Yarmouth and the Hartlepools, and occasional forays in the North Sea, one of which developed into the battle of Jutland, the German Fleet had remained inactive. On all the Seven Seas the Allied navies were dominant and the steel ring around the Central Empires was complete.

As a result, by 1916 seventy million Germans were living on severely reduced rations and thousands of them were slowly succumbing to the effects. On the other hand, supplies of every kind were flowing unchecked into the Allied countries from America and there remained to Germany but one weapon to combat both blockade and supply—submarine warfare in its unrestricted form.

This method had been urged by Admiral von Tirpitz as early as 1915, but had been vetoed by the Chancellor, who saw too clearly the inevitable results of such a policy and was determined to avoid at all costs a conflict with the United States. Again in March 1916 both Falkenhayn and Tirpitz urged upon the Emperor the necessity of declaring unrestricted U-boat warfare upon neutrals as well as belligerents, and again Bethmann Hollweg triumphed in the cause of reason, and to such good purpose that Tirpitz resigned from the Ministry of Marine.

The question was once more fully discussed at Pless two days after the appointment of Hindenburg and Ludendorff in August 1916, and on this occasion both agreed with the Chancellor in opposing the Naval Staff. The moment for unrestricted warfare was not thought propitious. Both the Chancellor and the Generals realized its probable effect upon neutral countries, but whereas the former dreaded the entry of the United States into the war, the latter were only thinking in terms of Holland and Denmark.

To the Supreme Command America was a strange and distant country, unorganized and undisciplined, presided over by a professional crank. Even suppose she could raise an army it would be years before it could be forged into a fighting machine, and its transport to Europe would produce further difficulties. "I am not interested in a contest between armed mobs," replied the great Moltke when asked in 1864 his opinion of the operations of Grant and Lee before Richmond, and the opinion of the German General Staff had changed little in fifty years.

The opposition of the Supreme Command was actuated by a fear that, with the issue of the Rumanian campaign still uncertain, if Holland and Denmark joined the Allies, there would not be sufficient troops available to meet the advancing Dutch and Danish divisions. They did not, however, reject the principle of unrestricted submarine warfare and extracted from the Chancellor the concession that "the decision to carry on the submarine campaign in the form of a 'War Zone' would depend on the declaration of the Field-Marshal." In other words, unrestricted submarine warfare was to start when Hindenburg and Ludendorff wanted it to start.

But the *Reichstag* would not allow this concession to go unchallenged. The parties of the Left, who were more closely in touch with the Government, strongly opposed both the expediency of the submarine campaign and the handing-over of power in such a wholesale manner to the General Staff. The parties of the Right espoused the views of the Supreme Command with equal violence. The debates were fierce and bitter. The climax came on October 16, when Erzberger, ever the friend and ally of Ludendorff, proposed in the name of the Centre Party, and secured adoption by a majority of the house, a motion momentous in the political life of Germany:

The Imperial Chancellor is solely responsible to the *Reichstag* for all political decisions in connection with the war. In taking his decisions the Imperial Chancellor must rely upon the views of the Supreme Command. If it is decided to initiate a ruthless submarine campaign, the Imperial Chancellor can be certain of the support of the *Reichstag*.

Constitutionally, this resolution marked the abdication of power by the *Reichstag* in favour of the General Staff and the confirmation of the military dictatorship of Hindenburg and Ludendorff. Its introduction was a pusillanimous attempt on the part of Erzberger to bring the existing situation into conformity with the Constitution. In effect, it began the destruction of the Bismarckian régime which was completed some eight months later, when, at the behest of the Supreme Command, the Emperor was forced to dismiss his Chancellor and to appoint as his successor a man whom he did not even know.

By the close of the year the situation had become more propitious for the introduction of a ruthless submarine warfare. The Rumanian defeats had heartened the High Command and the failure of the German peace offer of December, to which Hindenburg and Ludendorff had agreed after the capture of Douaumont by the French, had convinced them that a peace by negotiation was at the moment impossible. Moreover, it was imperative to strike a blow at the foreign munitions, supplies of the Entente and an end to the war must be sought. Conferences took place with the Naval Staff, whose statistics appeared convincing and who calculated that economically the case in favour of unrestricted submarine warfare was unassailable. Unfortunately, the statistics of the Naval Staff had failed to take into consideration certain doubtful factors, amongst them the capacity for endurance of the British people, and their economic calculations were not only academic but irrelevant. But in Ludendorff they found a ready convert, and Ludendorff worked upon Hindenburg.

How far the Marshal was himself entirely convinced of the necessity of this drastic step, it is difficult to say. It is certain that his native shrewdness must have instinctively warned him against a policy which failed completely to translate into action the will of the nation. It must have seemed all very worrying and irregular to him. But Ludendorff was convinced, and so completely had Hindenburg been absorbed into the personality of his coadjutor that he gave his agreement. As a result, an imperious telegram was despatched to the Chancellor by the Chief of the General Staff on December 26: "A ruthless submarine campaign is the only means of carrying the war to a rapid conclusion. . . . The military position does not allow us to postpone this measure." The Chancellor demurred. Ludendorff insisted. A council was called at Pless on January 9, 1917.

The Kaiser presided, pale and excited; to one side of him, correct and rigid, sat Hindenburg and Ludendorff; at the other, enthusiastic and confident, Admiral von Holtzendorf, Chief of the Naval Staff; opposite, the tall weary figure of the already defeated Chancellor. In attendance "the Hydra"—Valentini, Lyncker, Müller. Holtzendorf speaks first, full of the arrogance of victory. England will be defeated in six months, suing for peace. Holland and Denmark? They will not dare to move. America? "I give your Majesty my word as an officer that not one American will land on the Continent."

Hindenburg speaks briefly, laying stress merely on his belief that a decrease of the supplies of munitions from America to the Allies will result from the measure.

The Kaiser's eyes turn to Bethmann Hollweg. The Chancellor wavers. What is the use of going on? The demand is so unanimous, so confident. He is so tired. Deeply moved, he states for the last time his objection to unrestricted U-boat warfare, his great fear of the entry of America into the ranks of the enemy. He pauses and then surrenders. He adds that, in view of the changed views of the High Command and the unequivocal statements of the Naval Staff concerning the success to be expected, he wishes to withdraw his opposition.

The Kaiser, who has followed the Chancellor's remarks with great impatience and disapproval, declares immediately that ruthless U-boat warfare is thenceforth decided upon and that it is the duty of the diplomats to make clear to the neutrals the necessity for taking this step.

"*Finis Germaniae*," wrote Valentini in his diary.

On January 31 there were presented at Washington the Note declaring the commencement of unrestricted warfare and at the same time a statement of the German terms for peace. "The only German conditions," writes Ludendorff, "which ever reached the enemy from our side with any co-operation on my part." The reply of the United States was immediate and emphatic. Already shocked and enraged by the loss of American lives in the *Lusitania* and the *Arabic*, and at the torpedoing of the hospital ship *Sussex*, American public opinion was unanimously behind the President in his handling of the German declaration. Diplomatic relations between the United States and Germany were broken off on February 3, and war was declared on April 7. Three months later the first American troops landed in France, and by November they were in the fighting line.

If the error of the Supreme Command in the matter of Polish Independence had been detrimental, their blunder in insisting on the unrestricted submarine warfare was catastrophic. The risks involved were so great that it seems impossible that they could have been adequately weighed in the balance. Yet even writing *ex post facto*, with the full knowledge of what American intervention had meant, Hindenburg in his memoirs attempts to justify the decision on grounds of expediency. "In any case," he writes, "the adoption of unrestricted U-boat warfare, with its alluring prospects, increased the moral resolution of both the army and nation to continue the war on land for a long time to come."

How high a price this was to pay and how much more might have been gained by waiting is fully realized by Mr. Winston Churchill:

If the Germans had waited to declare unrestricted U-boat war until the summer, there would have been no unlimited U-boat war and consequently no intervention of the United States. If the Allies had been left to face the collapse of Russia without being sustained by the intervention of the United States, it seems certain that France could not have survived the year, and the war would have ended in a peace by negotiation, or, in other words, a German victory. Had Russia lasted two months less, had Germany refrained for two months more, the whole course of events would have been revolutionized. Either Russian endurance or German impatience was required to secure the entry of the United States.

The first six months of the Hindenburg-Ludendorff condominium had brought great military victories without achieving the annihilation of the enemy, and at the same time two momentous mistakes had been made which spelt the ultimate defeat of Germany.

· 5 ·

The consultation at Cambrai and the first tour of the Western Front in September 1916 had convinced the new High Command that the line must be shortened and rendered secure for defensive operations. With the spring heavy Allied attacks must be expected and the long line, bulging forwards and backwards into salients, could no longer be safely held by the diminished German forces. The capture of Douaumont had made a deep impression on the German High Command and had taught them a lesson. Despite the danger of shock to morale it was essential to withdraw to stronger defensive positions.

The line selected ran from Arras, west of Cambrai, through St. Quentin and Lafère, to Vailly-sur-Aisne, and here was constructed that powerful strategic position called officially the *Siegfried Stellung*, but known to history as the "Hindenburg Line." Work on these fortifications continued through the winter of 1916 and the early spring of 1917, and by March the German front had been re-established in a masterpiece of concrete and armour. Between the old line and the new the ground was systematically devastated. Houses were destroyed,[1] farms burned, orchards uprooted, and roads obliterated. The Crown Prince Rupprecht of Bavaria protested strongly to Ludendorff against the extreme rigour of the devastation, but his objections were overruled and he was forced to comply. Complete and utter ruin remained. Yet so skilfully was the operation carried out that the old line had been evacuated and the troops established in their new positions before the Allies were aware of what was afoot. Advancing cautiously, British and French troops found devastation such as they had not dreamed of, and before them frowned the bastions of the Hindenburg Line.

Into the construction of this position the Field-Marshal, on his recovery, had thrown himself heart and soul. This was war, far more acceptable to him than wrangling and fencing with politicians in Pless and Berlin. Ludendorff could attend to that. In February General Headquarters were moved from Pless to Kreuznach, a town in the Rhineland, pleasantly connected in Hindenburg's mind with memories of his period of service as Chief of Staff of the Rhine Province, and here he re-established the life of routine which had characterized his sojourn in Lötzen, Posen, and Kovno. War suited Hindenburg, as he said, "like a summer holiday." He slept well and regularly, ate enormously and drank sufficiently. The responsibilities of his position and the dangers of the situation made no inroads upon his constitution. His phlegmatic pachydermity saved him from those brain-storms and agitations which assailed Ludendorff's more sensitively attuned mind. A Wooden Titan, he stood strongly planted in the soil.

[1] Such few buildings as were left were mined. Two French deputies were blown up in the Town Hall of Bapaume and part of an English divisional staff suffered the same fate.

In Kreuznach, as elsewhere, he was the object of endless veneration. Youths, about to become his soldiers, serenaded him before departing for their depôts, and his quarters were daily decorated with fresh cut flowers by the young ladies of the town. He accepted these attentions with gruff acknowledgments; his rare demonstrations of tenderness were reserved for children.

Each day as he passed from his quarters to his office, a little boy in an infantryman's helmet stood stiffly to attention and saluted him with a toy rifle. With unsmiling gravity the Marshal regularly acknowledged the salute with the same punctilio he would have given to that of a real sentry. One morning the child appeared in a new glory. From somewhere he had acquired the headgear of a Prussian Uhlan and, bursting with pride, he awaited the arrival of the Marshal. He saluted as usual, but to his surprise Hindenburg stopped and regarded him gravely.

"You're wrong," he said. "You're not an infantryman now, you're an Uhlan. The cavalry salute like this." And before his astonished staff he went through the regulation movements of the cavalry salute. "Do it right next time," he admonished and passed on.

The boy never forgot, and each day gave his hero the salute in accordance with whichever head-dress he was wearing. Some weeks later on his birthday he received a photograph inscribed in that square unmistakable script, *"Meinem kleinen Soldaten —Hindenburg."*

It was at Kreuznach that the Marshal spent his seventieth birthday. The day was one of celebration and congratulations. The Emperor was his first caller and warmly greeted him; his staff followed, then representatives of the town and neighbourhood, then a long line of soldiers, recruits, and sick and wounded from the convalescent hospitals, and finally veterans who had fought with him in days long past. In the evening there was a dinner of honour and the Emperor proposed toasts. But an alarming rumour spread that the Allied airmen were about to celebrate the birthday by a raid of extraordinary proportions on G.H.Q. Lights were extinguished and the anti-aircraft artillery opened up a heavy barrage. "Thanks to the high rate of fire," Hindenburg records, "the available ammunition supplies were speedily exhausted, so that I could sleep in peace with the thought that I should be disturbed no more."

The raid did not materialize, but when they met next morning the Emperor produced a large vase filled with fragments of German shells which had been collected in the garden of his villa. There had been danger in Kreuznach that night after all!

The Hindenburg Line had barely been completed in time. Only a month elapsed between the evacuation of the old positions and the spring offensive of the Entente. For the Allies, too, had had a change of command. "Papa" Joffre had lost on the Somme the reputation he had gained on the Marne, and in his stead reigned General Nivelle, the brilliant captor of Douaumont, a disciple of shock tactics with a contempt for the policy of his predecessor, *"le vieux grignoteur."*

Great confidence was reposed in Nivelle. Mr. Lloyd George had such faith in him that, after the Calais Conference in February, he had agreed to a form of unified command and had ordered the reluctant Sir Douglas Haig to take orders from the new French commander. The dashing Nivelle carried before his optimistic impetuosity all opposition to his plans. He proposed to deal the Germans a staggering blow, and prepared to fight three battles simultaneously. Haig, despite his expressed preference for an advance in Flanders, was ordered to attack before Arras, while Nivelle planned a double offensive on the Aisne and on the Chemin des Dames.

In the preparation of these great battles Nivelle used none of the surprise tactics by which his reputation had been earned the previous October. For days the Allied intention to attack was heralded by the fury of massed artillery and trench-mortar fire. Then on April 9 Haig struck with irresistible force. The British assault swept over the first, second, and third German lines. The system of elastic defence had not yet been perfected and failed against so fierce an attack. The position was one of great crisis.

At Kreuznach there was consternation. Report after report arrived telling of the capture of this and that position. Had the *Siegfried Stellung* really failed? Pale-lipped staff officers asked themselves this question and turned from the answer with horror. This was Ludendorff's fifty-second birthday and he paced the operations room at G.H.Q., a prey to nervous anxiety. It was Tannenberg over again, and now there was no Hoffmann to restore confidence. But now as then, in the moment of acute crisis, Hindenburg rose magnificently to the emergency. Seated before the great map on which the sagging battle-line was charted from hour to hour, he remained calm and unmoved. Officers coming to report to him left his room with fresh courage and renewed confidence.

As the news grew worse and worse and the local disasters multiplied in number, Hindenburg walked through the offices of headquarters. He said little, only giving here and there a direction, but his massive presence and unexcited mien gave new hope to the staff. Returning to his own room, he found Ludendorff pale with apprehension; with one of his rare gestures of emotion the Marshal put his hand on his shoulder and said simply, "We have lived through more critical times than this together."

Hindenburg's unshaken confidence was justified. The moment of crisis came and passed, and disaster was staved off. The British failed to realize how very nearly they had come to breaking the Hindenburg Line and were unable to exploit the successes they had gained. In the meantime reinforcements reached the sorely tried Line. They had been drawn from the eastern front, which, mercifully for the Central Powers, was at the moment quiescent. Russia was in the throes of the First Revolution of 1917 and the Allied Powers had so far been unable to persuade the Provisional Government to undertake an offensive. Writing later, Ludendorff confessed that had the Russians won even minor successes in March and April it would have been impossible either to reinforce or hold the Hindenburg Line. But, as it was, the gaps were filled, the losses made good, and counterattacks restored the balance, at least for the moment.

By now, however, Nivelle had opened his own bombardment and guns of all calibres from Soissons to Rheims were raining death on the German lines. By April 16, the French Commander-in-Chief calculated, the enemy defensive zone would have been converted into a waste of rubble and corpses, and all that were lucky enough to escape physical destruction would at least have been morally broken. He therefore began his attack on that date. *"Notre heure est arrivée,"* he told his troops in an order of the day and bade them be in Laon the same evening. But the German defence had not been shattered and the French advance stuck fast upon the Chemin des Dames. By the second day's fighting it was clear that France had sustained her worst defeat of the war. Nivelle threw forward a third army to support the two already in action. All three were caught in the cross-fire of German artillery and, unable to deploy, great masses of troops were mown down where they stood. Haig tried to relieve the pressure by renewing his own attack but failed, and Nivelle refused to retire. Again and again he massed his divisions in a desperate attempt to bring off his *grand coup,* but in vain. By May the army was so demoralized that it would fight no more. The defeated troops were withdrawn and whole corps, infected with the virus of Bolshevism, mounted the red flag, threatening to march upon Paris. Nivelle, with the terrible stigma of *buveur de sang* ever attached to his name, vanished into obscurity, leaving to his successor, Pétain, the gallant defender of Verdun, the task of re-establishing the line and of liquidating the defection which defeat had bred in the French army.

For the moment all further danger of a French offensive had ceased, but there was little respite for the German defenders. In June the British renewed the attack by blowing up the Messines ridge and pressing on beyond it. This they followed up with a great drive in Flanders which continued throughout the summer. Again the German positions were threatened with disaster and again the calm presence of the Marshal maintained at headquarters that confident courage which in the end achieved success. In the main the lines held and disaster was averted if only by a narrow margin.

Despite these successes, however, there was little to cheer Hindenburg either in the military or the political situation. The heavy fighting of the spring and summer had made terrible inroads upon his reserves and there was no longer a possibility of replacing them. The Allies had succeeded in galvanizing the Russian Front into fresh activity and he dared not withdraw more troops from Hoffmann. Moreover, after six months of unrestricted submarine warfare, directed against Great Britain, a campaign which had unquestionably inflicted very heavy losses upon her shipping and had gravely affected her food supply, she showed not the slightest sign of collapse nor desire to negotiate. On the contrary, it became evident that a grimmer aspect had appeared in her attitude and that she was prepared to fight on to the end, whatever the sacrifice. Notwithstanding the proud boast of the Naval Staff at Pless in January, American troops were already landing at French ports and, although as yet unused to modern warfare, could before long be used in quiet sectors, thereby releasing veteran French and British troops for service elsewhere. American supplies and American credit had already vastly improved the Allied position, and the co-operation of the U.S. Fleet in the North Sea had rendered still more relentless the blockade of

Germany, which was slowly strangling soldier and non-combatant alike.

At home in Germany, on the front-behind-the-front, there were many signs of war-weariness and dissatisfaction. The supply of war material was failing both in quality and quantity, and the morale of the country was at a low ebb. Disbelief in a satisfactory outcome of the war spread like a blight over the country, and daily the section of the people who desired peace at any price increased. The Socialist deputies demanded a new franchise law for Prussia and openly threatened revolution in the *Reichstag*. The Chancellor himself was now certain of the ultimate defeat of Germany, and the High Command became convinced that they had not his full support. Ludendorff at once proceeded to deal Bethmann Hollweg the *coup de grâce*, and to replace him with a man who would work in closer harmony with the condominium.

· 6 ·

Ever since Bethmann Hollweg's opposition to an annexationist peace policy and the unrestricted U-boat campaign, his enemies in the parties of the Right, together with Erzberger, had planned his downfall. As early as February 25, 1917, they had met at the Adlon Hotel and had decided to urge the Kaiser to place the conduct of the war above politics and make Hindenburg Chancellor. The plan failed because the Marshal would have none of it. Nothing would induce him to take control of the civil as well as the military machine, and the conspirators retired baffled to bide their time. But between the Marshal and the Chancellor there was little love lost. They avoided one another as much as possible and, on the rare occasions when they shook hands, Hindenburg shuddered at the contact with the grey ghost of a man who seemed to portend disaster.

As the summer progressed, however, the attacks upon Bethmann Hollweg, both inside and outside the *Reichstag*, became
intensified. As fate would have it, he who, more than any other
man, had most strenuously opposed the unrestricted U-boat campaign, was now saddled by his enemies with the responsibility
both for its adoption and its failure. Ludendorff, anxious to
avoid a culpability that was most justly his, made haste to persuade the Marshal that it was essential, for the good of the country and in the cause of victory, that a change of Chancellors
should be made. In conference at Kreuznach, Bethmann Hollweg's successor was discussed by Hindenburg and Ludendorff,
with certain politicians and journalists. The choice lay between
Prince Hatzfeldt and Prince Bülow. Bülow was agreed upon,
and a trusted emissary was despatched to his Swiss retreat to
sound him on the matter. He consented and the conspiracy went
forward.

It was practically assumed from the start that neither of these
choices would be acceptable to the Kaiser. Bülow, after the *Daily
Telegraph* episode of 1908, saw no possible chance of being recalled by Wilhelm II, and even if he had been, his appointment
as Chancellor would have met with great opposition from the
Emperor Francis Joseph, who had not forgotten the offers of
Austrian territory which Bülow had made to Italy in an effort
to maintain her neutrality.

Of the two, Prince Hatzfeldt would, there is little doubt, have
been the sounder choice, for he enjoyed great popularity with all
classes. Almost the last of the *grands seigneurs*, Hatzfeldt held
a position unique in Germany. An unfortunate scandal shortly
before the war had, however, alienated the Kaiser's favours from
him, and his chances of appointment to the Chancellorship were
also, therefore, rather slight.

Apparently these unfavourable factors were either ignored or
discounted by those who sought a successor to Bethmann Holl-

weg, for Hatzfeldt was rejected by them not because he might prove unacceptable to the Kaiser, but because he might not prove sufficiently tractable to the views of the Supreme Command.

On June 19 Hindenburg wrote to the Chancellor urging upon him the necessity of reviving the spiritual energy of the country and the "will to victory." He deplored the hopeless tone of Bethmann Hollweg's policy. "A revival of our internal strength would be the most potent means of persuading our enemies of the futility of prolonging the war until their own means of existence are in danger of destruction. On the other hand, every complaint of disappointed hopes, every sign of exhaustion and longing for peace on our part, or that of our allies, any talk of the alleged impossibility of standing another winter campaign, can only have the effect of prolonging the war."

The Chancellor's reply disclosed so great a degree of hopelessness and depression that on June 27 Hindenburg appealed to the Emperor direct. "Our greatest anxiety at this moment," he wrote, "is the decline in the national spirit. It must be revived or we shall lose the war . . . for this it is necessary to solve those economic problems which are the most difficult and are of the greatest importance for the future. The question arises whether the Chancellor is capable of solving these problems—and they must be correctly solved or we are lost."

The next move was made by Erzberger in the Central Committee of the *Reichstag*, when on July 6 he made a bitter attack on the conduct of the war. He demanded, without actually attacking the Chancellor, that he should reverse his policy and return to the idea of defence which had been prescribed in the beginning. While the High Command would have to continue working at full pressure, it was essential to form a large majority in the *Reichstag* unequivocally in favour of a defensive war as it had been laid down on August 1, 1914. The world must be told that Germany desired a peace based on compromise without any forcible subjection of peoples or annexations, making clear the fact that Germany would fight to the last man were such an offer rejected.

Perturbed by these storm-signals, yet unwilling to part from the ablest Chancellor he had had since his dismissal of Bismarck, the Emperor sent for Hindenburg and Ludendorff to hear their views. They were received on the morning of July 7 and frankly proposed the resignation of Bethmann Hollweg and the succession of Bülow. The Emperor received both suggestions in silence and closed the audience without further comment. This silence was interpreted by the Marshal and Ludendorff as a sign of acquiescence; but in this they were speedily undeceived by those of their friends who were better acquainted with Wilhelm II's methods.

"What did the Emperor say when you suggested Bülow for Chancellor?" someone asked.

"He said nothing," Ludendorff replied.

"Then we had better look for someone else," said the other, "for that is a sure sign that the Emperor will not accept him."

The moment of crisis was rapidly approaching. On the following day the Chancellor in the *Reichstag* agreed to support the resolution to be put forward by the majority parties and at the same time promised the Socialists that the *Reichstag* franchise law should be applied to the elections for the Prussian Diet. Now or never was the moment for the High Command to act and, inspired by them, Stresemann, who had become leader of the Liberal Party in succession to Bassermann, fiercely criticized the Chancellor by name in the Central Committee.

The whole conduct of the nation's affairs [he declared] is being carried on under the motto "We shall not succeed anyhow." Essentially the prevalent defeatism is due to the fact that the nation believes that it is moving from one failure to another in this greatest of all wars. . . . This tension is more than the nation can bear in its present condition.

A political defeat of the utmost gravity is inevitable. . . . A Chancellor must succeed in having his way; if he fails, he must draw the necessary conclusions.

Here were Ludendorff's ideas clothed in the vigorous rhetoric of Stresemann, who had allowed himself to be the parliamentary agent of the High Command. It was the first time in German history that a member of the *Reichstag* demanded a change of Government in such tones and on the following afternoon the Chancellor asked leave to resign, a request to which he received a refusal the next morning (July 11).

But meantime the High Command had brought into play a new and more potent factor. Through the agency of Colonel Bauer they approached the German Crown Prince and impressed upon him the gravity of the position. The Crown Prince returned to Berlin from his headquarters and urged upon his father the necessity of Bethmann Hollweg's removal. The Emperor refused to dismiss his Chancellor, and on the advice of Bauer, the Crown Prince called a conference of the *Reichstag* party leaders on the morning of July 12. Bauer had already sounded out most of them and was satisfied of their dissatisfaction with Bethmann Hollweg.

It was a remarkable scene. For the first time in forty-five years a prince of the ruling house had thought fit to acquaint himself at first hand with a political situation. The interview was carried out in tune with the best Prussian traditions; shoulder to shoulder the party leaders, Erzberger, Westarp, Payer, Stresemann, David, and Martin, stood to attention while the heir to the throne cross-examined them, and Colonel Bauer took a record of their answers. The manner of their inquisition was anything but dignified.

The upshot of the "conference" was that, with the exception of the Social Democrat leader David, all the parties represented went on record as being in opposition to Bethmann Hollweg. Erzberger, on behalf of the Centre, offered a resolution to the effect that the Chancellor's continuance in office was "an obstacle to peace," but left it to him to determine the moment for his resignation; while Stresemann, for the National Liberals, informed the Vice-Chancellor, Payer, that the crisis was insurmountable unless Bethmann Hollweg resigned.

The Crown Prince returned to the Bellevue Palace in the afternoon and reported to his father the result of his enquiries. The two remained in close conversation, pacing up and down the linden alleys of the park. At seven in the evening the Chancellor arrived and was received discourteously. The Emperor complained peevishly that he had only consented to the Prussian franchise law in the expectation that the political crisis would be overcome thereby. Bethmann Hollweg replied that in any case the reform was long overdue, and passed on to speak of the peace resolution which the Majority parties proposed to bring before the *Reichstag*. The Kaiser complained that he had not been shown the text of the resolution and the Chancellor replied that he had come that evening for the express purpose of reading it to His Majesty. This he proceeded to do. The Kaiser's only comment was that the text must be telephoned at once to Hindenburg for his comment and within half an hour the reply of the High Command had been received. It protested against the omission of any thanks to the troops and demanded two other alterations. With these views the Emperor agreed.

At this moment the Supreme Command played its trump card. General von Lyncker, the Chief of the Emperor's Military Cabinet (that same Lyncker who had welcomed the newcomers on their arrival at Pless), entered the room with a message that Hindenburg and Ludendorff had telephoned their resignation from Kreuznach and that those of the whole General Headquarters Staff were on the way, the grounds given being that they were unable further to co-operate with Beth-mann Hollweg as Chancellor.

The Emperor was furious at this barefaced blackmail and told Lyncker to summon the Marshal and Ludendorff to report to him in Berlin immediately. But the Chancellor knew it was the end. There could be no choice in the matter; the country would never stand for the resignation of the High Command. A *"Kanzler-Krise"* might easily be transformed into a *"Kaiser-Krise"* and a revolution was not far off. Taking his leave of the Kaiser, he returned to the *Reichskanzelei* and wrote out his resignation. In order to embarrass neither his Emperor nor the Supreme Command, the Chancellor made no reference to the latter's ultimatum and gave the political situation as his sole reason for retirement. With him passed from the scene the most far-sighted and honest of Wilhelm II's statesmen, whose chief fault was that he saw too far ahead and lacked the courage of his own convictions.[1]

When therefore Hindenburg and Ludendorff arrived again at the Schloss Bellevue on July 13, they found that they had achieved their primary object in the elimination of Bethmann Hollweg. But here a hitch occurred in their plans and the prophecies of their friends were justified. It was conveyed to them privately that under no circumstances would the Emperor agree to accept Bülow as Chancellor and that, when the question of a successor was discussed, they would be wise in not pressing their candidate. There is little doubt that had they repeated their threat of resignation they could have forced the Emperor to accept whomsoever they pleased as Chancellor, for, so high was their prestige and his so low, that he had no other alternative

[1] The High Command did not hesitate to add insult to injury. Scarcely had Bethmann Hollweg returned from Berlin to his estate at Hohenfinow when a message arrived from Kreuznach offering him the position of Ambassador at Constantinople. The offer was coldly refused, but the incident had a curious parallel some fifteen years later.

but to accept any conditions which they cared to dictate. But they were unwilling to make a further test of their power, and without hesitation they abandoned the possible candidature of Bülow, though omitting to inform Erzberger of their change of plan.

Thus when, having refused to consider Count von Bernstorff and Count Hertling as possible Chancellors, the Emperor sent Lyncker, Valentini, the Chief of his Civil Cabinet, and General von Plessen, his aide-de-camp, to confer with Hindenburg and Ludendorff, it was possible to agree almost immediately on Dr. Michaelis, the Prussian Food Controller, as Bethmann Hollweg's successor. Ludendorff declared that he strongly approved of Michaelis, who had recently visited Kreuznach and left behind him the impression that as Chancellor he would be the right man in the right place. Though, in common with the greater part of the population of Berlin, the Emperor had no knowledge of his personality and had never even met him, he at once accepted Michaelis, and appointed him on July 14. Thus appeared the Chancellor of a Hundred Days.

At the Restaurant Hiller, Unter den Linden, where party politicians discussed the latest gossip over their luncheon, there was loud debate on July 14 as to the character of the new Chancellor, the news of whose appointment had just leaked through, though it had not yet been officially announced. Nobody knew him save as a vague signature at the bottom of ration-cards and *Erlasse*; he was just one of the many high officials of the Prussian Civil Service who had appeared as a result of the war. There entered Erzberger, who for some reason had not heard of the appointment and was still supremely confident that Bülow was to be the new Chancellor. Cries came from all sides; Erzberger was sure to know.

"Do you know the new Chancellor?" they asked.

"Well, my dear friends, I should scarcely put out one Chancellor if I didn't know who was going to succeed him."

"What, you really *know* Michaelis?"

"*Michaelis?*" gasped Erzberger, and nearly collapsed.

Just as the *Reichstag* resolution of the previous October had struck the first blow at the position of the Crown in the Bismarckian régime, so now with the dismissal of Bethmann Hollweg there vanished the semblance of constitutional government. In October 1916 the *Reichstag* had claimed responsibility "for all political decisions in connection with the war"; in July 1917, by conniving at the appointment of Michaelis, they voluntarily abdicated this right. For Michaelis regarded himself, quite accurately and not unnaturally, as the nominee and mouthpiece of the High Command, and made this clear to the *Reichstag* in his first appearance before that body on July 19. "I do not consider a body like the German *Reichstag* a fit one to decide about peace and war on its own initiative during the war," he declared, and frankly sought the advice of Ludendorff on every decision. "I begged him to excuse me," says Ludendorff, "but the Chancellor persisted, and we therefore decided to comply. At the same time, we were desirous of showing Dr. Michaelis what value we attached to confidential collaboration with the Imperial Government and both the Marshal and I frequently wrote in this sense to the new Chancellor."

Had the *Reichstag* had the courage to demand of the Emperor the dismissal of Michaelis there and then—which was the only course which the Majority parties could logically and honourably have pursued—much might have been saved; as it was, they meekly allowed both their authority and that of the Emperor to be usurped by Ludendorff, who in his own name and that of Hindenburg exercised dictatorial power over the country for the next sixteen months.

The *Reichstag* lost its power through lack of courage and,

even more, through not knowing what it wanted. From the first it realized the futility of Michaelis—"We separated after our first meeting with the Chancellor under such a cloud of depression that even Bethmann Hollweg's friends failed to derive any satisfaction from the embarrassment of his opponents," recorded Vice-Chancellor von Payer. But yet three precious months were allowed to elapse before the *Reichstag* attempted to assert itself. For a hundred days it tolerated the lacquey of the Supreme Command, and when it recognized its error it was too late.

The *Reichstag* of Imperial Germany looked for its salvation to a written Constitution, failing to realize that in national emergency it is practice and not theory that counts. Sixteen years later, in 1933, having learned nothing by previous misfortunes, the *Reichstag* of Republican Germany likewise placed its faith in solemn words and fundamental oaths. In both cases the result was equally disastrous for parliamentary institutions. There was, however, one great difference. In 1917 Hindenburg, as head of the Supreme Command, received the power; in 1933, as President of the Republic, he abdicated it. In both cases it is doubtful whether he realized what it was all about. In the first instance Ludendorff's influence in political affairs had become paramount with the Marshal, and, in the second, the Palace *Camarilla* played with him much the same rôle as "the Hydra" with the Emperor.

The degree to which the Supreme Command had taken control of the political life of the country was very soon seen in the handling of the Peace Resolution by the Chancellor before the *Reichstag*. This motion, originally sponsored by the Majority parties in an attempt to get back to the original statements of war aims of August 1914, had had to be amended and modified to meet the wishes of the High Command. These amendments had formed the subject of Bethmann Hollweg's last audience with the Kaiser, on July 12, and the party leaders had

THE WOODEN STATUE IN THE SIEGESALLEE, BERLIN

re-drafted the Resolution to include them, on the condition that the new Chancellor consent to make it the basis of his policy.

The Supreme Command, however, were still opposed in principle to any peace resolution at all. They were not in the least anxious to abandon the opportunity of annexing fresh territory to the Empire, if such came their way. The war had changed materially in character since its declaration in 1914; it had become a grim struggle for existence, and woe to the conquered. If in achieving victory—and this to Ludendorff still seemed possible in the summer of 1917—it were possible to secure spoils as well, so much the better! In addition, it was feared that the sentiments expressed in the Resolution would exercise an adverse influence on the spirit of the troops and on the determination of the people, while the enemy would construe it as a confession of weakness.

In conjunction with the Chancellor, therefore, the High Command first attempted to suppress the Resolution altogether, but in this they were foiled by the Social Democrats, who published the text in the *Vorwärts* for all Berlin to read. Ludendorff then attempted in a series of personal interviews to induce the party leaders to abandon the Resolution, and succeeded in detaching from the Majority Parties Stresemann's National Liberals, with the exception of a small Left Wing group under Richthofen. Scheidemann, Erzberger, and Payer were not to be shaken, and Ludendorff withdrew his opposition to the progress of the Resolution rather than precipitate an open conflict. Michaelis, however, was given instructions to render the final text of the Resolution as innocuous as possible.

The Conservatives and Pan-Germans of the *Vaterland Front* opposed the Peace Resolution with the greatest bitterness, both inside and outside the *Reichstag*, and, in so doing, they made free use of Hindenburg's name, a name which meant for many the last hope of a relatively tolerable end to the war. Covert representations were made to the Marshal from many quarters, that the more his name was invoked in the strife of parties, the more quickly would the last remnant of unity fall to pieces. Such diverse individuals as Scheidemann, the Social Democrat leader, Niemann, the representative of the High Command with the Emperor, and Haeften, their representative of the Foreign Office, urged upon him the necessity of taking steps to prevent the continued misuse. All efforts were in vain. So dominated was Hindenburg by Ludendorff that he was unable to dissociate himself. The propaganda against the Resolution continued and the Marshal's reputation in the country suffered accordingly.

The Resolution, as passed by the *Reichstag* on July 19, was indeed harmless in wording, consisting mainly in a repetition of the sentiment "We are not animated by any desire for conquest." It demanded a peace "by mutual agreement and reconciliation," and protested against all possible "acquisition of territory" and all "political, economic, and financial oppression." But in every document of this nature it is the spirit rather than the letter which ranks foremost in importance, and more important than either is the interpretation of both. For every man is free to interpret a principle for himself and this freedom of mental action was made clear by Michaelis, who gave his support to the Resolution "as I interpret it," emphasizing that he made this reservation on behalf of the Supreme Command.

But the *Reichstag* refused to recognize the danger arising from this ambiguity of phrase and the Resolution was passed by the votes of the Social Democrats, the Centre, and the Progressives, ironically enough, at the same time as new and enormous war credits. With justifiable triumph could the Chancellor write to the Crown Prince on July 25: "The hateful Resolution has been passed by 212 votes to 126, with 17 abstentions. I have deprived it of its greatest danger by my interpretation. One can, in fact, make any peace one likes, and still be in accord with the Resolution."

Indeed one could, and this had from the first been in the mind of at least one of its three leading sponsors. "You see, Your Highness," explained Erzberger, in discussing the Resolution with Prince Max of Baden, "this way I get the Longwy-Briey line by means of negotiation." At a later date it was even asserted that the Treaty of Brest-Litovsk accorded with the terms of the Peace Resolution!

The importance attached by the Supreme Command to their reservation to the Peace Resolution and their attitude of open contempt for the *Reichstag* was most clearly shown in connection with the Papal Peace Note of August 1917. At the end of June, before the fall of Bethmann Hollweg, the Papal Nuncio, Mgr. Pacelli (now Cardinal Secretary of State), had approached both the Emperor and the Chancellor on behalf of the Holy Father with a view to ascertaining the attitude of Germany in the matter of Belgium and Alsace-Lorraine. His conversations elicited the views that while Germany was prepared to restore to Belgium her independence, this must be accompanied by sufficient safeguards to prevent the country from falling under the political, financial, and economic domination of England and France. At the same time both the Kaiser and Bethmann Hollweg declared that if France showed signs of wanting peace the question of re-adjustment along the frontier of the *Reichsland* would present no difficulty.

On this somewhat flimsy basis the Vatican issued its Peace Note of August 1, and it was in anticipation of this that Erzberger had so vehemently championed the Peace Resolution in the *Reichstag*. The papal proposals were neither new nor startling. It was urged that peace was impossible unless the occupied territories were evacuated and that consequently Belgian independence must be restored, with safeguards to ensure her future independence of other Powers. Similarly, occupied German colonies and French territory must be mutually surrendered.

The reply of the British Government, delivered on August 21 and communicated by Pacelli to the Chancellor on the 30th, was a polite refusal. The British aims were re-stated in the triple formula of restoration, compensation, and guarantees for the future which later became the broad basis of the Treaty of Versailles. But at the same time it was pointed out that discussion of peace terms was idle until some official statement had been made by the German Government as to the future status of Belgium. Simultaneously the Supreme Command were informed both by the Foreign Minister, Herr von Kühlmann, and through their own channels of information, that if a satisfactory statement on Belgium were made there was a possibility of opening discussions with the Entente.

The task of drawing up the German reply was nominally one for the Government in conjunction with the *Reichstag,* and a Committee of Seven was set up to prepare a draft note. In effect, however, the terms of Germany's answer were determined at a Crown Council held at Schloss Bellevue on September 11. There were present the Emperor and the Crown Prince, five Ministers including the Chancellor and Kühlmann, together with the Marshal, Ludendorff, and Colonel-General von Falkenhausen. The latter, a hundred-per-cent annexationist, was for holding everything up to the North Sea. Ludendorff was prepared to give up the Flanders coast but insisted on the economic attachment of Belgium to the Empire, the independence of Flanders, the cession of Liége, and a lengthy occupation of Belgium by a German army. Hindenburg said nothing at all. The Emperor admitted that hitherto he had shared the views of General von Falkenhausen, but that recently Cardinal Hartmann had urged him not to press for annexation as the clergy in the new territories would be unreliable and the Walloons insubordinate. However, if the annexation of Belgium were no longer possible there must be compensation for Germany elsewhere, and he had in mind, apart from the complete destruction of British influence, the solution of the Flemish question, through the Autonomous Council of Flanders, and economic guarantees. No decision was reached and the Council dispersed.

Meanwhile the Committee of Seven was demanding that a definite statement on Belgium should be included in the German Note of Reply, but to this Kühlmann answered that a reference to the Peace Resolution was sufficient. Kühlmann himself was opposed to the annexation of Belgium, but he was equally opposed to making any public statement on the subject. To him Belgium was a valuable pawn which must not be surrendered too soon in the game. "Who told you that I am prepared to sell the horse 'Belgium'?" he asked in conversation with Colonel von Haeften, the representative of the Supreme Command at the Foreign Office. "It is for me to decide that. At present that horse is not for sale at all."

The reply of Germany to the Papal Note, which was handed to Pacelli on September 19, contained no mention therefore of Belgium and was but a spiritless document calling the attention of the Holy Father to the motives which had animated the adoption of the Peace Resolution in July. What, however, neither the *Reichstag* nor the Committee of Seven, nor indeed Kühlmann himself knew, was that Michaelis had, in collaboration with the Supreme Command, drawn up a programme regarding Belgium which provided for the permanent occupation of Liége.

On September 12, the day following the Crown Council, the Chancellor had written to Hindenburg enquiring whether the Supreme Command would be satisfied with a German occupation of Liége for some years after the conclusion of peace. The Marshal replied that he was in complete agreement with the view expressed by Ludendorff at the Council that, for the safety of the Rhineland, it was necessary that Liége should remain permanently in German hands. Michaelis therefore, on September 24, wrote secretly to Pacelli, and his letter contained the true reply of the Supreme Command to the Papal Note. "At the present stage," he wrote, "we are not yet in a position to comply with your Excellency's desire or to give a definite declaration regarding the intentions of the Government with reference to Belgium and the guarantees required. The reason does not exist in any objection on principle by the Government to such a surrender. Its extreme importance for the cause of peace is fully appreciated. . . . On the contrary the objection consists in the fact that certain essential preliminary conditions have not yet been fulfilled."

This communication, the full purport of which is sufficiently clear beneath its tortuous language, was despatched to the Nuncio without consultation with the Emperor or the Cabinet and without the knowledge of the *Reichstag* or even of the party leaders. From the dismissal and making of Chancellors the Supreme Command had passed to the formation and control of policy, and had now, through their tool the Chancellor, aspired to direct diplomatic negotiations. Their short-sighted policy of annexation had destroyed all hope of utilizing the not unpromising offer on the part of the Pope, and was later to lead them to greater excesses of error.

· 7 ·

On a grey day in March 1917, just at the time when German General Headquarters were being transferred from Pless to Kreuznach, the streets and squares of Petrograd were filled with mobs of men and women demonstrating against the government. This was no unusual sight in the Tsar's capital that winter, when strikes were frequent and the population daily became more hungry for food and more clamorous for peace. But on that day there seemed to be a new note in the roar of the crowds and a new determination. This was more than a demonstration, it was a revolt.

Suddenly there was a sound of galloping hoofs and there came the dread cry of "The Cossacks!" The crowds separated hurriedly to left and right, crouching in doorways and alleys to avoid the blows from the troopers' whips. And then a miracle happened. The Cossacks did not charge. Instead they rode quietly amongst the crowds, laughing and jesting with the people and exchanging with them the common salutation of "*Tovarish.*"

It was this gesture of fraternization that caused the Romanoff autocracy, which had ruled Russia for more than three hundred years, to vanish in a day, and it needed but the last tragic scene of abdication in a railway compartment at Mogilev, some two weeks later, to set the seal of ratification upon an already established fact.

By the Allies this new departure in the east was hailed with relief and satisfaction. Failing to appreciate the fact that one of the main causes of the overthrow of the Tsarist régime was a deep-seated revolution against the prolongation of an intolerable war, the governments of the Entente hastened to accord *de jure* recognition to the new Provisional Government and to urge upon it the necessity of prosecuting more relentlessly the campaign upon the Eastern Front.

For the Central Powers conversely the Revolution of March came as a disaster. Though hopes of a separate peace by direct negotiation with the Tsar's government had vanished with the proclamation of the Kingdom of Poland in the previous November, the corruption and inefficiency of the Imperial régime had been an indirect ally of Germany and had succeeded in bringing the war on the Eastern Front virtually to a standstill.

The Supreme Command, already occupied with its preparations to meet the Allied spring offensive on the Western Front,
cast about for some weapon with which to sabotage the Russian
Provisional Government. Far better informed as to the actual
state of affairs than were the Allies, the High Command at once
divined that the one weak spot upon which to work was the war-
weariness of Russia. The Provisional Government, confronted
with the problems of a country already disintegrating into
chaos, yet urged on by the continual demands of the Allies to
prepare a summer offensive, presented an exposed position to
the Central Powers, who were quick to take advantage of it.

It so happened that a powerful weapon, which ultimately
turned out to be a boomerang of the most deadly nature, was
ready to hand. In the city of Zurich there lived a group of Russian political emigrants and refugees to whom the news of the
March revolution in Petrograd came as the dawning of a long-
promised day. As bitterly opposed to the policies of the Social
Democrats and Liberals, who formed the Provisional Government, as they had been to the autocrats and oligarchs of Tsarist
days, they nevertheless recognized that, for the first time since
the abortive revolution of 1905, their chance had come. The
one great desire of this band of Bolsheviks, which included
Lenin, his wife Krupskaya, and Zinoviev, was to get back to
Russia at the earliest possible moment in order to capture the
revolution and transform it into a proletarian and anti-
Imperialist movement, with the immediate object of securing
a cessation of hostilities on all fronts. Equally it became of the
most urgent importance both for the Provisional Government
and for the Allied Powers that these would-be *saboteurs* of victory should remain where they were.

For this reason all applications of the Bolshevik leaders to
Petrograd for permission to return and to Great Britain and
France for assistance in doing so were met with a blank refusal,

and both Lenin and Zinoviev were plunged into the deepest depression. At this moment the *deus ex machinâ* appeared in the shape of the German General Staff.

The attention of the High Command had been drawn to the possibilities of conveying Lenin and his party from Switzerland through Germany to Sweden and thereby infecting the Russian Revolution with an anti-war virus which would destroy it, at any rate in so far as the army was concerned. The disintegration thus caused would be so great that in her own good time Germany could have what she wanted for the taking.

The plan commended itself to Ludendorff. Through Erzberger pressure was brought to bear on the Foreign Office, and an agreement was negotiated between the German Minister in Berne and the Swiss Socialist, Fritz Platten. In this unique international treaty between the editorial staff of a revolutionary newspaper and the empire of the Hohenzollerns the conditions of the journey were worked out with extraordinary detail. Lenin demanded complete extra-territorial rights for the train during the period of transit, and absolute freedom from supervision for the personnel of the party, their passports, and their baggage. No one should have the right to enter or leave the train throughout the journey (from this latter provision grew the legend of the "sealed" train). On their part, the emigrant group agreed to insist upon the release from Russia of a corresponding number of German and Austrian civil prisoners.

How far Ludendorff kept the control of these negotiations in his own hands it is difficult to say. It is certain that William II, Michaelis, and Hindenburg knew nothing of them, and both Kühlmann and Hoffmann, who might naturally be expected to have known, protest their complete ignorance. In his memoirs Ludendorff is anxious to throw upon "the Government" the responsibility for Lenin's passage, but the fact that neither the

Emperor, the Chief of the General Staff, the Chancellor, the Foreign Minister, nor the Chief of the Staff in the East were informed of the course of events, proves how completely at that period the First Quartermaster-General was "the Government."

Upon Ludendorff, and Ludendorff alone, must rest the responsibility for Lenin's return to Russia and all that it implied.

He sought to deal a deadly blow on his Eastern Front, and in this he was justified. In the same way that he sent shells into the enemy trenches, or discharged poison gas at them, so had he a right to use propaganda against the enemy. If by this means he could destroy Russia and drive her out of the war he was perfectly entitled to do so. As Lenin admitted at the moment of his departure, "If Karl Liebknecht were in Russia now, the Provisional Government would permit him to return to Germany." But Ludendorff did not accurately estimate the calibre of the men whom he sought to use and who, in their turn, were using him.

For while Ludendorff was saying to himself, "Lenin will overthrow the Russian patriots and then I will strangle Lenin and his friends," Lenin was thinking, "I shall pass through Germany in Ludendorff's car, but for his services I shall pay him in my own way." There was never for a moment the slightest illusion amongst the Bolshevik emigrants, nor amongst their non-Russian comrades, as to either the motive which prompted Ludendorff's action or as to their ultimate aim once they had seized the power in Russia. "We are fully aware of the fact that the German Government allows the passage of the Russian internationalists only in order thus to strengthen the anti-war movement in Russia," declared a group of international Socialists at the moment of Lenin's departure.

The train-load of political dynamite steamed out of the central station at Berne on April 8, 1917, and a week later (April

16), late in the evening, Lenin arrived in Petrograd to be greeted with a tremendous ovation. Standing on an armoured car he made his first public speech in Russia to a cheering throng of workers, soldiers, and sailors, and in the course of it made use of words which, had they been reported, should have awakened Ludendorff to a realization of what spirits he had conjured up —"The hour is not far when, at the summons of our comrade Karl Liebknecht, the German people will turn their weapons against their capitalistic exploiters."

The advent of Lenin and the anti-war activities of his supporters was not in time to prevent the summer offensive which the Allied Powers had cajoled the unfortunate Kerensky into making. It was duly launched on July 1, and the Russian troops fought with their customary courage despite their acute war-weariness and lack of equipment. Few events in the war were more tragic than this last Allied offensive on the Eastern Front, carried out by men whose one desire was for peace and to return home, and of whom, in many cases, only one in six or eight possessed a rifle. By sheer impetus they achieved a not inconsiderable advance, and within the first twenty-four hours had captured more than 36,000 prisoners.

But this offensive neither surprised nor disconcerted Hoffmann. The German counter-attack was begun on July 19, and it was then apparent how greatly the Russian morale had suffered. Bolshevik agents appeared in every division and the success of their work was only too clear; regiment after regiment revolted, murdered its officers, and then hesitated, not knowing what to do next. The front was paralysed. The German advance gave that last touch to the complete disintegration of the Russian army which the Bolshevik agitation had initiated. The effect was ghastly. A panic spread in the ranks of the army already in a state of utter dissolution. There was scarcely any question of resistance. The panic-stricken retreat paralysed

even the will of those individual regiments which were prepared to take up fighting positions. The troops melted away
before the eyes of their commanders.

Tarnopol fell at the end of July, 1917 and on September 2
the German armies crossed the Dvina, capturing Riga on the
following day. Only the difficulty of transport prevented a more
rapid advance, and hostilities on the Eastern Front were virtually brought to an end by the middle of October with the
capture of the islands of Moon, Dago, and Osel, in the Gulf
of Riga.

But of what was happening behind the Russian lines, of the
degree to which the seed of Bolshevik discord implanted by
Lenin with the aid of Ludendorff, was bearing fruit, Prince
Leopold of Bavaria and Hoffmann, sitting in the citadel of
Brest-Litovsk, knew little or nothing. They could not have known
that the opening of the July offensive had been the signal for an
abortive Bolshevik plot to arrest the Provisional Government in
Petrograd and to call upon every soldier at the front to leave the
trenches; nor could they foresee that the German counter-attack
would coincide with the unsuccessful Bolshevik *coup-d'état* of
July 17–19. Furthermore General Kornilov had not informed
them that after the fall of Riga he had tried to establish a military
dictatorship by force. They had no conception of the chaos which
reigned in the capital nor of the prodigious pace at which the
Provisional Government, deserted by its allies, was hurtling to
destruction. They only knew that the front had become sufficiently
quiet for troops to be taken out of the line, and transferred to the
west to be drilled and trained there for the new task before them.
But beyond this elementary yet important fact the German Headquarters were at a loss to knew what to make of the situation.

Thus they had no knowledge of the final collapse of Kerensky
and of the Bolshevik triumph of November 7. Their mystifica-
tion was increased when wireless operators began to pick up

messages addressed "To all," sent out by an unknown individual of the name of Trotsky, declaring the desire of the new Soviet Government for peace. "We cannot get a clear view of the Russian situation as yet," Hoffmann wrote in his diary on November 21; yet he urged Count Hertling, who had succeeded Michaelis as the Supreme Command's nominee for the Chancellorship, to declare Germany's willingness to negotiate.

The uncertainty persisted until November 26. "Whether they will [declare an Armistice] I cannot yet say," recorded Hoffmann on the morning of that day. "We have no clear picture of what is likely to happen in the interior of Russia in the immediate future."

But in the afternoon there arrived Trotsky's formal proposals for an armistice and Krylenko's wireless message proclaiming the definite cessation of hostilities. At last something tangible had happened and Hoffmann reported by telephone to Kreuznach.

"Is it possible to negotiate with these people?" asked Ludendorff.

"Yes, it is possible," was the reply. "Your Excellency needs troops and this is the easiest way to get them."

The Armistice was signed on December 16, but even before that date troop trains were streaming across from east to west,[1] where it was no longer a case of replacing tired divisions by fresh ones, but of really adding to the number of combatants.

As a short-term policy the assistance given by the German Supreme Command to Lenin had proved a complete success. Russia was out of the war, and it is clear beyond the need of demonstration what this meant to the Central Powers. For the

---

[1] The Armistice agreement prohibited the transfer of German troops to other parts excepting "such removals as had been commanded before the time when the Armistice agreement was signed." In view of the fact that orders had already been given to remove a very large proportion of the army to the west, Hoffmann "was able to concede" this point without any great difficulty.

Quadruple Alliance was held together at this point—the close of 1917—solely by the hope of the victory of German arms followed by a rapid peace. Bulgaria and Turkey still remained tolerably loyal, but the Austro-Hungarian Monarchy was showing grave signs of defection. The publication by the Bolsheviks of the secret Treaty of London, signed in 1915 to bring Italy into the war, had disclosed the fact that the Allied Powers were aiming at nothing less than the dismemberment of Austria-Hungary, and this revelation had had not unnaturally the most disquieting effect in Vienna. "Peace at the earliest moment is necessary for our own salvation, and we cannot obtain peace until the Germans get to Paris—and they cannot get to Paris unless their Eastern Front is free," wrote Count Czernin in his diary in November; and again in a letter to a friend at the same period, "To settle with Russia as speedily as possible; then break through the determination of the Entente to destroy us, and then make peace—even at a loss—that is my plan and the hope for which I live. . . . Let but old Hindenburg make his entry into Paris and the Entente *must* utter the decisive word that they are willing to treat."

"Old Hindenburg" at this moment was entertaining and expressing the most uncomplimentary views towards Count Czernin and his country in general. "Count Czernin did not realize of what his country was capable, otherwise he would never have talked to us in 1917 of the possibility of not going on any longer." The contempt for the Habsburg Monarchy which the Marshal had conceived, half a century before, at Königgrätz, had not been lessened by his contact with its armies under his command, and in a moment of exasperation at Kreuznach he was once heard to remark that the next campaign which Germany undertook must be against Austria!

However, despite his feelings of contempt for his allies, Hindenburg could not disguise from himself the fact that the views expressed by Czernin were fundamentally correct. An early peace was in every way as desirable for Germany as for Austria, and to achieve this, victory for the German armies was an essential. But the U-boat campaign had passed the peak of its success and was waning. It had failed to bring England to her knees and the pressure of the Allied blockade was again strangling the German people. If massed forces could be hurled against the Western Front it might be possible to break through, to take Paris and Calais, and to threaten England directly. But this presupposed a cessation of hostilities in the east.

At the same time, the arrival in France of large, if unseasoned, American reinforcements made it imperative for the Supreme Command to make their offensive as soon as possible. If the negotiations with Russia were successful, all would be ready by the middle of March. Therefore, as the Marshal wrote, "Could any notion be more obvious than that of bringing all our effective troops from the east to the west and then taking the offensive?" And Ludendorff adds, "It will be obvious with what interest we watched the peace negotiations."

The interest of the Supreme Command was not, however, confined to watching. From the first moment of the Armistice it was clear that in the peace negotiations which were to follow Hindenburg and Ludendorff intended to have the controlling influence. The salient point of their policy was that not an inch of soil which had been won by German arms should be surrendered and that those Baltic provinces of Russia which still remained under the occupation of Russian troops should at the earliest possible moment be incorporated within the German *Reich*. They favoured in fact a frank policy of annexation undeterred by the principles of the Peace Resolution of July.

In opposition to their views were those of the aged Chancellor Hertling, and of the more far-seeing Foreign Secretary, Kühlmann, who realized the very detrimental effect abroad which would be brought about by the conclusion of a peace of annexation. Kühlmann himself was already convinced that a victory in the field was impossible for the Central Powers, and that all that could be hoped for was a general peace of negotiation and compromise. When the time for that arrived any agreement now arrived at with Russia must necessarily be open to revision, and he therefore sought to provide himself with sufficient territorial bargaining material in the east to ensure against annexations on Germany's western frontier. He was strongly opposed to Germany's acquiring permanently any further territory.

The concrete grounds upon which these conflicting theories met were the problem of Poland and the ultimate future of Courland and Lithuania. The mistaken policy of the High Command which had resulted, with disastrous effects, in the proclamation of the Polish kingdom in November 1916, had only established the theoretical existence of that state. No attempt had been made either then or subsequently to define its political status, and the control of the occupied area still remained in the hands of the Governors-General of Warsaw and Lublin.

There were three possible solutions of the Polish problem. The first, the so-called "Austrian solution," provided for the union of Congress Poland with Galicia, the whole to become a partner in a Tripartite Habsburg Monarchy. This solution was favoured by the Habsburgs and by the Austrian Ministry but was strongly opposed by the Hungarian Prime Minister, Count Tisza, who felt that the political structure of the Monarchy should not be changed and that, if Poland must be added to it at all—and of the desirability of this he was not entirely convinced—it should form an Austrian province. Hindenburg and Ludendorff also objected to this solution, both strategically and politically, on the grounds that it would place a tax upon their alliance with Austria, which in the long run could not be borne.

There was also a "German solution," enthusiastically sponsored by Erzberger, though without any support from either the Chancellor or Kühlmann. This proposal envisaged the incorporation of both Poland and Galicia in the German Empire, Austria being compensated by Rumania. This plan was strenuously opposed by the Vienna government, which wisely enough was unwilling to throw away the substance for the shadow.

The Supreme Command had its own plans, plans which took little account of political considerations, and which were based exclusively upon military and strategic necessities. It was the desire of Hindenburg and Ludendorff to create a "protective belt," which would give greater security to East Prussia and lessen danger of an attack such as that made by the Grand Duke Nicholas in 1914. It was proposed to widen the narrow neck between Danzig and Thorn and to add, east of the Vistula, a broad strip of territory which would protect the Upper Silesian coal-fields. With the remainder of the dismembered Polish state the High Command were not concerned. It could become independent, provided that it established favourable economic relations with Germany, or it could be given to Austria.

Kühlmann, with the strong support of the Chancellor, opposed this solution of the General Staff on the ground that an addition of two million Slavs to the population of the German Empire was in every way undesirable, and while Ludendorff agreed with this view, he countered it with the words "this grave objection must give way before military necessity."

With regard to Courland and Lithuania the demands of the General Staff were equally emphatic. It was their wish to create two Grand Duchies connected with the Empire through the person of the Emperor himself, and so far had they impressed their views upon the local government, through the agency of the Commander-in-Chief in the East and in Courland of the Baltic baronial aristocracy, that elections for constituent assemblies had already taken place in both provinces. The Diet of Mitau had actually requested the Kaiser to become Duke of Courland, and though the Lithuanians had proved less tractable, hopes were still entertained of their eventual compliance.

To Kühlmann, whose one idea was to keep the question of the future of the provinces open for review in the course of a general peace settlement, the madness of the policy of cold-blooded annexation was only too abundantly clear. But his objections were of no avail. The High Command remained obdurate.

"But why," Kühlmann once asked Hindenburg during one of their not infrequently acrimonious discussions at Kreuznach, "do you so particularly want these territories?"

"I need them for the manœuvring of my left wing in the next war," was the Marshal's reply; and Ludendorff explained that Courland and Lithuania would improve Germany's food supply and bring her additional man-power in case she should, in a future war, have to rely once more upon her own resources.

From the first news of the Armistice proposals on November 26, the Imperial Government and the Supreme Command had conferred together on the terms to be presented to the Russians, and their discussion had only served to emphasize the degree of disagreement which existed between them. As usual the Kaiser was called upon to arbitrate, and he presided over a conference at Kreuznach on December 18, on the eve of Kühlmann's departure for Brest-Litovsk, at which the final terms of the instructions were to be fixed.

At this meeting the Emperor, who had previously been inclined to favour the "Austrian solution" for Poland, veered round to the views of the General Staff and expressed his agreement with their proposal of a "protective belt" on the Prussian-Polish frontier. In addition both he and the Chancellor endorsed the idea of establishing a personal union of Courland and Lithuania, either with the Crown of Prussia or with the German Empire, provided that the Federal Princes agreed.

Kühlmann again reiterated his dislike of this policy and repeated his belief that the question of the future of the two provinces should be left open. "I might withdraw my opposition against hoisting the German flag in the eastern border states, but I would energetically advise against ever nailing it to the mast there," he declared emphatically.

The Emperor vacillated; nothing definite was decided, and Kühlmann departed for Brest-Litovsk with a determination to do what he thought to be right. He did not regard himself as bound by the discussions at Kreuznach, which had ended in indecision.

Arrived at the conference Kühlmann found an unexpected ally in Hoffmann, who had been appointed to the German delegation to represent the views of the High Command, but who was too much of a realist to approve the fantastic annexationist schemes of Hindenburg and Ludendorff. Within the first few days of the conference the Foreign Secretary and the General drew more closely together in the face of stern realities. During a New Year's interval in the peace discussions Kühlmann returned to Berlin, bringing Hoffmann with him, and arranged for the General a private audience with the Emperor. So impressed was the Kaiser with Hoffmann, whom he had not seen since the days of the quarrel with Falkenhayn, that the General was invited to luncheon and asked to give his views on the Polish question.

Hoffmann was in a quandary. He did not share the views of the High Command, and yet was diffident in placing himself in opposition to them. He begged to be excused from giving his personal opinion.

"When your Supreme War Lord wishes to hear your views on any subject it is your duty to give them to him, quite irrespective of whether they coincide with those of G.H.Q. or not," replied the Kaiser.

At that Hoffmann began to talk. He gave the Emperor the views of a man who for the past eighteen months had been in constant touch with the situation and who had had practical experience of its difficulties. He pointed out that, notwithstanding the measures taken by Prussia during many decades, she had not been able to manage her Polish subjects and that consequently he could see no advantage to the Empire from the addition of a further two million Poles to its population. He was even more critical of Erzberger's so-called "German solution." He suggested that the new Polish border-line should be drawn in such a way as to bring to Germany the smallest possible number of Polish subjects. Only a small additional strip of territory, with not more than 100,000 Polish inhabitants, was necessary, near Bendzin and Thorn, to prevent the enemy artillery in any subsequent war from firing straight into the Upper Silesian coal-fields, or on to the chief railway station of Thorn.

Deeply impressed with the reasonableness of Hoffmann's argument, the Emperor, always swayed by what he had last heard, agreed with him, and at once had a map prepared in accordance with his proposals. This he produced next morning (January 2, 1918) at a Crown Council at the Bellevue Palace, to which not only Hindenburg and Ludendorff, but also Hoffmann had been summoned. The latter attended with no little apprehension, for though he had tried to get into touch with Ludendorff he had been unsuccessful, and the First Quartermaster-General was therefore still ignorant of what had passed between his subordinate and the Kaiser.

The Emperor opened the council by laying the map before them.

"Gentlemen," he said, "you will find on this map the future frontier between Poland and Prussia, as I, in my capacity of your Supreme War Lord, consider that it should be drawn." He then added, "I base my conclusion on the judgment of an excellent and competent expert, namely that of General Hoffmann, who is here."

For a moment there was silence, and then Ludendorff, his voice hoarse with anger, all self-control abandoned, shouted at the Emperor that he had no right to ask the opinion of a general over his (Ludendorff's) head. In no circumstances could the line drawn by the Emperor be considered as final. The Supreme Command would have to consider the matter further.

"We must certainly think this matter over carefully," muttered Hindenburg, in approval.

For a moment the Emperor hesitated in indecision. Should he assert himself and provoke a joint resignation? The Council sat about him, disturbed and uncomfortable. Finally he temporized.

"I will await your report," he said, and brought the painful scene to a close.

But the Supreme Command were not thus easily mollified. They considered that their authority had been flouted and their dignity aspersed. That the Supreme War Lord of Germany should have the right to consult one of his generals without their knowledge and consent, they vehemently denied, and they retired to Kreuznach in high dudgeon.

On January 7 the Emperor received not their promised report but a letter from Hindenburg in which occurred the following passage:

In the Polish Question Your Majesty has chosen to place greater reliance upon the judgment of General Hoffmann than upon that of General Ludendorff and myself. General Hoffmann is my subordinate, and bears no responsibility whatsoever in the Polish Question. The events of January 2 have been the cause of pain to General Ludendorff and myself, and have shown us that Your Majesty disregards our opinion in a matter of vital importance for the existence of the German Fatherland.

This letter, the origin of which lay undoubtedly with Ludendorff, was a direct challenge to the authority of Wilhelm II, both as Supreme War Lord and as King of Prussia, and showed to how great a degree the Supreme Command considered itself the deciding power within the Empire. They regarded their responsibility as covering every question that could remotely affect "the existence of the German Fatherland." Supreme dictatorship could not go further.

The Emperor dared not resist. In answer to Hindenburg's letter, the Imperial Chancellor hastened to inform the Supreme Command that a misunderstanding had arisen and that the Emperor had taken no definite decision in regard to Poland.

But though he abandoned Hoffmann's proposals the Emperor stood between him and the wrath of Ludendorff, who had demanded his dismissal as Chief of the Staff in the East and his appointment to the command of a division. By command of the Emperor, Hoffmann remained at his post at Brest-Litovsk, but the breach with Ludendorff was permanent. The symbol HLH was shattered. It had in fact become merely a gigantic L.

After this victory of the Supreme Command the final tenor of the peace terms of Brest-Litovsk were inevitable and assured. Kühlmann returned to the Conference determined that if he could not negotiate a sane peace he would at least demonstrate to the world that, stripped to its essentials, Bolshevism was but a new form of nationalism. For this purpose he engaged with Trotsky in a series of what the exasperated Czernin, who saw the sands of his country's life running out in the glass, described as "Spiritual wrestling matches." In the end Kühlmann succeeded; for, though Trotsky branded the Germans before the world as freebooters and military tyrants, the Soviet Foreign Commissar, when finally faced with a bare-faced annexationist policy, abandoned the rôle of world revolutionary and fought for his country with the tenacity of any patriot. He employed every artifice of diplomacy, including an attempt to make a separate peace with Austria, and in final despair adopted the desperate expedient of "Neither War—nor Peace," broke off the negotiations and returned to Moscow.

Hindenburg and Ludendorff demanded a resumption of hostilities. Kühlmann protested. With the double purpose of bringing about an immediate peace and of encompassing the fall of the Foreign Minister, the Supreme Command persisted in their demands. Kühlmann was not to be inveigled into political suicide. Though forced to submit, he refused to resign. "I am against the proposal of resuming hostilities," he said, "but I do not consider the question important enough for me to withdraw from the Cabinet." But he did not return to Brest-Litovsk.

War with Russia was resumed, and within a week the armies of the Central Powers had occupied Kiev and Odessa and had advanced to Lake Peipus, within 120 miles of Petrograd. Livonia, Estonia, and the Ukraine passed under German control. Then the Russians surrendered. They returned to Brest-Litovsk and on March 3 signed a treaty, which for a peace of humiliation is without precedent or equal in modern history.[1] Three weeks later the Supreme Command launched its great offensive in the west and the last furious gamble of the war had begun.

[1] By the Treaty of Brest-Litovsk Russia lost a territory (301,000 square miles) nearly as large as Austria-Hungary and Turkey combined; fifty-six million inhabitants, or 32 per cent of the whole population of the country; a third of her railway mileages; 73 per cent of her total iron and 89 per cent of her total coal production; and over 5000 factories, mills, distilleries, and refineries. By a supplementary agreement signed in August she paid to Germany an indemnity of 6,000,000,000 marks.

In nearly every respect the policy which the Supreme Command had imposed on the negotiators of Brest-Litovsk proved a failure, both psychologically and materially. The cold-blooded brutality of the peace terms silenced for ever those well-meaning pacifists in the Allied countries who had talked of a peace of understanding based upon the German Peace Resolution of July 1917. If it did nothing else, the Peace of Brest-Litovsk, as Kühlmann had feared and foreseen, showed clearly to the world what mercy the conquered enemies of Germany might expect. The effect in the Allied countries was of a grim tightening of the belt and an increased determination to destroy the régime which could make such a peace. No better antidote could have been provided in England to the early disasters which followed the opening of the March offensive.

For Germany, too, the moral effect was detrimental. The infiltration of Bolshevik propaganda, which had begun with the fraternization of the troops at the time of the Armistice, had increased with the return of prisoners of war from Russia, who had proved not unfertile soil for such a seed. It had made its first public appearance in Germany during the great industrial strikes of January 1918. It was destined to spread more quickly and much further. For although there was included in the treaty a provision that both the Soviet and German Governments should "refrain from any agitation or propaganda" against each other, there was never any pretence of respecting this agreement on the part of the Soviet Government. Joffe, its first Ambassador in Berlin, made no concealment of the fact. "The Soviet Government as a body and its accredited representatives in Berlin," he announced, "have never concealed the fact that they are not going to observe this agreement and have no intention of so doing in the future." For his brief tenure of office, which terminated with his expulsion in October 1918, he made the Soviet Embassy, Unter den Linden, the headquarters of

Bolshevik and Spartacist activities, and with considerable success prepared the way for the breakdown of November.

The weapon with which Ludendorff had sought to deal Russia so deadly a blow had indeed justified his expectations, but
he had not foreseen that it would be used against himself with
equally devastating effects.

Even the material advantages did not accrue to the extent
that had been hoped. The supplies of grain from the Ukraine
and of oil from Rumania, which were delivered in 1918 as
a result of treaty agreements, fell considerably below the
amounts which had been expected. And in the case of the
former, the major share went to Austria. The Ukrainian delegates, with whom the Central Powers had signed a separate
peace, had exaggerated the stocks of wheat and had ignored
the effects of the agrarian revolution. The imposing central
German-Ukrainian trading organization, which Gröner had conceived so excellently on paper, was able to procure, in effect,
very few supplies, and, in the opinion of Hoffmann, the Supreme Command would have been more successful if they had
commissioned a number of Jewish dealers to buy corn for them
in the open market.

But the most complete illusion of all was that the conclusion of peace with Russia had enabled the Supreme Command to transfer the very large majority of its forces from east
to west. This was far from being the case. A victor's peace must
be enforced. The political and economic conditions which the
Supreme Command had imposed on its captured territories
proved so irksome and unpopular that only by the most ruthless application of force could they be maintained at all.

Moreover at this period Ludendorff's paranoiac complaint
developed a Napoleonic complex. He saw himself creating and
distributing kingdoms as had the Emperor of the French after
Tilsit. He sent an expeditionary force into Finland to put down

a Bolshevik revolt. Another expedition penetrated to Batoum and Baku. A mission was sent to Odessa: an army of occupation was maintained in Rumania. In the Ukraine a régime had been set up under an hereditary Hetman, and grand-ducal governments were being organized in Lithuania, Courland, Livonia, and Estonia. In addition, the problem of Poland still required constant care and supervision.

To enforce the peace and to bolster up the fantasies of the Supreme Command, no less than a million soldiers had to be retained in the east in 1918. Admittedly they were older men, nearly all under thirty-five years of age having been sent to the west. But in the French and British armies there were a good many men over thirty-five years old, and if even half this million had been available for service in quiet sectors on the Western Front, other and younger men would have been released to take part in the offensive. Later in the autumn, when the German losses had reached a gigantic figure, the Supreme Command did indeed make transfer from the east to close the gaps. By October 1, 1918, barely half a million men remained with Hoffmann, but the transfers had only been made when Germany had been forced finally upon the defensive. When they were really needed—that is to say, in the first weeks of the offensive—they were not there. An additional five hundred thousand men in the west in April 1918 might very well have turned the scale in favour of Germany.

Thus the policy to which Hindenburg so unprotestingly gave his assent and name became the fatal lodestar of the German Empire, and while Ludendorff the soldier was demanding every man for the decisive battles in the west, Ludendorff the politician was wasting an army a million strong in the east.

Even granting that Hindenburg knew or realized little of what was in progress, and that he obediently followed Ludendorff's lead, it is impossible to exonerate him from a very large share of responsibility for the eastern policy of the Supreme Command and the consequent tragedy of Brest-Litovsk. The documents setting forth the case of the Supreme Command all appear over his signature. Throughout his life he had a sad weakness for signing what was placed before him, and in the last days it was not unusual for his immediate entourage not to trouble even to consult him but to send telegrams in his name. But these days had not arrived at that time. He was still capable at the age of seventy of understanding what he was told even if he did not always appreciate its real inwardness. But so completely was he dominated by the personality of Ludendorff that he accepted unquestioningly the views of his coadjutor.

· 8 ·

By the beginning of 1918 the position of the High Command in Germany was unique and supreme. They not only ruled but governed, and demanded a controlling voice in all internal and external affairs. With the callousness of mediaeval princes they jettisoned their nominees in office, and submitted the Emperor to the treatment meted out by the Carolingian mayors of the palace to the Merovingian kings. In the relations with their military colleagues they had learnt little from their own early difficulties with Falkenhayn. Unpalatable reports were either ignored or sharply criticized, and there grew up at General Headquarters that inevitable clique of "yes-men" which surrounds and vitiates the atmosphere breathed by all dictators.

The political and military situation of Germany at the moment greatly strengthened the position of Hindenburg and Ludendorff. It was admitted on all sides that a speedy end to the war was imperatively necessary. To bring this about there were two alternative methods; the favourable military position of Germany could be used for concluding a peace of conciliation or for an attack in the west. The peace policy was warmly favoured by Kühlmann and Prince Max of Baden, and had the secret support of German and Bavarian Crown Princes. The question of Belgium again arose, and it was urged on the Emperor that a clear and unequivocal declaration should be made renouncing all claims direct and indirect upon Belgian independence.

But the High Command would have none of it. Ludendorff had become convinced, even before the armistice in the east, that the sole hope of German victory lay in "a gambler's throw," a blow in the west as swift and as terrible as possible. "It will be an immense struggle," he wrote to the Kaiser, "that will begin at one point, continue at another, and take a long time; it is difficult, but it will be successful." He had reached this decision after a consultation with his chief staff officers on November 11, 1917, at Mons. The date and place are of interest, as is the fact that, at a conference where military decisions of the very gravest importance for the Central Powers were to be taken, neither the Supreme War Lord, Wilhelm II, nor the Chief of the General Staff, Hindenburg, were present.

The Emperor, almost certainly against his better judgment, finally decided for the High Command. In so doing he delivered himself into their hands and sealed the fate of his Imperial house. Having committed himself to the thesis that "Germany's fate depended on one card," he could no longer rid himself of HL who claimed to have that card up their sleeve. Herein lies the secret of the period of unequalled supremacy which Hindenburg and Ludendorff enjoyed from December 1917 till the October of the following year, a period during which they made no small contribution to the ultimate downfall of the House of Hohenzollern.

The Chancellor, Michaelis, having fallen foul of the Social-Democrats in the *Reichstag*, was replaced in November 1917 by the aged Bavarian statesman, Count Hertling, who, feeling himself primarily the nominee of the Supreme Command, did his best to translate their policy into action. Though his ripe experience and high character rendered it impossible for him to adopt the views of Ludendorff *in toto*, his advanced age and lack of vigour made him feel unequal to embarking on a controversy with the Supreme Command.

The earliest opportunity for Hindenburg and Ludendorff to test their increased strength was over the peace terms of Brest-Litovsk, and in this case they were eminently successful, riding rough-shod over Emperor, Chancellor and Foreign Secretary. But they had been deeply affected by the Emperor's change of front under Hoffmann's influence at the Bellevue Conference on January 2, and although they had received assurances that the Kaiser had completely withdrawn his opposition to their views on the Polish question, they were persuaded that the time had come to have the seal of imperial approval placed upon their strongly-held views regarding "responsibility."

A memorandum to the Emperor was drawn up which stands unique in the history of war and politics. On the Emperor was placed the full responsibility of the new offensive then under preparation in the west, in which the Supreme Command would make every effort to secure a decisive victory, bringing with it the annihilation of the enemy. But they could only do this on condition that they enjoyed the fullest confidence of the Emperor, and had a guarantee that a victorious and dictated peace should crown the victory. It was for the Emperor to decide, but if he dared to hold a different view he must find other generals.

> We must defeat the Western Powers in order to assure the position in the world which Germany needs [writes Hindenburg to his Emperor]. It is for this purpose that Your Majesty has given orders for the Battle in the west to be undertaken, a battle which will constitute the greatest effort made by us during the war, and involving the heaviest sacrifices. After the events of Brest-Litovsk I cannot but doubt that, when peace comes to be negotiated, Germany will not obtain the concessions which her position demands and to which our sacrifices entitle us. . . . It is Your Majesty's privilege to decide. . . . The heavy task which Your Majesty is placing upon the men who will have to prepare and conduct the operations in the west, in conformity with Your Majesty's instructions, makes it necessary that they should feel certain of enjoying Your Majesty's fullest confidence. Both the armies and their leaders must be upheld by the feeling that the political success will correspond to the military success. Most humbly I beg Your Majesty to decide on this fundamental principle. Personal consideration for General Ludendorff and myself cannot be allowed to count in matters where the safety of the State is concerned.
>
> (*Signed*) VON HINDENBURG, G.F.M.

It was the old policy of a pistol to the head, only in a more barefaced manner. "The Field-Marshal and I will resign" had been Ludendorff's clinching and final argument from the earliest days, and it had now become an almost unassailable one. What was demanded was not a share in, but a control of, foreign policy in its widest sense. The proposal was as preposterous as it was impudent, and both the Emperor and the Chancellor were very naturally furious and alarmed.

In an interview with Hertling, Hindenburg and Ludendorff were given clearly to understand that, while the Supreme Command had the right to assist in peace negotiations in a consultive capacity in so far as military matters were concerned, the sole and final responsibility for the conclusion of peace must rest with the Chancellor, the Emperor being the final court of appeal. This view received the official approval of Wilhelm II in a letter replying to Hindenburg's memorandum. After thanking him for his "soldierly frankness and outspokenness," and while admitting the right of the Supreme Command "to give unrestrained expression to their views," the Emperor went on to say: "The final decision must rest with me. I have passed on your memorandum to the Chancellor and am in agreement with his views. I expect henceforward that you and General Ludendorff will be able to give up further objections and to devote yourselves whole-heartedly to your proper function of conducting the war."

This was a brave reply and gave the impression that the Emperor was about to reassert his position. But in effect the Supreme Command were little concerned by it. They realized that behind this bluster neither Wilhelm II nor Hertling had the courage to denounce a dictated peace. They knew that they had already established a sufficiently strong control over the Foreign Office through their representative, Colonel von Haeften, to ensure their views remaining paramount, and they were confident that, though the Emperor might summon up enough valour to reprove them, he did not dare to take up their challenge and accept their resignations.

To prove their domination, they launched a new attack in a direction very singularly offensive to the Emperor, since it was against one of his personal entourage and challenged his undoubted right to appoint his own staff. On January 16 Hindenburg wrote to the Emperor demanding the dismissal of the Chief of his Civil Cabinet, Herr von Valentini, a man who had for years enjoyed his closest friendship, and who deeply resented the encroachment of the Supreme Command upon the Imperial prerogative. The reasons for the requested dismissal were that Valentini had had a large share in the responsibility for "the dangerous policy of Bethmann Hollweg," of which the failure to make sufficient political exploitation of military successes had remained as a legacy. In a supreme moment of hypocrisy Hindenburg urged the Emperor to replace Valentini by a man who "viewed the situation clearly and impartially, and who would openly and manfully inform Your Majesty as to the state of affairs." It was exactly these qualities which Valentini possessed and for which he was to be sacrificed; it was, moreover, a man of these qualities which was so sadly lacking in the Marshal's own environment.

The Emperor obeyed. He dared not, in the final analysis, refuse. Gone were the brave days when with a light-hearted assurance he had dismissed Bismarck. Gone even was the spark of courage which had enabled him to dispense with Falkenhayn. Now at the demand of the Chief of the General Staff he dismissed a faithful servant whose chief fault was his loyalty. In these days monarchical government could scarcely be said to exist in Germany and it was almost impossible to recognize the Emperor as a force. His passion for marginalia discloses the disgruntled realization of his new position.

When Kühlmann in the *Börsen-Zeitung* launched a guarded and anonymous attack on the Supreme Command, the Emperor peppered it with exclamations of approval, whose tenor showed how clearly he appreciated that his position had suffered both with the *Reichstag* and with the General Staff. "Again and again," wrote Kühlmann, "there comes a cry from the German people for a statesman to lead them. Conditions however are not such as to allow any statesman to become great." "Very true," was the Imperial marginal comment; "either he is unpopular with the *Reichstag* or Kreuznach or both." The article continued that "in the conduct of foreign affairs the Foreign Office is no longer paramount—a preposterous state of affairs." Against this

Wilhelm II wrote: "Naturally; the Kaiser is ignored by both sides."

Complaints arose also from the German commanders on other fronts that their views were ignored. Marshal von Mackensen in desperation sent a report to the Emperor direct, expounding his views on the situation in the Balkans and in the Austro-Hungarian Empire. The report is endorsed in the Imperial script: "Mackensen's views wholly coincide with my own. Up to the present, however, I have been unable to obtain a hearing for them from the Chief of the General Staff."

In the internal government of the country and in the regulation of relations between capital and labour the Supreme Command also endeavoured to make its influence supreme. Through the Home Commands, whose control Ludendorff removed from the Minister of War and placed under himself, and by means of martial law and a formidable array of military regulations, there was created an executive authority entirely independent of the Imperial Government.

The High Command allied itself with the industrialists and landowners, and supported their war aims. It was particularly severe in its relations with organized labour. Strikes in time of war were high treason, and strikers therefore were treated with considerable severity. They were tried by court-martial to avoid the risk of mild sentences, and for this purpose suitable officers were appointed as Judge-Advocates-General and Crown Prosecutors. The great strike of January 1918, which involved more than half a million workers, chiefly in Berlin, was dealt with in a most ruthless and efficient manner. A state of siege was proclaimed, the labour press forbidden, and all strike meetings broken up by the police. One leader was arrested and received a sentence of five years' detention in a fortress. Thousands of workmen on the Army Reserve were called to their regiments, and finally seven of the great industrial concerns were placed under military control and the men ordered to resume work on pain of punishment in accordance with the utmost rigour of martial law.

The strike collapsed, but the effect on the country was so serious that, in a letter to the Minister for War on February 18, Ludendorff recommended that in future industrial disputes should be settled "in general without the employment of force." "Nevertheless," he added, "it is necessary to be prepared for all eventualities, and it is for this reason that I have consented to leave the desired troops in Germany." In reality he was so much disturbed that he sent a secret order to each army commander instructing him to keep two battalions ready for use against the civilian population.

To these disastrous policies at home and abroad Hindenburg was lending his name and accepting implicitly a considerable share of responsibility. He became disturbed at the increasing number of disputes in which the Supreme Command was becoming involved. Again and again he acted as peace-maker between Ludendorff and the Emperor, Ludendorff and the Chancellor, Ludendorff and the party leaders, but when the final choice came he had no will of his own. The "happy marriage" with Ludendorff had developed into a harmonious married life in which, in the words of the Marshal, the relationships of the individuals "are one in thought and action, and often what one says is only the expression of the wishes and feelings of the other."

· 9 ·

The principle of launching a great attack in the west having been accepted in November 1917, preparations went steadily forward throughout the winter and early spring. As the weeks drew on towards the day when all must be ready, it was found necessary for the Supreme Command to be in closer touch with the headquarters of the Army Groups and armies which were to play the principle parts in the forthcoming battle, and the Great General Headquarters of the German Army were accordingly moved from Kreuznach to the little Belgian watering-place of Spa, where Hindenburg and Ludendorff took up their quarters in the Hôtel Britannique in the early days of March. Advanced headquarters were established at Avesnes, just across the French frontier. The Kaiser did not take up residence either at Spa or at Avesnes, but lived in his special train during the eventful weeks which followed. The train was moved about according to the military situation.

During one of the periodic visits of the High Command to the front from Avesnes the German Army was nearly robbed of its controlling brains. A faulty switch-box caused a heavy munitions train to collide broadside on with the train of the Supreme Command, derailing it and smashing several of the cars to splinters. Apart from the fact that Hindenburg and his *alter ego* were unceremoniously tumbled out of bed, no harm was done. There were no casualties; not even the maps were damaged.

As at Pless and at Kreuznach, numerous important visitors arrived at Spa to pay their respects to the two lengendary figures who were now regarded as the sole props of the Quadruple Alliance. Amongst these was the Crown Prince Vaheddin of Turkey, and in his suite was a young major-general, recently transferred from the Syrian Front, who, in company with many of the younger Turkish generation, nursed a bitter resentment against Germany for her dealings with his country.

To the Crown Prince the Marshal gave a most optimistic review of the military situation of the Central Powers, including that in Syria, but in a hasty aside to the Prince the Turkish officer assured him that the details given of the Syrian Front were completely incorrect and that he strongly suspected the rest of being largely bluff.

Later Ludendorff arrived and gave them a more detailed account, especially of the preparations for the great offensive. The Crown Prince, who was quite ignorant of everything military, nodded somnolently, but the Turkish general wanted to know more.

"What is the line you expect to reach if the offensive is successful?" he asked.

The Marshal, nettled at being cross-examined by so young an officer, replied in general terms:

"We usually aim at a point that is decisive to us. Any further action depends on circumstances."

"There!" cried the general to Prince Vaheddin, "even the Chief of the German Staff doesn't know his objective and trusts to luck to get him through."

That evening there was a banquet given by the Emperor in honour of his guests. Under the influence of the Imperial champagne, the Turkish general again approached Hindenburg.

"Your Excellency," he said, "the facts you supplied this morning to Prince Vaheddin about the Syrian Front were quite wrong. I know, for I was there, and the cavalry division of which you spoke exists only on paper. However, let that pass. Would you, as a favour, tell me in confidence what is the objective of this new offensive?"

The Marshal looked down from his great height upon this presumptuous young man, and completely ignoring his questions gave him a cigarette to keep him quiet.

In days to come, which none could then foresee, both were destined to become presidents in their own countries, for the cock-sure young Turk was Mustapha Kemal Pasha.

In fact, the plans for the offensive were, of course, considerably more definite in form than the Supreme Command had seen fit to tell the Turks! The general aim was by a series of terrific blows to shatter the enemy's continuous entrenched position, to make it impossible for them through lack of reserves to hold together in open warfare, and to defeat their separate armies. If it proved impossible to reduce them to complete impotence, at least the war-will—and more particularly the *Vernichtungswille* ("desire for annihilation")—of their peoples must be so broken as to make it impossible for them to await the long and uncertain process of reconstructing their shattered fortunes with American aid.

Such was the general conception. To bring it to fruition there was a variety of alternatives, the merits of which were canvassed and sifted. On January 21, however, Ludendorff, again in the absence of Hindenburg, came to a final decision. The blow should fall with its full weight upon the British army, on a seventy-mile front from Vimy Ridge to Barisis-sur-Oise. This course was chosen partly because Great Britain was regarded as the mainspring of the Entente; partly because the Supreme Command considered the British less skilful tactically than the French,—"The Englishman did not understand how to control rapid changes in the situation. His methods were too rigid," was Hindenburg's opinion;—and partly because it was rightly calculated that the French would not "run themselves off their legs and hurry at once to the help of their Entente comrades." The tactical break-through was not in itself an objective; its *raison d'être* was to gain an opportunity for applying that strongest form of attack, envelopment; to drive a wedge between the British and French armies and defeat them severally.

The execution of the offensive was entrusted to the Army Groups of the German and Bavarian Crown Princes, who assembled between them forty-three divisions to be launched against the fourteen divisions of the British Fifth Army. This gave the Germans odds in their favour of over three to one, and this overwhelming superiority in numbers discounted the fact that the place, date, and even the time of assault were eventually known to the British, in spite of the elaborate German precautions to preserve secrecy.

On March 18 Hindenburg and Ludendorff moved up to Avesnes. At that time the exact date for the opening of the offensive had not been fixed, but it was felt that if any element of surprise was to be preserved it must be launched as soon as possible. The weather was stormy and rainy almost the whole of March 20. The prospects for the morrow were uncertain, but at noon it was definitely decided that the battle should begin on the morning of the following day. The orders had been drawn up on March 10 over the Kaiser's signature with the day and hour of attack left blank; now they were brought to Hindenburg and he countersigned them.

The early morning hours of March 21 found the whole of northern France, from the coast to the Aisne, shrouded in mist. At 4.40 a terrific bombardment from seven thousand guns opened with a crash on the forty-mile front of the British Fifth Army. The higher the sun mounted into the sky the thicker the fog became. At times it limited the range of vision to a few yards. Even the sound-waves seemed to be absorbed in the grey veil. Back in Avesnes, Hindenburg and Ludendorff could only hear a distant, indefinite roll of thunder coming from the front. At a little after 9 o'clock the creeping barrage began, and at the same time the grey waves of German infantry began to advance through the fog. The greatest struggle in history had opened. The "Kaiser's Battle" was on.

At first only vague reports reached Avesnes; recitals of objectives reached, contradictions of previous reports, rumours and alarms. Only gradually, as the mist began to dissolve and the sun to triumph, was it realized that the British line had been broken through at all points. By the evening it was clear that the right and centre of the German advance was held up before the British second line, but the left had swept forward far beyond St. Quentin. The delay, however, was disposed of on the following day, and the attack pushed further and further westwards. Hundreds of guns and enormous quantities of ammunition and other booty fell into German hands and long columns of British prisoners were marched towards the rear. Péronne was captured on the 23rd, and on that same day the first long-range shells fell upon Paris. An advance now seemed possible on Amiens, that nodal point of the most important railway connection between the war zones of Central and Northern France. If it fell into German hands the Allied field of operations would be divided and the tactical break-through would indeed have been converted into a strategical wedge between the French and British armies, which might even develop into a political cleavage between the two countries. Forward, then, against Amiens!

The evening of March 24 saw the fall of Bapaume and the old Somme battlefield was behind the German lines; wide sections of the English Front had been utterly routed. What remained of the Fifth Army had been placed under the command of the French General Fayolle and was retiring on Amiens. On the 26th the French considered the position of the British so critical that at the Conference of Doullens, when Haig entered the room, Pétain whispered to Clemenceau, "There is a man who will be forced to see his army capitulate in the open field."

But the force of the German attack was slackening; the pace was too fast and the calibre of the men was not equal to the strain. The success of a break-through is not only a question of tactics and strategy, it is essentially one of reinforcement and supply. The German losses had been very heavy, the price of the advance was ghastly, for the first time in the war they had two soldiers killed for every British, and three officers killed for every two British. Their consumption of material exceeded their captures, and the quality of the food and equipment served out to the men, much of it *Ersatz* in character, began to tell unfavourably.

Here was the nemesis of that fatal earlier policy which had been the lodestar of the Supreme Command since 1916. A million troops immobilized was the price of aggrandizement in the east, and half that number would have turned the scale in the west during the last week of March. According to both Sir Douglas Haig and General Mangin, only a few cavalry divisions were necessary to widen the gap between the French and the British, thus severing the two armies. These were not available on the Western Front, but at that moment three cavalry divisions were occupied in the Ukraine propping up the unpopular and unsavoury government of the Hetman Skoropadsky. As it was, the drive for Amiens fell short by ten miles and flickered out in heavy fighting around Villers-Brétonneux, Hangard, and Moreuil. By April 4 the "Greatest Battle of the War" was over; its most far-reaching effect had been the appointment of Foch as Allied Commander-in-Chief.

But this was by no means the impression made in Germany, where the advance of the army and the enormous captures of men and material were hailed with enthusiasm. For the last time a wave of optimism swept the country, and with it came a great re-awakening of the Hindenburg Legend. Both were anxiously and immediately exploited. The battle was christened *"Die Kaiserschlacht,"* and the Emperor conferred upon the Marshal the highest military order of Prussia, the Grand Cross of the Iron Cross with Golden Rays, which had been created for Blücher after Waterloo and which even the great Moltke had not received. The fact that this honour, usually regarded as the crowning award at the close of a victorious campaign, should be given to Hindenburg at a moment when the final issue of the battle was still in serious doubt, cannot have escaped him, for at this moment he writes to his wife: "What is the use of all these

orders? A good and advantageous peace is what I should prefer.
It is not my fault in any case if the struggle ends unfavourably
for us." This is not the tone of a commander assured of victory.

To exploit the successes against the British in the south and
to take advantage of the weakening of the enemy line through
the transfer of reserves, the Supreme Command planned a new
stroke in the north across the valley of the Lys from Armentières
to La Bassée, the ultimate object being the capture of Calais and
Boulogne. Beginning on April 9, the anniversary of Nivelle's
fatal attack, it too met with initial success. The great natural
bastion of Kemmel Hill was captured from the British; the
Portuguese divisions ceased to exist as a fighting force; Armentières, Bailleul, and Wytschaete fell into German hands and they
stormed again the battered ruins of Messines. The British were
in great jeopardy, and the gravity of the situation was reflected
in Haig's now historic order of the day: "With our backs to the
wall."

But again at the critical moment the last ounce of weight was
missing from the German onslaught. Discipline was slackening
and considerable time was lost while the troops pillaged the captured British stores for the luxuries which the Allied blockade
had so long denied them. The heavy losses were beginning to
tell more and more, and there were no fresh divisions to throw
into the line. On the other hand, new British divisions were arriving from Italy and Palestine, and American troops were now
entering France at the rate of 125,000 a month.

The second great attack had failed in its final objective. The
Allied line sagged and bulged but it remained unbroken. Neither
Amiens nor Calais had been reached and the tide was beginning
to turn. Once again Hindenburg and Ludendorff gathered their
strength for a further effort. But their strength was not what it
had been. Only forty-one divisions were available for this third

great attack delivered against the French on May 27 along the heights of the Chemin des Dames, with Paris as the objective.

The attack, however, was a complete surprise. The French had considered the position impregnable and had regarded the absence of a previous German attack on this section as a recognition of the fact on their part. Hindenburg himself was inclined to believe the story told to him by an officer who had taken part in the preparations on the Ailette, that the croaking of the frogs in the streams and marshes had been so loud that it was impossible for the French to hear the sounds made by the approach of the German bridging trains! Whatever the cause, the French were taken off their guard and were rapidly thrown back across the Aisne and as far as the Marne. Again the Allied front was dented perilously and again the German assault proved just too weak to break it. Mangin's counter-attack in June 1918 near Compiègne, south of Noyen, and the historic action of the American troops at Chateau-Thierry brought the third German attack to a standstill before the gates of Paris. The action closed on June 8 and both sides paused for a breathing-space.

The outcome of the offensive had been entirely contrary to the hopes, expectations, and promises of the High Command. In spite of every effort they had not been able to inflict a mortal wound upon their adversaries in either a military or a political sense. There was no sign of surrender on the part of the Entente. On the contrary, each military reverse seemed only to increase their determination to carry on the struggle to the bitter end.

Such was not the case within the Quadruple Alliance. Separatism in Hungary, disruption and revolt in Austria, reared their heads and hissed at the Dual Monarchy. In Germany the fruits of Brest-Litovsk were ripening and the corrosive doctrines of Bolshevism were making rapid inroads upon the morale of the Home Front. Divisions transferred from the East brought the infection with them, as did exchanged prisoners of war, and the army in the West began to feel its influence.

The fact that, despite the very large gains in territory, the German offensives of March, April, and May had failed in their fundamental object of breaking the Allied line, was not generally appreciated in the country, where the tactical successes of the army were still the cause for great rejoicings. Amongst the leading men of Germany there were, however, those who had entirely lost hope of victory and were anxious only to make peace while the power of taking the offensive still remained with the army. The Crown Prince of Bavaria, Prince Max of Baden, and Kühlmann, who had held this view longer than any of them, all urged upon the Chancellor the necessity of a peace offensive.

The Supreme Command remained silent as to the reality which lay hidden behind their apparent victory, but their views leaked through to the Imperial Government by indirect channels. "General Ludendorff," wrote Prince Rupprecht to Hertling on June 1 [a full week before the end of the battle of Soissons], "shares my view that in all probability a crushing defeat of the enemy is out of the question; he is now resting his hopes upon the success of a *deus ex machinâ* in the shape of an internal collapse in the Western Powers."

Prince Max had conveyed the same warning to the Supreme Command themselves. Dining at Avesnes on May 19 and sitting between the Marshal and Ludendorff, he begged them to promise him one thing, that they would warn the Government before the last offensive strength had been thrown in, for then it would be high time to make peace. Everything, he assured them, depended on whether Germany went to the conference table with an army still capable of striking, so that a further appeal to arms could be made if impossible terms were put forward. At the moment both agreed with him, but the Prince feared that his plea would soon be forgotten.

The difficulties of the situation were not lessened by the fact that at this critical moment the Supreme Command and the head of the Foreign Office had become bitter enemies. The breach which had opened at the Bellevue Palace on January 2 had never been bridged. An attempt at reconciliation had been made by Colonel von Haeften, the representative of the Supreme Command at the Foreign Office, but it had failed, both sides displaying an almost child-like obstinacy.

Haeften, however, shared the views of Kühlmann and Prince Max of Baden as to the gravity of the situation, and in June he made a further effort. In a memorandum, with which he arrived at Avesnes, he declared: "Unless our statesmanship gets to work on a definite plan before the conclusion of the military operations, there is no prospect of a peace of statesmanship; and only a peace of statesmanship corresponds with our interests."

By this time the High Command had themselves realized the necessity of at least exploiting politically the intervals between battles. They gave approval to Haeften's proposals for a peace offensive. Ludendorff actually agreed that victories alone could not bring peace. "It is high time," he said to Haeften, "that something was done," and he sent the memorandum to the Chancellor with a covering letter. Haeften returned to Berlin almost jubilant and reported his conversation to Hertling and Kühlmann, adding that he believed that the Supreme Command would now agree even to a declaration on the restoration of Belgian independence. Kühlmann commissioned him to prepare and carry out the political offensive.

The Foreign Secretary himself believed that he was on the threshold of establishing confidential conversations with the Allies, and this belief was strengthened by the reports he had received from England via the Hague and by the famous letter of Lord Lansdowne, and the speeches of Mr. Asquith and General Smuts. Armed with the news which Haeften had brought him from Avesnes that the Supreme Command themselves no longer believed in victory by force of arms alone, he seized upon the occasion of a debate on foreign affairs in the *Reichstag* on June 24 to make a reply to these tentative feelers from abroad.

The speech contained nothing that was not obvious and nothing that was not completely substantiated by the events of the months which followed. But Kühlmann was speaking in what appeared superficially to be a breathing-space between two great German victories. He emphasized that in order to achieve peace an understanding must be sought between Germany and the Entente. "Without some such exchange of ideas, in view of the enormous magnitude of this coalition war and of the number of powers involved in it, including those from overseas, an absolute end can hardly be expected through purely military decisions alone, without any diplomatic negotiations." The remainder of the speech was an appeal to the Majority parties in the *Reichstag* to take their stand on the Peace Resolution of a year before and to take the initiative once more.

But the *Reichstag* rose against him almost to a man. Count Westarp declared for the Conservatives, "Just as our good sword has brought us peace in the east, so too will our sword bring us peace in the west." Stresemann and Posadowsky followed with bitter criticisms, and the Socialist leaders, Scheidemann and Ledebour, delivered themselves in the words of Prince Rupprecht, of "nasty speeches which undoubtedly make negotiations far more difficult."

But from Avesnes there came a bellow of rage. It was impossible to deny the truth of what Kühlmann had said, but he had blurted out publicly what should only have been whispered *sub rosa*. In the Headquarters mess the word "traitor" was used quite openly, and immediately steps were taken to procure Kühlmann's dismissal. By telephone Ludendorff, in language scarcely coherent, cancelled Haeften's projected political offensive, while

Hindenburg in a telegram to the Chancellor expressed "extreme indignation" at Kühlmann's speech, which would have a "profoundly depressing effect" upon the morale of the army and people alike. The Supreme Command, he added, "could no longer work with the Foreign Secretary." An imperious summons was issued to Count Hertling to report at Spa on July 1.

On that occasion the Imperial Government was arraigned before the Supreme Command. The Chancellor sought to defend his colleague "like a teacher trying to excuse a bad essay by one of his pupils to a school inspector." Kühlmann was overwrought, Hertling pleaded; he was exhausted, had no time to prepare his speech adequately, had not even had time for lunch. Hindenburg replied that a Foreign Minister must find time to prepare a speech of such importance, and added: "the Supreme Command has never tried to disguise their suspicions of the Foreign Secretary." They could no longer work with him.

The Kaiser arrived next day. The Chancellor and the Marshal both appealed to him. Again Wilhelm II was faced with this grim dilemma. The Imperial Government or the High Command? The Constitution or the Condominium? Again under the threat of resignation he surrendered. He did more, he surrendered abjectly. At the Crown Councils of July 2 and 3, all thoughts of a peace offensive were abandoned. The Emperor and the Chancellor subscribed to the foreign policy of the High Command. The Austro-Polish solution was finally dropped, and Poland was required to pay a contribution to the expenses of the war. Belgium, it was agreed, "must remain under German influence to prevent a hostile invasion from ever advancing through it again." It was to be divided into two separate states, Flanders and Wallonia, and Germany required a long military occupation, the Flanders coast and Liége being the last points to be evacuated. The Admiralty representatives even put in a claim for a neutral zone on the east coast of North America, but the Emperor stopped short of this colossal folly and declined to include it in the peace terms.

The Emperor returned to Berlin and on July 8 dismissed Kühlmann. In so doing he deprived Germany of the services of her most far-sighted war statesman, with the exception of Beth-mann Hollweg, and destroyed the last hope of securing a peace of understanding. By July 12 the Emperor was back in Spa, full of confidence and ready to witness the overwhelming success of his armies which should bring him a peace of victory.

The "Kaiser's Battle" was indeed entering on its last phase, but not in the sense that the Emperor and the High Command had hoped. The battle of Rheims, which opened on July 15, was, in the words of a neutral eye-witness, "brilliant but hopeless," for, whereas on the Marne the German divisions crossed and drove forward half-way to Epernay before they were held by a force of French, American, and Italian troops, east of the city of Rheims they met with frightful defeat and were stopped dead, losing as many as 30,000 killed. Two days after it had been launched the offensive had withered away. Orders were issued to withdraw behind the Marne. On the following day, July 18, came the first Allied counter-offensive and the initiative passed finally out of German hands.

It was the beginning of the end. With two million fresh young American troops in France, Foch put forth his new strength, and it was only with great difficulty and by much hard and costly fighting that the Germans were able to bring the Allies to a stand-still on the line of the Vesle on August 2.

Even then Hindenburg and Ludendorff had not emerged from the Valley of Delusion. During the period of comparative quiet which followed August 2, the new Foreign Minister, Ad-miral von Hintze, arrived at Avesnes and put the question as to whether the Supreme Command were still certain of finally and decisively beating the enemy. To this Ludendorff replied with "a decided *yes,*" and the Admiral returned to Berlin reassured, and hopeful that it might be his "pleasant and promising part to crown an assured victory with a victorious peace."

A few days later came Colonel Niemann, the representative of the Supreme Command with the Emperor, with a further enquiry: "Can I assure His Majesty that Your Excellency will shorten the line?" he asked Ludendorff. "It appears to me that the positions in which our counter-attacks have left us are awkward for defence and require too many troops." "Defence?" cried Ludendorff. "I hope that in a few days, as soon as the men have pulled themselves together, our attack on Amiens will be in full swing again!"; and he actually began to plan four minor offensives. Only the Athenians before Syracuse or the French before Moscow showed such a lack of appreciation of the real military situation as the German High Command evinced in the summer of 1918.

But there came a day on August 8 when even Ludendorff was disillusioned. On that "black day of the German Army" the first of the Allied hammer blows was delivered by the British east of Amiens. A considerable defeat was suffered by the German divisions and the order to counter-attack could no longer be carried out. For the first time whole divisions failed and in many cases allowed themselves to be captured without resistance. From then until November the German armies, fighting bravely and stubbornly, were engaged in a retreat for which little or no preparation had been made.

The events of August 8 were not merely a military defeat of grave importance. They were tantamount to a vote of no-confidence passed by the German Army on the Supreme Command. Ludendorff realized this to the full, and there is little doubt that from this realization dates the mental deterioration which showed itself so clearly in the weeks which followed. "There is no more hope for the offensive," he said gloomily to von Haeften on August 12. "The generals have lost their foothold." One of his periodic *crises de nerfs* seized upon the First Quartermaster-General. He proposed his resignation to the Kaiser, who reassured him as to his personal feelings towards him, and gave him "quite special proofs of his confidence." Ludendorff urged the Field-Marshal to replace him if he thought it advisable, but Hindenburg refused.

For the prevalent epidemic of disillusionment had failed to touch the Marshal. Though in 1919 he wrote in his memoirs that he had "no illusion about the political effects of our defeat of August 8," and was wont to reiterate in the days of his presidency that as far back as February 1918 he had known that the war was lost, these reflections in retrospect may be classed with the oft-repeated assertion of George IV that he had led a charge at the battle of Waterloo. No one took them very seriously, but "they had often heard His Excellency say so."

The truth is that at this time the Marshal really knew very little of what was going on about him. Separated by an army of officials from a nation which regarded him with almost superstitious adoration, he lived in an entirely false atmosphere of optimism, and Ludendorff saw to it that only those had access to him who represented the nation's "will to victory," a will which was slowly growing weaker. Even his position at Spa had become anomalous. He had little or no military functions, and when one of his former general staff officers, General von Kuhl, was asked as to what part he played, he was hard put to it to reply. After considerable reflection he asserted that the Marshal "helped to see that General Headquarters did not get slack in their work." He was not kept closely informed on the current military situation. The reports of the divisional commanders were always received by Ludendorff alone; and Colonel Bauer, the chief of the Operations Section, admitted that "towards the

end we did not tell him even where the army corps were sta-
tioned." Consequently he retained his illusion much longer than
Ludendorff, with the result that at the Crown Council which met
at Spa on August 14 to consider the situation he adopted a more
optimistic tone than his colleague.

Ludendorff had previously informed Hintze in confidence that
he had no longer any hope of breaking the resolution of the
enemy by means of an offensive, and that his only hope now lay
in a strategic defence which would eventually succeed in wearing out the Allies. But at the Council, in the presence of the
Emperor, the Crown Prince, and the Chancellor, he confined
himself to criticism of the Home Front and did not mention the
military situation. It was left to Hintze, who had been rudely awakened by his conversation of the day before, to survey the position and to repeat to the Council what Ludendorff had told
him, namely, that the enemy could no longer be beaten by military operations. Hindenburg, however, took a considerably more
optimistic view. "It will be possible," he assured the Emperor,
"to maintain our troops on French territory, and thereby in the
end enforce our will upon the enemy."

The impression conveyed was both disastrous and erroneous.
To those at the Council it appeared that, whereas Ludendorff
no longer believed in a victorious conclusion of the war, the
Marshal still had hopes that, with God's help, it was not beyond
attainment, and they preferred to believe Hindenburg. The last
possible opportunity of a negotiated peace was therefore allowed to slip by, for it was agreed that the situation was not so
acute as to warrant a direct peace offer to the Allies, but only
that negotiations should be opened as soon as possible through
the mediation of the King of Spain and the Queen of the Netherlands.

The policy of self-deception was carried still further. Not
even these specified negotiations were seriously undertaken, and

on August 21 the Chancellor informed the *Reichstag* that "there is no ground for doubting our victory." As late as September 15 he repeated this assertion to the party leaders, assuring them that the war would be carried on to the bitter end, that no peace offer was contemplated, and that the time for one was not yet ripe.

Such were the disastrous repercussions of the first occasion on which Hindenburg adopted a seriously divergent view from that of Ludendorff, for although within the circle of the High Command he was taken at his true worth and occupied the position of "a greatly respected zero," outside of Avesnes, to Germans high and low he was HINDENBURG, the conqueror of the east and west, a Titan, an epic hero, a Siegfried, who would triumph against all adversities. The star of the Hindenburg legend still shone brightly, and its rays dazzled the intelligence of many who should have shown better judgment. Undoubtedly the Marshal spoke as he believed, but his beliefs were as ungrounded as those of others built upon his words.

But disillusionment and nemesis were hot-foot upon the way. Upon every front, in France and Flanders, in Syria and Palestine, in Macedonia, and along the Piave the Allied legions, refreshed with victory, were pressing hard upon the tottering fortress of the Central Powers. By September 26 all the ground gained by such bloody sacrifice in the summer offensives had been lost, and once again Germans and Allies scowled at each other across the Hindenburg Line. In the south-east the outer bastion of German defence was falling, for on the 25th news came from Sofia that a Bulgarian Armistice had become an immediate and unavoidable necessity. Despairing cries came too from Vienna and from Constantinople. The Quadruple Alliance, which had for so long existed upon the sole support of German divisions and supplies, was fast crumbling now that the source of this cohesive force was drying up.

The Home Front too was cracking. The miseries occasioned

by the Allied blockade became daily more harrowing. Workmen fainted in the factories, women collapsed in the streets, few children even had sufficient to eat. What food there was was of the loathsome *Ersatz* variety, repulsive and lacking in nutriment. With hunger came the spectre of revolution. The clamour for constitutional reform and the introduction of democratic government could no longer be silenced. It made itself heard in the *Reichstag* and in the press of the Left; it found support in the hearts of many soldiers returning to the front from leave at home; it was utilized by Socialists and Communists alike, though with different ends in view. Above all, the intense war-weariness of the masses made itself evident in the enthusiastic organization of meetings for the purpose of "supporting a peace of understanding along the lines of the *Reichstag* Peace Resolution of July 19, 1917." These meetings were banned by the military authorities.

To meet this grave situation the aged and inert Hertling was utterly inadequate. The Centre Party refused him their support and passed into opposition. It was only a matter of days before his Cabinet must fall.

These events deprived Ludendorff of all judgment and sense of proportion. As each disquieting report succeeded another at Spa, his mind became more and more confused and his imagination more fantastic. His nerves had given way again and he was consumed with a passion for self-justification. He had convinced himself that, at the Council of August 14, he had definitely urged the beginning of peace negotiations. He had erased from his memory all reference to his actual advice of "strategic defence which should gradually wear down the enemy's fighting spirit." He was now persuaded that everything was lost and became obsessed by the terror of an immediate collapse of the German armies in the field. To prevent the awful circumstances of Germany's thus finding herself stripped, helpless, and at the mercy of her enemies, an armistice must be proposed at once and an offer of peace made to the Allies on the basis of President Wilson's Fourteen Points.

It is doubtful whether Ludendorff had ever read this document, or if he had, whether he had regarded it as anything more than a conglomeration of vague generalities. His conception of such an offer envisaged a gradual withdrawal of German troops from France and Belgium to prepared positions on their own territory where the struggle could be resumed if the Allied peace terms proved intolerable. In no way was the word "armistice" connected in his mind with the word "capitulation."

It was late in the afternoon of September 28 when the First Quartermaster-General reached this decision, and summoning his aides, he went to inform Hindenburg. His face, as he passed through the hall of the Hôtel Britannique, was livid and haggard above his field-gray uniform, with the Cross *Pour le Mérite* glittering at his throat. When he reached the Marshal's room he could scarcely speak, but controlling himself with an effort, he gasped out that an armistice must be concluded at once—*at once*. There was not a moment to lose.

It took more than a moment to convince old Hindenburg that he was hearing aright. He had seen Ludendorff in a state of nerves many times since August 1914, but never to this degree. But when full realization dawned on him, bringing the shattering of his illusions, his phlegmatic character came to his rescue. He was deeply stricken, but he kept his iron control. To the nerve-racked man before him he extended both his hands and took the other's right hand in them. It was a gesture which was to become historic in German politics, and those who experienced it learned to fear it. With tears in his eyes he gave his silent acquiescence to his colleague's verdict. Later in his career his tears and his silence were to become notorious.

A little before noon on the following morning (September

29) in the Château de la Fraineuse, the Chief of the General Staff and the First Quartermaster-General stood before their Supreme War Lord with the melancholy duty of confessing to him that he and they were defeated men, and that this fact must be proclaimed to the world within twenty-four hours. Wilhelm II behaved with great dignity of manner, and displayed a nobility unusual in him. He did not reproach the Marshal, who, but six short weeks before, had talked of maintaining himself on French territory to "enforce our will upon the enemy," nor the General who, at the same time, had urged a "strategic defence which should wear down the enemy's fighting spirit." This was no time for repining. The Emperor was faced with the question not merely of terminating the war, but whether he could keep his throne. One means remained by which the German people might be rallied to their loyalty to the dynasty and to the defence of their country *à l'outrance*. The supreme power, which Wilhelm II held as absolute monarch in time of war, must be transferred to the people themselves, and must be vested in them. Parliamentary government must be conceded at once as the forerunner of a new constitution. It was the only hope. Hintze, who had arrived from Berlin that morning, urged immediate action. Ludendorff feverishly supported him. What was needed was a "Revolution from above."

Quickly and quietly the Emperor made his decisions. He accepted the unavoidable with fortitude and concurred in the proposal for an immediate armistice. After some hesitation and an attempt at procrastination, he took the final political plunge, and signed the most difficult document of his career, the proclamation of a parliamentary régime. The same day he had faced defeat at home and abroad, by the evening he appeared a broken and suddenly aged man.

On September 30 Count von Hertling, with his Cabinet, resigned. So passed from the stage the third of Germany's war

Chancellors. The first had had to go because he was "too slack" for the High Command; the second because he was unable to bring the requirements of the High Command into accord with the growing war-weariness of the people; and the third, an aged and dying man, was now departing when the High Command had lost their grip of the situation. The search for the fourth continued.

Ludendorff's panic had communicated itself to the whole General Headquarters. It was impossible to wait for a new Cabinet to be formed; the armistice request must go forth at once. This demand was communicated to Berlin by Grünau, the Foreign Office representative at Spa, and he added: "he [Ludendorff] said he felt like a gambler, and that a division might fail him anywhere at any time. I get the impression that they have all lost their nerve here."

At length, in the afternoon of October 1, came the news that Prince Max of Baden was considering the formation of a government and, in consideration of this, Hindenburg telegraphed to the Vice-Chancellor that if by that evening it was certain that a new Cabinet would be formed, he agreed to delaying action for twenty-four hours; on the other hand, "if there should be any doubt as to the formation of the Cabinet, I am strongly of opinion that the declaration to the Foreign Powers should be issued tonight."

That same day the Bulgarians signed an armistice and Hindenburg left for Berlin to meet the new Chancellor. With him went Major von dem Bussche of the General Headquarters Staff, who was to break the news to the party leaders.

There is something strangely ironic in the fact that the first democratic Chancellor of Germany should have been a Prussian Major-General, a Prince, and the heir to a Grand Ducal throne. Yet the choice of Prince Max was not altogether an unfortunate one. He had shown distinct democratic tendencies, and his realization of the necessity of peace made him acceptable to the Left. Moreover, his generous work with the Red Cross and for prisoners of war had earned the sympathy and admiration of friend and foe alike. But he was too much of a "border-line man," and during the six weeks of his Chancellorship he alternated between a policy of war-like cunning and a childish belief in humanity. His best-intended actions were never in time, and this he realized in the bitterness of the after years. "I thought I should have arrived five minutes before the hour," he wrote, "but I arrived five minutes after it."

His Cabinet, composed for the first time of responsible Ministers, included Solf as Foreign Secretary, Erzberger as Minister without Portfolio, General von Scheuch at the Ministry of War, and such Socialist leaders as Scheidemann and Bauer. The new Chancellor's mainstay and support throughout these troubled weeks was, however, his private secretary and *alter ego*, Kurt Hahn, to whom must be given the credit for such constructive moves as were made by the Prince.

At a Crown Council in Berlin, on October 2, the Prince and the Marshal met before the Emperor. Hindenburg repeated Ludendorff's demand for an immediate truce: "The Army cannot wait forty-eight hours." Prince Max demurred. The position, he argued, was very grave and undoubtedly an offer of an armistice must be made, but such precipitancy as was demanded by the High Command was suicidal. It would be interpreted by the Entente as a capitulation. The change of régime and an appeal to the Fourteen Points smacked too strongly of a death-bed repentance to be regarded abroad as anything else but a policy of desperation, and the Prince was better informed as to the American mentality than the Marshal. He remembered a conversation he had recently had with Max Warburg. The best Americans, the banker had said, were gentlemen, but there were also the self-opinionated individuals who knew nothing of Europe. If Germany humiliated herself now, not the good type, but the bad, would be masters of the situation. "In that case Wilson will not be able to maintain himself against the party machines. He will demand the German Republic."

These larger issues the Chancellor endeavoured to explain to Hindenburg in support of his policy of delay. Let there be an armistice offer by all means, but there must be at least a fortnight in which to prepare the ground.

But the Prince found a united opposition against him. Hindenburg repeated Ludendorff's arguments like a good child that has learned its lesson, and the Emperor supported him with unusual violence. "The Supreme Command considers it necessary; and you have not been brought here to make difficulties for the Supreme Command," he told the Chancellor tersely.

There is little doubt that, left to himself, Hindenburg might well have been disposed to agree with Prince Max's view. He was still unconvinced that the situation was as desperate as Ludendorff believed it to be, and he was alternating between moments of optimism and depression. His natural tendency, born of a phlegmatic and nerveless character, was to fight on; on the other hand the tremendous influence of his partner "in marriage" was against this. It is even possible that he had come to Berlin in a scarcely realized attempt to escape the defeatist atmosphere of Spa, for it was the first time that he had attended a Crown Council without Ludendorff. "I hoped I could fight down pessimism and revive confidence," he writes, "for I myself was still firmly convinced that in spite of the diminution of our forces, we could prevent our enemy from treading the soil of the Fatherland for many months."

But even at a distance the influence of Ludendorff was strong upon him. To all the Prince's arguments he repeated obstinately the demand for an immediate truce, saying, what in his heart he did not really believe, that he could not give any assurance that a further enemy offensive would not end in disaster. The Prince pressed him further. If the Supreme Command believed that the situation was so desperate, it was for them to raise the white flag in the field.

Hindenburg did not like it being put that way. He was not skilled in debate and had never taken an important decision without Ludendorff, who had usually taken it first. While preserving his stolid exterior, he was inwardly sorely perplexed. He could only repeat the brief which he had learnt, but he agreed to give his final opinion in writing to the Chancellor next day. As soon as the Council was over he rang up Ludendorff at Spa, and the letter which followed bears signs of joint authorship:

The Supreme Command adheres to its demand made on Sunday September 29, for the immediate despatch of the Peace offer to our enemies.

Owing to the breakdown on the Macedonian front, whereby a weakening of our reserves in the west is necessitated, and in consequence of the impossibility of making good our very heavy losses in the battles of the last few days, there no longer exists any prospect, according to human calculation, of forcing peace upon our enemies.

The enemy is regularly bringing new and fresh reserves into action. The German army still holds fast and repulses all attacks with success. But the position gets worse every day, and may force the Supreme Command to make serious decisions.

In these circumstances it is imperative to stop fighting in order to spare the German people and its allies further useless sacrifices. Every day lost costs thousands of brave soldiers' lives.

VON HINDENBURG, G.F.M.

This letter is of great historical importance, in that it states clearly and definitely the causes of Germany's collapse and the need for an immediate armistice. By putting his signature to it the Marshal had, despite his subsequent protests to the contrary, accepted the responsibility, whatever may have been his private opinion. Of equal importance is the fact that no mention is made in the letter of the "stab in the back" theory of which the Marshal subsequently made so great a feature.

Meantime, on the order of the Supreme Command but without the knowledge of the Chancellor, the party leaders had been assembled in the *Reichstag* Building to hear a statement on the military situation by Major von dem Bussche. They came in that firm belief of eventual German victory which had been engendered by four years of ceaseless official propaganda and lies. Not one of them had the slightest idea of the gravity of the position; Ludendorff had fooled them as he had fooled the German people, the Kaiser, and Hindenburg, and, as the staff officer proceeded with his statement (which bore many marks of similarity with that which had just been sent to the Chancellor, though written at least two days earlier), it was as though the ground rocked beneath them. Certain sentences flashed at them like burning arrows. "According to all human calculation, there exists no longer any possibility of compelling the enemy to plead for peace . . . the enemy is able to make good his losses through the assistance of America . . . we can no longer win." And then at last the final stab: "The Supreme Command have seen fit to propose to his Majesty that an attempt be made to put an end to the struggle . . . every twenty-four hours can impair the situation and give the enemy a chance to discover our real weakness."

His listeners were dumbfounded, utterly crushed. Ebert went white as death and could not utter a word; Stresemann looked as though someone had struck him. "We have been lied to and betrayed," cried Heydebrand, and the Prussian Minister, von Waldow, staggered to his feet, muttering "There's only one thing left now; to put a bullet in one's head." Only the extreme Left, the Independent Socialists, were jubilant. Haase rushed up to

Ledebour, beaming. "Now we've got them," he cried. And he was right. In this last effort to convince the party leaders of the correctness of their views, the Supreme Command had destroyed the last remnant of unity on the Home Front. Henceforth the Independent Socialists and many others were for peace at any price, not excluding therefrom the abolition of the monarchy, a subject which was indeed being discussed at that moment.

In a last despairing effort to persuade the Supreme Command to play for time, Prince Max made one final appeal to Hindenburg on the afternoon of October 3, pointing out to him that even under the best possible circumstances a precipitant peace move would mean the loss of Alsace-Lorraine and of the purely Polish districts of Eastern Prussia—so much was implicit in the acceptance of the Fourteen Points as a basis of negotiation. To this the Marshal replied, after the inevitable telephone conversation with Ludendorff, that the Supreme Command were quite prepared for the loss of the small French-speaking portion of the *Reichsland*, but that any surrender of German territory in the east was out of the question.

It became more and more evident that the Chancellor had read the Fourteen Points and the Supreme Command had not and so the situation became more gravely complicated. Berlin and Spa were not speaking the same language at this moment, and the effect would have been laughable had it not been so starkly tragic.

But Hindenburg had a further moment of weakening. At a meeting of the Cabinet he gave expression to his own more optimistic views and declared that if the terms of the Entente were too humiliating he was for "fighting to the last man"; but as Count Roedern, the Finance Minister, acidly pointed out, this act of gallantry, which was possible for a single battalion, was not to be expected of a people of sixty-five millions. Fighting to the last man had become a favourite phrase of the Supreme

Command; already Prince Rupprecht's army had coined the bitter phrase that "The Prussians will fight on to the last Bavarian."

Prince Max grasped at this new vacillation on the part of Hindenburg as one clutching at a straw. Through Haeften he made a final offer to Ludendorff. A peace offer should be issued at once, but not coupled with a request for an armistice. Ludendorff refused utterly and absolutely, and repeated his original demands. He was anxious to get Hindenburg back to Spa and to come himself to Berlin. He knew well—who better?—that if a course of action were put to the Marshal in the name of duty and loyalty he would follow it blindly, and he feared that such an appeal might be made at the last moment. But the resistance of the Chancellor was at an end. With a heavy heart he signed the note which lay drafted upon his table, and, in the small hours of October 4, Germany's appeal for an armistice was flashed across the Atlantic.

Hindenburg returned to Spa, more wearied by his few days in Berlin than he had ever been by many arduous weeks of active service. He was out of place in that atmosphere of politics and intrigue, and he was glad to be back in an environment which he knew and understood. He devoted himself to the organization of defence and the carrying-out of the retreat, which continued steadily. For the front still held, as he had always believed it would, and though the repeated blows of the Allies forced the German army to give ground, it still fought with courage and tenacity, inflicting heavy losses in many deadly rear-guard actions.

Throughout those sultry October days, Ludendorff dashed frenziedly between Spa and Berlin, now endeavouring to bully the Government into some form of action, now almost suppliant in his appeals for half a million more men for the defence of the country. But he was dealing with different types of politicians to those which he had been used to bend to his will. Scheidemann and the other Majority Socialists in the Cabinet had no reverence for the military traditions. They were not impressed either by his threats or by his cajoleries. They were bent upon peace, the peace that had been so passionately demanded by the Supreme Command, and they faced with perfect equanimity the prospect of the First Quartermaster-General's resignation, if that became necessary.

And indeed Ludendorff had ceased to be an asset either to the High Command or to his country. His nerves had broken completely now, and even his reason seemed affected. As early as the end of August the Tsar Ferdinand of Bulgaria, while on a visit to Spa, had drawn the attention of the Kaiser to Ludendorff's highly nervous condition, and had suggested that some measures be taken to lessen the overwhelming burden of his responsibilities. There were whispers that he had suffered a stroke at Spa on that fatal 29th of September, and his conduct certainly justified such a belief. The glory had departed.

As the pre-armistice negotiations proceeded, so did Hindenburg's anxiety and indignation increase. The reply of Woodrow Wilson was couched in courteous terms. The President made a condition and put a question. An armistice could only be granted upon Germany's agreeing to evacuate all occupied Allied territory, and it was asked for whom the German Government spoke; was it "on behalf of those forces of the Empire that have hitherto been fighting?" Hindenburg was quite ready to agree to the provision for evacuation, it had been part of Ludendorff's original plan to withdraw to prepared positions on German territory; and the Chancellor was able to assure the President that the German Government spoke in the name of the German people and the majority of the *Reichstag*.

So far so good. The negotiations seemed to be proceeding "according to plan." The front was still holding out. Hopes revived. But here again nemesis appeared. On October 12, the very day of Prince Max's Reply to President Wilson, there occurred the last horror of that unrestricted U-boat warfare which, Hindenburg consenting, had been so relentlessly forced by the Supreme Command on a reluctant and protesting Bethmann Hollweg. The passenger-boat *Leinster*, on the Dublin-Holyhead route, was torpedoed, with the loss of nearly two hundred British and American lives, and for days bodies were washed up on the English and Irish coasts to be identified by waiting relatives.

A wave of anger swept over the Allied countries, and this indignation was reflected in Wilson's Second Note (October 14). No armistice agreement could be entered into with Germany so long as her armed forces "continued the unlawful and inhuman practices in which they still persist," and which the Allies regarded justly "with horror and with burning hearts." If an armistice should be granted it could only be upon terms which would guarantee the maintenance of the present military superiority of the Allies. Finally, Germany's attention was drawn to the fact that one of the terms which she had accepted was "the destruction of every arbitrary power anywhere that can separately, secretly and of its single choice, disturb the peace of the world; or, if it cannot be destroyed at present, at least its reduction to virtual impotency." The German Government fell within this category. It was within the choice of the German people to change it, and it was implied that peace would only be granted when they had done so.

This condition was not included in the Fourteen Points but was made in the course of the President's address at Mount Vernon on July 16, 1918, which had become annexed in the nature of a supplement to the Fourteen Points. Its sentiments were in marked contradistinction to those expressed some eight months before by the President, in a Message to Congress on December

4, 1917, when he declared: "We do not intend to inflict any wrong on the German Empire, nor to interfere in any way in its internal affairs."

The new Note was in very different language. It was gradually becoming clear that the Allies aimed not only at the capitulation of the German army in the field but at the abdication of the Emperor and the creation of a Government based upon accepted democratic institutions. To Hindenburg the first of these demands appeared to be the more outrageous. Like many others at the time, he refused to read into the latter part of the President's Note a demand for the abdication of the Kaiser. Such a thing was unthinkable to him. It remained for Hoffmann, who had never suffered from delusions, to tell Solf bluntly that the "arbitrary power" which President Wilson wished to see "destroyed" before granting an armistice was the Emperor.

Hindenburg and Ludendorff were again united in that happy state in which their "thoughts were one before they found expression in words," for Ludendorff had swung around and was in agreement with the Marshal that the military situation was not sufficiently bad to warrant the acceptance of such humiliating terms. The Supreme Command now demanded a *guerre à l'outrance* on any terms. They supported the idea of a *levée en masse* which they had rejected with scorn when Rathenau had proposed it a week earlier. Ludendorff assured the War Cabinet, on October 17, "on his conscience that a break-through (by the Allies) was unlikely." Within a few weeks the campaigning season would be over, and with half a million more men he could retire to the Meuse, last out the winter, and begin again in the spring. Above all, the Belgians must be told that peace was still far off, and that "the horrors which are inseparable from war may befall Belgium once again, so that 1914 will be child's play compared to it." Hindenburg supported him whole-heartedly. There could, he thought, be only one finale, unless they succeeded in creating

HINDENBURG WALKING WITH THE KAISER AND LUDENDORFF AT SPA, APRIL 1918

one last reserve from the resources of the people at home. A rising of the nation could not fail to make an impression on their enemies and on the army itself. The Chancellor was disposed to agree, and Ludendorff left Berlin for Spa in the belief that his views had triumphed. It was a happy homecoming; the great twin-brethren were at one again.

Left alone, Prince Max characteristically hesitated. Could he really take the responsibility of breaking off negotiations and prolonging the war, with all its suffering? Must he be branded as the man who delivered Germany naked and defenceless to her enemies? Between these two alternatives the Prince might well falter. Misery and suffering surrounded him. Influenza scourged Berlin. On October 15 over seventeen hundred people died of it. The Chancellor was to become infected himself. Starvation stalked the streets. "Better an end with terror than terror without end," advised Scheidemann. But Karl Liebknecht, the Spartacist, raised a cry still more dangerous, and preached it publicly in the streets and halls of the capital: "If we get rid of the Kaiser we shall get a decent peace."

The Chancellor yielded to humanitarianism. He prepared a Reply to Wilson in almost fawning terms, abandoning submarine warfare, and accepting the new military conditions laid down by the President. It drew attention to the recent drastic changes in the German Constitution and expressed the hope that no demand would be made "which would be irreconcilable with the honour of the German people or with opening a way to a peace of justice."

From Spa, Hindenburg and Ludendorff protested energetically against the tone of the German Reply, and then, failing to prevent its despatch, dissociated themselves from all responsibility connected with it. Their protests were repeated even more vehemently when, within forty-eight hours, Wilson's Third Note reached Berlin. The President consented to recommend to the

Allied Powers the negotiation of an armistice on the terms agreed, but he added that if it was still necessary to treat "with the military authorities and the monarchical autocrats of Germany . . . they must demand not negotiations for peace but surrender."

Here was no mincing of words. The last veil was torn from the Allied demands, and gone was the final hope of those who had cherished the thought that the Kaiser's power might be limited in some form of restricted monarchy such as that obtaining in England, Belgium, or Scandinavia. There could be no ambiguity about the last sentence of the President. It meant, in bald language, that the Emperor must go.

The receipt of Wilson's Reply, with its cold brutality of phrase, moved the High Command to take drastic action. Hindenburg despatched a personal protest to the Chancellor, against the policy of the Government, who "talk only of reconciliation and not of fighting the enemies which threaten the very existence of our country." On the same day (October 24) two telegrams were despatched from Spa. The first was to the Chancellor and contained a denial of the statement that the Marshal had demanded an immediate offer of peace, or that he had said that it had become only a matter of hours. The second was a circular message from Hindenburg to all Army Group Commanders, describing the armistice conditions as unworthy of Germany and unacceptable to the army, and ordering a fight to the finish.

In face of very serious objections from the Gallwitz Army Group, the second telegram was withdrawn, but not before it had reached the battalion staffs of at least one army, and not before one military wireless operator, an Independent Socialist, had had time to transmit the text from Kovno to the *Reichstag* members of his party.

The explanation of this incident is difficult to find. The first telegram contained a deliberate lie, the second involved an equally deliberate act of insubordination. The question is: Did the initiative come from Hindenburg himself or from Ludendorff? Was it the last occasion on which the Marshal acted under the influence of the First Quartermaster-General, or was it the first and only moment in Hindenburg's life when he acted on the impulse of the moment? Certainly Ludendorff was privy to the whole affair, which was entirely in accordance with the views which he had recently re-espoused. Later he attempted to excuse his own part in the business by saying that he did not know it was contrary to the wishes and policy of the Government. He also stated that, contrary to the usual custom whereby documents were brought to him for signature before being taken to the Marshal, this telegram had already been signed by Hindenburg when it reached him.

On the other hand, it is not incompatible with Hindenburg's nature to believe that the whole thing was his own idea. It was in him to wish to escape from responsibility and blame, a feature of his character which became more and more apparent in after years. He must not appear to posterity as the one who had taken the lead in a movement which had ended in the demand for the capitulation of the German army and the abdication of the Emperor. In the light of later events, these may well have been the motives which urged him to impulsive action. For later the passion for exculpation led him further and caused him, on November 1, to write to the Chancellor a letter remarkable for its humility of language, in which he excused himself from the responsibility for the telegram of October 24, on the grounds that it had been "put before me with the statement that it embodied the views of the Government."

Whatever the causes, the effects were of tremendous importance. The Chancellor was prepared to ignore the first telegram on the grounds that in the excitement of the moment the Marshal had forgotten the wording of his telegram of October 1 and the arguments he had used on the following day to Prince Max himself. The second, however, could not be passed over. Not only was it an act of bad faith on the part of the Supreme Command, but it was also a breach of the new Constitution, which placed the military forces under the control of the Chancellor and ruled absolutely against the joint responsibility with the Imperial Government which the Supreme Command had always claimed. Prince Max had but one course open to him. He went immediately to the Emperor and offered the resignation of himself and his whole Cabinet. Either they or the Supreme Command must go; the Emperor must choose.

No other event could illustrate so forcibly the sweeping changes which had taken place in Germany during the month of October. The new German democracy had been challenged and had taken up the gage. The Supreme Command, the maker and breaker of Chancellors and policies for the past two years, now stands itself impeached before the Imperial throne; the threat of resignation, so often used by Ludendorff, is now the weapon of the Chancellor. The boot is on the other foot!

It was fortunate for Hindenburg that the attack both of the Chancellor and the Majority in the *Reichstag*—where a furious debate had taken place on the 25th—was directed against Ludendorff personally and not against the Supreme Command as a whole; fortunate, because, though the laurels on the Hindenburg legend were still green enough within the Fatherland, with the army as a whole they had withered visibly. At that very moment Lerssner, the Foreign Office representative at Spa, was warning the Government, "on the score of his many years' experience at Headquarters," against "having faith in any promise which the High Command might make." He added that a change in the High Command would be well received by the greater part of the army, "as confidence in the present High Command has gone."

But it was Ludendorff's head that the politicians were demanding on a charger, eager to avenge the many insults which they had received at his hands. For this reason the Chancellor overlooked completely Hindenburg's share in the authorship of the telegrams of October 24—indeed he was anxious to retain him, in order not to alarm the country—and concentrated the force of his attack upon the First Quartermaster-General.

The end came quickly. The Emperor summoned Hindenburg and Ludendorff to appear before him on October 26, at the Schloss Bellevue, where little more than fifteen months before they had forced him to dismiss Bethmann Hollweg. There, speaking to Ludendorff alone and ignoring Hindenburg, he addressed the General in terms which could only provoke a request to be allowed to resign; a request which was instantly granted.

Hindenburg remained. He did, it is true, make a half-hearted request for *démission,* which the Kaiser, whom the Chancellor had implored to keep Hindenburg at all costs, somewhat brusquely refused; but the Marshal did not see fit to draw attention to his own part in the affair of October 24 nor to say one word in the defence of a man who had been his almost hourly companion for four tremendous years. Just as he had done nothing to save Hoffmann, to whom he also owed much, from the wrath of Ludendorff, so now he allowed the Kaiser's wrath to fall upon the head of Ludendorff without even attempting to take his own due share. For, whatever military reputation he had achieved, Hindenburg owed it to Ludendorff, with all the latter's faults, and he fully realized the fact. For four years and more he had allowed himself to be idolized, knowing full well that the greater share of the praise was Ludendorff's. Their "happy marriage" had been a very fortunate one for him, for although their partnership had involved blunders and errors of gigantic size, the blame for these had somehow stuck to Ludendorff and the glory to himself. He could either have shared the

blame and credit of his chief adviser or have declined responsibility by divesting himself of much of the praise that had been
so lavishly given him. He did neither. He remained the Wooden
Titan, into which the worms of decay had already entered.

· 10 ·

Hindenburg returned to Spa on October 27 cast down in
mind and spirit. His scale of values had received a severe blow,
and his world, which for seventy-one years had been such a very
secure one, was beginning to crumble around him. Despite his
protests, the Imperial Government had accepted every one of
Wilson's humiliating conditions and were now awaiting a sign
from the Allied Powers as to their fate. For the first time, the
protests of the Supreme Command had been rejected and swept
aside, with a brusqueness that was bewildering. The generals
had received scant courtesy whilst in Berlin. But worst of all had
been the change of mien in the Supreme War Lord. Only three
weeks before, in Hindenburg's presence, the Emperor had told
the Chancellor peremptorily that he was not there to put obstacles in the way of the Supreme Command; yet yesterday he
had greeted his Generals coldly, had dismissed Ludendorff
abruptly, and had refused Hindenburg's own resignation. The
change, though characteristic of Wilhelm II's volatility of spirit,
was disconcerting to the old Marshal.

And now he was alone. For the first time since August 23,
1914, when he had met Ludendorff on the station platform at
Hanover, the dominating personality of his partner was absent.
Their parting in the General Staff building in the Königsplatz
had been painful, for Ludendorff had made no secret of the
fact that he thought the Marshal should have insisted on resigning also. Hindenburg himself felt that he had returned from
the graveside of a particularly dear friend. He was now con-

vinced, however, that he had followed the straight path of duty.
He had chosen between his comrade and his country, or, as he
preferred to put it, his Emperor's command. So long as he could
be ordered by his War Lord to take a course of action, his soldier's soul responded with confidence; in later years he had to
find consolation in the assurance of his advisers that what he
did was his duty. But that day had not yet come, and he was still
in the happy position of having above him one to whose superiority of rank he could bow.

These days of loneliness were full of incident. Everywhere
the cause of the Central Powers was failing. From Vienna and
Constantinople came the news that armistices had been requested, and the breakdown of the Austro-Hungarian army necessitated a withdrawal of troops in the West to form a Bavarian
army of defence on the Tyrolese frontier. Sole responsibility for
these decisions fell upon Hindenburg, and he struggled gallantly
to keep abreast of his ever-increasing load of care until the arrival of Ludendorff's successor as First Quartermaster-General.

There had been no question as to who should succeed Ludendorff. Both the Emperor and Hindenburg had at once agreed
that General Gröner was the one man who could fill the vacancy.
His appointment had been made on the same day that his predecessor had resigned, but as he was at that moment at Kiev, it
was impossible for him to reach Spa before October 30.

Gröner undoubtedly stands out as one of the great tragic figures of German military history, for it was laid upon him to
play a part in his country's service which caused him to be
scorned and vilified by his fellow soldiers. Few soldiers have
given more selfless service to the nation than has Gröner, and
few have been treated with such base injustice.

A Württemberger by birth, Gröner was the son of a paymaster.
He entered the Württemberg army and quickly distinguished
himself by his coolness of judgment and his genius for organi-

zation. He became an instructor at the *Kriegsakadamie,* and his courses were eagerly followed by the young officers who came under his influence; to them he seemed inspired, but throughout his military career he felt himself to be a lonely man, unable to fit in completely with the rigidity of the Prussian military machine.

When, however, the General Staff was reorganized after the younger Moltke's appointment as its chief, it became clear that the two officers who must necessarily receive high appointments were two lieutenant-colonels, Erich Ludendorff and Wilhelm Gröner. A sharp rivalry grew up between them. Neck and neck, they easily outdistanced all others in competing for the "plum" position of the General Staff, the head of the Operations Section. But after a lengthy consideration Gröner was passed over, for the sole reason that his father had been a paymaster, and he was not therefore of the old military caste. Ludendorff was not an officer's son either, but there had been officers in his family for generations, and this turned the scale in his favour. He became Chief of Operations, and to Gröner fell the parallel post of Chief of Transport.

The fundamental changes in mobilization and operations which Moltke made in the Schlieffen Plan with Ludendorff's approval, met with the liveliest opposition from Gröner, who was firmly convinced of the error of weakening the right wing and of making the sudden attack on Liége. He feared that too much faith would be placed in the 42-cm. mortars which Ludendorff had ordered for use against the Belgian fortress, and he warned against the over-estimation of technical inventions which tended to destroy the creative imagination of Staff officers, rendering them too prone to mental rigidity in warfare.

The alternative plan which Gröner urged upon Moltke was one which, had it been adopted, might have altered the course of the early weeks of the war. Gröner was satisfied that it was possible to defend the line of the Vosges with a very small number of troops. Two army corps could therefore be withdrawn from Alsace and concentrated on the lower Rhine, near Emmerich, thereby making the German right even stronger than Schlieffen himself had intended. In view of the fact that Joffre was pledged in advance to an offensive policy, he would, it was reasoned, have been forced to violate Belgian neutrality, and thus enable the Germans to fight the first decisive battles of the war under favourable political and military conditions.

Between the proposals of Ludendorff and Gröner, Moltke characteristically hesitated; finally he attempted a compromise, adapting part of Gröner's scheme into the larger framework of Ludendorff's plan. This resulted, in 1914, in two divisions being immobilized in trains on the lower Rhine without anyone seeming to know why they were there. Certainly Moltke seemed to be cursed with the *main malheureuse*.

But it was to Gröner that the undying credit belonged for the amazing perfection with which the transport of troops and guns and *matériel* functioned during the first two years of the war. Germany had the strategic advantage of interior lines, and of this Gröner made full use. In the summer of 1916 he was promoted general and placed in charge of the Army Food Supply Department, and in the autumn of that year he became head of the War Office, with special executive control of the Supreme Command's economic programme for the intensification of production. In this capacity his flair for organization added greatly to his reputation. The trade-unions officials had declared their refusal to work with a representative of General Headquarters, but in an astonishingly short space of time Gröner had won their co-operation, at first unwillingly and in spite of themselves, but soon in genuine admiration of his qualities and fair-mindedness. His success was to his own detriment. Ludendorff became jealous of the one man in the army who, with the possible exception of Hoffmann, was his equal, and the great industrialists resented and suspected his good relations with the workers. Gröner was removed from his work of organization—Scheidemann declares bluntly that he was "sacked" and speaks savagely of those who "treated so shabbily this distinguished man"—and placed in command first of a division and later of a corps on the Western Front. When, however, the thankless task of executing the economic provisions of the Treaty of Brest-Litovsk had to be discharged, it was felt by all that Gröner was the one man who could fill the post, and he was consequently appointed head of the trading corporation in the Ukraine. It was here that the summons to take up the mantle of Ludendorff reached him.

On his arrival at Spa, Gröner found himself faced with a series of problems which demanded of him a ruthless energy, utter self-denial, and the renunciation of all glory and all gratitude. With quiet courage he assumed his new responsibilities and showed nobly that he possessed in full measure the qualities required.

From the outset, however, his task was vastly complicated by the presence at Spa of the Supreme War Lord. Wilhelm II had found the atmosphere of Berlin, with its ever heightening clamour for his abdication, increasingly uncongenial. To the Chancellor's almost frenzied protests at his desertion of the capital at such a moment, he replied that, now that Ludendorff had gone, he must personally assist Hindenburg, but to Admiral von Hintze, who had recently been appointed Foreign Office representative at Spa, the Emperor said, "Prince Max's Government is trying to throw me out. At Berlin I should be less able to oppose them than in the midst of my troops."

So Wilhelm II made his "flight to Varennes," and arrived unexpectedly at General Headquarters on October 30, to the intense surprise of the Marshal and of Gröner, who had himself only just reported a few hours before. As a result there grew up at Spa two distinct groups with very often divergent policies. At the Hôtel Britannique were Hindenburg and Gröner with the Headquarters Staff; and a little outside the town, at the Château de la Fraineuse, was the Emperor attended by his Adjutant-General, von Plessen, a former aide-de-camp of Wilhelm I, who was seventy-seven years of age and whose mind alternated between the two themes of "shoot them down," and "the Emperor must have only good news"; by the head of his Military Cabinet, the jovial and convivial General von Marschall, and by others of his military suite. Thus Spa became both the military and the dynastic storm-centre.

For the question of the Kaiser's abdication was now the foremost problem on the board. Prince Max was desperately anxious that he should resign the throne, at least apparently of his own free will without pressure being brought to bear on him by the Government. The Crown Prince would also have to renounce his right of succession, and it was hoped by means of a constitutional monarchy and a Council of Regency to save the throne for his eldest son, Prince Wilhelm, then a child. This view was supported by nearly all parties except the Independent Socialists on the Left and the National Conservatives on the Right. Had the Kaiser been in Berlin even he could not have failed to realize the essential soundness of the proposal, but in the feudal atmosphere of Spa he was still entirely opposed to abdicating and firmly convinced that there was absolutely no reason for his doing so.

To Hindenburg the Emperor's attitude seemed entirely correct and reasonable. The presence of his Supreme War Lord at Spa was a great pleasure to the Marshal. He was always glad to be in the company of the Emperor, and in this he was inspired in no degree by a sense of snobbery, but rather by that me-

diaeval fealty of the paladins of Charlemagne. No one was less
of a mystic than Hindenburg, but there was innate in every
officer of the old Prussian military caste a strange sense of awe,
almost of superstition, in respect of the sovereign to whom they
had sworn their oath of loyalty. It was the last remnant of rule
by Divine Right and was fostered by the German court to an
even greater extent than, for example, at the far more ancient
court of Vienna.[1] This respect was more deeply held by Hindenburg's generation than by that which followed. It was, for instance, almost entirely absent in Ludendorff. But Hindenburg
would gladly have gone out to battle at the command of his
"Most Gracious Kaiser, King, and Lord"; indeed he would have
rejoiced to have had the issue thus simplified.

He was soon, soon to have an opportunity of expressing
his views on the dynastic question. Prince Max of Baden, still
suffering under the combined shock of a severe attack of influenza and the flight of the Kaiser from Berlin, had passed the
intervening days in a fruitless effort to find an emissary who
should go to Spa and there so far penetrate "the majesty that
doth hedge a king" as to bring the monarch to a sense of realities. Unable to go himself, he sought vainly for someone who
was prepared to fulfil a task which must almost certainly in-
volve the displeasure of the sovereign. He begged Prince
August-Wilhelm, the Kaiser's son, to go, and, when he would
not, Prince Frederick Charles of Hesse and others. All refused.
At last a sufficiently courageous man was found in the Prussian
Minister of Interior, Dr. Drews.

Drews arrived at Spa on November 1, and was received by
the Emperor in the presence of Hindenburg and Gröner. The

---

[1] Count Czernin, for example, sharply criticizes the custom of kissing of hands
on leaving the Emperor's presence which at Berlin was "something quite ordinary." "At Vienna one would never have seen high officials kissing the Emperor's
hand. Even the most servile would never have stooped to it" (*In the World War*,
p. 62).

Minister reported the now daily demands in the press for the Emperor's abdication, and the growing support for such an act throughout the country; the Federal States, the political parties, high industrial and financial circles, all alike awaited anxiously the decision of the Kaiser to sacrifice himself for the sake of the dynasty. Further delay could only end in abdication under pressure and the destruction of the monarchy.

The Emperor refused point-blank, and reproached Drews for even broaching the subject to him. "How comes it," he demanded, "that you, a Prussian official, could reconcile such a mission with the oath you have taken to your king?" Hindenburg and Gröner fiercely supported him. If the Emperor abdicated, the army would become nothing more than a band of brigands and marauders straggling back to Germany, the Marshal declared; the officers would resign and the troops would be without leaders. Gröner used even harsher language and denounced both Drews and those who had sent him in no uncertain terms, and his characterization of the Chancellor was made with such blunt ferocity that the Emperor had to come to the Minister's rescue and soothe his ruffled feelings.

But he was delighted with his generals. "Drews is supposed to be hard of hearing," he said to his aide-de-camp later, "but they both shouted so loud, that he couldn't have missed a word, and how splendid to see the solemn Gröner so carried away. I was delighted to see a South German so ready to defend the King of Prussia. The brave Suabian!"

"The brave Suabian" was facing greater realities than his War Lord. Gröner had left for the front after the interview and there strained every nerve to disengage the army in a rapid retreat to the Antwerp-Meuse line. It was a difficult device to execute. Precious war material was within reach of the enemy in this line, and 80,000 wounded lay in advance or field hospitals which must be evacuated. The retreat was slower than

had been hoped. The final blow came on November 4, when
the British broke through the line between the Scheldt and the
Sambre, east of Valenciennes. The German rear-guards were
thrown into complete confusion and could not recover themselves. From then on the German army, in the opinion of its
opponents, was incapable either of accepting or refusing battle.

Gröner realized the situation in all its hopelessness. He returned to Spa and conferred with the Marshal. He hastened to
Berlin and bluntly informed the Chancellor: "We shall have to
cross the lines with a white flag. Even a week is too long to
wait. It must be Saturday (November 9) at latest." The Fourth
Wilson Note had just arrived, saying that Marshal Foch would
receive "properly accredited representatives of the German
Government," and would communicate to them the terms of an
armistice. Prince Max pointed out to Gröner that the chief
obstacle to favourable terms was the refusal of the Emperor
to abdicate. Would not Gröner himself dissipate the illusions
at Spa and make the Emperor realize the truth?

But Gröner was still bitterly opposed to this course. "I am
utterly devoted to the cause of the Emperor," he informed the
Cabinet.

"Perhaps the Field-Marshal . . ." someone suggested; and
Gröner turned upon him, shouting:

"The Marshal would consider himself the lowest kind of
scoundrel if he abandoned the Emperor, and so, gentlemen,
would I and every honourable soldier. If the attacks against
the Emperor continue, the fate of the army is sealed; it will
break in pieces, and if that happens the wild beast will break
out in the bands of irregular soldiery pouring back into Germany."

That same day he met Ebert and Scheidemann, and other
Social Democrat and trade-union leaders, men with whom
he had collaborated on friendly terms in 1916 and 1917. All

trusted him, and Ebert begged him to urge abdication upon the Emperor. He himself, said Ebert, was in favour of a monarchical régime, based upon the trade unions and controlled by a parliamentary system, but this was impossible under the present Emperor or the Crown Prince. The last chance of saving the monarchy was to entrust one of the imperial princes with the regency.

Again Gröner refused to consider taking any steps with regard to an abdication, or even to broach the subject to the Emperor. But he was shaken. The honest reasoning of Ebert had affected him more deeply than had the distracted pleadings of Prince Max. In his own mind he formed the impression that the abdication of the Emperor could not be long postponed, though he could not as yet bring himself to have any direct share in it. He hoped that the report which he would make to the Kaiser would influence him in the required direction.

In his heart of hearts Gröner would have liked to have seen the Emperor seek death in the front line. He had said as much to Hindenburg, and to Plessen and Marschall, immediately after the Drews interview. "He should go to the front," he advised, "not to review troops or to confer decorations but to look for death. He should go to some trench which was under the full blast of war. If he were killed it would be the finest death possible. If he were wounded the feelings of the German people would completely change towards him." The two Court Generals were horrified at the idea, and Hindenburg disapproved of allowing the Emperor to run such risks, but there can be no doubt that Gröner's reasoning was both patriotic and practical.

Arrived back at Spa on November 6, Gröner gave the Emperor and Hindenburg the gloomiest possible view of the situation. The country was face to face with revolution; the fleet was in open mutiny, and the army could no longer be relied on. Bolshevik propaganda and the desire of the people for peace at any price had done their work. The Government's authority was no longer existent and the troops in the interior would refuse to fire on the insurgents. Under these circumstances the Emperor's abdication was well-nigh inevitable, and an armistice must be immediately and unconditionally accepted.

These were very different sentiments to those to which Gröner had given vent before the unfortunate Drews only a week before, and in which Hindenburg had concurred. At that moment the First Quartermaster-General had only just arrived from Kieff. He had been neither to the front nor to Berlin. He had visited both now and, though his loyalty to the Crown remained unswerving, his clear-sighted realization of facts and his common sense could no longer allow him to delude himself as to the ultimate issue, and with his conclusions Hindenburg was again forced to agree.

On the following day the Armistice Commission arrived at Spa. Its composition had caused much discussion. It had become known at General Headquarters even before the receipt of Wilson's last Note, that the Allies would not treat with a representative of the Supreme Command but only with a commission appointed by the German Government. There was little competition to lead this body, but by dint of persuasion, cajoling, and flattery, Erzberger had, most reluctantly, been jockeyed into this position. He had accepted provisionally and had accompanied the rest of the Commission to Spa, but so uncertain was it that he would really cross the lines that General von Gündell had been warned for duty to take his place if he should "run out" at the last moment. It was Hindenburg who finally persuaded him. With tears in his eyes and clasping Erzberger's hand between both his own, he besought him to undertake this terrible task for the sacred cause of his country. Touched and not a little flattered by this personal appeal from the old Marshal, Erzberger consented to serve, greatly to the relief of General von Gündell, and at noon set out with the Commission to put his signature to a document which was to be his own death warrant.[1]

This event virtually closed the hostilities on the Western Front and the entire attention of Spa was centred on the dynastic problem. The tempo was rapidly increasing. The mutinous sailors of the fleet, whose revolt on November 4 had been the first signal of serious civil disturbances, now controlled Kiel, Hamburg, and Bremen. Hindenburg's own city of Hanover, as well as Brunswick and Cologne, had mounted the Red Flag, and in Munich the House of Wittelsbach had been deposed and the Bavarian Soviet Republic installed. The revolution was in being.

In the afternoon of November 7 the Chancellor telephoned that he had received an ultimatum from the leaders of the Social Democratic Party. If the abdication of the Kaiser and the Crown Prince had not been announced by noon next day an immediate revolution was threatened, as it would be impossible to prevent the rank and file of the party from joining the Independent Socialists and Spartacists. "A revolutionary gesture is necessary to forestall the revolution," Ebert had declared. Prince Max added a request to be allowed to resign, and made a further plea to the Emperor to avert catastrophe by announcing his intention of abdicating as soon as an armistice had been signed and it was possible to issue writs for a National Constituent Assembly.

The Chancellor also telegraphed Admiral von Hintze to press this proposal with all the zeal at his command, and the Admiral repaired to General Headquarters. He begged the Marshal and Gröner to come with him to the Château de la Fraineuse and put forward this new solution, which was a compromise between the immediate demands of the Majority Socialists and the intransi-

---

[1] Erzberger was assassinated by Nationalist gunmen in 1921, for the part which he played in the Armistice negotiations.

gent obduracy of the Emperor. But the generals refused. Hindenburg protested that he had given his final opinion to the Kaiser and would have nothing to do with the matter. Gröner was equally adamant, though he was more reserved in his opinion than the Marshal. He had been reading reports from the interior. Hintze went alone to the Château and was met with yet another blank refusal. Wilhelm II appeared absolutely resolved to keep the Crown.

Thus at the close of November 7 there was an open breach between Spa and Berlin. The Emperor had spoken personally to the Chancellor by telephone in a "fury of indignation" and had twice more that evening refused to abdicate. So far he was supported both by his military suite and by the High Command. Hindenburg had again assured the Emperor of the army's unswerving devotion to his person, but Gröner had already warned him that in the event of a civil war the troops would not fight.

By the following morning everyone at General Headquarters, except Hindenburg, had been convinced that the necessity for the Emperor's abdication was not only imperative but immediate. The army chiefs had reached the same decision at which the Imperial Government had arrived a week earlier. It was clear, however, that so long as Wilhelm II believed he had the support of his army he would not consider renouncing the throne. The obvious person to acquaint him with the real state of affairs was the Chief of the General Staff; but Hindenburg was not yet convinced of the need, and had he been so, was constitutionally incapable of enlightening the Emperor.

So the day continued in a welter of illusions. The Emperor declared his intention of restoring order in Germany at the head of his army, and ordered Gröner to prepare plans accordingly. Hindenburg was rather relieved at the prospect of action at last. This sitting and waiting, this negotiating back and forth with Berlin, irked him. If it was his Emperor's command that he should lead troops against the rebels, he would do so; any action, even the detestable action of civil war, was better than restless inactivity.

But the moment of his disillusionment was at hand. It was September 21 over again. Now, as then, it was the First Quartermaster-General who forced him to realize the truth. In a heart-to-heart talk, in the same room in which he had had that momentous interview with Ludendorff, Hindenburg heard from Gröner the cold and unassailable facts of the case. The troops in the interior had gone over to the revolution; the field army was no longer *Kaisertreu*. Soldiers' and Workers' Councils were being formed all over Germany and had in their hands the great railway centres and supply depôts. The supplies for the army itself could not last longer than three or four days. A repressive operation, such as the Kaiser desired, was not only impossible but lunatic.

Gröner had made similar statements before, both to the Emperor and to the Marshal, but now he spoke with the conviction of despair, and there was no refuting him. The time for deception, whether of self or others, was at an end.

While Hindenburg was still bowed with the weight of these new realizations, the Emperor's Adjutant-General, Plessen, arrived to receive the plan of operations which Gröner had been instructed to prepare. To him the First Quartermaster-General repeated what he had so recently told the Marshal. Plessen was utterly taken aback. He protested violently. Completely cut off from the field army and breathing only the Byzantine atmosphere of the court, he still believed in a spirit amongst the troops which no longer existed. In any case the Emperor and the High Command, he cried, must not capitulate to "a handful of revolutionaries, a band of infamous sailors."

Patiently Gröner repeated the facts of the case. Such an

operation as the Emperor envisaged would mean that a civil war would have to be carried on in addition to the rear-guard action against the enemy. The army was in no condition to bear such a double burden. Nothing but complete collapse could result from the enterprise.

Dumb with misery, Plessen turned to Hindenburg. The two septuagenarians, grown grey in the service of three Emperors, confronted each other in an agony of despair. The Marshal could give no comfort. With a heavy heart, he said, he associated himself with Gröner's opinion. Sobbing, Plessen left the room.

For Gröner there remained one ray of hope, the proposal which Ebert had made to him in Berlin two days before. The Social Democrats would shortly have the game in their hands. Ebert himself was a monarchist. By this means only could the throne be saved. Later that evening he conferred again with Hindenburg. After a long discussion they agreed on all points. The Emperor must abdicate in favour of one of his younger sons, or of the eldest son of the Crown Prince. But there must be no question of his leaving the country. Such an action would discredit the monarchy forever. He must retire to one of his estates. They shook hands on it and Gröner retired to his own quarters. Twice during the night he was to be called up by telephone from Berlin, first by Colonel von Haeften and then by Vice-Chancellor von Payer, both begging him to urge upon the Emperor the necessity of immediate abdication and flight. To both he returned a refusal. He had done his duty. He had warned the Emperor as early as November 6 that the army could no longer be depended upon. That very evening (November 8) he had repeated the fact to Plessen and to Hindenburg. He had the Marshal's promise of co-operation in the policy which both believed to be correct and proper to pursue in the interests of the monarchy.

But Hindenburg had another visitor that night. Admiral von

Hintze came to him very late and eloquently placed before him the arguments for the immediate abdication and flight of the Emperor. He must renounce the throne the next day and go to Holland. It is probable that Plessen had gone straight to Hintze after he left the Marshal and Gröner, and told him, in an hysterical state, the doleful news which he himself had just learned. At any rate this would confirm Hintze's own view that the cause of the House of Hohenzollern was lost, and he put it to the Marshal that in this case the one paramount consideration was the safety of the Emperor's person. This could only be secured by flight.

Torn between two conflicting interpretations of his duty to his Emperor, Hindenburg was deeply vexed in spirit. He had agreed with Gröner and had given him his word, but Hintze's arguments were so cogent and so plausible. The tragedy of Ekaterinburg recalled itself to him. He could not run the risk of allowing his Kaiser and King to be captured by a mutinous soldiery and dragged a prisoner to who knew what end. That must be avoided at all costs. Wearily he concurred with the Admiral and retired to pass what was for him almost a thing unknown, a restless night, during which, it was remarked, the light in his room was put on and out many times.

However agonized these hours of darkness may have been for the Marshal, he should not have spent them in inactivity. To do so was a dereliction of duty both to his Emperor and to his colleague Gröner. It was well known to him, and to all at Spa, that the Emperor's refusal to abdicate was based on the belief that his armies were still loyal to him. This basis Hindenburg now knew to be false, and so false as to have recently convinced him that further delay might endanger the very safety of the monarch. In view of this conviction it was his obvious duty, as Executive Chief of the Armies, to acquaint the Emperor with this situation without a moment's delay, regardless of his sleep, and to insist that he take action at once. In addition there was his clear obligation to tell Gröner immediately of his change of mind, and if possible to win his approval.

But from this double duty Hindenburg flinched and held back. He was incapable of going to the Emperor, as a Prussian officer to his War Lord, and telling him that the army was no longer true to him. It was a disloyal action of a vassal to his lord, and all the innate forces of the military caste within him rebelled in horror against the very thought. He had not the courage for such a task; another must undertake it, and that other must be Gröner.

November 9, the last day of Imperial Germany, dawned cold and gloomy. A thick blanket of fog enshrouded Spa, deadening all sound and seeming to form a barrier against the outside world. But through the fog the telephone wires brought worse and worse news. At a very early hour it was known that a general strike had broken out in Berlin, that the masses were in the streets, and that the trusted Jäger battalions of veteran infantry had mutinied and deposed their officers. With such inauspicious tidings the day began.

A conference of divisional, brigade, and regimental commanders had been called to meet at G.H.Q. at 9 o'clock, where they were to be consulted on the loyalty of their troops. The Marshal had promised to address them, and shortly before the time he went to Gröner's room. His face, bearing traces of his night's agony, was of a sickly greyish colour, profoundly sad and dejected. His fists were tightly, almost convulsively, clenched; his eyes red, as though from much weeping. Hoarsely and abruptly he told Gröner of his change of front, that he had been persuaded by Hintze into consenting to the immediate abdication and flight of the Hohenzollerns, and that in an hour they were to make this recommendation to the Kaiser. Gröner was shocked out of his usual calm. He protested against this sudden *volte face*. He objected that he could not accept such a complete change of policy at a moment's notice. Hindenburg apologized. "He had not been able to find time" to tell Gröner earlier. There was no more time for discussion; the conference of officers awaited them.

The Marshal addressed the officers briefly, but the picture of the situation that he drew for them was in such sombre colours that, when he ceased speaking, there was "a silence as of a tomb; not a word, not a whisper." Poor old Plessen, who had joined the meeting unexpectedly, made no attempt to restrain his tears and held his handkerchief to his eyes. Gröner, who had recovered his poise, remained impassive and unfathomable. At the close of the address Colonel Heye was left in charge of the meeting and the Supreme Command went on their way to the Château de la Fraineuse.

During the drive from the Hôtel Britannique no word was exchanged between Hindenburg and Gröner. The Marshal was in the grip of a fierce emotional struggle. His lips quivered and he bit them to regain his self-control. At the château, in a garden room, they found the Emperor, and with him Plessen, who had preceded them. Marschall, Hintze, and the Crown Prince's Chief of Staff, General Count von Schulenburg. The morning was cold, the room was closely curtained, and a wood fire burned in the grate. Leaning against the fireplace, the Emperor stood and shivered.

The Emperor asked the Marshal for his report on the situation. Hindenburg made an effort to speak, but his voiced choked and he could not. The last vestige of reserve was gone. With tears running down his face he begged his Emperor's leave to resign. He could not as a Prussian officer say to his War Lord what must be said to him. He had therefore ordered General Gröner to give to His Majesty the considered opinion of the High Command.

So it was Gröner, "the brave Suabian," who was to be the scapegoat. As an officer of the army of Württemberg he could use language which could not sully the lips of a member of the Prussian military caste. Upon the shoulders of this lonely South German was laid the task of disillusioning the King of Prussia.

In a quiet and controlled voice Gröner repeated what he had said to Hindenburg and to Plessen the previous day. An operation against the interior of Germany was impossible; it was no longer a question of suppressing an insurrection, but of civil war. The railway centres and supply depôts on the Rhine were in the hands of the rebels and many troops in the interior had joined the revolution. They could and would cut off supplies from the field army, which itself could no longer be depended upon. Mutinies had already taken place, and Aix-la-Chapelle and Verviers were in the hands of the insurgents. The army was no longer in a condition to fight. There were no more reserves.

While carefully avoiding any direct reference to the dynastic question, Gröner had so phrased his statement as to leave the Emperor under no other impression than that his abdication was imperative. Wilhelm II stood speechless with perplexity, sunk deep in consternation. Not so Schulenburg. This dashing and courageous officer took up the challenge and championed the cause of monarchy, that same cause which Gröner had sought so zealously to save. He challenged every statement made by the First Quartermaster-General. In eight to ten days, he declared, it would be possible to gather on the Rhine a force of picked men upon which the Emperor could implicitly rely. When the army was told that the navy had betrayed it, it would not hesitate to fight on the Home Front. A beginning must be made by sending loyal troops to reduce the mutinous garrisons at Aix-la-Chapelle and Verviers by smoke-bombs, gas, and *Flammenwerfer*. Order must be restored city by city.

At this fighting speech old Plessen regained his nerve. "His Majesty cannot simply and quietly capitulate to revolution. The expedition against Aix-la-Chapelle and Verviers must be put in hand at once."

Gröner listened with an almost grim humour. How little they knew the situation! Plessen's fantastic views were excusable, he had always been "all for gunfire," but how could Schulenburg talk such nonsense when only yesterday twelve out of sixteen representatives of his Army Group had confessed that their troops were unreliable for service in the interior. The report was lying now on Gröner's office table at G.H.Q. Courteously but firmly he repeated his views. The suggestion of Schulenburg and Plessen would render chaos unavoidable.

Meanwhile the Emperor had come to a decision. He would renounce the idea of reconquering the country. He wished to spare the Fatherland the horrors of civil war. He would remain at Spa until an armistice had been signed, and then return home quietly at the head of his army.

Gröner heaved a sigh. So the Emperor had not understood the situation after all. He had still not realized that the whole revolutionary movement was directed against himself. The time for diplomatic phrases was passed, he must speak clearly now.

"Sire, you no longer have an army. The army will march home in peace and order under its leaders and commanding generals, but not under the command of Your Majesty, for it no longer stands behind Your Majesty."

The Emperor turned upon Gröner, his eyes blazing with anger.

"Excellency, I shall require that statement from you in black and white, signed by all my generals, that the army no longer stands behind its Commander-in-Chief. Have they not taken the military oath to me?"

"In circumstances like these, Sire, oaths are but words," replied Gröner sadly.

This was too much for Schulenburg. Forgetting the August Presence, he bellowed at Gröner at the top of his voice that neither the officers nor the soldiers would so disgrace themselves as to desert their Kaiser and King in the face of the enemy.

"I have other information," was the cold reply.

Stung by Schulenburg's venom, Hindenburg at last broke the absolute silence he had preserved throughout the meeting and came to the support of Gröner, but he spoke half-heartedly, as if to placate the Emperor and his fellow-Prussians. The sentiments and principles of Count Schulenburg must be shared by every Prussian officer, but most unfortunately he, no more than General Gröner, could take responsibility for the loyalty of the army either at home or in the field.

As if to give further point to this statement, there came a laconic telephone report from the Commandant of Berlin. "All troops deserted—completely out of hand."

In considerable agitation the Emperor adjourned the Council. It was just eleven o'clock.

By twos and threes they drifted through the French windows and into the garden. The Crown Prince arrived. On his way he had been met with "curses and cries and fists raised in the grey mist," yet he urged his father to return with him to his headquarters.

More than an hour passed in talk and argument; continued gasconades by Schulenburg, repeated negatives from Gröner, a stolid silence from the Marshal. Every now and then Hintze would join them from the château with some further report from Berlin or with a more imperative demand for the Emperor's abdication.

The Emperor began to talk excitedly. If the worst came to the worst he would abdicate the Imperial crown of Germany, but not the throne of Prussia. He would stay with his Prussian troops, who would remain loyal to him. He glanced at Hindenburg, as if for approval, and the Marshal, his gaze fixed on the distance, nodded silently. Schulenburg took up the idea joyously. In any and every case the Emperor must remain King of Prussia. He should gather his Prussians around him and then see what the *Reich* would do. Prussian officers and soldiers would not tolerate the *débâcle* which would follow the disappearance of their King.

"Will they fight for their King against the people?" asked Hintze pertinently, and Schulenburg, his dream-bubble suddenly pricked, had to admit that they would not. "But in any case," he repeated furiously, "the Emperor must remain King of Prussia."

"A fortnight ago such a solution might have been salutary, but it is too late now," said Gröner to Hindenburg; and again the Marshal nodded abstractedly.

In the midst of their discussions, Colonel Heye appeared bringing with him the report of the conference of officers. The thirty-nine representatives had been asked two questions; first: "Would it be possible for the Emperor to regain control of Germany by force of arms, at the head of his troops?" and to this only one affirmative answer had been returned, while twenty-three were in the negative, and fifteen ambiguous. To the second question, "Would the troops march against the Bolshevists in Germany?" the replies had been, eight "yes," nineteen "no," and twelve "uncertain." In summing up the results of his enquiries, Heye told the Emperor: "At the present moment the troops will not march against Germany, even with Your Majesty at their head. They will not march against Bolshevism. They want one thing only, an armistice at the earliest possible moment. Every hour gained is of importance."

A long pause followed Heye's report. The feeling of despondency increased. Blow seemed to be following upon blow in calculated justification of Gröner's statement. The Kaiser broke the silence. Would the army return to Germany in good order without him? he asked. Yes, said Gröner; no, said Schulenburg. But Heye had the last word. "It is only under the command of its generals that the army will return in good order to the Fatherland," he said in his usual sonorous tones. "From this point of view the army leaders have their troops well in hand. If Your Majesty wishes to march with them the troops will ask nothing better and will be delighted, but the army will fight no more, either at home or abroad."

"His Majesty has no need of an army in order to take a walk," said Admiral von Hintze bitterly; "what he needs is an army that will fight for him."

At this moment the Admiral was called into the château.

The Chancellor was once more on the telephone. Very soon Hintze returned with an even graver face. Prince Max reported that the situation in Berlin had become so extremely menacing that the monarchy could no longer be saved unless the Kaiser decided upon immediate abdication.

The Emperor received the message in silence. His face was livid and he seemed suddenly to have aged by years. Once again his eyes sought those of Hindenburg, as if appealing for help and strength. He found nothing. The Marshal stood motionless, silent, and met the gaze of his War Lord with a look of despair.

With a visible effort the Emperor gave his decision. He would abdicate as German Emperor but not as King of Prussia; he would hand over the command of the German armies to Hindenburg but would remain himself with the Prussian troops. It was Wilhelm II's last attempt at compromise, and having made it, he dismissed his generals and went in to lunch.

The meal in Hindenburg's quarters was a sad and silent one. Little was eaten, for, like sleep, Hindenburg's usual hearty appetite had deserted him. He found consolation, however, in a cigar. Suddenly, a little after two o'clock, the most astounding messages began to flood in upon him from Berlin. Disregarding the Emperor's statement, the Chancellor, in a last despairing effort to save the monarchy, had, on his own responsibility, announced the abdication by the Emperor both as the German Emperor and as King of Prussia, and the renunciation by the Crown Prince of his claims to both thrones. Prince Max himself had resigned, handing over the Chancellorship to Ebert, who would appoint a Regent.

Scarcely had the Marshal had time to realize the full meaning of the message when its tremendous sequel followed. The Prince's gesture had come too late to be effective. The Spartacists had seized the Imperial Palace, and Liebknecht, from its steps, had proclaimed the Soviet Republic. This act had thrown Ebert's supporters into a panic, and he had been unable to restrain the impetuous Scheidemann from proclaiming the Socialist Republic from the portico of the *Reichstag.*

So in the course of a brief hour the Kaiser had been relegated from the position of chief actor in the drama to that of spectator, for the struggle was now no longer one of dynastic aspirations, but of Bolshevism against Social Democracy. The only question now concerning Wilhelm II was what to do with him, and to this problem Hindenburg applied himself.

With Gröner, Hintze, and Schulenburg he considered the situation in the light of the most recent information. It did not take long to agree that no other alternative to flight presented itself. The roads back to Germany were blocked by the revolutionaries. The Second Guard Division, which was charged with protecting G.H.Q. from a possible attack by mutinous troops from Aix-la-Chapelle, was at that time not believed to be entirely trustworthy. The troops at Spa were already organizing a Workmen's and Soldiers' Council. Manifestly the Emperor must go, and go at once. The advantages of Holland and Switzerland as a place of refuge were canvassed, and, for a number of reasons, the former was preferred. Hintze was instructed to make the necessary arrangements with the Foreign Office.

One further ordeal was in store for Hindenburg on this terrible day, and one of which this time he could not avoid the responsibility. To him was delegated the duty of informing the Kaiser of the decision taken. With Gröner and Hintze he drove back to the château. The Kaiser had not yet recovered from his surprise and anger at Prince Max's "act of violence." He was beside himself with rage, and was still furiously refusing either to abdicate as King of Prussia or to leave Spa. "My God, are you back here again already?" was his greeting to the deputation. Then turning on Gröner, he said passionately, "You no longer have a War Lord," and from that moment refused to look at or address him again.

Standing before his Emperor, Hindenburg made his report. He was calm now and had overcome his emotion of the morning. Lucidly he set forth the reasons why he was no longer able to guarantee the Kaiser's safety at Spa. In conclusion he said: "I cannot accept the responsibility of seeing the Emperor haled to Berlin by insurgent troops and delivered over as a prisoner to the Revolutionary Government. I must advise Your Majesty to abdicate and to proceed to Holland."

The Emperor was convulsed with rage. Did they think he dared not remain with his troops? No one answered. In a deathly silence Wilhelm II paced the room. Finally he came back to the group, and in quieter tones confirmed the order to Hintze for the preparations for his departure.

Admiral von Scheer was announced, and before him and his Staff officers the Emperor requested Hindenburg to repeat what he had just reported. The Marshal did so, concluding with the words: "Would to God, Sire, it were otherwise."

In a calmer mood, the Emperor agreed that if things were really as bad as the Marshal said he could not allow himself to be surprised at Spa. He would abdicate as German Emperor, but never as King of Prussia. Scheer supported Hindenburg, saying that it was no longer possible to rely upon the navy.

"I no longer have a navy," said Wilhelm II bitterly, and left the room. It was then five o'clock.

Sadly Hindenburg returned to the Hôtel Britannique. He did not know that he had seen his Emperor for the last time. He only knew that he could bear no more that day. In the morning he would come again and receive his War Lord's final commands. But no more to-day.

Later that evening Plessen came to him with the news that the Kaiser would leave for Holland next day. Hindenburg suggested that he should go at once to the Imperial train, but Plessen persuaded him against it. His Majesty, he said, was overtaxed by all he had gone through. He should not be disturbed again to-night. To-morrow would be plenty of time.

The Marshal was relieved. He too was worn out with the emotions of the day and the previous night. He must have rest to give him strength for the morrow, when he should take over the Supreme Command of the Armies from the Emperor. He retired early, and over G.H.Q. there was an atmosphere of calm after storm.

But there was to be no handing over of command on the morrow. Very early in the morning the Imperial train, its splendours of cream and gold unnoticed in the darkness, slipped quietly from its siding and vanished towards the Dutch frontier. When Hindenburg awoke, the church bells were ringing but his Emperor had gone.

It was Sunday, November 10.

For the remaining sixteen years of his life Hindenburg was to be haunted by the memories of these November days and the part he had played in them. For though, thanks to Schulenburg, Waldersee, and others, Gröner was maligned and traduced by the officers of the Old Army, the Prussian nobility and the Junkers were left in no doubt by the Kaiser as to where, in his estimation, the blame for his abdication and flight really lay. Ruminating in retrospect at Doorn, Wilhelm II became convinced that while Prince Max of Baden and Hindenburg were jointly responsible for his abdication, the responsibility for his flight was entirely the Marshal's.[1]

[1] Where the true responsibility for the Kaiser's flight into Holland lies, remains a mystery. Undoubtedly the immediate responsibility for advising the Kaiser's departure from Spa was Hindenburg's, but the idea was not his own and had its origin much further back. It was not in any case a chance improvisation conceived in a moment of panic provoked by the progress of the Revolution. Scheidemann states that as early as the end of October the Emperor knew that the Dutch frontier was open to him, and he alleges that a request had been made to the Queen of the Netherlands to give him asylum by none other than the King of England (*Mémoirs of a Social Democrat*, vol. ii. p. 538). It is a fact that a high Dutch military official, General van Heutsz, ex-Governor-General of the Dutch East Indies, visited Spa on the night of November 8. Moreover, it had been announced in Holland as early as November 7 that the Kaiser would take up his residence in the district of Apeldorn, and Niemann, the representative of the Supreme Command with the Emperor, asserts that "at Berlin there had been foresight enough to secure that all the necessary arrangements had been made. . . ." The inference is that the Emperor's journey to Holland had been arranged without the knowledge of the Emperor, and Dr. Maurice Beaumont, in his admirable study of these November days, raises the question of the possibility that certain high officials were convinced that Wilhelm II would be forced inevitably to go to Holland and had made arrangements accordingly (*The Fall of the Kaiser*, p. 246).

If this suggestion is correct, the circumstantial evidence all points to Admiral von Hintze. In his capacity of Foreign Office representative with the Supreme Command he would certainly have met the Dutch General van Heutsz on the evening of November 8. Had he seen him before he paid his late visit to Hindenburg and obtained his agreement to the immediate abdication and flight of the Emperor? It was certainly the Admiral who persuaded Hindenburg against the opinion of Gröner to which he had already agreed. It was Hintze who voted with Hindenburg in favour of Holland as against Switzerland during the conference with Schulenburg on the afternoon of November 9, and to him fell the task of making the arrangements for the Kaiser's departure. These arrangements were not set on foot before 5 o'clock in the evening, and yet by 4.30 on the following morning all was ready for the departure. In view of the chaotic state of things in Berlin at the moment, this was incredibly quick work if the ground had not already been prepared. The actual orders for departure were issued as early as 12.30 A.M.

As against this there is the Admiral's own statement that when, very early on

Though Hindenburg was later forced publicly to accept this responsibility, he was never entirely sure himself whether he had been responsible or not. He was always most anxious to excuse and to explain his conduct on November 9, and did not hesitate to throw a large share of the blame upon Gröner, regardless of the fact that Gröner had definitely advised against the flight to Holland, and that it was he, Hindenburg, who had changed his mind at the last moment. "You all blame me, but you should blame Gröner," he once said to the Nationalists; but they were unconvinced, and it remained one of their strongest holds over him in his later political career, that he had demanded the armistice which destroyed the German army and had sent his Kaiser over the frontier. They never ceased to impress upon him that it was his duty to himself and to Germany to restore the Kaiser and to rehabilitate the army, and these two considerations played an important part both in persuading him to accept the Presidential candidacy and finally to accept Adolf Hitler as Chancellor.

· 11 ·

The sudden departure of the Kaiser had simplified the problem of Hindenburg's own personal line of conduct. There was now at any rate no question of his accompanying his War Lord into exile. He had been left behind. There remained, however, the question of his immediate position. Technically speaking, his appointment to the Supreme Command of the German armies had been dependent upon Wilhelm II's remaining King of

the morning of November 10, he came to the station at Spa, he found the Imperial train already gone. There is also the fact that when the Kaiser arrived at the Dutch frontier at 7.30 in the morning he had to wait six hours while urgent telephone conversations were held with the Hague. It is possible, of course, that the Emperor left earlier than the Admiral had expected and that the prepared schedule was thus thrown out. In any case the weight of circumstantial evidence is against von Hintze.

Prussia. But now everything was changed. The Emperor had vanished without making any act of abdication. What was a loyal Prussian soldier to do? But here again Fate had answered the question for him.

While Hindenburg had slept the sleep of emotional exhaustion on the night of November 9, Gröner had been making history. He sat alone for a long time, reading and re-reading a document which a courier had brought that afternoon to Spa. It was the terms for an armistice which Marshal Foch had handed the day before to Erzberger. They were staggering in their severity, yet they were no more harsh than the terms which Hindenburg and Ludendorff had imposed on Russia and Rumania. This fact was of little consolation to Gröner, who realized that the conditions meant abject surrender and that Germany had no choice but to accept them. So crushing were the terms of the Allies that only a strong government in Germany could ensure their execution. And had Germany a strong government?

In deepest thought Gröner reviewed the situation before him. Wilhelm II's last words to him that afternoon had released him from his allegiance to the German Emperor, and he was not vitally concerned with saving the King of Prussia. But he was a good German, and deeply and genuinely he was concerned for Germany in her extremity. What was his duty? His Emperor had fled, his own King, Wilhelm of Württemberg, had abdicated, releasing his officers from their oaths to him; there remained only Germany, and his duty was to her.

Five hundred miles away in Berlin was a man whom Gröner knew and trusted, Fritz Ebert, the saddler, the last Imperial Chancellor and the first *Reichspräsident* of Germany, who, having failed to save the monarchy through no fault of his own, was now straining every effort to save the revolution. Gröner knew him for an honest and courageous man who, given the chance, would build up a strong Government in Germany. At the moment, however, he was in grave danger. His Cabinet, scarcely formed, was being attacked fiercely by the Independents and the Spartacists. If he failed to keep control, Bolshevism would sweep the country. With the support of the army, the Social Democrats and trade unions could restore the authority of the central Government and at least save Germany from the horror of civil war. Gröner saw his duty clearly: it was to Germany. He picked up the telephone.

Alone, behind locked doors in the Chancellor's room, Ebert sat collapsed in his chair. His sweat-soaked collar and disordered clothes bore witness to the efforts of the day. He was exhausted. All day he had fought and struggled, first for the monarchy, then for the revolution, and latterly for the very life of the Social Democratic Party. For Haase and Liebknecht were beating him; they had refused to support the Government, and all over Berlin Independent and Spartacist agitators were at work. At any moment civil war might break out. It would be the Commune over again.

Through the windows came the cheers and jeers of the crowds in the Wilhelmstrasse and from Unter den Linden the strains of the "Internationale." The Chancellor rose and paced the floor. His glance fell on the telephone on his desk. A private line connected him direct with Spa. If only he knew the attitude of the army. Could he depend on the corps of officers?

Suddenly, as if in answer to his question, the telephone bell rang. Ebert picked up the receiver with a hand that trembled. Then he almost wept with joy. . . .

"Gröner speaking."

Was he willing to protect Germany from anarchy and to restore law and order? the First Quartermaster-General wanted to know. Yes, he was, said Ebert. Then the High Command will maintain discipline in the army and bring it peacefully home, Gröner replied.

But the Chancellor wanted guarantees. What was the attitude of the High Command towards the Workers' and Soldiers' Councils? Orders had been given to deal with them in a friendly spirit, was the reply. What do you expect from us? asked the Chancellor. The High Command expects the Government to co-operate with the Officers' Corps in the suppression of Bolshevism, and in the maintenance of discipline in the army. It also asks that the provisioning of the army shall be ensured and all disturbance of transport communication prevented.

Ebert had one more question:

"Will the Field-Marshal retain the Command?"

Gröner hesitated a moment, then in a confident voice he answered:

"Yes, the Field-Marshal will retain the Command."

"Convey to the Field-Marshal the thanks of the Government," was Ebert's reply.

So when Hindenburg awoke on the morning of November 10, his course of action had already been decided for him. Very early came Gröner, bringing with him the armistice conditions and the report of the pact he had made with Ebert. There before Hindenburg opened a new path of service. One last questioning of conscience, one final clash of loyalties, and the struggle was over. Without sacrificing his personal loyalty to the Crown, he placed his services at the disposal of the Republic and of the army.

To many hundreds and thousands of loyal officers the collapse of the German army meant that the very foundations of their thoughts and feelings were tottering. They were faced with the hardest of all inward struggles. "I thought," writes the Marshal, "that I could help many of the best of them to come to the right decision in that conflict by continuing in the path to which the wish of my Emperor, my love for the Fatherland and Army, and my sense of duty pointed me." By so doing he not only

materially contributed to the saving of the Revolution from laps-
ing into Bolshevism, but also made the new régime a little more
acceptable to his fellow officers and thereby rendered counter-
revolutions considerably more difficult.

It was his greatest and most noble deed; greater than the victories of Tannenberg or the Lakes, greater far than anything
which occurred in his later life. For this act many deeds less
noble may be forgiven him.

Hindenburg, having shouldered this new and heavy responsibility, at once began upon the grim tasks which it involved.
The armistice terms which Erzberger had sent must be accepted
or rejected by noon the next day and the Government was anxious for his opinion. There was only one opinion to be given,
but in his telegram to the Minister of War, the Marshal suggested certain points on which mitigation of the terms might be
gained. If it was impossible to gain these modifications, "a fiery
protest should be raised," but—and here lay the whole essence
of the matter—"it would nevertheless be advisable to conclude
the agreement."

The armistice came into force at 11 o'clock on the morning of
November 11, and on the following day the German army began
its march homeward, very quietly, in column of route. Not the
least triumph of Gröner's genius for organization was that the
armies of the West were brought back home quickly and without
mishap. The greatest tact was required in dealing with the new
"spokesmen" which each unit was permitted to elect, but though
revolutionized, the military machine remained practically intact,
and, with the exception of some regrettable incidents in the
Rhineland, discipline was strictly maintained.

General Headquarters were transferred on November 15 to
Wilhelmshöhe in Cassel. Here indeed was tragic irony. When,
in 1870, Paul von Hindenburg, a dashing young subaltern of the
Third Foot Guards, newly decorated with the Iron Cross, was

pressing on to victory and Paris, there was lodged in this Palace of Wilhelmshöhe, where once Jerome Bonaparte had ruled as King, and a deposed and captive Emperor, his nephew, Napoleon III. Now, half a century later, in those same rooms, sat Marshal von Hindenburg, a defeated man, even though decorated with the Iron Cross with Golden Rays, and across the frontier his own Emperor was in exile. The wheel had turned full cycle.

But at Wilhelmshöhe Hindenburg was greeted with every mark of respect and confidence. A special order was issued authorizing him and his staff to be allowed to carry arms, and Grzesinski, chairman of the Workers' and Soldiers' Council of Cassel, published a proclamation of welcome. "Hindenburg is fulfilling his duty to-day in a manner which endears him to us as never before. Hindenburg belongs to the German nation." For the first time a German Socialist was publicly honouring a Prussian General.

And so, in these November days at Wilhelmshöhe, the Hindenburg Legend was rekindled. It had burned very low a month before and had all but flickered out. But in making the greatest and hardest decision of his life, in offering his services to the Republic, the Marshal had reawakened the confidence and the affection of the German people. Evidence of this increased popularity was to be seen on all sides. "The majority of red cockades which are on sale in the streets are portraits of Hindenburg," announced a Berlin newspaper. "Hindenburg's face has been painted over red, but the paint comes off very easily, and Hindenburg's face appears once more." This and many other portents marked the metamorphosis of the Legend. And very much of this renewed popularity Hindenburg owed, all unwittingly, to Gröner, whose timely negotiations with Ebert had made possible "the approach to Democracy."

But despite this revival of his personal prestige, Hindenburg, during these early days at Wilhelmshöhe, was a sad and lonely man. Now he was alone indeed in the midst of new and bewildering events which in nearly every case were alien to all his conceptions of life. He no longer had his War Lord to esteem and obey, and though he worked in close collaboration with Gröner, there was nothing of that warmth of feeling, that harmony of "marital bliss," that had characterized his relations with Ludendorff. Ever between them was the memory of November 9, like a spectral barrier, and Hindenburg had the uncomfortable feeling that Gröner knew.

There was, moreover, little to give him comfort. Germany's hopes and honour were in ashes, and at home anarchy and chaos still threatened. The army which Hindenburg had brought back home had had a strange welcome. The veterans, who had fought as gallantly under the bitter circumstances of defeat as in the intoxicating excitement of victory, were greeted by the revolutionaries with jeers and cat-calls, hailed as tyrants and lackeys of tyrants, and execrated as the butchers of the Imperial régime. Officers were particularly singled out for attack, and in many cases were brutally manhandled, their epaulettes torn off, their decorations trampled in the mud, and every indignity heaped upon them.

Despite his efforts, Ebert was unable to keep the pledges which he had given to Gröner. His position was all but impossible. The Social Democrats showed neither aptitude nor capacity for keeping control of the situation. The machinery of government was breaking down, and the Independents and Spartacists seized upon every circumstance which could inflame the people against the Cabinet. The refusal of the Allied Governments to raise the blockade was grist to Liebknecht's mill, and if Bolshevism had triumphed in Germany in the winter of 1918, the blindness and stupidity of the diplomacy of the Entente Powers would have been very largely to blame.

Unable to combat these revolutionary movements, Ebert endeavoured to conciliate them. The Congress of Worker's and Soldiers' Councils, which opened in the Prussian House of Deputies on December 16, adopted a resolution grossly offensive to the army in general and the High Command in particular. "As a symbol," the motion declared, "of the destruction of militarism and the abolition of blind obedience, all badges of ranks are to be removed and no arms carried by soldiers off duty. . . . The rank and file are to elect their own leaders. . . . Speedy measures are to be taken for the abolition of the standing army and the constitution of a national guard."

The wording of this resolution recalls Kerensky's famous Order No. 1, which played such havoc with the discipline of the Russian army, but Ebert was anxious to placate the Congress, which was on the verge of being carried into the Spartacist camp. He proposed to give authority to the resolution.

Almost every evening when his colleagues had left him, the Chancellor made use of the army wire to Wilhelmshöhe, the secret of which was unknown to his staff, to confer with Gröner, who was thus able to keep his finger on the pulse of the Government. Now Ebert told him that, reluctantly enough, he would have to put the resolution abolishing insignia into force. Gröner advised against it. The Marshal would never stand for it, and Gröner did not feel justified in urging him to do so. The spirit of the resolution struck at the very heart of military discipline, which, in any case, had sadly deteriorated.

Gröner was correct in his prophecy as to the Marshal's reaction. Hindenburg was furious. Already he had come into conflict with the Councils by forbidding any unit of the field army to carry the Red Flag and by opposing the right claimed by the troops to elect and depose their officers. The terms of the resolution were too much. If carried into effect, the army would melt away through lack of discipline. "You may tell the Chancellor," he said to Gröner, "that I decline to recognize the ruling of the

Congress with regard to the executive authority of our officers; that I shall oppose it by every means in my power, and that I shall not allow my epaulettes or my sword to be taken from me." At the same time he telegraphed to all troop commanders that no change was to be made in the army regulations. Ebert begged the High Command to reconsider its attitude. "It is not we who began the quarrel," replied Gröner, "and it is not our business to put an end to it."

The High Command triumphed, and the resolution was never put into force. The incident, however, might well have terminated the good relations between Wilhelmshöhe and Berlin, had not the Spartacist Rising of January 1919 overshadowed all other considerations.

In the crushing of this revolt, and the subsequent deaths of Karl Liebknecht and Rosa Luxemburg, the High Command at Wilhelmshöhe had no part. The operations against the insurgents were conducted by the Majority Socialist, Gustav Noske, who had suppressed the naval revolt at Kiel and was therefore now entrusted by Ebert with a similar task. Noske used for his attack on Berlin the troops of the Guard Cavalry Division, some veteran Jäger battalions, and certain of the volunteer corps which were springing up all over the country for local protection. Nominally of course these troops were under Hindenburg's authority as Commander-in-Chief; actually, however, they were commanded by Generals Hoffmann and Lüttwitz, who accepted orders from Noske direct, and it was by Guard Cavalry officers that the Spartacist leaders were murdered.[1] By the middle of January the revolt had been crushed with such efficiency that those involved in its suppression had earned the nickname of

---

[1] Not the least tragic aspect of the murder of Rosa Luxemburg is the fact that at the time of her death she had actually recanted Communism. She was arrested as she left a secret meeting with certain Majority Socialists at which she had become convinced of the fundamental unsoundness of Communist principles and had declared her intention of leaving the Spartacist ranks.

"Noske's Butchers," and the way was at last open for the meeting of the National Assembly at Weimar.

The task of withdrawing the armies of the West was completed by the New Year, and early in February 1919 General Headquarters were removed to Kolberg, in Pomerania, on the Baltic, the scene of the rise to fame of the great Gneisenau. Here Hindenburg and Gröner gave their attention to the Eastern Front, where bands of irregular volunteers were waging a guerilla warfare against the Soviet forces. The arrival of the Victor of Tannenberg was hailed with delighted enthusiasm. The glories of August 1914 would be repeated. Hindenburg would again save East Prussia from the Russians. Military ardour ran high.

The Marshal issued a rousing proclamation: "You volunteers and young comrades, who are determined to risk your lives in the defence of the Ostmark, remember the brave men of 1914. And you, old comrades who fought with me at Tannenberg and the Masurian Lakes, come quickly to our help. Do not let my appeal to the sons of Germany fall upon deaf ears!"

It was his plan to raise an army of veterans and volunteers and throw the invader out of the Baltic provinces, and immediately there was a keen response to his call. Soldiers who could find no employment and were tired of being insulted, youths who had been too young to fight, all answered his appeal. But alas for their hopes. From Trier, where was the G.H.Q. of Marshal Foch, the Allied Generalissimo, there came a command to halt. No offensive operations were to be undertaken and no advance was to be made beyond a demarcated line.

Hindenburg was furious. He implored the Government to reject these demands, but Ebert replied by asking the High Command if they were prepared for a resumption of hostilities. To this of course there was only one reply possible. Raging impotently, Hindenburg bowed to the inevitable and confined himself to reorganizing the defence of the German Eastern provinces.

Little by little, however, the new Germany gained strength and confidence, but not without blood and violence. In March occurred the second Spartacist Rising, and this again was suppressed by Noske, now Defence Minister, with great severity. In this operation the reorganized military forces of the State, the *Reichswehr*, were used for the first time, and Noske's handling of this new army, still scarcely formed from the conglomeration of *Freikorps*, regulars, and volunteers which remained as residue from the war, greatly impressed Hindenburg and Gröner. Between the Old army and the New a mutual respect was born. "The High Command," wrote Gröner to Noske on March 18, "has confidence in the Government, limited confidence in the Ministry of War, and unlimited confidence only in the Minister for National Defence."

As the spring progressed, the attention of Germany and of the whole world turned toward the Peace Conference. The hopes and fears of all, the ideals of those who dreamed of a New World, the ambitions of those who sought the permanent destruction of Germany, centred about Paris. The old legions of hatred did battle with the new forces of understanding, and apart, anxious and uncertain for the future, the world waited apprehensively.

In Germany itself there were still those who hoped for a peace based upon the Fourteen Points, which, though severe, might yet be acceptable; and there were those who still dreamed of armed resistance should the conditions of peace prove too humiliating. There was no great understanding of the real military and political position resulting from Germany's defeat. It was a common belief that the unbeaten German army had only broken off an unequal struggle to secure just peace terms, which America had offered. There was little or no conception of the deep-seated hatred which had grown up in the countries of the Entente against a people who had countenanced the sinking of passenger vessels, the bombing of women and children, and the deportation of Belgian civilians. The question of war-guilt was barely recognized, and the policy of Scheidemann, who had become Chancellor when the Weimar Assembly elected Ebert as President of the Republic, not only fostered these misconceptions, but was itself based upon them.

The High Command shared none of these illusions. Both Hindenburg and Gröner knew that little could be hoped from an enemy who had exacted such ruthless terms of capitulation in the field, and neither of them had any belief in the possibility of a resumption of hostilities. Gröner, however, considered that, in the last emergency, a campaign of passive resistance could be carried out with effect; but he prayed that this might not be necessary.

There came at last the day when the conditions of peace were handed to Count Brockdorff-Rantzau. They were published in Berlin on May 7, and at once a wave of rage and protest swept the country. Even those who had condemned the war policy of Imperial Germany, such as Prince Lichnowsky, the former Ambassador in London, and Dr. Walter Schücking, the international jurist and pacifist, joined in appealing to the Government to reject, at whatever cost, terms of so humiliating a nature. President Ebert issued a proclamation against "A Peace of Violence," and, as a sign of mourning, ordered the suspension of public amusements for a week. The Chancellor declared that "the peace conditions are unacceptable and impossible of execution," and with one voice the press demanded either rejection or negotiation.

For more than a month the battle raged in Berlin, in Weimar, and in Paris. As a result of such negotiation as was permitted them, and very largely on account of the reports which General Malcolm, head of the British Military Mission, was sending from Berlin, to the effect that the new spirit in Germany was establishing itself slowly but surely and every day more visibly, the German Peace Commission were able to secure certain important modifications of the original terms; but when the revised and final demands of the Allies were received on June 17 they were still of so crushing a nature that again there arose a national demand for their rejection. But it was not as unanimous as before. The Independents were now in favour of accepting the terms at any price. Though the Allied blockade had been lifted, there was still a terrible scarcity of essentials; of clothing, underwear, boots and shoes; even of bread there was a shortage. "Sign, then there'll be bread," became the slogan of the Independents, who now threatened armed revolt if the treaty was not accepted. On the other hand, the Army Associations officially declared through their officers that they would refuse to serve the Government if the dictated peace were signed.

Scheidemann and his Government were still unanimously in favour of rejection; Ebert supported them. The final word, however, lay with the High Command, for it was idle to pretend that rejection would not bring with it the resumption of hostilities. Ebert turned once more to Gröner.

The issue was passionately debated between Weimar and Kolberg. The question which confronted the High Command was whether the fighting spirit of the German nation was still capable of further resistance. Would the nation, in fact, prefer to accept a humiliating peace rather than face the alternative of making a last desperate stand involving in all probability its final overthrow?

After two days of bitter mental conflict, reason triumphed over a very natural desire for resistance. The reply of the High Command to the Government was as follows:

In the event of a resumption of hostilities we can reconquer the province of Posen and defend our frontiers in the east. In the west, however, we can scarcely count upon being able to withstand a serious offensive on the part of the enemy in view of the numerical superiority of the Entente and their ability to outflank us on both wings.

The success of the operation as a whole is therefore very doubtful, but as a soldier I cannot help feeling that it were better to perish honourably than accept a disgraceful peace.

VON HINDENBURG, G.F.M.

The sentiments expressed in the final paragraph were laudable and patriotic in the extreme, but in writing them, the Marshal had ignored the fact that he himself had advised the acceptance of the armistice conditions, no less humiliating, in his telegram to Erzberger on November 10. The desire for exculpation was beginning to show itself, and became more apparent as the struggle over the treaty proceeded and the opposition of the Right and the Old Army officers became more and more vehement.

Seizing upon Hindenburg's reply, the Independent Socialists attacked the Government in the Assembly, and so weakened its position that Scheidemann resigned on June 20. A new Cabinet was formed, depending for its support on the Majority Socialists and the Centre, with the Socialist, Gustav Bauer, as Chancellor, and Erzberger, Hermann Müller, and Noske in key positions. Again the fight was on. A compromise resolution was eventually carried, authorizing the acceptance of the treaty with the exception of the articles (227-8 and 230-1) which demanded the surrender for trial of the Kaiser and other "war criminals" and the admission of Germany's war guilt.

To this counter proposal the Allied and Associated Powers replied with an ultimatum. The treaty must be accepted or rejected as a whole within forty-eight hours; in the event of rejection, hostilities would reopen. This reply was received at Weimar about 11 o'clock on the evening of Sunday, June 22, and created something approaching a panic. But here Erzberger, taking up the fight for signature, suddenly appeared in a new light. For the first time in his career he played the part of a statesman rather than of a politician. With the support of Professor Haguenin, the French agent at Weimar (without whose work it is improbable that the treaty ever would have been signed), he defeated the waverers amongst his own followers of the Centre and brought them into line with the Independent Socialists and Majority Socialists, forming a solid bloc in the Assembly upon which the Government could rely for support. "Erzberger has the reputation of being a pure self-seeker in politics," wrote an Allied general from Berlin, when all was over, "but during the past week he has played a fine and patriotic rôle. I almost call it noble."

But the Cabinet itself was divided. It met at 10 o'clock on the morning of June 24 and reached no agreement. It adjourned. At 11 o'clock there came to Noske General Maercker, whose veterans had taken a prominent part in crushing the Spartacist revolts; all the higher *Reichswehr* commanders, he said, were prepared to resign from the army. They would proclaim Noske Dictator of Germany and reject the treaty. Noske considered the proposal, hesitated, and—to his eternal honour—refused.

The Cabinet met again at midday. Still no agreement. The sands were running out. The final vote of the Assembly must be taken that evening, and the Government must come before it with a united policy, or resign. Grimly the Chancellor adjourned the meeting again until 4.30.

In the meantime Ebert telephoned to Kolberg. He would only agree to sign the treaty if the High Command had come to the final conclusion that there was no chance left of armed resistance. If G.H.Q. still believed in the smallest possibility of success, Ebert declared, he would throw the whole weight of his influence in favour of rejection. What he must have before the decisive vote in the Cabinet that afternoon was the considered opinion of Hindenburg, and he would telephone again at 4 o'clock to receive it.

Again the responsibility of decision had been placed upon the Marshal, and again he had not the courage to shoulder it. Upon his decision depended peace or war; war, with all its hopelessness and its reawakened horrors, or peace, with its surrender of Alsace-Lorraine, the Polish Provinces and the Colonies, with its crushing indemnity, with its admission of war guilt, and finally, most terrible of all for Hindenberg, with its surrender of the Emperor for trial. He had forced his Emperor to abdicate, he had urged him to run away, must he now take responsibility for the decision which should deliver him over to his most implacable enemies? The nightmare of Spa seized hold on him again; yet war was impossible.

The great tragedy of Hindenburg's life was that his mental conflicts were never between right and wrong, but always between right and right. It was the clash of fealties which tore his soul, and the result of the struggle was usually that he was loyal to neither. So now he reached an impasse. He could not advise the resumption of hostilities, and equally he could not take the responsibility for accepting the treaty. In the greater issues he lacked moral courage.

Half an hour before the appointed time they met in Gröner's office, the Marshal still in a state of indecision. Gröner asked him what the reply should be. "You know as well as I do that armed resistance is impossible," said Hindenburg. "You realize all that this decision means?" Gröner asked. The Marshal, without answering, walked slowly to the window. How well he knew all that it meant, and in that moment Hindenburg had made up his mind. He had not the courage to give the decision to Ebert. He looked at his watch. It was a quarter to four.

"There is no need for me to stay," he told Gröner. "You can give the answer to the President as well as I can"; and he left the room. Some time later, after the fatal call had been made, the Marshal returned and laid his hand upon Gröner's shoulder. "The burden which you have undertaken is a terrible one," he said.

That night the National Assembly voted to accept the Peace Treaty, but in the chronicles of Weimar it is written: "What finally decided the matter was a trunk-call from General Gröner to President Ebert, in which the former stated that, if fighting were resumed, the prospects of a successful issue were hopeless, adding his firm conviction that in the end even the army would approve the acceptance of the conditions."

Hindenburg's name does not appear.

For the second time Gröner had become the victim of Hindenburg's lack of courage, and, in the eyes of the army, the "treachery of Weimar" was added to the "treason of Spa." From the charge of disloyalty to the Emperor Gröner sought to defend himself, and in 1922 a Court of Honour pronounced that he had "acted according to his conscience, holding that thus he could best serve the interests of his country." But in the matter of Weimar he remained silent in face of the attacks and calumnies which were repeatedly levelled against him over fourteen years; and in this time the Marshal said no word in his defence or ever denied that the whole responsibility of the fatal decision rested with Gröner.

Why, a group of his friends once asked Gröner, did he make no effort to protect his name and reputation? "Because I believed that in the interests of the New Army the myth of Hindenburg should be preserved," he replied. "It was necessary that one great German figure should emerge from the war free from all the blame that was attached to the General Staff. That figure had to be Hindenburg."

The Marshal's work was over. The peace terms had put an end to the German Great General Staff and, on the same day that the treaty was signed in the room where, half a century before, he had seen his King proclaimed Emperor, Hindenburg concluded his "second life" with his retirement from the army. His proclamation of farewell, with its sincerity of appeal and noble simplicity of language, has become a historic document. It had been drafted by Gröner.

Soldiers [it read] upon my retirement my thoughts revert in the first place, with deep emotion, to the long years during which I was permitted to serve three Royal and Imperial Masters . . . and at the same time with feelings of deep sorrow to those sad days when our Fatherland collapsed. The self-devotion and loyalty with which officers, non-commissioned officers, and men have stood by me have been a great consolation to me in those unspeakably difficult times. For this I would ask you all, and especially the volunteer corps who have so manfully mounted guard on the eastern front, to accept my lasting thanks. I have, however, to make a request as well as to express my thanks. Whatever you may think as individuals about recent events is entirely your own affair; but as regards your actions I would beg each one of you to be guided solely by the interests of his country. Personal views must be subordinated to the general welfare—however difficult this may seem. It is only by the united efforts of all of us that we can hope with God's help to raise our unhappy German Fatherland from its present depths of degradation and restore its former prosperity. Farewell. I shall never forget you!

HINDENBURG.[1]

[1] The signature itself is of interest. The proclamation is the only public document signed by Hindenburg, at this period of his life, without the "von" of nobility or the initials G.F.M. (General-Field-Marshal). He was writing on this occasion as one German soldier to others.

3

WEIMAR AND NEUDECK

✠

HANOVER again; Hanover and retirement, but not the obscurity of 1911. Then Lieutenant-General von Hindenburg, one of the many general officers retained *à la suite* of their regiments, had passed unnoticed on the streets and had gone unrecognized on little domestic shopping expeditions. But now on July 4, 1919, the City Fathers, in all the dignity of their silk hats and frock-coats, met the Field-Marshal at the station with an address of welcome and conducted him with all ceremony, not to his old first floor flat in the Holzgraben, but to the fine, new villa in Seel-horststrasse which Hanover had presented to its first citizen of honour.

It was a strange home-coming and his first since his departure on the eve of Tannenberg. On that night he had waited alone, without even an aide-de-camp, for Ludendorff; now, with his son Oskar, and Colonel von Kügelgen in attendance, with the notori-ous Oberbürgermeister Tramm to welcome him, with a guard of honour in uniform, immaculate almost as if there had been no war, he passed to his new home through great throngs of cheer-ing troops and citizens. At the villa his wife awaited him, and in that reunion with her, the first for many months, was his real homecoming.

Throughout the privations of the war and the terrors of the

revolution, when Hanover had been among the first cities to hoist the Red Flag, Frau von Hindenburg had bravely gone about her business and had kept up her courage by alternate readings in the New Testament and the campaigns of 1870–71. She had found great comfort in the friendship of Countess von Crayenberg, whose niece was now so soon to become Oskar von Hindenburg's wife, and together they had passed through the trials and acknowledged the honours which came to the wife of a great soldier. She had taken up residence in the new villa, but at once offered to return it to the city when the revolutionary government took over control in November 1918. To his great credit, the Mayor, Leinert, who later became President of the Prussian Diet, refused even to consider such a proposal, and gave strict orders that she was to suffer no discomfort or indignity.

Her quiet courage was now rewarded; her husband had come back to her, a defeated general but a hero in the hearts of his countrymen, and the glory of the homecoming seemed to make amends for the weary months of waiting.

The enthusiasm of the welcome did not pass in a day. A perpetual crowd stood before the house in the Seelhorststrasse and wherever the giant figure of the Marshal appeared in the streets, all traffic ceased and the crowd gave itself up to joyful demonstration. His celebrity became a burden to him. Hating ostentation and devoid of personal ambition, he chafed at the restrictions which his popularity placed upon him. "My wife has just gone into Hanover to do some shopping. I used to like doing it myself but I can't any longer. If I cross the Georgstrasse there's such a crowd that the traffic has to stop," he complained to a visitor.

The flood of presents which had poured in on him after Tannenberg now recommenced with redoubled force. From rich and poor came gifts appropriate and otherwise. The house became

a museum both from the value of the gifts and from the personalities of their donors. A Turkish carpet from Enver Pasha; a
great group of bronze elks from the province of East Prussia to
her saviour; the silver axe of the Hungarian regiment of which
he was Colonel-in-Chief; the watch which Napoleon had used at
St. Helena; all these stirred memories within him whenever his
glance fell upon them. In one corner of his study hung a particularly cherished relic, a naval flag, the beloved *schwarz-weiss-
rot*, now prohibited by the Republic. They were the colours of
the battle-cruiser *Hindenburg*, scuttled in Scapa Flow after her
surrender. A young lieutenant had wrapped them round his body
before jumping overboard, and had brought them back to the
man whose name the ship had proudly borne, and to the woman
who had launched her.

But between Hindenburg and the peace of his retirement the
memories of Spa rose like a spectre. How differently things had
worked out to what he had dreamed they would. He had been
wont to say to his intimates at Spa: "As soon as peace is signed
I shall ride with the Emperor through the Brandenburger Tor
to the palace and take part in the festivities there; then I shall
take a cab to the station, go back to my dear old wife, and no
one will ever see me again." To the burden of responsibility for
Wilhelm II's flight was added the fear of the Emperor's extradition and trial, for which the Allied press still clamoured, and
this possibility haunted the Marshal continually.

His first act on laying down his active command was to send
a letter to Ebert assuming full responsibility for all the actions
of the High Command since August 1916, including the orders
of the Emperor, which, he declared, had been given in every
case on his personal advice. At the same time he wrote direct to
Marshal Foch, as Generalissimo of the Allied Armies, "in the
name of the old German army," asking him to refrain from
pressing for the surrender of the Emperor:

As the supreme head of an army which through centuries has upheld the tradition of true soldiers' honour and knightly sentiment as its highest ideal, you will be able to appreciate our feelings. I am ready to make any sacrifice to keep this shameful humiliation from our people and our name. Therefore I put my person entirely at the disposal of the Allied Powers, in place of my royal master. I am convinced that every other officer of the Old Army would be prepared to do the same.

To this appeal the French Marshal made no reply.

The gesture made, Hindenburg settled down to the preparation of his case for posterity. It was a great season for the production of memoirs. On both sides generals and admirals, victorious and unsuccessful, rushed into print in justification of their records and of the particular parts which they had played. Some wrote their own defence, some were incapable of doing so. In Germany, Ludendorff produced two volumes of detailed recollections, and two more on the work of the General Staff. From neither work does he emerge a very dignified figure. In Holland "ghost-writers" had found a happy hunting-ground amongst the exiled Hohenzollerns. At Amerongen the journalist Rosen was busy upon the Kaiser's recollections, while at Wieringen a famous novelist was engaged upon a similar task with the Crown Prince. So too at Hanover, with General von Mertz and a journalist as his collaborators, Hindenburg prepared his own story, not from "any personal inclination to authorship, but in answer to the many requests and suggestions that have been made to me." With such speed did they work that by September a thick volume of some hundred and fifty thousand words was published, entitled *Aus meinem Leben*.

As a literary production or as a contribution to history, the memoirs are unimpressive and disappointing. Pompous and stilted in style and vague in language, they are remarkable rather for what is omitted than for what is told. Considering the author's career and the material at his disposal, it is surprising to find only one mention of Schlieffen's name and none at all of Hoffmann's. On the other hand both the Kaiser and Ludendorff are referred to throughout in the most laudatory terms, as if these passages were dictated by the pangs of conscience. The events of Spa are dismissed in a single paragraph, a master-piece of evasive discretion. "I was at the side of my All-Highest War Lord during the fateful hours. He entrusted me with the task of bringing the army back home. When I left the Emperor in the afternoon of November 9, I was never to see him again! He went to spare his Fatherland further sacrifices and enable it to secure more favourable terms of peace."

In the last chapter, "My Farewell," the Marshal showed that he had already imbibed the belief which he was later to make famous as the "stab-in-the-back." Regardless of the reasons which he himself had given to Prince Max of Baden for the collapse of the front, he now pronounced a phrase which was to become the fighting slogan of the German Nationalists and, after them, of the National Socialists. "Like Siegfried, stricken down by the treacherous spear of savage Hagen, our weary front collapsed"—here was a basis for the myth that the German army was not well and truly beaten but had been betrayed by the Revolution.

The book concluded with a flight into the future, a prophecy so strangely accurate that it was later turned to great political account:

Comrades of the German Army once the proud and mighty famous Army! How can you talk of despondency? Think of the men who gave us a new Fatherland more than a hundred years ago. Their religion was their faith in themselves and in the sacredness of the cause. They built up a Fatherland, not on a foundation of doctrines strange to them but on those of the free development of the individual within the frame-work of the whole body-politic, and on his sense of responsibility to the State. Germany will tread that path once more as soon as she is permitted to do so. I have an unshakeable conviction that, as in those days, our historical continuity with our great and glorious past will be preserved and restored where it has been broken. The old German spirit will descend upon us again, though it may be that we shall first have to go through the purifying fires of passion and suffering. . . . When our national ideals and our national conscience have resumed their sway among us, we shall see how moral values have been struggling to birth in our present grievous trials and the Great War, on which no nation is entitled to look back with more pride than the German people, so long as it remained true to itself. Then, and then only, will the blood of all those who fell believing in the greatness of Germany have been poured out not in vain. In that hope I lay down my pen and firmly build on you—Young Germany.

The ideal which Hindenburg had in mind was the future restoration of the monarchy ("from the tempestuous seas of our national life will once more emerge that rock—the German Imperial House—to which the hopes of our fathers clung in the days of yore"). But his "farewell message" conjured up a dream and a vision for the realization of which Adolf Hitler claimed to stand. The words might well have been written for him. On these grounds, and on these grounds alone—the rehabilitation of the German nation and of the German army— was he able to claim the support of the Marshal for the Revolution of 1933; and when Hindenburg's political testament came to be written, at a moment when Nazi fortunes had fallen decidedly low, Hitler insisted that these words should be incorporated in it. The Marshal had wrought more than he knew.

On November 1, 1919, the Allied and Associated Powers presented to the German Government a list of 830 German citizens who were arraigned under Article 228 of the Treaty of Versailles as persons "accused of having committed acts in violation of the laws and customs of war," and their surrender for trial was demanded. It was one of the many senseless humiliations heaped upon a defenceless Germany. The list of "war criminals"—they were thus designated before trial—included many hundreds of humble persons, engineers who had destroyed industrial plants during the retreat across France and Flanders, naval officers charged with offences against Allied shipping, doctors accused of neglecting wounded prisoners, former U-boat commanders, and even one woman, who was held responsible for ill-treatment of prisoners!

But in order to escape the accusation of "one rule for the rich and another for the poor," the victorious Powers had added to the list those whom they regarded as morally responsible for the crimes committed by their subordinates. The arch-criminal, of course, was the Kaiser, but his case had been covered separately under Article 227 of the Treaty. Besides, the list of those "wanted" included nearly every leading figure in German public life during the war, the German Crown Prince and the Crown Prince of Bavaria, the ex-Chancellors von Bethmann Hollweg and Michaelis, Count Bernstorff, the former Ambassador in Washington; Field-Marshals von Hindenburg and Mackensen, Generals Ludendorff and von Falkenhayn, Grand-Admiral von Tirpitz, and Admiral von Scheer, who had commanded the High Seas Fleet at Jutland.

The German people saw, with rage and shame, their most distinguished leaders publicly branded as criminals and the Government, who had signed the Treaty under duress, could not, even had they wished, have arrested men who had done their duty to their country as they had conceived it. No one believed that a trial before courts in foreign countries would carry with it any elements of justice, and therefore the verdicts would have no moral force whatever. Moreover, the offences with which these were charged were the merest humbug, and it is difficult to understand how any responsible statesmen could have seriously condoned such a proceeding.

The Government was in no position to execute the demands of the Allies. It was still threatened with counter-revolution from the Right, and any attempt to arrest the distinguished personages on the Allied list of "criminals" would have been the signal for an armed uprising of all the conservative elements in the country. An attempt was made to secure a few voluntary surrenders. The German Crown Prince and Prince Rupprecht of Bavaria both offered to give themselves up on behalf of all. The great sociologist, Max Weber, called on Ludendorff to try and persuade him to join them. Ludendorff, forgetting the claim which he had made at Pless for joint responsibility, referred him to Hindenburg, who had been his nominal superior. Weber replied that all the world knew that, in effect, he, and not Hindenburg, had controlled the High Command. Ludendorff grinned bitterly—"Yes, thank goodness," he said. But he refused to surrender all the same.

Hindenburg made no move at all. He had offered himself in the place of his Emperor, he would make no effort on his own behalf. "If they want to shoot an old man like myself who has only done his duty and nothing more, let them come and take me," he replied to a deputation who came to beg him not to give himself up.

The voluntary surrender of great representative Germans would, in fact, have embarrassed the Powers not a little, though it is possible that some of the minor and less sophisticated defenders of Liberty and Democracy would have been delighted to hang their former opponents as criminals. But the German Government, with a united country behind it, felt strong enough to make a first gesture of resistance. It refused to surrender the persons named in the Allied list but offered instead to have them tried before the Supreme Court of the *Reich* at Leipzig. To this the Powers agreed, secretly glad to be free of an embarrassment which their own senseless rashness had brought about.

A few lesser fry were put on trial; there were a number of acquittals but some convictions, particularly in cases where deliberate brutality could be proved, and the affair was allowed to fall into decent obscurity.

But the great ones of Germany were not to go entirely free of public censure. Deeply stirred by the charges made against the country of having provoked the war and of having committed acts in contravention of international laws and customs, the National Assembly appointed a committee of investigation, which, on the motion of the Independent Socialists, was also empowered to enquire into the charge against the former Imperial Government of having refused to make peace in 1916–17. If the enquiry should bring to light the direct culpability of any individual in Germany, it was proposed to bring him before the *Staatsgerichtshof,* the newly-constituted High Court of Justice. The Committee had power to subpoena witnesses, and many of the distinguished "criminals" on the Allied list appeared before it, including Count Bernstorff, Bethmann Hollweg, the former Vice-Chancellor Helfferich, and Admiral von Kapelle. The public interest centred upon whether Hindenburg and Ludendorff would be summoned to give evidence.

The Independent Socialists demanded that no exceptions should be made under any conditions. Hindenburg had been Chief of the General Staff and in this capacity had exercised very great influence on policies of the day; without question his testimony must be heard. The Nationalist press was beside itself at the very idea of Hindenburg's conduct being investigated. The thing was incredible even on the part of such scoundrels as the men of Weimar; on no account must the Marshal be subjected to this indignity.

But while the Nationalist press fulminated, the Nationalist leaders held conclave. Helfferich's house in the Hitzigstrasse was becoming the centre of reaction and counter-revolution.

Here came Ludendorff and others of the late army leaders, together with veterans of the *Vaterlandfront* and the old Conservative Party. What better thing for the cause of reaction than to capture Hindenburg, to inculcate him—no very difficult task —with the belief that the German army had been betrayed on the Home Front, and use his appearance before the Committee of Enquiry for a grand attack upon the republican régime? Ludendorff supported the suggestion warmly. He had already refused to appear before the Committee unless Hindenburg were called also. The recollection of joint responsibility seemed to have returned.

So in the latter days of November Hindenburg came as a conquering hero to Berlin. A special saloon car brought him from Hanover, and at the Friedrichstrasse Station a guard of honour was awaiting him. Two regular army officers were attached as honorary aides-de-camp and two steel-helmeted sentries were posted in front of Helfferich's villa while the Marshal was his guest. Here for the first time since October 26 of the previous year he saw Ludendorff again. Their meeting was cool but not hostile. Huge crowds cheered Hindenburg at his every appearance, but these in turn provoked counter-demonstrations by the Independent Socialists, who missed no opportunity of depicting in flaming terms the dangers of reaction. So fierce did the faction feeling become that reprisals and disorders threatened. The Government became seriously alarmed; they were none too secure in their position and a "state of siege" still existed in Berlin.

Throughout his visit Hindenburg's own attitude was irreproachable, and when matters became really serious he, in consultation with Noske, issued a dignified address to the people of Berlin, thanking them for their reception and appealing to them for reason.

The thought of Germany's future fills my mind to-day as it did during the war [he told his admirers], but in view of the 'state of siege,' which still obtains in Berlin, I appeal for a cessation of all demonstrations which disturb traffic and public order. My unity in thought and will with the people of Berlin gives me the assurance that this appeal will not be misunderstood.

Would that this same common sense had assisted him in his conversation with Helfferich and Ludendorff. But he was lending a willing ear to their views, and was imbibing from them the belief that already had found expression in his own memoirs. He was being indoctrinated with the false theory of the "stab-in-the-back," a misquotation from a statement by a British General, but a theory in justification of which many innocent Germans were to suffer when the National Socialists came into power. For in this doctrine was the germ of many of Adolf Hitler's attacks against the Social Democratic Party.

Hindenburg and Ludendorff appeared before the Committee of Enquiry on November 18, 1919. In plain clothes they drove to the *Reichstag* building through streets lined with troops and mounted police who kept back the cheering and jeering crowds. In the Königsplatz, later to be re-christened the Platz der Republik,[1] they were greeted with a storm of hoots and hurrahs. The *Reichstag* itself was heavily guarded. Barbed wire barred the entrance of the side doors, and machine-guns were posted at each corner. The two commanders were greeted at the entrance by Herr Warmuth, the Nationalist member of the Committee, who conducted them up the staircase to the central committee-room, where a great bunch of chrysanthemums, tied with ribbons of the national colours of *schwarz-weiss-rot*, decorated the witness-box.

The Committee was really very anxious to show every con-

---

[1] The change of name took place immediately after Ebert's death in 1925; the square resumed its old name after the Revolution of 1933.

sideration to the Marshal and, as evidence of this, it had been agreed that he should not be cross-examined by a Social Democrat chairman, but by Gothein, the Democrat member, a man of old Prussian Civil Service traditions. His selection as presiding officer was not a happy one.

As Hindenburg glanced round the crowded committee-room, he recognized faces he had not seen for a long time. The long, bearded face of Bethmann Hollweg recalled their last clash before the Emperor in the summer of 1917, and Count Bernstorff's yellow, furrowed features brought back other memories. The sound of Gothein's voice recalled him to the present. "We would willingly have spared Your Excellency the inconvenience of this journey," the little man was saying, "had not General Ludendorff attached so much importance to it." Without giving any sign of having heard him, the Marshal, with some deliberation, took his seat.

The clerk rose to administer the oath, when Ludendorff interrupted him. Before taking the oath, he said, he wished to make a statement on behalf of the Field-Marshal and himself. Their position was ambiguous. According to the provisions of the *Strafprozessordnung*, to which the proceedings of the Committee had to conform, they had the right to refuse to give evidence. They regarded it, however, as the right of the German people to hear the truth, and had therefore come forward of their own accord. They then took the oath.

Gothein began his cross-examination: "When did the General Headquarters first consider that the declaration of the U-boat war should not be later than February 1, 1917, and why?"

Hindenburg completely ignored the question. He produced a typewritten document from his pocket. He proposed, he said, to read a memorandum explaining the principles of all their actions during the war. The chairman ruled that this could not be allowed as it would entail the expression of personal opinion, whereas it was the business of the Committee to discover facts. Taking no notice of him at all, the Marshal began to read aloud. He did not read well. It had been unrehearsed, and he put emphasis on the wrong passages. He was not at his best.

. . . The war had no parallel in history. Battle areas became gigantic. The masses of armed men attained a strength hitherto undreamed of, and the technical feature assumed a predominating significance. War and world economics became intertwined as never before. Our relative strength in men, machines, munitions, and resources was from the beginning highly unfavourable for us. Never were the *imponderabilia* of war so important, such as the morale of the troops and the requirements made upon the central authorities and local leadership. . . . The unshatterable will for victory was imperative. But this will to conquer was inextricably bound up in the assurance that we were in the right. It was not a question of personal determination, but an expression of the will of the people. Had it not existed we would not have been justified in assuming command. The General Staff was trained according to the system of the great military philosopher, Clausewitz, which looks upon war as the continuation of policy by means other than those of statesmanship. Our peace policy had failed. I know with absolute certainty that the German people, the Kaiser, the Government, and the General Staff did not want war. . . .

Here the chairman rang his bell. "I must protest," he cried. "That is an expression of opinion."

The Marshal looked at him coldly for a moment, then in a loud voice replied: "The historian will have to decide the issue." He continued to read:

. . . The military authorities were of course prepared for the possibility of war, which was, perhaps, unavoidable. That was what they were there for. . . . In spite of the superiority of the enemy in men and material, we could have brought the struggle to a favourable issue if determined and unanimous co-operation had existed between the army and those at home. But whereas the enemy showed an ever greater will for victory, divergent party interests began to manifest themselves with us. These circumstances soon led to a disintegration of our will to conquer. . . .

Again the chairman's bell. "That is an expression of opinion as to the internal political situation," cried Gothein.

Without paying the slightest attention, the Marshal continued to describe the effects of politics on the army and its final permeation by the revolutionary spirit. "Owing to this, our will to victory was undermined. I looked for energy and co-operation, but found pusillanimity and weakness."

"But that again is an expression of opinion!" Gothein was almost weeping with rage and humiliation. Somebody laughed softly, and the members who sat on either side of the chairman pulled him down by his coat-tails. Hindenburg proceeded to his peroration, unperturbed; he was speaking now in a voice of such sepulchral depth that all ears were strained to catch his words:

Our repeated requests for the maintenance of stern discipline and the strict application of the law met with no results. Our operations in consequence failed, as they were bound to, and the collapse became inevitable; the revolution was merely the last straw. As an English General has very truly said, "The German Army was stabbed in the back." [1] It is plain enough upon whom the blame lies. If any further

[1] There were, in effect, two British Generals who were inadvertently responsible for the origins of the theory of the "stab-in-the-back." The first was Major-General Sir Frederick Maurice, whose book *The Last Four Months*, published in 1919, was grossly misrepresented by reviewers in the German press as proving that the German army had been betrayed by the Socialists on the Home Front, and not been defeated in the field. General Maurice issued a *démenti* in the German press, but it was impossible to overtake the lie once it had been launched, and both Helfferich and Ludendorff made use of the reviews in their conversations with Hindenburg.

The other officer was Major-General Malcolm, Head of the British Military Mission in Berlin. Ludendorff was dining with the General and his officers one evening, and with his usual turgid eloquence was expatiating on how the High Command had always suffered lack of support from the civilian Government and how the Revolution had betrayed the army. In an effort to crystallize the meaning

HINDENBURG AT SPA, JUNE 1918

proof were necessary to show it, it is to be found in the utter amazement of our enemies at their victory.

The deep silence which followed the conclusion of the Marshal's address was broken only by the crackling of the paper
as he replaced it in his pocket. The chairman, who had recovered
his composure, now repeated his opening question.

"From the time we assumed the Supreme Command we regarded the ruthless U-boat war as essential," replied Hindenburg. "In the beginning of 1917 it was clear that U-boat warfare
was necessary to help the hard-pressed Western Front. It was the
only way to end the war. Were we with equanimity to allow our
soldiers to be torn to pieces by American shells and their wives
and children to be starved by the blockade? The U-boat war was
the only weapon with which we could oppose these measures."

After that he left the submarine warfare to be dealt with by
Ludendorff, who embarked on an endless campaign of bickering and verbal skirmishing with the Committee. Only once more
did the Marshal intervene to declare that his views and Ludendorff's had always coincided. At noon the Committee adjourned
the hearing *sine die*, as Hindenburg said he was fatigued and
could not be sure when it would be convenient for him to attend
again.

It had not been a very creditable affair, for in view of their
statement that they had come voluntarily before the Committee
Hindenburg and Ludendorff had treated it with rank discour-
tesy. They were at pains to emphasize this in the statement which
they issued to the press on their return to Helfferich's house.
They had worn civilian dress, they declared, because they felt
they would have been paying too great a compliment to some

---

of Ludendorff's verbosity into a single sentence, General Malcolm asked him: "Do
you mean, General, that you were stabbed in the back?" Ludendorff's eyes lit up
and he leapt upon the phrase like a dog on a bone. "Stabbed in the back?" he
repeated. "Yes, that's it, exactly. We were stabbed in the back."

members of the Committee of Enquiry by appearing before them in their Prussian uniforms and orders. Altogether a mean and petty episode, and one unworthy of Hindenburg's stature. Moreover, the harm done was incalculable. Hindenburg's statement regarding the "stab-in-the-back" became a notorious slogan and added much fuel to the flames of discord which the Nationalists were fanning. It contributed materially to the state of mind which later on produced the campaign of political assassination; among its victims were Erzberger—whom Hindenburg himself had persuaded to head the Armistice Commission—and Rathenau. The Marshal's desire for exculpation had overridden his sense of justice and truth.

The year 1920 was one of continued anxiety and uneasiness for Hindenburg. The spectre of Spa was ever with him, and he was ridden by the nightmare of the Kaiser's extradition. Five days after the official coming into force of the Peace Treaty on January 10, the Allied Powers despatched a Note to Holland demanding the surrender of Wilhelm II. The Dutch Government refused—it was not bound by the provisions of a treaty to which the country was not a party. A month later, the legal executors of the treaty, the Conference of Ambassadors, again applied for the Emperor's extradition, and again, on March 5, the Dutch Government rejected the demand, declaring it to be incompatible with sovereignty and national honour. It was agreed, however, that Wilhelm II's place of exile should be moved from Count Bentinck's house at Amerongen, which was within a few miles of the German frontier, to the more remote castle of Doorn, and to this compromise the Allies agreed with great relief, since they had at last realized that no court of justice could legally try the Kaiser, and that in consequence his surrender would be a source of very considerable embarrassment.

Safe at last from all dangers of being handed over to his enemies, the Emperor began to take steps to elicit from Hinden-

burg a full admission of his responsibility for the flight from
Spa. The sighting-shot was fired during the spring of 1921, in
the course of a correspondence with the Marshal on the question
of war-guilt. The Emperor, in a lengthy memorandum, supplemented by "Comparative Historical Tables," sought to show
that neither he nor the Imperial Government was guilty of complicity in bringing about the war. To this Hindenburg replied
fervently: "I agree with Your Majesty to the uttermost depths
of my soul—in my long term of military service I have had
the good fortune and honour to enter into close personal relations with Your Majesty. I know that the best of all the efforts
of Your Majesty throughout your reign were towards the maintenance of peace. I can realize how immeasurably hard it is
for Your Majesty to be eliminated from active co-operation for
the Fatherland." This was so, the Emperor replied, in a later
letter; such an elimination was the cause of "burning anguish in
my soul." And he added: "As you know, I forced myself to
the difficult and terrible decision to leave the country only upon
the urgent declaration of yourself . . . that only by my so
doing would it be possible to obtain more favourable armistice
terms for our people and spare them a bloody civil war."

Here was an uncompromising and unequivocal statement calculated to leave the Marshal under no misapprehension as to
the Kaiser's views on responsibility. During the entire correspondence, which extended over eighteen months, Gröner's name
did not appear. Both the Kaiser and the Marshal knew the truth
of that story.

But there was a tragically human side to this early exchange
of letters in March and April 1921. Both men were under the
shadow of approaching bereavement. The Empress Augusta and
Frau von Hindenburg were both dangerously ill at this time
and the anxiety of the two husbands is touchingly referred to in
the letters. "I beg to thank Your Majesty most respectfully for

your gracious interest in the illness of my wife. She is not yet out of danger." "The condition of Her Majesty has become worse. My heart is filled with the most grievous worry." The Empress lived two years longer, but by the middle of May Hindenburg was a widower, even more lonely than before.

Some time later the correspondence with the Emperor was resumed. Finally, in July 1922, Hindenburg shouldered his burden of responsibility. He wrote from Hanover to the Emperor:

MOST SERENE HIGHNESS, GREAT AND MIGHTY KAISER!
    MOST GRACIOUS KAISER, KING, AND LORD!

I take the responsibility for Your Majesty's resolve to go into exile, a step taken on that unhappy ninth of November as a result of the united demand of all your advisers.

I have already given as the reason the menace of the danger that Your Majesty sooner or later might have been arrested by mutinous troops and might be surrendered to the enemy at home or abroad. The Fatherland had at all costs to be spared such insult and disgrace. On these grounds I advised, in the names of us all, at the meeting on the afternoon of November 9, that the journey to Holland be undertaken, an exile which I considered to be only of short duration. Even to-day I am still of the opinion that this proposal was the right one.

It is incorrect to say that on the evening of November 9 I pressed for immediate departure, as has recently been stated against my will. For me there exists no doubt that Your Majesty would not have taken the journey to Holland had you not thought that I, the Chief of the General Staff, considered this step imperative in the interest of Your Majesty and of the Fatherland.

As is written in the Protocol of July 27, 1919,[1] I only learnt of Your Majesty's departure after it had already taken place.

In conclusion of this statement I beg in all respect to be allowed to assure Your Majesty that I have always pledged unbounded loyalty to my Kaiser, King, and Lord, and will always do so, and am therefore

[1] This document, covering the events of November 9 at Spa, had been jointly prepared by Hindenburg. Admiral von Hintze, Colonel-General von Plessen, and General Count von Schulenburg. Its discretion and reticence are a tribute to its authorship.

willing to take the responsibility for the decision taken on November 9.

In deep respect and great gratitude, I remain always Your Imperial and Royal Majesty's most loyal subject,

VON HINDENBURG, G.F.M.

By this letter Hindenburg publicly accepted the burden of responsibility that was historically his, and thereby delivered himself to the Monarchists and Nationalists, who never ceased to urge certain policies upon him in expiation. The spectre of Spa became an almost inseparable part of his existence, he was never to escape from it again, and the major policies of his life thereafter were to be guided by it.

The Emperor delayed two months before sending his reply from Doorn, and when it did come it was not very handsome. He was glad, he wrote, that this matter had been cleared up once and for all, but he had had to wait a long time before the persons principally concerned could be persuaded to come forward and declare publicly

that I was forced to depart from Spa on the urgent advice of my political advisers and against my own conviction. I thank you for having now taken this step, which is necessary not only in the interests of historical truth, but equally for my personal reputation and the honour of my House. . . . Convinced that you were loyally discharging a difficult task, you gave to your Kaiser and King the counsel which you thought it your duty to give as a result of your considered view of the situation. Whether that view was correct cannot be finally decided until all the facts of those unhappy days are known.

Such was Hindenburg's reward. His sovereign graciously accepted his gesture of assuming responsibility, but intimated that it was very late in coming and that he was not at all convinced that the Marshal's conduct, though loyal in intent, was justified by events. Hindenburg had not succeeded in appeasing his Emperor and had given to the Nationalists that hold over himself which they desired. From thence to the end he was a hostage in their hands, urged on to adopt policy after policy, to veer from one course of action to another, always with the same end in mind, to restore the monarchy and thus lay the spectre of Spa for ever.

In these years of his second retirement from the army Hindenburg took no part in the public life of Germany. Unlike Ludendorff, who drifted more and more rapidly into open opposition to the Republic, he maintained a dignified silence. Of the Kapp *putsch* of 1920, the Communist risings of 1923 in Saxony and Thuringia, and the Nazi revolt in Munich during the same year, he remained an impassive spectator, and if he thought anything at all of Adolf Hitler after this last escapade, he probably shared the opinion of Professor Maurice Gerothwohl who, in editing Lord D'Abernon's diaries in 1928, said that the National Socialist leader had "vanished into oblivion."

The Marshal lived his life in peace and in such contentment as any German could find in that tragic period of his country's fortunes. He shot chamois in Bavaria and made such additions to his collection of pictures of the Madonna that the walls of one room of the house at Hanover became completely covered with paintings, etchings, plaques, and ikons representing the Holy Mother and Child. The period of the war, and more particularly of the years 1918–19, had exhausted him more than he had at first realized. He was dead tired, and there is no doubt that during these years of rest and quiet he acquired those great reserves of strength which enabled him to survive the trials of office to come. He possessed the priceless faculty of being able to shut himself off at certain intervals from all cares and to indulge in complete mental relaxation, by means of the physical joys of the chase or the aesthetic pleasure of his collection.

His public appearances were rare and were usually limited to the dedication of some war-memorial or to some re-union of ex-Service men. The outcome of one of these affairs was so tragic that for a long time he would not attend a meeting again. It was at Königsberg in June 1922. The Marshal had agreed to take the salute of a Nationalist parade and to address a demonstration. The social unrest, which accompanied the steady decline of the mark, was at that time already far advanced, and in order to avoid the danger of a clash the Prussian Minister of Interior forbade members of the *Reichswehr*, school children, and public officials to attend the meeting. Despite this order there was a very great attendance. Former officers of State, the leaders of the Nationalist Party, the Association of ex-Officers, and generals of the Old Army, all flocked to Königsberg. The Marshal attended in full parade uniform and received a tremendous ovation; his car was filled with bouquets flung by his admirers. But the Communist Party had organized a counter-demonstration, and the inevitable clash occurred; serious riots took place in which a number of people were killed. Hindenburg was so appalled at the outcome that for over a year he refused to appear in public again.

It was only the tenth anniversary of Tannenberg in 1924 which tempted him forth from his seclusion, when, with Ludendorff, Mackensen, François, and Seeckt, now commander of the *Reichswehr,* he dedicated the memorial at Hohenstein before a gathering of more than a hundred thousand people. To him fell the honour of striking the foundation stone; and he struck three times, dedicating each blow in clear, measured tones. The first, he said, was struck to the fallen in grateful memory, the second to the living for remembrance, and the last to the future generation, that they might vie in achievement with their ancestors. But in the whole celebration there was a sense of incompleteness, the feeling that something was lacking. Hoffmann was not there.

Despite Hindenburg's reserve and retirement, his name was

kept continually before the public eye, sometimes in the strangest
and most embarrassing connection. In the *Reichstag* elections in
1924 there appeared a variety of strange and irresponsible political parties which invited the support of the voters. Amongst
these was the League of Herr Hausser, an "Apostle," who had
but one slogan, "Who loves his Fatherland better than the axe,
vote Hausserbund!" His gospel, which was preached in working-
class districts by long-haired disciples of both sexes, with quaint
robes and sandalled feet, called for an immediate alienation of
superfluous capital. Those who did not comply voluntarily with
its demands after the establishment of a dictatorship were to be,
without more ado, decapitated, and the dictator whom it was
proposed to appoint to carry out this somewhat drastic programme was Hindenburg!

For Germany the years of Hindenburg's second retirement
were years of the darkest and most bitter internal conflict. Saddled with the burden of a peace to which her signature had been
forced, Germany resisted step by step the execution of the treaty
provisions. The first act of defiance in the refusal to surrender
the "war criminals" had been followed by others, chiefly in the
field of disarmament and reparation payments, and the spirit of
the country was steadfastly opposed to "fulfilment." For this attitude of mind the Allies were themselves very largely responsible. A harsh peace had been followed by the continuation of a
war mentality towards Germany, and no attempt was made to
give assistance to the German Government, who were at first not
unwilling to do their best to carry out the treaty provisions.
Germany was the malefactor upon whom a crushing sentence had
been imposed; no help must be offered her in carrying out this
sentence, but, if she did not do so, further and more dire penalties awaited her.

Men were not wanting on the side of the Allies who viewed
the situation in a saner light, and foremost amongst these was

Major-General Sir Neill Malcolm, head of the British Military Mission in Berlin, whose reports had played an important part in moderating the original conditions of peace. Most Germans are unaware of what they owe to General Malcolm, but from those who know and understand he has earned undying gratitude, and even to-day, within the Third Reich, his name is still one to conjure with.[1] Before the Revolution of 1933 many Germans in the highest positions in the State expressed to the writer the belief that but for General Malcolm's timely advice to successive Chancellors, the Weimar Republic would have almost certainly fallen a prey either to forces of Bolshevism or Reaction, and that before his departure in 1921 he had, through his own personal connections, opened the way for the policy of the Locarno Agreement.

From the moment the Treaty of Peace was signed the General urged a spirit of helpfulness upon the Allied Governments.

Now that peace is signed [he wrote on June 30, 1919], I think we should do all that we can to support the German Government, and show it sympathy. It will be attacked by the military on one side and the Independents on the other. Either, if successful, would be disastrous for the country and a danger to Europe. We *need* a stable Germany. . . . If we could in any way alleviate the strict execution of the peace terms it would be a very great help. Germany can only be controlled either by promises of help towards reconstruction or by military action. Threats will hardly control her.

The Allied Powers failed to act on this eminently sane advice, which was based not upon false sentimentality but upon sound common sense. They insisted upon the most exacting fulfilment of the peace terms and made no concessions which were not wrung from them by the sheer inexorability of facts. Had, how-

[1] The release of Friedrich Ebert, the son of the former *Reichspräsident*, from a Nazi concentration camp in the winter of 1933 was largely due to a letter to *The Times* from Sir Neill Malcolm.

ever, the counsel of General Malcolm, and of other similarly enlightened individuals, been followed, it is more than probable that the National Socialist Party would either never have come to exist, or would at least have found its grave on the Odeonsplatz at Munich, where, as Lord D'Abernon wrote scathingly in his diary, "Hitler's courage was unequal to the occasion." Nor probably would Hindenburg have been elected President of the Republic, for it was the intransigency of the Allies that supplied the Nationalists with their political *raison d'être*, providing them with those cogent arguments with which, when the occasion arose, they were able to hale the old veteran forth once more to save Germany from the Social Democrats.

Obstinacy bred obstinacy. Faced with the cold insistence of the Allies abroad, and threatened from the Right and from the Left at home, it was impossible for the new Germany to acquire a strong government. A procession of Chancellors passed through the palace in the Wilhelmstrasse, like the ghostly kings in Macbeth, each holding a mirror. Bauer, Fehrenbach, Wirth, Marx, and Cuno, each fell as his predecessors had fallen, and wherever a statesman arose in Germany, Nationalist gunmen meted out to him the penalty of "treason." In this form death came to Erzberger in the Black Forest during 1920, and to Rathenau in the suburbs of Berlin a year later, their only crime being that of *Erfüllung* [1] (Fulfilment).

The policy of obstinate resistance, pursued *nolens volens* by successive German Governments, reached its climax in 1923 with the invasion of the Ruhr and, its corollary, the campaign of passive resistance. Europe seemed faced with a hopeless deadlock and a complete financial debacle was threatening in Germany which would inevitably have its repercussions throughout

[1] Seven years later, in 1929, André Tardieu, speaking in the French Chamber on this series of assassinations, demanded: *"Est-ce qu'il faut mourir, pour prouver qu'on est sincère?"*

the world. It was the darkest moment which post-war European history had so far known. Then, just as the gospel of fulfilment had all but perished, it found a new apostle in Gustav Stresemann. "The man and the hour had met."

The metamorphoses of politicians into statesmen is among the many strange developments which have taken place in Germany since the war. Matthias Erzberger, the intriguer, Walter Rathenau, the advocate of a *levée en masse*, Gustav Stresemann, the jingo annexationist and mouthpiece of the High Command, all had travelled since 1918 the road to Damascus, and in the course of their journeys had "seen a great light." These men were the founders and martyrs—for Stresemann, though he more than once escaped an assassin's bullet, nevertheless gave his life for the cause—of that Policy of Fulfilment which in later years was so nearly carried to success by their great compatriot, Heinrich Brüning. Their failure, and the consequent tension in Europe, was certainly not due to their lack of effort.

On September 26, 1923, Stresemann took the most momentous decision of his career and in the foreign policy of the Weimar Republic, by abandoning the policy of obstinate resistance for that of constructive negotiation. He declared the cessation of passive resistance in the Ruhr, and thereby paved the way for the Micum Agreements between the German industrialists and the Allied Commission of Control. By so doing he had taken the first step along the road to the Dawes Plan in the following year, to the Locarno Agreements and the entry of Germany into the League of Nations, and to that ultimate realization of his dream, the evacuation of the Rhineland, which he himself was not destined to see.

Though Hindenburg was but a spectator of these events, their repercussions did not leave him untouched. In the height of the storm of radicalism and protest which swept the country after the murder of Rathenau, the Chancellor, Josef Wirth, had decláred passionately in the *Reichstag*, referring to the instigators of the policy of assassination, that "This enemy stands on the Right." This well-merited denunciation of the Nationalists' campaign of terror and assassination found its echo in Hanover, where Hindenburg was publicly accused in the City Council of being the secret head of a national league of assassins, and mobs, who once had brought him in triumph to his home, now demonstrated outside it, clamouring for his immediate removal from the city. So venomous did the attack become that he threatened to disinter the body of his wife and go and live in East Prussia.

The storm subsided, however, and peace reigned once more around the home on the Seelhorststrasse. The Marshal was never again disturbed by hostile agitation, and the only inconvenience he suffered was from the popular ovations which soon recommenced whenever he stirred abroad. The years of his retirement had a mellowing effect upon him, and the mental scars of the war were gradually obliterated. In his Hanover retreat and in the deep quiet of the Bavarian mountains he recaptured the peace of mind which had long eluded him. The spectre of Spa, though still unlaid, was more remote from him now, and deep reflection was maturing his judgment of the new world in which he lived. Had he written his memoirs in 1924 they might well have been worthier of him, and it is improbable that he would have endorsed so readily the fallacious theory of the "stab-in-the-back."

He was seventy-seven years old, and it seemed as if the remainder of his days would be passed in the dignified retirement which he had so well deserved. *"Ich will meine Ruhe haben,"* he would answer to all attempts to lure him into public life, and better would it have been for him and for his memory could he have had it. But again Fate willed otherwise. All unknown to Hindenburg his days of peace were numbered. His third "life" was about to open before him.

· 2 ·

On February 28, 1925, died Friedrich Ebert, last Imperial Chancellor and first President of the German Reich. Not perhaps a great man as judged by the world's standards, he was one for whom no German need feel anything but admiration. Great courage, firm singleness of purpose, and no little statesmanship were his outstanding attributes, and lesser men would have shrunk from the overwhelming responsibilities which the former saddler, joiner, and café-keeper was called upon to take up at the moment of his country's downfall. He was a man of destiny *malgré lui*, but though reared in a school of party strife and factional hatred, once greatness was thrust upon him he assumed with it a dignity and a nobility of spirit that were unexpected. Though his patriotism was often and bitterly impugned by his opponents, in reality it never wavered for an instant. It was not that fanatical, self-defeating breed of patriotism which works for immediate results only and takes no thought for the morrow, but rather was it one which was ready to bear all things for the moment if by so doing a richer heritage might be bequeathed to future generations. Thus, having been prepared to resist acceptance of the Peace Treaty to the uttermost so long as a reasonable chance of resistance remained, once the treaty had been signed and ratified, he fearlessly championed its fulfilment. In him Erzberger, Rathenau, and Stresemann had found a loyal supporter.

During Ebert's presidency Germany had risen from the ashes of her defeat, and at his death she stood on the threshold of re-entry into the family of European nations. The Weimar régime had, like the infant Third French Republic in 1871, survived the flight of its Government from the capital in the face of armed revolt, and Ebert had returned from Stuttgart, like Thiers from Versailles, if not in triumph, at least bringing with

him the beginnings of stability. The country had gradually revived economically and politically, and had gained once more a
position among the Powers. That wizard of German finance, Dr.
Hjalmar Schacht, and the Finance Minister, Hans Luther, had
reduced the monetary circulation and confined it within economic limits, in addition they had made huge reductions in
personnel and abolished economically unproductive organizations, thus completing the liquidation of the socialist legislation
of the war and the revolution. Politically, Ebert himself had
resisted the separatist activities in the west and had cemented the
Reich of Weimar into a more stable edifice. Stresemann, having
rehabilitated the country in the eyes of the world, was on the eve
of greater triumphs.

Ebert's sudden death, at the age of fifty-four, was a disaster
for Germany and for Europe, for his work, though within an
ace of success, was still uncompleted. Germany was standing at
the cross-roads between democracy and reaction, and though for
a moment political strife was stilled, it needed but the spark of
a national election for the old hatreds to blaze up again in all
their fury. Thus, while Ebert was borne with funereal pomp and
dignity to his burial men asked themselves apprehensively who
his successor would be.

By the Constitution the election of a president must take place
within a month of the termination of the period of office of his
predecessor, or, alternatively, from the date of vacancy, by the
"common, equal, direct, and secret vote" (*allgemeine, gleiche,
unmittelbare und geheime Wahl*) of every citizen, male and
female, who had reached the age of twenty. To be elected, a
candidate had to receive an absolute majority of the votes cast,
and if this were not secured, a second ballot was held in which
only a simple majority was necessary.

Clearly, then, there was not much time to spare, and negotiations were at once opened between the party leaders to find a candidate who could unite the forces of the moderate parties, or even have, in the second ballot, the support of the Nationalists or the Social Democrats. The obvious man for this choice was Otto Gessler, the bullet-headed Bavarian leader of the Democratic Party, who had succeeded Noske as Minister of Defence after the Kapp *putsch* in 1920 and had held that office ever since. Gessler, who, like Gröner, was the son of an N.C.O., had risen to be Bürgermeister of Nürnberg and had been Ebert's most intimate friend in political life. He had done much to cement the loyalty of the *Reichswehr* to the Weimar régime, a fact which had largely contributed to the successful handling of the National Socialist and Communist risings in the autumn of 1923. He had all the innate "canniness" and some of the cunning of the *petit bourgeois* mind; his public record was a good one and he seemed an eminently suitable successor to Ebert.

The candidature of Gessler was strenuously opposed by the extreme Nationalists, but he was acceptable to the majority of the parties, and negotiations had progressed so far that at a meeting in the *Reichstag* of the members of the Centre Party it was announced that there was a safe majority for him as the candidate of a *bloc* composed of the Social Democrats, Centre, Democrats, and the German People's Party. His nomination seemed assured when suddenly in the lobbies a whisper began to circulate connecting Gessler's name in liaison with a certain Berlin lady of high position. It was a malicious slander spread by the extreme Right, but it had the desired effect. Throughout the *Reichstag* building, where meetings of other political parties were being held, the rumour ran like a flame, followed by a further canard, emanating this time from the extreme Left, that, if Gessler were adopted as a Majority candidate, the French Government would at once make revelations regarding their dossier on the secret military organizations such as the Black *Reichswehr, Orgesch,* and others.

It was, however, the imputation against Gessler's good name that did him most harm. The members of the parliamentary *fraktionen* knew well that the allegation was untrue, but the slander caught hold upon the imagination of the delegates from the country and the provincial towns. Hours passed in fruitless efforts on the part of Gessler's friends to convince a majority of representatives in the parties that the rumour was false. Excited debates took place in every committee-room, and in the corridors the Nationalists rubbed their hands with glee. They had defeated the one move which they feared most, the adoption of a Majority candidate; the forces opposed to them would now be divided, and a Nationalist candidate stood a very good chance of heading the poll.

In part they were right. Gessler's nomination was dropped and there remained neither the time nor the inclination to find another Majority candidate. Though for the Republicans the only point of real importance was that a genuine Republican of proved loyalty should be elected, the Republican parties were now hopelessly divided, each putting forward a separate candidate for the people's choice.

Meanwhile in the Nationalist camp there was a hasty call-over of possible candidates for the throne once their electoral candidate had triumphed at the polls and had fulfilled his task of restoring the monarchy. Too much attention was given to these day-dreams and too little to the selection of the candidate himself. Eventually a bargain was struck with the German People's Party, whereby their candidate, Dr. Jarres, the Bürgermeister of Duisberg, should appear as the joint nominee of the two parties acting together as a *Reichsblok.*

There were dissensions in the parties of the Right also. Ludendorff, whose part in the Munich *putsch* of 1923 had been tacitly ignored at the subsequent trial, announced his intention of standing as the nominee of Adolf Hitler, who had recently been released from prison and was slowly and painfully rebuilding his political machine. It was the reappearance of Ludendorff in the arena under such a banner which provoked Hindenburg to break his silence on political subjects. In the name of their former friendship he wrote to Ludendorff begging him, as the first and last favour he would ever ask, to withdraw from the contest in which he could only meet with ignominy and defeat. But the Marshal's advice was never even acknowledged. Ludendorff, contemptuous of wise counsel, plunged into the fight with that same fanatical hatred of the Weimar System which had prompted his support of Kapp and Hitler. His defeat was no more humiliating than he merited, but by this time his reason was definitely affected, and he had adopted the worship of Thor and Odin, to whom altars were erected in the garden of his villa in Munich. To this eccentricity was later added the phobia that the destruction of German culture, and, indeed, of European civilization, was being encompassed by an unholy and surprising combination of world-Jewry, the Grand Orient, and the Roman Catholic Church!

On March 29, 1925, seven major candidates offered themselves to the electorate: Jarres, for the *Reichsblok;* Otto Braun, Prime Minister of Prussia since 1921, for the Social Democrats; Wilhelm Marx, a former Chancellor, for the Centre; Ernst Thälmann, for the Communists; Held, the Bavarian Prime Minister, for the Bavarian People's Party; Hellpach, for the Democrats; and General Ludendorff, for the National Socialists. The fight was bitter, no holds were barred. But, as had been obvious from the first to everyone except the *Reichsblok,* there could be no complete victory for any one candidate. The results of the ballot were:

Jarres	.	.	.	.	10,400,000
Braun	.	.	.	.	7,800,000
Marx	.	.	.	.	3,900,000
Thälmann	.	.	.		1,900,000
Hellpach	.	.	.	.	1,500,000
Held	.	.	.	.	1,000,000
Ludendorff	.	.	.		280,000

A second ballot was necessary. Both the Right and the Left had learned their lesson. Only by concentration could victory be won. A hasty reorganization of party machinery began in both camps. For the Republican parties the issue was a simple one. The Social Democrats, Centre, and Democrats allied themselves into *Weimarblok*, Braun and Hellpach giving way to Marx as candidate. This combination on the return of the first ballot could command a total of some thirteen million votes, and against it the possible concentration of the *Reichsblok* with the Bavarian People's Party and the National Socialists could not expect, on the same basis, more than twelve millions. Manifestly, if the forces of the Right were to triumph, a new candidate must be found, an outstanding personality who could not only steal votes from his opponents, but could rally to the Black-White-Red standard that floating vote whose unpredictable voice decides the issue in all elections.

Within the camp of the Nationalists, among the Junkers and the industrialists and ex-officers, were "tumult and affright." The chances of half a dozen possible candidates were canvassed and rejected. An Imperial Prince? No—no member of the House of Hohenzollern could oppose Marx with any hope of success. A general? Von Seeckt, the enigmatic commander of the *Reichswehr?* Again no, for, though he was the hero of Gorlice and the Rumanian campaigns, he had exercised since then dictatorial powers in Saxony and Bavaria, shedding the blood of Communists on the one hand, and of Nazis on the other, and this was no recommendation to the electorate. A great industrialist, such as Krupp von Bohlen or Thyssen? Here again, no, for these men were too representative of Big Business and all that that implied.

A week of precious time went by in vain dispute. Then came inspiration. As in a similar quandary at Coblenz eleven years before, the name of Hindenburg was proposed—though this time by the name of Hindenburg and not of Beneckendorff—and as before it was received first with surprised scepticism and then with general approval.

There had been some thought of his opposing Ebert for the presidency in 1920, when, with the formal inauguration of the Constitution, it was suggested that the president, who had only been elected by the National Assembly, should seek re-election by popular vote. The Kapp *putsch* had, however, put an end to any such proposal, and Ebert had been hastily confirmed in his office. Hindenburg himself had never seriously considered the matter, and would not, at that time, have been a desirable choice.[1] Again, in the selection of the *Reichsblok* candidate before the first ballot in March 1925, the *Landrat* Winkler, the leader of the Hanoverian delegates to the Nationalist party convention, had proposed Hindenburg's name, but had withdrawn the suggestion in face of considerable opposition, both from the German People's Party and from his own. He had, however, notified Jarres that he reserved full liberty of action if a second

[1] There is little doubt that, had the Kapp *putsch* succeeded, Hindenburg would have been hustled into the presidency to pave the way for the Kaiser's return. In the course of a conversation on December 7, 1919, with the famous American journalist, Karl von Wiegand, Colonel Bauer, who a few months later became one of the military leaders of the *putsch*, said, "We intend to restore the monarchy on the English model, and the election of Hindenburg would help us to that end"; and the notorious Nationalist cleric, Pastor Traub, said of the Marshal only a week before the *putsch* began, "He is not a man who would bar the way to a future Kaiser, on the contrary, he would prepare it."

ballot were necessary, and now his renewed proposal of the Marshal as candidate was greeted with relief and applause.

Of course the Nestor of Germany was the man; his picture was in every house and on every schoolgirl's dressing-table. His dignified silence throughout the early struggles of the Republic was in itself a strong recommendation, and the Hindenburg Legend was still strong in the land. Moreover—but this was only whispered in the inner circles of the party—was he not the Man of Spa, and must he not redeem his name from the slur of having sent his Emperor into exile, for which he had publicly admitted the responsibility? His yearning after Imperial yesterdays was notorious, and his famous dictum of the "stab-in-the-back" before the Committee of Enquiry was recalled with satisfaction. Above all, was he not the Arch-slave of Duty? Here was the man whose name would mobilize an army of voters and who, once selected, could be relied upon to make an end of the detested and ignoble Weimar System.

But there were obstacles which must be overcome before the Nationalists could get their way. Their allies of the German People's Party must first be "squared" and Jarres eliminated, and there was always the probability that Hindenburg would not stand. The German People's Party were not easily brought into line. They were still resolved to stand or fall by Jarres, and in this they were supported by Seldte and his ex-Service men's organization, the *Stahlhelm*. Stresemann was particularly opposed to the candidature of Hindenburg, but not upon personal grounds. Stresemann still retained that romantic admiration for the Marshal which had led him to champion so fervently the cause of the Supreme Command before the war-time *Reichstag*. His conversion to the Policy of Fulfilment had in no way dimmed his veneration for Germany's greatest public figure. But three months before, in the greatest confidence, he had opened the negotiations which ultimately resulted in the Pact of Locarno, the first international agreement to be freely negotiated by Germany. To speak of it then would have meant death both for him and for his project, for the extreme Nationalists would not, and later did not, shrink from plotting his assassination, and such knowledge of the negotiations as had been made public had provoked the fiercest opposition. Stresemann knew his Europe well enough to foresee how foreign countries would react to the election of the incarnation of Prussian militarism, and a "war criminal" to boot, as President of the Reich, and, great as was his admiration for Hindenburg, still greater was his life's ambition to free the Rhineland from foreign occupation.

Passionately he exhorted Jarres not to withdraw in favour of Hindenburg, advancing every argument which might prevent such a disaster. The Marshal was too old and too ignorant of politics. He would be the tool of the Nationalists and would be used to undo all the work of the past six years; alternately, it was unjust that this great figure should be exposed to the rough-and-tumble of an electoral contest and to the venomous intrigues of political life. Under no consideration must Jarres withdraw.

But Jarres was unable to resist the pressure of the Nationalists, and in any case he had little real desire to exchange the minor problems of the city of Duisburg for the gigantic tasks of the Presidency. He turned a deaf ear to Stresemann's pleadings, gracefully withdrew his name as candidate of the Right, and returned thankfully to the obscurity from which he had been dragged.

So far the Nationalists had got their way, but their greatest difficulties were to come. Their first tentative embassy to Hanover was met with a brusque, almost ungracious refusal. Hindenburg was suffering from a form of bronchial catarrh which would not yield to treatment, and this made him even more disinclined to re-enter public life. He had never been a party man, he said, and he had no intention of becoming one now.

He was shrewd enough to suspect that this sudden and anxious appeal to him was being made out of a desire to exploit him for party purposes. The deputation withdrew disheartened. Others took their place, but without any better success. Another week went by and still Hindenburg was adamant. To all the entreaties of Ditfurth, of Schiele, of Schlange, and of Schmidt, he made the same reply: *"Ich will meine Ruhe haben."*

"The Devil take you all!" was his exasperated dismissal of Schmidt. "I don't mind if he does, so long as we have you for Reichspresident!" was the reply.

His refusal became known in the press. The Nationalists were at their wits' end. Only a fortnight remained until the second ballot and they were still without a candidate. Could nothing be done to break the Marshal's resolution? In desperation Winkler turned to Grand-Admiral von Tirpitz for advice and it was the crafty old sailor who provided the solution. He had always believed in Hindenburg, and, it will be remembered, as early as January 1916 had wished him to become military and political dictator of Germany. Now his belief was coloured by a more intimate knowledge of the Marshal's mind, and he knew upon which chord to harp with success. The Marshal's chief objection, he said, was to standing as a *party* candidate; this idea therefore must be dropped. An appeal must be made to him to go to the electorate, not in the Nationalist, but in the National interest, and his sense of duty could not allow him to refuse such a call.

It was Tirpitz, with his tremolo voice and his long beard flowing in a silver fork over his coat, who came to Hanover to make the supreme appeal. He was a year younger than Hindenburg, but half a century older in guile and political cunning, and he handled the Marshal with a master's technique. To every objection barked out in the harsh military voice, the Admiral made a soft-toned reply which demolished the Marshal's arguments. Gradually Hindenburg ceased to argue and sat listening to Tirpitz's brilliant exposition of his case.

He quite understood, said the Admiral, the very natural disinclination of the Marshal to stand as a party candidate, but that was not the real issue at all. This was no factional fight but a national crusade. He depicted for the Marshal the state of the country, and particularly the situation in Prussia, and then added his irresistible call to duty. The country was crying out for a "saviour" and in its need it turned again to the great figure who had never forsaken it. A great sacrifice was being asked of Hindenburg, no doubt; his age and his distinguished record unquestionably entitled him to a peaceful retirement, but throughout that long life had he not always looked upon subordination of self to duty as the highest form of service? The Fatherland was calling to him to save it from national discord and foreign domination, the great mass of the people looked to him for guidance. Could he refuse their appeal?

Thus Tirpitz in his silvery voice played upon the sensibilities of Hindenburg. He had caught the Marshal by his sword-knot and had struck the one note of appeal which he could never resist. But Tirpitz had hidden from Hindenburg the fact that the support which could be expected from the electorate was not nearly so great, nor the demand of the Fatherland so unanimous as he had depicted. He had not mentioned the scruples of Stresemann or the opposition of the *Stahlhelm*. He had led the Marshal to believe that if he accepted the nomination, he would meet with very little opposition.

Hindenburg had been definitely shaken by Tirpitz's eloquence. If the country really was in so bad a condition and he was the only man who could save it, had he the right to refuse? Devotion to duty was with him a fetish, service a guidon which he had always followed. Yet there was his loyalty to his Emperor, renewed publicly only three years before. Again the clash of fealties, the hesitation, the choice between right and right.

He had wavered from his former inflexibility, but he would not give a definite answer. He must, he said, have three days to think of it. To-day was April 6? He would give them his decision on the 9th.

But Tirpitz returned to Berlin well satisfied. He knew his man and he knew that he had implanted in his mind that seed of doubt which would blossom forth in the flower of acceptance. For him there was little uncertainty as to the answer which Hindenburg would give.

Nor was he wrong. For three days the Marshal pondered his decision in Hanover. His election would mean a complete break with his former traditions, he would become the salaried servant of the Republic and the chief guardian of its Constitution. Hitherto he had never pledged himself. A brief note to Ebert from Spa, confirming the agreement made with Gröner, was his only official connection with the Weimar System. But now . . . ? There was his loyalty to his Emperor. Had he not written in 1922—and the letter had appeared in the press—that he would "remain always Your Imperial and Royal Majesty's most loyal subject"? To be sure, the Kaiser had answered him somewhat ungraciously; still, his declaration stood. But Germany? Germany was calling for him. He had fought for her in war, he had served her in the darkest hour of defeat, now he must answer again the call to the service of peace. The pomp and panoply of the presidency meant nothing to him, no man abhorred civilian display and ostentation more than Hindenburg. No man was more lacking in personal ambition. Far rather would he have preferred to remain in peace at Hanover and drink his glass of wine by the bank of the Leine. But to the call to duty there could only be one answer. He must serve.

He did not, as was widely reported, ask permission of the Emperor to accept the candidature. He arrived at his decision after deep personal reflection and consultation with his family and closest friends. He would stand for the presidency; if elected he would take the oath to the Constitution and would loyally defend it—until a further path of service was opened before him. But when, on April 9, 1925, he sent his answer to Berlin he had no other intention but the loyal and honest fulfilment of the new task which, unwillingly enough, he had agreed to undertake. Nothing, however, could change his personal loyalty to his Emperor; whatever his public views might be, his personal beliefs would remain the same. Had not Ebert, though President, remained a Socialist? With this balm he soothed his conscience. It was the inevitable sequel to his frequent clashes of loyalties—compromise, that compromise which Carlyle has called the "grave of the soul."

In the campaign which followed Hindenburg took little personal part. Much was promised in his name of which he knew nothing, and he passed through experiences which must have made him regret that he had ever agreed to stand. The mud and vitriol of an election was all so new to him, so alien to his soldier's notion of chivalry towards an enemy. While he ignored with stoical calm the venomous attacks of the opposition press upon himself, he was naïvely appalled to find similar vileness in the papers of the *Reichsblok* concerning Marx. "I will not allow such things to be said on my behalf," he told his personal staff. "I insist upon my political opponents receiving fair play from my supporters." The staff smiled a little cynically and promised "to see to it." The attacks on both sides continued.

Easter messages were issued to the electorate by both candidates. Hindenburg attempted to strike a personal note, but it was as empty as that of Marx; its chief interest was his evident difficulty in successfully reconciling his appearance as a candi-

date for the presidency of a republic with his well-known monarchist beliefs. He attempted to escape the issue by stressing
the essentially non-party character of the presidency.

My life lies open to all the world [he declared]. I believe that in
time of need I have done my duty. If this duty were to bid me now
as President of the Reich to work within the articles of the Constitution, without respect for party, persons, origin, or profession, I shall
not be found wanting. As a soldier I have always had the whole nation
before my eyes, and not its parties. Parties are necessary in a parliamentary state, but the Chief of the State must stand above them. . . . Just
as the first German President, even as Protector of the Constitution,
never concealed his origin from the ranks of labour, no one will be
able to expect of me that I should surrender my political convictions.

In this way the curious mental process of compromise was
made public. Ebert had been able to retain his republican beliefs whilst he was President of the Republic, therefore, he,
Hindenburg, could remain personally a loyal monarchist whilst
filling the same office. It was an argument which was difficult to
follow and betrayed more naïveté than one would have credited
to the Marshal.

His only other public announcements were made at a reception given to the German and foreign press, and a radio-broadcast
on the eve of the poll. The press reception was a *Bier-Abend* and
a very jolly affair. Hindenburg was in excellent form and
greeted his guests with the words: "I've asked you to come here,
gentlemen, in order to show you that I don't come riding on a
cannon nor yet in a bath-chair. I know that you all want from
me a statement on foreign policy, but I can't give it to you as
I'm not yet *Reichspräsident*, and in any case the Chancellor is
responsible for the conduct of foreign policy and not the President."

He answered an endless flood of questions with unfailing
good-humour and a generous display of elephantine wit. The

questions themselves ranged from the general to the personal, each inquirer vying with his neighbour as to how much information he could squeeze out of the old veteran. Most of them concerned peace and war, and the Marshal replied that he personally shared the opinion that Germany could gain only from peaceful development at home and abroad, and that he believed, as a military expert, that the country was incapable of defending itself against the smallest of her neighbours.

"What was the greatest day of your life, Field-Marshal?" somebody wanted to know, expecting as a reply some grandiloquent reference to Tannenberg. "The first time, when I was a cadet, that I was allowed to eat as many cakes and as much whipped cream as I liked," was the Marshal's answer.

"How many decorations have you?" asked another.

"Seventy-seven," was the reply; "one for each year of my age, but I didn't get one every year."

The climax was reached when a French journalist asked the Marshal to autograph a postcard which he proposed to send as a greeting to Marshal Foch. Hindenburg lost his laughing air. Instantly his thoughts went back to his unanswered offer of July 1919, and he replied grimly, "That gentleman has long since refused to know me, and I never write to strangers."

The broadcast address was not such a success. Hindenburg had never seen a microphone before, and was nervous and embarrassed. He spoke somewhat haltingly and kept time by beating with his clenched fist on the table before him. To the listening public his voice came accompanied by an obbligato of thumps, but as they strained their ears they could hear him declaiming before all the world his determination, born of personal experience in youth and in old age, to avert the horrors of war. The rest was an appeal for, and a promise of, unity at home and patriotic behaviour, and both listeners and speaker seemed relieved when the address was over. But, like many a man making his first broadcast, Hindenburg, as soon as he had finished, forgot his great unseen audience, and so it came about that in thousands of German homes he was heard saying with evident relief to the official beside him, "Well, thank God that's over."

Throughout the rest of his life he never conquered his dislike for the microphone, and when, later, it became necessary for him as President to address the German people by wireless, a phonograph record was made of his speech and released at the appointed moment to the listening public, who fervently believed that it was the President himself who spoke to them.

Polling-day, Sunday April 26, was spent by Hindenburg at Gross-Schwülper, the estate of Oskar's mother-in-law, the Baroness von Marenholtz, near Brunswick. He was quite untouched by the general excitement and passed the day walking in the park and playing with his grandchildren. About 9 o'clock in the evening the results began to come in, and it was evident that the Marshal was not going to have an easy victory. The towns, the strongholds of Social Democracy and of the trade unions, were for the *Weimar-Blok,* and more than once during the evening Marx was heading the poll. But the country districts, where the great landowners could influence the choice of their peasants, voted for Hindenburg, and gradually his tally began to mount.[1] Even then he would not have been successful were it not for the stirring-up of Protestant feeling against the Catholic Marx in Prussia, Thuringia, and Saxony, and in the country round Halle and Magdeburg, where the Social Democrats and even the Communists forsook their party allegiance and voted for Hindenburg.

At his usual hour of 10 o'clock the Marshal went uncon-

---

[1] People voted for Hindenburg for a variety of reasons. One Bavarian peasant girl told her friends that she had seen a picture of him "holding a candle" and had given her vote for him because she thought he must be a good Christian man. What she had actually seen was a photograph of Hindenburg grasping his Field-Marshal's bâton!

cernedly to bed, but his son Oskar sat up with paper and pencil till a late hour beside the radio. By midnight it was certain that the Marshal had been elected with a slight margin of votes, and in the small hours of Monday morning the final figures were announced:

Hindenburg	.	.	.	14,655,766
Marx	.	.	.	13,751,615
Thälmann	.	.	.	1,931,151

It had been a very close thing, less than a million majority, and no absolute majority at that; but they had won nevertheless, and Oskar went to bed happy.

At 7 o'clock next morning he brought his father the news of victory. "Well," replied the newly-elected President testily, "why did you want to wake me up an hour earlier to tell me? It would still have been true at eight"; and back he went to sleep. On being called at his usual hour, he awoke to a graver view of the position. His natural piety was touched and he said very seriously: "May God bless the choice of the German people and make it a prosperous one."

Messages of congratulation poured in from all quarters, and amongst the first was a telegram from Marx offering to his victorious opponent his loyal co-operation in the future. Hindenburg was greatly touched by this gesture, and reaffirmed to his staff his firm intention to be strictly impartial. "I propose to hold out the hand of fellowship to my late opponents as if they were my most trusted friends," he declared; and he certainly justified his words in the case of Marx, for twice within the next seven years he called him to be Chancellor.

Many others sent him their congratulations, and among them was Franz von Papen, Catholic nobleman, former military attaché in Washington, *Herren-reiter*, and deputy for the Centre

Party in the Prussian Landtag. Papen had not at this stage reached that felicitous relationship with the Marshal which he was later to enjoy, but he was sufficiently alive to future possibilities to desert the cause of his party and his party's candidate, Marx, and to campaign zealously for Hindenburg on the grounds that the political future of the Centre Party was threatened if it allied itself with the Left in electing a President. He was successful in drawing away a considerable number of Catholic votes to Hindenburg, and on the latter's victory he telegraphed that he would not wish to be "missing from the ranks of those who offer their thanks to their great leader, who, at this vital moment, has been willing to make sacrifices in order to take the fate of the nation into his trusted hand." Papen added that even as a Centre Party deputy he had not ceased to urge support for the Marshal on the principle of "the Fatherland above Party." With this move began that strange friendship which continued unbroken for more than nine years, until Hindenburg's death. It was a comradeship so wholly disastrous for Germany that it is the more curious to note that it was the only friendship in Hindenburg's life that was not marred by any suggestion of treachery on his part.

A host of visitors descended upon Hanover; the Chancellor and other high State officials, and the leaders and artificers of the *Reichsblok*, all came to pay their respects to the new Chief of State. Luther was agreeably surprised. In discussing the arrangements for the inauguration ceremony, he found Hindenburg most friendly and helpful, and it was in this attitude that the Nationalists were to receive the first of many shocks experienced during the coming months. It had been fully expected that Hindenburg, despite his campaign statements, would refuse to take the oath to the Constitution and would not recognize the Black-Gold-Red of the *Reichsbanner*, which had superseded the *schwarz-weiss-rot* of Imperial Germany, as the national colours. But, to the delighted surprise of the Chancellor, the President-elect raised no objection either to oath or to flag, merely stipulating that the form of oath should not be civil but a religious one, taken upon the Gospels.

Otto Meissner, too, called upon Hindenburg.

Few men, with the exception of Adolf Hitler, have influenced the post-war history of their country more than this seemingly very typical square-headed German Civil Servant, and the full story of the strange part which he played is still to be written. Born in Alsace, the son of a German immigrant and an Alsatian mother, Otto Meissner had studied constitutional law, but had found employment as a Civil Servant in the State Railways of the *Reichsland*. His experience in this capacity led to his transfer during the war to the Ukraine, where Gröner was reorganizing the railway system. Here Meissner met Rudolph Nadolny, who became his immediate superior and whose fortunes he followed during the troublous days of the Revolution. Nadolny became secretary to Ebert at Weimar, and Meissner was closely associated with him throughout that period of tragedy. When the office of the President came to be organized, Nadolny became Secretary of State, but when, in 1920, he was appointed Ambassador to Angora, his assistant, Meissner, succeeded him in his high office.

In that position, which, after fifteen years, he still occupies (1936), he has swayed the policies of post-war Germany to no little extent, and with considerable political agility has succeeded in serving and pleasing three such diverse personalities as Ebert, Hindenburg, and Hitler! To call him a turn-coat would be too drastic; to accuse him of premeditated treachery would be unfair; but, doubtless with the best possible intentions, he has provided in modern times the most outstanding example of a political Vicar of Bray.

At this moment, in 1925, however, Meissner came to Hanover with certain apprehensions. The Nationalists, who were anxious to get rid of him as a representative of the detested System, had let it be known that the new President, in exercising his right of appointment, would choose as his Secretary of State Lieutenant-Colonel von Feldmann, an old friend and a member of his former Staff who had been chief of his election bureau in Hanover, and Meissner approached the house in the Seelhorststrasse in uncertainty as to his future.

But here again Hindenburg disappointed his followers. He recognized in Meissner the man who, under Ebert, had formulated and defined the office of the presidency which the Weimar Constitution, itself drawn up in haste, had left vague and undetermined. He realized that in the tasks ahead of him Meissner's vast knowledge and experience of procedure and custom, and of the parliamentary routine, of which he himself was ignorant, would be of greater service to him than the pleasing companionship of the loyal Feldmann, and he expressed his feelings in characteristic terms: "When a lieutenant becomes a company-commander he keeps the old sergeant-major." He therefore confirmed Meissner in his office, and, in so doing, made a decision which was to be no less important in his life than his meeting with Ludendorff.

For Hindenburg's third "life" was to be very largely influenced by his new "marriage" with Meissner, a union in which the latter, like Ludendorff, held the rôle of the dominant husband, and with very much the same effect. For, as Hindenburg had been malleable in Ludendorff's hands so was he in the hands of Meissner, upon whom he leaned more and more with advancing years; and, similarly, just as for the first period of their partnership Ludendorff's influence over the Marshal had been for good rather than otherwise, so in the early years of office Meissner guided the feet of the President through the difficult paths of constitutional government. The tragic sequels were also similar. Ludendorff, in the grip of megalomania, carried his chief, perhaps unwillingly, into the seas of tortuous intrigue till the inevitable shipwreck overwhelmed them both. Meissner, perhaps unwittingly, allowed his unknowing leader to fall into the hands of the *Camarilla*. Death saved Hindenburg from a full realization of the truth.

And yet there had to be a Meissner, for, if Hindenburg had been appointed as a figure-head in 1914, he was infinitely more so in 1925. It was inevitable and essential that some shadow-figure, some *eminence grise*, should stand behind him and prompt his actions. The full portent of their relationship was defined at that very moment with terrifying accuracy of proph-ecy by Theodore Lessing. "From the very moment when this least political of men is mis-cast for a political rôle another will be the decisive factor," he wrote. "This man, through and through, is a man of service; there are not even the beginnings of a personality capable of deciding, measuring and considering. Here the sole essential will always be the instruction, the tradi-tion, the consensus that 'one certainly must' or 'one certainly must not.' . . . He will remain the 'good shepherd and pro-tector' only so long as some clever man is there who will interest him in his duties and arrange them for him. A nature like Hin-denburg's will ask until he dies—'Where can I serve?' . . . It may be said, 'Better a zero than a Nero.' Unfortunately, the course of history has shown that behind a zero lurks always a future Nero." [1]

The ceremony of inauguration was arranged for May 12, and the President-elect left Hanover the day before. His way

---

[1] How truly the writer had foreseen the tragic course of events he was to prove terribly in his own person, for no sooner had the "Nero" appeared than Theodore Lessing was murdered by Nazi gunmen on neutral Czechoslovak territory (Septem-ber 1933).

to Berlin was one continuous triumph. No Emperor or King received such a welcome. The *Bürgermeister* Tramm was at the station to bid him farewell, and with him Noske, now President of the province of Hanover, the fiery revolutionary of 1918, scarcely recognizable beneath the frock-coat and top-hat of officialdom. At the capital it was the same, cheering masses, rigid ranks of troops, the shrill cries of children, and flowers everywhere. Twice before in his life he had ridden victoriously through the Brandenburger Tor; once in 1866 following the King of Prussia, and again in 1871 in the train of the German Emperor. It had been his fond hope that he might be granted a third triumphal entry with Wilhelm II, but this had been denied him. Instead, the triumph was his own and, acclaimed as a sovereign, he passed upon his way.

He slept that night in the palace of the Chancellor, which he had not entered since the eve of Ludendorff's dismissal. What ghosts and memories were stored within those rooms! The great bulk of Bismarck, whose life's work Hindenburg had helped unwittingly to shatter; his fellow soldier Caprivi; Hohenlohe, the princely statesman; the intriguing Bülow, whom he had tried with Ludendorff to recall; the grey ghost of Bethmann Hollweg; the pathetic figure of Michaelis, scuttling across the stage, the puppet of the Supreme Command; the grey-bearded shadow of the senile and incapable Hertling; and Max of Baden, that transient, embarrassed phantom. Memories of dead and living thronged the palace, and one likes to think that the spirit of Ebert revisited his old room and, brooding there a while, a little apprehensively perhaps, over the great recumbent figure of his successor, wished him good fortune in the great tasks before him.

But, undisturbed by any recollection of the past, Hindenburg slept the exhausted sleep of the very old, and awoke upon the threshold of his third official "life." The only memory that was to haunt him till his death was that of an exiled monarch, to whom he still pledged loyalty but in whose place he now ruled. The spectre of Spa could not have been far from him that morning. "Nevertheless"—the motto of his house—with a firm voice, in the ringing tones of a Prussian officer, he took the oath before the assembled *Reichstag:* "I swear by God, the Almighty and the All-knowing, that I will devote my powers to the welfare of the German people, increase its benefits, turn danger from it, guard the Constitution and the Laws of the *Reich,* conscientiously fulfil my duties, and do justice towards everyone, so help me God."

· 3 ·

Thus, at the age of seventy-eight, Hindenburg found himself embarking upon a new career of the elements of which he was entirely ignorant and for which he, of all men, was supremely unfitted by nature. No one was more essentially non-political in mind than Hindenburg, and his natural and expressed aversion to politics made him tend more and more to confide to other and less scrupulous hands the reins of office which should not have left his own control.

This tendency to delegate authority was the more important because of the powers conferred upon the President by the Constitution. He was elected for seven years—though in 1925 no one expected that Hindenburg would survive his term, let alone successfully weather a second election—and represented the German people to the world; alliances and treaties were concluded in his name and he could nominate and dismiss the Chancellor, and, on the latter's advice, the Ministers of the *Reich.* The Constitution gave him authority to compel the Federal States, if necessary by force of arms, to fulfil the obligations incurred under the Constitution and the Laws of the *Reich,* and he had power to suspend provisionally the fundamental liberties of the citizen, if in his opinion such action was required for the maintenance of public law and order.

Ebert had wielded these powers with understanding and discretion, and in creating them the Fathers of the Constitution at Weimar had always envisaged the presidency as being occupied by an experienced republican and democrat, never by a military veteran with expressed monarchist sympathies and no political knowledge. But in this negative quality he was highly representative of the German people as a whole, who are among the least politically minded in the world. That they elected Hindenburg at all is an indication that they obeyed the dictates of sentiment rather than of political sense, for a people schooled in politics would not have elected a monarchist who had never been anything else but a soldier to be the head of a democracy. For the consequences of this strange act on their part the German people must bear a share in the responsibility.

In the Cabinet of Dr. Luther, which Hindenburg inherited from his predecessor, two personalities stood out as representative of the only stable factors in the German political world. Stresemann and Gessler, representing foreign policy and the army, were destined to occupy their respective Ministries, the one for six and the other for eight years, during which time their policies remained unchanged and directed towards the fulfilment of a certain goal. In many respects these policies were at variance. Stresemann sought by means of the Policy of Fulfilment to assure peace in Europe and to secure the evacuation of the Rhineland; Gessler's policy was based almost entirely on the negation of *Erfüllung*. His ambition was to build up, within the specifications and restrictions of the Treaty of Versailles, as efficient and as well-equipped a Defence Force as possible, but parallel with these official activities ran the military rapprochement with the Soviet Union, and the surreptitious encouragement, or at least condoning, of such illegal organizations as the Black *Reichswehr*.

It is characteristic of Hindenburg and of the anomalous conditions which prevailed in the Weimar Republic after his election, that the policies of both Stresemann and Gessler, in so far as he understood them, received his approval, and the foundation and evolution of both were factors of primary importance in his career.

Gustav Stresemann had begun his tenancy of the German Foreign Office in September 1923, and had signalized the immediate change in the external policy of his country by terminating the campaign of passive resistance, by which Germany, at a ruinous cost to herself, had rendered sterile the French invasion of the Ruhr. By so doing he took the first step along the seemingly endless road to the realization of his great ideal, the evacuation of the Rhineland by Allied troops, an ideal which was the motive force of his foreign policy. Less than a year later the negotiation of the London Agreements, in August 1924, placed reparation payments upon a business footing under the Dawes Plan, based for the first time not merely upon Allied desires for reparation but on Germany's capacity to pay. Further fruits of Stresemann's policy were a forty-million-pound "Dawes Loan" to Germany and, in addition, a vast influx of short-term credits given by private American and British finance houses to German states and municipalities. Germany had become rehabilitated in the eyes of the world, and international confidence in her economic and financial probity had been restored.

The change in the external position of the country enabled Stresemann to take a further step, which he had meditated for long in his own mind and in confidential conversations with the British Ambassador in Berlin, Lord D'Abernon. With the departure from office of the first Labour Government after the elections of October 1924, it became evident that Great Britain would reject the Geneva Protocol, that still-born child of the united socialistic idealism of Mr. MacDonald and M. Herriot. The moment had arrived when an alternative proposal, more in tune with the British thesis of "special arrangements to meet special needs," might succeed where the "umbrella" principle of the Protocol had failed, and, greatly daring, in February 1925 Stresemann put forward very tentatively, and with great secrecy, his plan for a multilateral pact of security and guarantee in Western Europe. Germany, he asserted, would be prepared to enter with Great Britain, France, and Italy, into a mutual understanding not to go to war with one another, the suggested substitute for the settlement of disputes being the negotiation of arbitration and conciliation treaties between the contracting parties. More important still was the additional statement that Germany was prepared to accept a pact expressly guaranteeing the existing territorial status (*gegenwärtiger Besitzstand*) *vis-à-vis* France.

The importance and daring of this proposal are evident. Despite the campaign of terror and assassination which had been waged by the extreme Nationalists against those German statesmen who had attempted to reach an understanding with the Allies, Stresemann was now offering not only to renounce war with the former enemies of Germany, but to recognize for all time the permanent separation of Alsace-Lorraine from the *Reich*. Had not the strictest secrecy been preserved as to the terms of the offer, Lord D'Abernon wrote in his diary, "there can be little question that Stresemann would have been turned out of office, and there is a strong possibility that he would have been assassinated."

But the secret was well-kept, and Stresemann's proposals were received with reserved approval in London and Paris. On two conditions—the inclusion of Belgium in the pact and the willingness of Germany to enter the League of Nations—Great Brit-

ain and France were prepared to treat the German project as a
basis of negotiation, and Stresemann willingly accepted their
counter-proposals. Then, and only then, did he feel sufficiently
secure to make public his policy, and, as he had expected, a
storm of obloquy and execration broke over him. Stresemann's
contention that his proposals involved for France the permanent
abandonment of a French frontier on the Rhine neither impressed nor satisfied the Nationalists. For them this policy of
Fulfilment and Renunciation (*Erfüllung und Preisgabe*) was
rank treachery. Not only would the proposed pact abandon forever Alsace-Lorraine to the French but it would set the seal of
solemn re-affirmation upon the accursed Treaty of Versailles.
Stresemann must go; his policy meant only further humiliation
for Germany.

It was at this critical moment that Ebert died, and at one
stroke the German political situation was thrown into the melting pot and Stresemann was robbed of his most powerful supporter. With infinite difficulty he concluded the agreement with
the Nationalists for a *Reichsblok,* with his own nominee, Jarres,
as candidate, and it may be understood how bitterly disappointed he was when he found himself unable to prevent Jarres
from withdrawing in Hindenburg's favour in the second ballot.
Nor was he at fault in his forecast. Allied opinion was critical
indeed of the Marshal's nomination and election. "Behind him,"
wrote *Le Temps,* "are enlisted all the forces of reaction and
revenge, which hope that he will hasten the day of Germany's
military resurrection"; and the *Nation Belge* tersely summed
up the situation in a single phrase, *"aujourd'hui Hindenburg—
demain le Kaiser";* while even *The Times* devoted a leading
article to the dangers of military leaders of democracies, drawing the inevitable parallel with Marshal MacMahon.

But the Nationalists were overjoyed. With Hindenburg elected
they could scotch, once and for all, these scandalous negotiations.

The veteran of 1870 would never agree to the permanent renunciation of Alsace-Lorraine. Here was an additional reason for Hindenburg's candidature. But here again the Marshal disappointed them.

An attack of angina pectoris, the result of weeks of anxiety and nervous strain, prevented Stresemann from accompanying the Chancellor on his visit to the President-elect at Hanover, but Luther's first act on his return to Berlin was to go to the sickroom of the Foreign Minister. With pleasure and surprise, he told Stresemann that where he had looked for opposition and obstruction he had encountered co-operation and understanding. What about foreign policy? asked Stresemann. Hindenburg had repeated the stock views of the Nationalists against the Security Pact and the League of Nations, Luther replied, but he did not think that in the final analysis he would make difficulties.

Stresemann's first meeting with the new President did not take place until May 19. A strange contrast they must have made; the towering mass of Hindenburg's great frame, still a little unaccustomed to presidential morning-dress, beside Stresemann's shorter figure, with its square, heavy, bloated face, smooth pink cheeks, and little twinkling eyes. He was the personification of the caricature German on the English music-hall stage, except for his hands, which were small and white, delicate as a woman's. He too was agreeably surprised by the helpful attitude of the Marshal. "He showed himself most objective," Stresemann wrote that night in his journal, "and appeared to understand the importance of our security proposals; and the indignant cry of the Nationalists, 'Renounce Alsace-Lorraine? Never!' never passed his lips." With regard to the League of Nations Hindenburg was more reserved, and evidently viewed it with personal repugnance; but Stresemann was impressed with his anxiety to clear Germany from the accusation of war-guilt, and, for his part, Hindenburg was delighted to discover the steps which Stresemann had already taken to combat this allegation.

So well did the interview proceed that, at its close, Hindenburg turned to his Foreign Minister and demanded brusquely: "If things are as you say, why are you always so furiously attacked?" "I replied with some irony," says Stresemann, "that I had frequently asked myself that same question!"

But though in principle a sense of understanding had been established between the two, Hindenburg's ignorance of politics and diplomacy rendered it very hard for Stresemann to keep him informed of the progress of negotiations, and there must have been many moments when he longed regretfully for the constructive criticism and support of Ebert. On June 9 he records, "I find it extremely difficult to discuss with him [Hindenburg] complex questions of foreign policy, because his grasp of the subject is very limited."

Still, Stresemann was fortunate in having only Hindenburg's ignorance and not his opposition to contend with, for the Nationalists brought every influence to bear upon the President that was unfavourable to the Foreign Minister, and saw to it that only statements critical of Stresemann were laid upon the Presidential table. At this moment their domination over Hindenburg was not, however, complete. Oskar's influence with his father had not yet reached that fatal degree which it afterwards achieved; moreover, the Palace *Camarilla* did not, as yet, exist, and under Meissner's guidance the President maintained his support of Stresemann's foreign policy.

Stresemann, his flanks secured, as it were, pressed forward with his two parallel series of negotiations with the Allied Powers, the first directly with Great Britain and France regarding the pact of security; the second, with the Conference of Ambassadors in reference to the final disarmament of Germany and the evacuation of the first Rhineland Zone. Gradually and with infinite difficulty the security negotiations proceeded towards success. Stresemann agreed to the French proposal that the East European Allies of France, Poland and Czechoslovakia, should be included among the contracting parties, but refused Germany's acceptance of her frontiers with these two states as permanent. The most he could concede was that Germany would forgo the right to change these boundaries by armed force, and with this France had to be satisfied. At long last, at the Conference of Locarno in October, the agreements were initialled, Great Britain, France, and Italy agreed to sponsor Germany's nomination for membership in the League of Nations and to a permanent seat on the Council, and Stresemann wrung the additional concession from them that the Locarno Agreements should mark the beginning of the movement towards Allied disarmament, to which, by the terms of the Treaty of Versailles, the disarmament of Germany was to be but a "prelude."

In the parallel negotiations with the Conference of Ambassadors, Stresemann had an equally uphill battle, and it was here that his policy ran foul of that of Gessler and the *Reichswehr*. Stresemann's foreign policy had received a great set-back when, in January 1925, the Conference of Ambassadors had announced that in view of the non-fulfilment by Germany of the disarmament clauses of the Peace Treaty, the Allies could not proceed with the evacuation of the First Rhineland Zone, which, according to Article 429, should be completed at the end of five years. With Stresemann's assertion that the disarmament of Germany was complete, a statement which was patently inaccurate, the Inter-Allied Commission of Control refused to agree, producing documentary evidence in support of their contrary view, and the Conference of Ambassadors chided Germany with extreme acerbity for her breach of faith.

Throughout the year Stresemann sought every means, on the one hand, of urging the *Reichswehr* to give no grounds for further complaint, and, on the other, of convincing the Allies of the complete compliance of Germany with all the military and naval clauses of the treaty. Under the mellowing influence of the security negotiations, the Allied attitude became less formidable, and by the time the Locarno Agreements were initialled, it was possible to announce that the evacuation of the First Rhineland Zone would begin with the ceremony of signature in December. "In thus making the beginning of the evacuation coincide with the signature of the Locarno Agreements," wrote Briand to Stresemann, "the Conference [of Ambassadors] expresses the confidence of the Governments represented upon it that the signature will inaugurate a new era in their relations with Germany."

Hindenburg's first year in office closed in a blaze of glory. The achievement was Stresemann's, but it was not without a bitter struggle. The Nationalists, having thrown every obstacle in the way of the negotiations, made a final desperate effort to prevent the ratification of the Locarno Agreements. Stresemann, on his return to Berlin from Locarno, had to leave the train some distance outside the city, reaching his house by devious ways and under police protection. Vile and stupid stories were spread about him; he was paid by the French—his wife, it was said, was the sister of Mme. Poincaré, just as once it had been rumoured that Rathenau's sister had married Radek—and the press was vindictive as only the press of Germany can be. "If the Cabinet has agreed that Stresemann should state his views on Locarno before the *Reichstag* Committee on Foreign Affairs, it is merely allowing him the right of defence conceded to any murderer or similarly unprofitable member of society, though there are many members of our party who regard Stresemann as something worse than a murderer," wrote Colonel von Rodenberg in the Nationalist *Preussische Landeszeitung*.

Within the Cabinet the Nationalist members attacked the Foreign Minister fiercely and threatened to withdraw altogether from the Government, if it persisted in supporting Stresemann's policy of treachery and renunciation. But here help came from a source whence it would least have been expected. Hard-headed old Gessler fought beside Stresemann in this moment and added his bitter irony to the latter's eloquence. "Renunciation?" he drawled in his slow Bavarian voice, at one Cabinet meeting. "You can't call it renunciation when a one-legged man is asked to give up dancing competitions!"

Throughout these days of crisis Hindenburg stood solidly behind Stresemann. Despite the frenzied efforts of the Nationalists to persuade him not to sign the bill of ratification, and to force Stresemann to resign, he listened to the wiser counsel of Meissner—"Germany must not and cannot pursue any other foreign policy"—and gave the Chancellor and the Foreign Minister every necessary support. The Nationalists were at last disillusioned. The hopes which they had built upon Hindenburg's election had been shattered one by one, and they could now only make good their threat of withdrawing from the Government and leave Stresemann in possession of the field. "We had dreamed that Hindenburg, turning his marvellous popularity to account, would dissolve the *Reichstag* and appeal to the nation," wrote old General Litzmann, his contemporary and former comrade-in-arms, in bitter disappointment. "Then he would have won an even greater victory than at Tannenberg."

But at last the treaties were signed and ratified, and by the end of January 1926, the last British soldier had left the First Rhineland Zone. In March, Hindenburg made a triumphal entry into the liberated city of Cologne. Great were the rejoicings, and splendid the celebrations of freedom. Cologne was *en fête* to do honour to its veteran President, the legendary hero of Germany, who had led it out of captivity. Immense festivals were planned in his honour, torchlight processions turned night into day, and the strains of *"Deutschland über Alles"* were heard everywhere.

The President made a number of addresses, notably one in the great *Messehalle* before a huge concourse of people, and all remarkable for their tact and moderation. But one thing mars the record of the festivities. Hindenburg again displayed that curious negative vanity, which had enabled him to accept for four years of war, the credit and honour that were due—at least in major part—to Ludendorff. Throughout the triumph of his tour, he took to himself the plaudits of the crowd, and never once in his addresses saw fit to pay tribute to Stresemann, who had achieved all and who was slowly giving his life for the liberation of the Rhineland. How differently had Blücher behaved towards Gneisenau, letting no opportunity escape to bear testimony to the work of his lieutenant. This weakness in Hindenburg's character was complementary to his fear of responsibility. Where was praise, there he gathered it to himself, but in moments of great trial, such as at Spa and at Kolberg, he was found wanting.

At the moment, when Hindenburg was passing in triumph through the liberated First Zone, Stresemann was facing a serious rebuff at Geneva. A special Assembly of the League of Nations had been convened for the admission of Germany and the stage was set for the logical sequel to Locarno. And then came the anticlimax! In guaranteeing a permanent seat on the Council to Germany, the Great Powers had promised more than they could fulfil. Within the League there was equality of vote, and no bloc, however powerful its members, could dispose of Council seats thus lightly. Other claims were advanced and a deadlock ensued. For ten days Stresemann and the German delegation waited like shivering neophytes without the portals of the Assembly, the involuntary and disgusted observers of the humiliating paralysis of the League.

It seemed as if Fate had at last deserted Stresemann and espoused the cause of the Nationalists, who clamoured for his withdrawal from Geneva. "Withdraw! withdraw!" they demanded, seeing therein a last means of sabotaging the Locarno policy. Here was presented to Stresemann an opportunity to regain much of the popularity and the support which he had lost. To leave Geneva now and return to Berlin would have meant a royal welcome, and the certainty of a *Reichstag* majority, but for what? The work of Locarno would have been destroyed, and Germany would have returned to the policy of Obstinate Resistance. The high courage and great statesmanship of Stresemann was proof against such a temptation. "The triumph is too cheap for me," he replied to Emil Ludwig, who urged upon him the necessity of withdrawing. A new spirit had been born at Locarno, a spirit of mutual respect and trust, and Stresemann stood by his fellow artificers in this moment of their common humiliation. His loyalty was rewarded. When he did leave Geneva on March 16, it was with the renewed respect and heightened admiration of all parties, and with the profound assurance that, when the Assembly met again in September, a solution would have been found.

Throughout this crisis, as before, Luther and Stresemann received the firm support of Hindenburg. The most experienced republican Chief of State could not have behaved more irreproachably than did the Marshal in these days of difficulty. Unobtrusive, he took no part in the public conflict, but, acting as ever under the spur of Meissner, he gave encouragement at the critical moment when it was most needed. His greatest critics cannot reproach him for the correctness of his attitude towards his Foreign Minister at this moment.

But Stresemann could not entirely escape the consequence of the Geneva fiasco. On his return he had to yield to the demands of the Nationalists and the *Reichswehr* in signing the treaty of neutrality and non-aggression with the Soviet Union. No sense of pique provoked this new diplomatic departure, but the sheer necessity of conciliating his political opponents. The rapproche-

ment with the Soviet Union had never been a tenet of Stresemann's policy, it belonged to the policy of the *Reichswehr*, who
needed Soviet assistance in their endeavours to evade the military provisions of the Peace Treaty. That strange Bolshevik liaison which began in 1920 and only ended with the advent of
Hitler—when military evasion was no longer necessary—was
dictated throughout from the Bendlerstrasse and not from the
Wilhelmstrasse, though there in Maltzan, and in Brockdorff-
Rantzau at Moscow, were found willing collaborators.

In the years that followed, Stresemann's failing strength was
devoted unflaggingly to every means which might complete the
evacuation of the Rhineland and re-establish Germany as a
world power in the new community of nations. As his health declined, it became a race with death, and the increasing tempo
of the contest inevitably affected his judgment unfavourably.
The record of his efforts was one of set-backs and advances. The
final admission of Germany to the League was followed by the
mirage of Thoiry, when Briand's eloquence opened before
Stresemann's eyes a vision of Franco-German co-operation for
the peace of Europe. There followed disillusionment and momentary despair. The reappearance of Poincaré revived bitter
memories of the Ruhr and of Versailles. But still the efforts were
not relaxed, no opportunity was neglected.

The immediate acceptance by Germany of the Kellogg-Briand
Pact was a strategic success of the first water, and for its signature
Stresemann came, with the shadow of death already on his face,
as the first German Foreign Minister to enter Paris since 1870.

And ever behind him stood Hindenburg in strong support.
Chancellors came and went, the victims of internal policy, but
each retained Stresemann in office, and the President remained
a rock upon which he could lean in moments when the struggle
with his enemies and with his fate threatened to overwhelm him.
This continued support of Stresemann, in season and out, for

five years, is among the highest achievements of Hindenburg's
political career. Admittedly the impetus came from Meissner,
but as Hindenburg had been absorbed into Ludendorff's personality in war, so was he dominated by Meissner in peace. The
tragedy came in each case with a change in the character of the
dominant partner, when the wax of Hindenburg's personality
bore the imprint of intrigue in place of statesmanship.

There came inevitably the last round in Stresemann's losing
fight with death. It had never been believed that he would return
from Paris alive. Those who met him there, of whom the writer
was one, were shocked at the livid greyness of his face, and the
weary effort of every movement. But he rallied under the stimu-
lus of necessity and opened his last struggle with France for the
evacuation of the Rhineland, and a final settlement of reparation payments. The French demanded an Eastern Locarno as the
price of evacuation. Stresemann refused. The Young Committee dragged out its weary sessions, fraught in themselves with
the drama of death, and produced its report in June 1929. In
August the statesmen met at the Hague to consider its adoption.

Stresemann was conserving the last particle of his strength
now, but his judgment and will-power were weakening. Did he
really believe that Germany could meet the heavy obligations
imposed by the Young Plan? Should he have accepted these
new burdens on behalf of his country with that whisper of uncertainty in his mind? Within his grasp was the final realization
of the goal toward which his whole policy of seven years had
been directed. It was the price of his acceptance, and he had no
more strength to fight. Perhaps against his better judgment he
accepted the Young Plan, and on August 29, with a joyful heart,
put his signature to the Agreement for the Evacuation of the Second and Third Rhineland Zones. It was the last of that series of
documents with which he had raised Germany from the position
of a pariah to the dignity of a world Power. Six weeks later he
was dead.

· 4 ·

"We shall wait in vain for the awakening in our country of that public spirit which the English and the French and other peoples possess, if we do not imitate them in setting for our military leaders certain bounds and limitations which they must not disregard." When Baron von Stein wrote these words over a hundred years ago, the new military machine with which Gneisenau and Scharnhorst had evaded the military provisions of the Treaty of Tilsit and had greatly contributed to the overthrow of Napoleon, was making its bid for the political domination in Prussia. Though, since the days of Frederick the Great, the influence of the Prussian army had been strong, it was not until the forerunner of the German Great General Staff was created in 1807 that it reached that unassailable position which, with two intervals, it has continued to occupy until the present day.

The great military leaders of the Liberation period, Blücher, Gneisenau, and Scharnhorst, though sharing different views on foreign policy, loyally supported Stein and Hardenberg in their policy of reform, and, with them, fought the opposition of the vacillating monarch, Frederick William III; yet Stein was aware of the danger to the monarchy and Government if the control of the military machine should at some future time fall into less scrupulous hands than those of his colleagues.

It was for this reason that he sought to confine the position of the army within certain bounds and limitations—the army having captured the nebulous and "woolly" patriotism generated by the activities of the *Tugenbund;* and there was a danger that a dominant school of thought would arise convinced that true patriotism could only be expressed through the medium of militarism.

At one moment only in the later history of Royal Prussia did the civil Government and the army preserve the delimitation of their respective functions. Under Wilhelm I, the Chancellor, the Minister of War, and the Chief of the General Staff worked together in harmonious accord, and it was assumed that when Bismarck, Roon, and Moltke were agreed upon a policy, the agreement of the King would also be forthcoming.

This close collaboration, though it spelt destruction for the enemies of Prussia, raised that country from the status of a titular vassal of Austria to that of *primus inter pares* among the German states, and finally to the controlling position of Imperial power. The four worked together as colleagues and not as rivals, and it is impossible, for example, to conceive of any of them treating the old King with that frank brutality which on occasion the Supreme Command and even the Chancellor meted out to his grandson. It was for the army to win victories, the Chancellor to govern, and the King to rule, and during this period each performed his function with excellent results.

This was the first exception to the rule of the domination of the army. The second was that brief period in 1918–1919, when the military caste were discredited, the authority of the generals ineffective, and the army in a state of disintegration. Deprived of its Emperor the army had lost the symbol to which its singular loyalty had always been pledged. Its leadership was in the dust, it owed allegiance to no man, and its power and numbers had been shattered by defeat and the crushing terms of the Armistice. It was within the power of German Social Democracy at that time to confine the military leadership of Germany within the bounds which Stein had sought so zealously to impose a hundred years before; that it failed to do so was due partly to its own ineptitude, partly to the skill of the military caste, and partly to the insistence of the Allied Powers on such humiliating military clauses in the Treaty of Peace that it became incumbent upon every German soldier to encompass their evasion.

It is recorded that a German statesman enquired of an American acquaintance visiting Berlin soon after the Armistice, what sort of terms Germany might expect. "Military terms," was the reply. "But what about Wilson?" "In spite of Wilson," said the American sadly. "Thank God," exclaimed the German, "for in that case we shall overcome the revolution and secure our national freedom so much sooner!"

He was right. Under a milder treaty the democratic German Republic might have continued to flourish instead of languishing in agony for fourteen years. The harsh terms of the Treaty of Versailles made reaction inevitable, and played into the hands of the waiting militarists.

By the end of 1919, the army which Hindenburg and Gröner had brought home from France had been reduced to the figure prescribed by the terms of the Armistice. The chaotic condition of the country made it impossible for those demobilized to be absorbed into civilian life and they swelled the ranks of the starving unemployed, roaming the country in bands and ripe for any mischief. From these grew up the Free Corps, those privately owned and organized armies formed to protect the eastern frontier against the depredations of the Poles, to crush the incipient Communist risings which threatened in many parts of the country, and to keep alive some semblance of the old German military spirit.

Meanwhile such of the Old Army officers as could bring themselves to follow the example of Hindenburg and Gröner, and co-operate with, rather than serve, the Republic, grouped themselves round the Minister of Defence, Noske, and convinced him of the necessity of building up a strong force from the stable elements which remained of the Imperial army. There were men amongst the Social Democrats and the Centre who foresaw the danger of this move, and urged passionately that the new army should be a purely republican guard and not a force drawn from elements essentially antagonistic to the Weimar régime.

Noske's view, however, prevailed; when the new *Reichswehr* was constituted it was largely recruited from members of the Free Corps and volunteers who had seen war service, and with this force the second Spartacist Revolt of March 1919 was effectively crushed. This feat earned the respect of Hindenburg and Gröner, and the latter used his influence with Ebert to have Seeckt, by far the ablest of Germany's executive officers, appointed General Commanding the new army.

A strange man, Hans von Seeckt; at first glance a typical Prussian officer, with his thin, red turkey-neck, surmounted by an inscrutable face and the inevitable monocle. Just another general, one thought, as he entered a room, and that impression remained until he took his hands from behind his back, and one was amazed at their beauty. Long, thin, artistic, they might have belonged to Benvenuto Cellini or to Chopin. Not a soldier's hands, and no one who possessed them could be an ordinary soldier. Seeckt was not. He was a genius; a genius at making bricks without straw, and at fashioning a military machine, nominally within the restrictions of the Peace Treaty, which struck admiration and apprehension into the heart of every General Staff in Europe.

But the danger of creating the new army from the old soon became apparent. It was one thing to crush a Communist revolt, but a very different one to operate against the remainder of the Free Corps and Old Army troops under Lüttwitz, who joined the Kapp *putsch*. "There can be no question of setting the *Reichswehr* to fight these people," Seeckt declared to Noske. "Would you force a battle at the Brandenburger Tor between troops who a year and a half ago were fighting shoulder to shoulder against the enemy?" The Kapp *putsch* was defeated by the general strike of the trades unions and the threat of a march on Berlin by bands of armed workers. Throughout that fateful week the *Reichswehr* preserved a silent and, in some cases a very benevolent neutrality.[1] It was not a very meritorious episode in its history.

In the reconstruction of the Government which followed the *putsch*, Noske retired to Hanover as Provisional President, to be succeeded by Gessler, and Gröner entered the Cabinet as Minister of Railways. The Government had not felt strong enough to make an example of Seeckt for his conduct; indeed they could not afford to lose him, and with the support of Gessler and Gröner, he proceeded to perfect his reorganization.

It was no ordinary army that he succeeded in creating. In the rank and file the worker element was excluded, and recruits were accepted mainly from the agricultural districts. By his own example and influence Seeckt broke down the prejudice which many of his old comrades felt towards a "professional" army and persuaded members of the nobility and the military caste to become officers. For this remarkable army of one hundred thousand men it was found necessary to have a ministerial staff of three hundred officers and six hundred and seventy staff officers—and this despite the fact that under the Peace Treaty the German Great General Staff had been declared dissolved and its reconstruction illegal—and in addition there were fifty-five generals. The eighteen regiments of cavalry prescribed by the treaty were commanded by three generals of divisions and nine inspectors with the rank of general, and forty-two thousand horses were required for them. One hundred and twenty-three

---

[1] In some localities, principally in Prussia, the troop commanders openly sided with Kapp and Lüttwitz. There were, however, notable exceptions. Colonel von Hammerstein, who had married Lüttwitz's daughter, was ordered by his father-in-law to be with his troops at a certain place. He refused and was placed under arrest in his own headquarters. On the failure of the *putsch*, when Kapp fled, Hammerstein was released and promptly arrested his father-in-law, holding him until the order arrived from Seeckt for his release, as it had been decided that the military leaders, Lüttwitz, Erhardt, Bauer, and Pabst, should be allowed to escape.

colonels appeared in the Army List, of which twenty-three were in the *Reichswehr* Ministry, and in 1926 the military budget amounted to 776.6 million marks.

In proportion to its size it was the most expensive army in the world, and the ratio in numbers of officers to men suggests more the army of one of the smaller Latin American republics. Actually, of course, the whole organization was based on the possibility of rapid expansion, in which case every man of the hundred thousand would be a potential non-commissioned officer. In furtherance of this theory each battalion of the *Reichswehr* retained the "tradition" of one of the regiments of the Old Imperial Army, and while this system kept alive the old military spirit, it also had the added advantage of providing the nucleus for immediate expansion should the necessity and opportunity arise.

By the Constitution the President was *ex officio* Commander-in-Chief of all the armed forces of the *Reich*, but under Ebert there were never any illusions on this point. Seeckt had created the *Reichswehr* and it was loyal to him alone. All civilian influence had been completely excluded, and when the Government wanted to use the army for its own defence it had first to ask the permission of the General Officer Commanding. "Will the *Reichswehr* stick to us, General?" asked Ebert of Seeckt, at the Cabinet meeting summoned so hastily in the small hours of that November morning when the news of Hitler's rising arrived from Munich; and Seeckt, who alone of those around the table seemed to be collected and composed, replied with his sphinx-like smile, "The *Reichswehr, Herr Reichspräsident,* will stick to me."

With the election of Hindenburg to the presidency all this changed. A Field-Marshal was a very different chief from a Socialist trade-union leader, and immediately the army pledged its loyalty to the Marshal, not in his capacity as President but as its Commander-in-Chief. In this it was merely reverting to type. Under the Empire the army had owed allegiance only to the Emperor, and Hindenburg had assumed the position as Chief of State which the Emperor had once occupied. Besides, was he not their old commander? The older soldiers had served under him in the war, and the younger had imbibed from them and from their fathers and brothers the glories of the Hindenburg Legend.

In his person, therefore, Hindenburg wedded the army to the republic, and whilst he remained President nothing could shake this loyalty. Every attempt by Hitler, both before and after he became Chancellor, to seduce the *Reichswehr* from its personal allegiance to the President met with ignominious failure, and it was not till after Hindenburg's death that he was able to exact from them an oath of fealty.

The army of which Hindenburg found himself Commander-in-Chief in 1925 resembled its Imperial predecessor in one particular respect. It was above politics, because it dominated them. With zealous care it had been removed from political control and no disruptive influences existed within its ranks. It never played politics, but no Government could stand a week without its support. In the words of Gröner: "The *Reichswehr* had become a factor which no one could pass over in political decisions."

This situation appealed enormously to Hindenburg. Lord D'Abernon had summed up his reaction exactly when he recorded the thought, "The President—essentially a soldier—instinctively distrusts anything but force." And while he tolerated and supported Stresemann's policy of diplomatic *rapprochement*, he lent a more willing assistance to the policies of the *Reichswehr*.

Of these the most important was the liaison with the Soviet Union. This was the child of Seeckt, and one of the most re-

markable anomalies of the Weimar period was this close relationship between the German and Soviet General Staffs. In the
days immediately following the war, the military leaders of
Germany were sharply divided on the Bolshevik issue. Hoffmann, who had been an eye-witness of the revolution and knew
too well the devastating effects of Bolshevik propaganda upon
his own troops, regarded Moscow as the root of all evil, and
advocated the sinking of differences between Germany and the
Allies in a crusade against the common enemy. The possible
results of this policy are worth consideration, for, had Germany
been allowed to exploit Russia from the outset, it is improbable that she would have reached that state of desperation which
made National Socialism an inevitable evil. Gröner, also, had
seen Bolshevism at first hand during his service in the Ukraine
in 1918, and he viewed both it and its works with fear and
repugnance.

Seeckt too had served on the Eastern Front—was he not
the hero of the break-through at Gorlice, for which Falkenhayn
took the credit?—but he had fought the Imperial Russian armies
and not the Bolsheviks. He knew the Russians to be good fight-
ers, whether they were well or badly led, and saw in the new
Red Army something which, properly handled, could be made
a valuable instrument for his policy. Germany, he argued, had
been virtually ostracized from the European society of nations
and must needs therefore consort with the other outlaw state,
the Soviet Union. Moreover the U.S.S.R. was the one state
friendly to Germany and unfettered by the Treaty of Versailles,
which possessed full liberty of manufacture and use of those
categories of weapons and military equipment which the Peace
Treaties forbade to the *Reichswehr*. On the other hand, the Red
Army only lacked that training and discipline which German
instructors could impart to make it a very considerable factor
in Germany's future policy. Admittedly the Soviet Union was

a dangerous ally, but she was better at that juncture than no ally at all.

This liaison with the Red General Staff became the keynote of Seeckt's policy almost from the first moment of his assuming command of the *Reichswehr*, and was formally enunciated to his staff and collaborators in February 1920 during the outcry against the surrender to the Allies of the Emperor and the other "war criminals." Seeckt informed his lieutenants that if the Government consented to surrender the old heads of the army, the *Reichswehr* must oppose it by every means in its power, even if such opposition entailed the reopening of hostilities with the Allies. In this case the troops in the west would retire fighting, step by step, behind the line of the Weser or the Elbe where defensive positions would already have been prepared, but in the east they would launch an offensive across Poland, join hands with the Red Army, and, having crushed the Poles, would march westwards to meet the French and British.

These desperate measures of Seeckt's never materialized, but in them lay the germ of the threatened "Red Army on the Rhine" with which the *Reichswehr* were to make so great a play in future years. Moreover, Seeckt found in Maltzan, the head of the Eastern Department of the Foreign Office, a ready ally. Between them they so worked upon Rathenau that the Treaty of Rapallo, signed with the Soviet Union during the Genoa Conference of 1922, set the official seal upon the unofficial relations which had already existed between the two general staffs. The treaty was complemented by a secret military agreement which enabled Seeckt to send each year to Russia a certain number of officers to act as instructors for the Red Army, and a further number to gain all the experience they could in the handling of heavy artillery, tanks, armoured cars, and other weapons forbidden to Germany.

The Nationalists warmly supported Seeckt's policy as an alternative and corrective to Stresemann's policy of conciliation, and Count Brockdorff-Rantzau, the first German Ambassador in Moscow since Mirbach's assassination in 1918, was amongst the most able and fierce opponents of Locarno. The great triumph of this school of thought was when, after the fiasco at Geneva in March 1926, Stresemann was compelled by expediency to yield to their demands and conclude with Moscow the treaty of neutrality and non-aggression.

This, then, was the extraordinary state of affairs with which Hindenburg found himself confronted on assuming office as President and Commander-in-Chief. In the sphere of foreign policy a tug-of-war was in progress; Stresemann supported by the Social-Democrats, the Centre, and his own People's Party (though he never knew at what moment his own followers would stab him in the back), were seeking by means of the Policy of Fulfilment to restore Germany's position as a Great Power by peaceful and conciliatory means, whilst the army, supported by an unnatural alliance of the Nationalists and the Communists, sought, by evading the disarmament clauses of the treaty and by a military understanding with the Bolsheviks, to prepare for that day when Germany should feel herself sufficiently strong and recovered from defeat to assume by her own act her former position as a Great Power.

Hindenburg's natural proclivities led him to support the army, but like Hoffmann he feared Bolshevism, and was greatly relieved when, during his first interview with Stresemann, he was assured that no alliance between Germany and the Soviet Union existed. Meissner's influence and his own genuine desire to fulfil his constitutional duties caused him to back Stresemann, even in the teeth of Nationalist opposition, but little by little he drifted back into the military fold, thanks to the zealous care and intrigue of a certain individual in the *Reichswehr* Ministry.

For when in 1925 Hindenburg reappeared as the *tête d'armée*, the real force behind the *Reichswehr* was virtually unknown. It was not Seeckt, or Gröner, or Gessler, but a young staff colonel who occupied a little room in the Ministry overlooking the Landwehr Canal. Kurt von Schleicher, the son of an old Brandenburg family and a hereditary member of the military caste, had begun his military career in 1900 as a subaltern in Hindenburg's old regiment, the Third Foot Guards, and had there formed a close friendship with Oskar. For this reason he had been a frequent visitor at the flat in the Holzgraben during Hindenburg's first retirement in Hanover, where his natural charm and wit, in addition to his excellent qualities as a soldier, soon made him a favourite with the old General. While Oskar remained with his regiment, Kurt had designs on the staff. At the *Kriegsakademie* he had attracted the attention of Gröner, who considered him, with Willisen and Hammerstein, among his most brilliant pupils, and when Gröner was appointed to the Transport Section of the General Staff, he had Schleicher transferred to his department. Except for a brief period of service on the Eastern Front, after the Armistice of Brest-Litovsk, during which he was awarded the Iron Cross, Schleicher's record throughout the war was that of a *Schreibtischoffizier* (an "office" soldier) and he discharged his duties with great efficiency. With no doubts as to his own capabilities, he let no opportunity slip—and there were very many at General Headquarters—to make acquaintance with the great ones who surrounded him, and the witty young dandy became an essential figure in many important circles.

He had never been a favourite of Ludendorff's, however, and Gröner's succession to the post of First Quartermaster-General was a stroke of luck for him. For his old chief plucked Schleicher, now a major, from his duties in the Press Department of General Headquarters and made him his personal adjutant. In this capacity he was present at the momentous interview with Hindenburg on the morning of November 10, and added his voice to Gröner's in persuading the Marshal to support the existing Government in Berlin simply because it was a Government. Together they weathered the trials and depression of the Revolution. These days, though dark, were not without their adventurous moments, and on one occasion in Berlin, Gröner and Schleicher, alone and on foot, forced their way to Ebert's rescue through a howling mob in the Wilhelmstrasse, which had virtually imprisoned him in the Chancellery.

The supreme ambition of Schleicher was the possession of power without responsibility, and the march of events immediately following the signature of peace materially aided him in realizing this ideal. While Gröner turned civilian in good earnest, Schleicher capitalized his previous contacts and secured for himself a vague and undefined but secure position in the Ministry of Defence, and from here, in the little room overlooking the Landwehr Canal, he began to play that game of politics and intrigue which was to carry him to the Chancellor's palace and to end with a murderer's bullet.

Not that he was an intriguer for the pure love of intrigue— he was too intelligent for that; his plots were always directed towards some larger end which would justify them should they become prematurely discovered. Thus it was Schleicher who ably assisted Seeckt in rendering the army free from politics by creating it an Olympian *imperium in imperio;* and it was Schleicher who, having had a large share in the creation of the Free Corps and the recruiting of the *Reichswehr* from amongst their members, maintained the residue—the Black *Reichswehr, Orgesh,* the Erhardt's Brigade, and the rest—as unofficial appendages of the Ministry of Defence which could be sponsored or disavowed at will.

Sociable, engaging, and a successful ladies' man, Kurt von Schleicher gradually found himself in a position where his advice and opinion were sought by politicians, hostesses, journalists, and any foreign observer who visited Berlin. Outside the official circle and the growing body of his acquaintances, his name was unknown to the country at large, yet he came to know all there was to be known in the political world of Germany, and eventually perfected for his advantage a far-reaching system of "something which, when practised by our enemies, we call espionage." There was to be a time when not a telephone conversation of importance took place in Berlin but its content was reported to him, and his agents were in every Ministry and Government office. Not since Holstein was there so pertinacious a pryer into the secrets of the official world.[1]

All this was not achieved at once, but with the advent of Hindenburg, Schleicher's position was at once strengthened and enhanced. His intimacy with Oskar, now his father's personal adjutant, gave him free access to the Palace, an asset of which he took full advantage. With Oskar and Hammerstein both, like himself, formerly of the *Dritte Garde,* he formed a small but powerful clique which, though originally intended to counteract Meissner's influence, succeeded eventually in winning his co-operation; and from this grew that sinister Palace *Camarilla* which in years to come completely dominated the President.

It was necessary, however, for Schleicher's purpose that he should have not nominal, but virtual control of the *Reichswehr,* and between him and this attainment stood the obstructing per-

---

[1] In a book intended to glorify Schleicher and published before he became Minister of Defence, Dr. Heinz Brauweiler says, "He is a specialist for the watching of inner political activities. . . . He knows all the politicians and how to handle them. Naturally he does handle them" (see *Generäle in den deutsches Republik,* p. 33). Schleicher's name, *anglicé,* means "creeper."

sonalities of Seeckt and Gessler. For though Seeckt was strongly influenced by Schleicher's views, he was by no means his puppet, and Gessler was equally averse to being any man's tool.

Seeckt was the first to go, in 1926, and the manner of his going was peculiarly vile. Together with Schleicher, he had planned secretly to permit the eldest son of the Crown Prince, the potential Wilhelm IV of Prussia, to take part in the annual manœuvres with the rank of lieutenant. Schleicher, fully cognizant of the plan, allowed it to proceed to a point where it became irrevocable and then, by devious means, apprised the press of the Left of what had taken place. At once a howl of fury arose from the Republicans, and the Government was criticized abroad for a breach of the "Locarno Spirit." Stresemann, on the eve of securing the admission of Germany to the League, was nonplussed in the face of these accusations of monarchist intrigues, and the very existence of the Cabinet was threatened. With profound reluctance Gessler was forced to recommend to the President that Seeckt be asked to resign, and Hindenburg was himself unwilling to lose the services of one whom he knew to be amongst the ablest of Germany's soldiers. The influence of the *Dritte Garde* group was, however, paramount, and under their united efforts the President was persuaded to dismiss Seeckt from the command of the army which he had created with such brilliant success.

Schleicher's nominee for the moment was Heye—he was anxious in reality to keep the place warm for Hammerstein. Gessler concurred in the choice, and Hindenburg appointed him as Seeckt's successor. But the pompous, though not incompetent Heye, who, on that fatal November morning at Spa, reported on the results of the Conference of officers, had in the meantime turned democrat with a vengeance. He had a tendency to persuade non-commissioned officers to give him their views on their superiors, and his influence on the morale of the army was anything but satisfactory. His tenancy of command was short and inglorious, and in 1930 Schleicher achieved, without difficulty, his dismissal and the succession of Hammerstein as active head of the *Reichswehr,* despite the rival claims put forward on behalf of Stülpnagel and Blomberg.

Gessler was the next victim. In disposing of him, also, Schleicher displayed a lack of scruple which was startling. The secret activities of the Ministry of Defence in the field of rearmament had not been confined to the army. The navy, too, had had its clandestine relations with foreign Powers, and to these both Gessler and Schleicher had been privy. In 1929 details connected with certain contracts for the building of submarines in Spain and Sweden were brought to light and the press and parties of the Left again assailed the *Reichswehr,* this time directing their attack against the person of the Minister. It is not established, though it was widely rumoured at the time, that Schleicher had, in this case, as in that of Prince Wilhelm, communicated the facts to the press, but it is a fact that, though he had shared Gessler's knowledge of the illegal activities and had warmly encouraged them, he made no attempt to defend his chief, either openly or with the President. On the contrary, when Gessler's resignation was demanded by the Left, Schleicher urged Hindenburg to agree, and Gessler was sacrificed with the same cold-blooded disloyalty as Seeckt had been.

The problem of his successor affected both Hindenburg and Schleicher very closely. With Seeckt, the presiding genius of the *Reichswehr* gone, the position of the Defence Minister assumed new importance and responsibility. Moreover, it seemed inevitable that a soldier should hold the position. The possible candidates were three in number, Willisen, Schleicher's fellow pupil under Gröner, whose brilliant war record well fitted him for the position, Count von Schulenburg, with equally excellent qualifications, and Gröner himself. But for Schleicher there was no hesitation of thought; from the moment of Gessler's resignation, he settled in his own mind that his patron, Gröner, must succeed him. For Gröner trusted him and believed almost implicitly in his views. He would often refer jokingly to Schleicher as his "son," and it was already being rumoured that "Kurtchen" might in fact become his son-in-law.

At first glance the matter presented grave difficulties when it was remembered in what disfavour and contempt Gröner had been held by his brother officers. But times had changed and views with them. The Court of Honour in 1922 had cleared Gröner's conduct at Spa, albeit somewhat frigidly, and the "treachery of Weimar" loomed less large than it had ten years before. Schleicher's canvassing on Gröner's behalf met with practically no opposition, and even Schulenburg, his archantagonist at Spa, and latterly, with Waldersee, his principal traducers, refused point-blank to allow himself to be considered in competition to him, so strongly did he feel that Gröner alone could fill the position. "We must have Gröner at all costs," he telegraphed to Treviranus. "We have all been mistaken about him."

The chief opposition came, not unexpectedly, from the President himself. Gröner was a link with his past which Hindenburg would have severed, and he did not at once give his consent. For alone of living mortals Gröner knew the truth of what had passed at Spa and Kolberg, and would, in the frequent contact which must be maintained between Commander-in-Chief and Minister of Defence, prove a constant and irritating reminder of these two not very noble episodes in the Marshal's career.

But there was no gainsaying Schleicher; with subtlety of argument and cajolery, he, and with him Oskar, bore down the President's objections. The welfare of the *Reichswehr* demanded that Gröner should defend its interests in the Cabinet and in

ONE OF THE THREE-MARK PIECES SPECIALLY ISSUED FOR THE TENTH ANNIVERSARY OF THE WEIMAR
CONSTITUTION (AUGUST 11, 1929)

On the right is Hindenburg and on the left is the symbol of loyalty to the Constitution. These coins have been withdrawn
from circulation.

the *Reichstag*. None other had so long and so complete an experience of the military machine as he, and none could serve its interests better. Under the weight of such arguments as these, Hindenburg withdrew his opposition and once again the combination of Spa and Wilhelmshöhe and Kolberg was re-established. With the success of this intrigue Schleicher's position had become unassailably powerful. With his friend as active commander and his patron as governmental chief of the *Reichswehr*, he virtually controlled the army.[1] In addition he took advantage of Gröner's appointment to create for himself a new position approximating that of Permanent Secretary in civilian ministries. The scope and influence of this position, which carried with it the control of the intelligence services and of the relations between the army and the *Reichstag*, gradually grew and expanded, and with it Schleicher's personal powers increased steadily. He was promoted to Lieutenant-General in 1929, and two years later attained the right of immediate access to the President. Thus both in his official capacity and unofficially as a friend of Oskar's and of the family, Schleicher could exercise his influence upon Hindenburg. No longer was it merely a matter

---

[1] It is not intended to convey the impression that either Gröner or Hammerstein lent themselves willingly or knowingly to any of Schleicher's subsequent political intrigues. It was simply because they both trusted and believed in him that his influence was so powerful. Gröner was long in awakening to the manner in which he had been used and manipulated by his protégé, and when he came to disagree fundamentally with Schleicher, the latter, as will be seen later, had no hesitation in adding him to his list of victims. Hammerstein, from the time he took over the active command of the *Reichswehr*, firmly pursued Seeckt's policy of keeping both the officers and the rank and file out of politics. Nor did he himself indulge in intrigue of any kind. Yet his personal affection and admiration for Schleicher never faded, and of this he gave signal proof on an historic occasion. After the murder of Schleicher and his wife, on June 30, 1934, at a moment when any display of sympathy with a victim of the massacre rendered the sympathizer liable to danger of life and liberty, Hammerstein, his wife, and three others only, of Schleicher's former friends, attended his funeral and had the experience of being refused access to the chapel by S.S. guards, who also confiscated the wreaths they had brought with them for the grave. Hammerstein also took a large part in the campaign by the *Reichswehr* for the "rehabilitation" of Schleicher and Bredow which achieved its ultimate success in February 1935.

of resisting republican influences, he was now in a position to dominate the inner political life of the country.

· 5 ·

It was against this background of foreign policy and militarist intrigue that the internal politics of Germany, with which Hindenburg himself was more intimately concerned, developed. For throughout the life of the Weimar Republic its lurid domestic history was dominated by external affairs and the influence of the army upon government. The *Reichstag* elected in 1924, which Hindenburg inherited from Ebert, was unique in the annals of German post-war parliamentary institutions in that it contained young men of all parties who had seen active service. The elections for the National Assembly and for the *Reichstag* of 1920 had ignored this great element of national life, but in 1924 they had asserted themselves and at once a new spirit began to permeate the political world. For amongst the new young deputies the old fellowship of the war transcended the bitterness of party strife, and such men as Treviranus, the dashing naval lieutenant-commander, Brüning, the machine-gun officer, and Bredt, the company commander, could never allow their common bond of union as holders of the Iron Cross to be submerged in the controversies in which their membership in the Nationalist, Centre, and Economic Parties inevitably involved them. This comradeship of the war even extended beyond the Right and the Centre to the Left, and was the means by which many crises were overcome and many others avoided.

Yet this saved Hindenburg little vexation. The complexities of political intrigue and the petty jealousies of Party Leaders were as incomprehensible to him as they were irritating, and there were many moments when he regretted the sacrifice he had made, longingly remembering his peaceful retirement on the banks of the Leine. The whole thing was so essentially alien to all that he had been brought up to, and the complete lack of military precision irked him still more; he longed to be able to instil some discipline into the quarrelsome politicians who surrounded him.

He could not comprehend the difficulties which his Chancellors experienced in obtaining a parliamentary majority, and could never understand why they frequently found it necessary to resign. "Why did he go?" the Marshal would enquire of Meissner. "He was quite a nice man." "Yes," Meissner would reply, "but he couldn't find a majority." "Oh well," Hindenburg would conclude, "he suited me very well, but if they want a new one I don't mind."

Almost at once those who had voted for Hindenburg received a bitter disappointment when the Luther Government began to make public its plans for new taxation and revaluation. His supporters during the election campaign had made sweeping promises on Hindenburg's behalf of lower taxes and a complete revaluation of internal debts, and for this reason many of those who, during the war, had patriotically subscribed to German War Loans, voted for the man in answer to whose appeal they had loaned their money to the Government. Now Hindenburg was reaping the whirlwind which had been sown in his name by other hands during the war. From 1917 onwards every appeal to the investing public to buy War Loans had been made over the Marshal's name, and they became popularly known as "Hindenburg Loans." The man who had appealed to them for their money might reasonably be supposed to protect them from a devaluation of their holdings and from increased taxation, at least so argued many of the electorate, and they voted accordingly for Hindenburg.

Now, however, came the awakening from so pleasant a dream. Luther, anxious to keep, through his internal policy, the support of the Right for Stresemann's efforts in external affairs, ignored almost entirely the claims of the small-holders of War Loans and pandered to the demands of Nationalist landowners and big business. While investors in War Loans only got a very small revaluation, the holders of mortgages got 25 per cent of the nominal value. At the same time a law was forced through the *Reichstag* giving special relief in taxation for the forming of large industrial and banking combines.

The result of these measures was twofold. The finances of the *Reich* were allowed to proceed in a fundamentally unsound direction, especially when in the following year the turnover tax was lowered, and the popularity of the President suffered a grave falling-off amongst many of his former supporters, who transferred their allegiance to the Social Democrats and even to the Communists.

By the close of his first eight months of office Hindenburg, for one reason and another, had disappointed the hopes of very many of those who had elected him, and the withdrawal of the Nationalists from the Government after Locarno caused a Cabinet crisis which extended over the Christmas holiday. The prolonged negotiations and bargaining made the President fretful and petulant. "The depressing spectacle of these perpetual Government crises must be put an end to," he declared in his New Year message to the country; and after a still further delay, he sent for the Party Leaders and told them that their squabbles must find a solution in a Cabinet by 10 o'clock that evening. As a result, Luther formed a Minority Government commanding a majority of only ten in the *Reichstag*, and dependent for its social legislation upon the Social Democrats.

Immediately, however, a new problem arose for the President of a nature peculiarly distasteful to him. The vexed question of the indemnification of the ruling houses and princely families of Germany for properties confiscated during the Revolution, was one which stirred the country to its depths, for it involved not only legal questions, but the most profound moral issues. Expropriation without compensation was emphatically championed by the Left, while the Right regarded the issue both as an attack upon dynastic principles and upon the sacred rights of private property. Hindenburg, as a Prussian and a member of the military caste, was a fanatical believer in private property, and was aghast at the idea that the possessions of his King should be expropriated. The idea that compensation should not be paid was, of course, unthinkable, and the whole influence of the President, despite Meissner's warnings as to the constitutional necessity of remaining impartial, was cast into the scale in support of the Right.

Nevertheless, when the matter came to a referendum, in the first ballot fifteen and a half million voters—five and a half million more than had voted for Hindenburg's election—were in favour of the Socialist proposal of expropriation without compensation. Hindenburg had taken no public part in the campaign. He did not intend to do so now, but in the height of his indignation at the result of the ballot, he wrote a private letter to Herr von Löbell, the former Imperial Minister of Interior, who had been the chairman of his election committee in 1925 and was now the leader of the fight against expropriation:

That I, who have spent my life in the service of the Prussian Kings and the German Emperors, feel this referendum primarily as a great injustice, and also as an exhibition of a regrettable lack of traditional sentiment and of great ingratitude, I do not need to explain to you. The very foundation of a constitutional state is the legal recognition of property, and the proposal of expropriation offends against the principles of morality and justice. . . . I trust therefore that our fellow citizens will reconsider their decision on this matter, and will undo the mischief they have done.

For a Marshal of the Imperial Army and an old servant of the royal house to give vent to his feelings in these terms was indeed natural enough, but that the constitutionally elected head of a democracy should give expression to such sentiments to one of the protagonists in the dispute, even in a private letter, was very wrong indeed. Far worse was the sequel. To the horror of all who still held Hindenburg's name in esteem and respect, his letter to Löbell appeared as a placard next morning on every kiosk and hoarding in the country. Friend and foe alike were shocked and embarrassed both by such an abuse of confidential correspondence and by so complete a departure by the President from the constitutional path of political impartiality, which he himself had made such a display of following. The reaction, though unfavourable to Hindenburg, was satisfactory for the cause which he had so wrongly espoused. When the final ballot was taken the majority of the voters reversed their decision, and not only was the expropriation proposal defeated, but many thousands of acres, as well as castles and palaces and fifteen million gold marks in cash, were added to the fortune of the exiled Hohenzollerns.

The defeat of the expropriation measure did not console Hindenburg for the abuse of his confidence and the public odium which he had incurred. He was dissatisfied and disappointed, sick to death of political worry and intrigue, and tired of all the party leaders without exception. More and more he chafed against the restrictions which his office placed upon his personal liberty of action, and the more heartily did he regret ever having allowed himself to be inveigled into this "gilded cage." His heart was full of scorpions, but, unlike Macbeth, he had no "dear wife" to whom to turn.

In an attempt to bring about a reconciliation with the Nationalists and to please, at least on one point, the very disgruntled President, Luther chose this moment to introduce a measure to allow German diplomatic missions abroad to fly the black-white-red colours of Imperial Germany in addition to the black, red, and gold of the *Reichsbanner,* which the Weimar Constitution had substituted as the official flag. Though the Social Democrats attacked the bill as a concession to reaction, there is no doubt that had the Chancellor played his cards properly, he could easily have secured a majority for a measure which was very dear to the tradition-loving heart of the old President. Luther, however, threw the game away. He held no conferences with the party leaders to ensure a majority for the bill, nor did he even warn the members of the Cabinet at what time it was coming up for discussion. He tried to force it through on a "snap vote," with the result that it was lost by a very small majority. A new disappointment for Hindenburg, but more was to follow. The Chancellor persuaded the President to enact the measure by an administrative decree, and this was accordingly done. In the storm which followed Luther's position was so much shaken that he was forced to resign, and once again the President found himself in the vortex of a Cabinet crisis.

This time a complete deadlock ensued. The extreme Nationalists under the leadership of Hugenberg would not enter a Cabinet with the Centre, whom they accused of being agents of the Vatican; the Centre countered with the allegation that the Nationalists were deliberately working for a financial and economic debacle in order to fish in troubled waters. In 1928, the mandate of Parliament would expire and a General Election was due, in which, according to every indication, the Social Democrats would greatly increase their number of seats at the expense of the Nationalists. Until then the Centre favoured the formation of a minority Government, relying on the neutrality of the Left, or a non-party Cabinet consisting of high officials, although in principle they did not refuse to co-operate with the Nationalists.

Negotiations dragged on drearily. Hindenburg wanted a Government of the Right and Centre. He told the Nationalists that the time had come when they must show what they could do in a responsible position. They refused. Hindenburg's patience was at an end. Disgusted and wearied of the business of Government, he informed the Party Leaders that he proposed to resign from the presidency and return to that peaceful retirement from which he had been dragged unwillingly and by false pretences. "I have made my sacrifice for Germany," he told them, "but I find no one willing to follow my example."

His fit of petulance had the desired effect. The majority in the Centre Party, as well as in the Nationalist Party, on the authority of Hindenburg, succeeded in overcoming the opposition in their Parties. Forthwith Hindenburg on January 10, 1927, issued to Marx his Order for the Day in terms which no German Chief of State had ever addressed to a Chancellor.

> You are directed, *Herr Reichskanzler,* to form without delay a Government composed of a majority of the Right and Centre Parties in the *Reichstag.* At the same time I appeal to the parties in the *Reichstag* in question to waive their personal objections and divergencies of opinion in the interests of the Fatherland; to co-operate under your leadership, and to unite behind a Government which is determined to work, not in the interests of any one party but for the good of the Fatherland, and in strict observance of the Constitution. The duty of the new Government, although the parties of the Left are not included in it, is to safeguard the legitimate interests of the working classes with no less zeal than the other essential needs of the State.

On the basis of this lecture to Parliament the Coalition with the Right was formed. A semblance of enduring government had been created, but it was but a breathing-space before the political hurricane of the Young Plan burst upon the country.

· 6 ·

Thus, at the close of his eightieth year, Hindenburg appeared a pathetic figure, isolated from the veneration of his people and surrounded by a thickening web of intrigue. Disquieted by the tortuous ways of politicians, disgruntled and lonely in his high office, he regarded himself as having been betrayed by his friends who had haled him forth from the peace of his retirement under false pretences. Willingly, in 1927, would he have resigned the presidency and returned to Hanover. Only his stern sense of duty kept him in harness. "I have made my sacrifice," he would say, "but none has followed me."

In this spirit of dissatisfaction Hindenburg was naturally receptive of any suggestion or proposal calculated to please him, and it was the great desire of the new Chancellor to find, if possible, some means whereby the Marshal's disappointment might be relieved. In his search Marx hit upon the one remaining point of the Marshal's electoral programme which had escaped destruction, the promise of legislation for the settlement of small-holdings in East Prussia and the provision of financial assistance for the settlers.

As early as 1917, Hindenburg had pledged himself to devote his energies after the war to the settlement of ex-Service men in East Prussia, and it was with genuine pleasure that he had seen the insertion in his electoral programme of promises which would enable him to redeem his word. The series of political crises, which tormented his first years of office, had prevented any action being taken in the matter, and now he welcomed the introduction of the necessary legislation. With the inclusion of the Right in the Government the danger of opposition was lessened, and the measure was brought forward in the *Reichstag* as a private motion by that *enfant prodigue* of the Nationalist Party, their Chief Whip, the irrepressible Treviranus.

But, though the small-holdings scheme had the approval of the Nationalists in the *Reichstag*, the great land-owners of East Prussia were filled with dire forebodings at what they conceived to be so revolutionary a proposal. To them it was but a step from the splitting up of derelict estates into small-holdings for ex-Service men, to the expropriation of their own estates. The measure, though it was designed to raise the value of land in the east, was considered a first move in the direction towards Bolshevism, and the powerful *Landbund* of East Prussia took counsel among themselves as to how they might circumvent it.

A solution was propounded by the veteran leaders of the *Landbund*, Baron von Oldenburg-Januschau and others, a solution which would not only safeguard the estates of all East Prussian land-owners, but would vastly enhance their influence over the President. Let them, it was suggested, make the President one of themselves and then their interests would be his. Ready to hand was a most appropriate means, Neudeck, the family property of the Hindenburgs, which had, since the death of the President's sister-in-law, passed into strange hands. This should be purchased by public subscription and presented to Hindenburg as a national gift on his eightieth birthday, which fell in October. In this way the Marshal would himself become a landed proprietor in East Prussia and would take good care that their common interests were safeguarded. At the same time an alternative to his Bavarian retreat would be provided for the President's vacations and the great conservatives of East Elbia would have him almost continually under their influence.

No little irony was attached to the proposal. In the first place, Neudeck itself had only been included in the boundaries of East Prussia since the peace settlement, when as a result of the creation of the Polish Corridor certain former territory of West Prussia was, for frontier reasons, transferred to the neighbouring province. Thus, Hindenburg's eligibility to join the circle of East Prussian grandees was directly due to Woodrow Wilson's determination to give Poland access to the sea!

Moreover, the suggestion of the *Landbund* was very subtle. It touched the weak spot in Hindenburg's otherwise simple character, for whatever there was in him of vanity and *Snobbismus*, took the form of the land-hunger sometimes felt by great soldiers who have risen from families of smaller social standing. Like the great Duke of Marlborough, Hindenburg had a secret desire to be a member of the landed aristocracy. The fact that he was a Field-Marshal, President of the German *Reich*, and Commander-in-Chief of its armed forces, could not entirely obliterate that inherited sense of resentment and inferiority which his family had felt towards the older nobility of East Prussia. There was a further consideration. Throughout the centuries a permanent struggle was carried on in the Vistula district between the Germans and the Poles, with varying fortune for each individual land-owner, and though even under Polish rule the German peasants and towns' population remained on the whole German, the landed proprietors pursued a policy of vacillation, coalescing to some degree with the Polish nobility. To these families the more implacable Germans attached a local nickname, a word meaning "Polonophil," which carried with it all the contempt of the intransigent for the adaptable. At one period or another the family of Hindenburg had earned this scornful sobriquet and the fact had always rankled in the Marshal's mind. To become one of the territorial elect would clear the family name for ever, and this consideration undoubtedly weighed with him.

For these and other reasons Hindenburg welcomed most warmly the proposal of the national gift. His ideas for Neudeck were not pretentious. It was enough for him that he should once again own the family estate and become a recognized member of the East Prussian landed caste. Had the choice been left to him he would have preferred to keep the old house as he had known it in his youth, a remembrance of his childhood. But not so Oskar, his son. The younger Hindenburg was not entirely content with his position as personal adjutant to the President.

He aspired to greater things and had been heard to say that he must not be regarded merely as his father's son. In the matter of Neudeck he was emphatic. The gift must only be accepted if the simple country house was rebuilt as a *Schloss* worthy of the President of the Republic—and his son. So importunate was he that his father concurred, and the condition was agreed to by the donors.

But the scheme was not so easily accomplished. The cost of purchasing Neudeck and of rebuilding the house in accordance with Oskar's ideas was estimated at a million marks, and it was originally intended that the gift should be made to the President by the landed proprietors of East Prussia. But despite the eloquence of Oldenburg-Januschau, his fellow members of the *Landbund* would subscribe no more than 50,000 marks. When this fact became known, Hindenburg was so humiliated that he seriously considered refusing the gift altogether, and only the protests of his son prevented his doing so. Equally, many of the great industrialists in southern and western Germany were ashamed at the niggardliness of the East Prussians, who, having proposed the idea of a gift, would not, or could not, raise the necessary funds. Pocketing his pride, Oldenburg-Januschau suppressed the traditional contempt of the lords of the land for the industrial magnates, and came to them cap in hand. At the same time, to save the face of all concerned, the Government brought pressure to bear on the banking and commercial communities.

The necessary sum was raised and the business of rebuilding set in hand. But again Oskar gave rein to his grandiose ideas. When the house was nearly finished, he declared to the Committee of Donors that he could only persuade his father to accept Neudeck if the interior decoration was in better style and the stables and farmery were stocked with horses and cattle. Once more the worlds of industry, commerce, and finance were ap-

pealed to, for the land-owners of East Prussia frankly refused
to contribute another *pfennig,* and once more, rather than see
the old Marshal still further humiliated, they complied, but with
contempt for Oskar's conduct.

So the unfortunate episode of Neudeck drew to its apogee,
but not before Oskar had once more asserted himself. On October 1, 1927, Oldenburg-Januschau and the aged "Paint-King"
Duisberg presented the title-deeds to the Marshal, on behalf of
German agriculture and industry, but it was not discovered until three years later that, thoughtfully but illegally, the deeds
had been registered in Oskar's name to avoid death duties and
that payment of other taxes had been deferred.

In all this haggling the President had had no part, nor is it
even known that he was a party to the plot. His only complicity
was his acquiescence to Oskar's importunities.

The great land-owners had succeeded in their object. Hindenburg had become one of them, and they did not overlook the
advantage to themselves of Oskar's social aspirations. His influence with the President was well known and had been admirably demonstrated, and they fostered his friendship and his
grand ideas.

But the business of Neudeck had not entirely escaped public
criticism. The sums spent on the manor had become known and
a certain resentment was caused thereby. Well-meaning friends
of the President suggested to the *Reich* and Prussian Governments that a welcome and expedient gesture would be to persuade Hindenburg to allot some outlying portions of the estate
for the settlement of ex-soldiers. This advice was taken, but the
effect on the President was unexpected. The small-holdings lay
between Neudeck and Deutsch-Eylau, the nearest point on the
railway, so that whenever Hindenburg drove from the station
to the manor he had to pass through them. Gradually, as he
became more completely assimilated into the East Prussian

atmosphere, he began to harbour a certain resentment at the fact that part of his family property should be saddled with small-holders. Little by little this state of mind began to affect his whole outlook on the governmental policy of land settlement in East Prussia, and under the pressure of his fellow landlords, his attitude changed from one of support to hostility. In this matter, at least, he had been captured by the *Landbund*.

Hindenburg's eightieth birthday was the occasion for a further demonstration of the great popularity among the German people which he continued to enjoy for a further six years. Gifts of all kinds flowed in upon him—varying from a series of views of old Berlin painted on porcelain, the gift of the State of Prussia, to a live rabbit from a newspaper boy!—and tributes of loyalty and affection arrived from every corner of the *Reich*. On his actual birthday, October 2, the day after the gift of Neudeck, the Chancellor presented him with the proceeds of the "Hindenburg Fund," raised by common subscription throughout the country and to be devoted to war widows and crippled ex-Service men. A new postage stamp was printed and the mint issued coins bearing his effigy.

A short while later, in unveiling the marble busts of Ebert and Hindenburg in the hall of the *Reichstag*, its President, the Socialist Löbe, paid a high tribute to the Marshal's political impartiality: "From the day of his accession to office he has acted as the representative of the whole nation and not as the spokesman of a party, and he has always raised his voice on behalf of conciliation and compromise." Six years later, when suffering the horrors of a concentration camp, Löbe may well have recalled these words with irony and bitterness.

Now, if ever, Hindenburg was the *Vater des Volkes*, and well would it have been for him had he rested content with the plaudits of his countrymen and had not exchanged the summer hospitality of his Bavarian friends for the dignity of an East Prus-

sian landlord. As Mr. Winston Churchill has written of his great
ancestor, for whom the wary Godolphin had proposed an anniversary thanksgiving by Act of Parliament rather than the gift
of the manor of Woodstock, "It would have been better for Marlborough's happiness if something like this had been done; for
the course adopted was to lead him into many embarrassments
and some humiliation."

Two days' march to the south and east from Neudeck lies the
battlefield of Tannenberg, and here, in this same autumn of
1927, Hindenburg was the central figure of the greatest patriotic
demonstration which post-war Germany had then seen. The occasion was the dedication of the Tannenberg Memorial, a vast oc-
tagonal fane designed as an arena for military gatherings on a
grand scale, and every opportunity had been taken by the forces
of the Right to give the affair as monarchical and reactionary a
flavour as possible. To avoid passing through Polish territory,
Hindenburg was conveyed from Swinemünde to Königsberg in
the cruiser *Berlin,* and on his arrival was the guest of the Kaiser's agent, Herr von Berg, at the castle of Markienen. Thus the
procedure followed the keynote struck at the laying of the foun-
dation-stone two years earlier, when the Chairman of the Memorial Committee had declared that the blows of his hammer "had
welded anew the Crown of Imperial Germany." The Republican
and Jewish ex-Service men's associations had been excluded, the
Stahlhelm alone of the veterans' associations taking part, and in
protest against this predominance of the *schwarz-weiss-rot* the
Prussian Government refused to be represented.

But all the great military figures were there. Hindenburg, gigantic and lonely; Mackensen, fresh-complexioned and slim,
whose proudest boast it was that his waist-line had remained unchanged from lieutenant to field-marshal; and Ludendorff, pon-
derous and grey. Hindenburg and he had not met since the presi-

dential election and now they bowed coldly and did not shake
hands. Later in the day, when Ludendorff rose to speak, Hindenburg had not waited to hear him, and at the end of the ceremony
Ludendorff left almost alone. Hoffmann was not there—he had
died in the previous July.

It had been agreed between the Chancellor and the President
that the demonstration should not be purely commemorative, but
should be the occasion for Germany's long-awaited reply to the
accusation of war-guilt. Here on the battlefield of Tannenberg
the man who had commanded Germany's armies and who presided over the fate of the German people should refute once
and for all the slur which the Treaty of Versailles had put upon
Germany.

Both the subject and the setting were ill-chosen. Whether the
accusation had been justified or not, Germany would have been
better advised to allow it to lapse by tacit consent than to demand
the impossibility of its public withdrawal. In any case, it was
unwise to make the occasion for this demand a demonstration to
commemorate and glorify that spirit of military imperialism on
which the Allies had based the accusation.

For Hindenburg, however, it was a matter of personal honour
and obligation. The allegation had been laid by the Allies at the
door of the Kaiser and the military caste, and he considered it
his bounden duty to vindicate his War Lord and his fellow soldiers. Willingly, then, he had lent himself to the idea, and now,
in the uniform of his Masurian regiment, to which his Emperor
had appointed him colonel-in-chief, he delivered, in his deep,
sepulchral voice, the speech which Marx and Stresemann and
Meissner had prepared for him:

> The accusation that Germany was responsible for this greatest of all
> wars we hereby repudiate; Germans in every walk of life unanimously
> reject it. It was in no spirit of envy, hatred, or lust of conquest that we
> unsheathed the sword. . . . With clean hearts we marched out to de-

fend our Fatherland, and with clean hands did we wield the sword. Germany is ready at any moment to prove this fact before an impartial tribunal. In many graves, the symbol of German heroism, rest men of every party without distinction. . . . May every discord therefore break against this monument.

There is no doubt that the declaration of innocence, delivered in booming tones, which amplifiers intensified and radio carried to the four corners of the country, represented the conviction of the vast majority of the German people, but the effect abroad was anything but favourable. The speech had been made to gratify the demands of the Nationalist Party and had not been intended as the opening of a campaign for repudiation. Consequently, the Foreign Offices and public opinion of the world were completely unprepared for so emphatic a declaration, and at once doubts, never entirely absent from Allied minds, arose as to the honesty of Stresemann's Policy of Fulfilment. For Stresemann had been a party to the speech and had had the major share in its preparation. The Foreign Minister's health was already at a low ebb and his nerves were on edge. The Tannenberg speech was but one of a series of unaccountable provocations which he offered at this time—he publicly taunted Poincaré with preferring the Ruhr to the Locarno Policy; he defended the decision to build a new battleship, and allowed a Nationalist Minister to hint at rectification of the Eastern frontiers. This strange surrender to the Nationalists was greatly detrimental to Stresemann's foreign policy, and the effect of Hindenburg's speech had to be explained away before he could proceed with his plans for a final settlement of the reparations problem and the evacuation of the Rhineland, matters of far greater material importance to Germany than the academic discussion of war-guilt.

But Hindenburg was happy. His eightieth year had closed in far more pleasant circumstances than he had expected. He had received a touching demonstration of the affection of his countrymen; he was a landed proprietor of East Prussia; and he had made a public profession of innocence in defense of his Kaiser and King. With greater contentment than he had known for months, he returned to the grave political problems which confronted him.

· 7 ·

Both within and without, Germany was faced with crisis and uncertainty. In internal affairs the Marx Government, which Hindenburg had brought into being with such difficulty, was continually threatened with disaster. No sooner had it weathered the storm from which resulted the resignation of Gessler and the appointment of Gröner to succeed him as Minister of Defence, than it was confronted by a more serious crisis in the closely connected problems of the increase of salaries in the Civil Service and the question of education in the confessional schools.

The increase of salaries to Civil servants had been promised by all parties in the presidential contest of 1925, and particularly by the Nationalists in the name of Hindenburg. In 1927 the Marx Cabinet set out to redeem these pledges, but was at once hampered by the parlous condition of the budget. The advice of the Agent-General for Reparation Payments, Mr. Parker Gilbert, was sought, and an agreement was reached with the Cabinet whereby, provided that the rise in salaries should not exceed 10 per cent, the Agent-General would not criticize it in his next report. At the same time it was agreed between the leaders, under the influence of the young men of the Nationalist and Centre Parties, that the increase of salaries should not be voted before the law relating to confessional schools was passed.

In effect neither of these undertakings was kept. Not only did the Government put the bill for the increase of salaries before the *Reichsrat* while the final draft of the bill regarding the confessional schools was not yet completed, but, in so doing, the

Finance Minister announced an average increase of 16½ per cent in the salaries of all Civil servants. But in the case of the middle grade (*mittlere Beamten*) Civil servants the increase was as much in certain cases as 40 per cent. The result was chaos and opposition from all sides; the cost of living rose by from 5 to 15 per cent; the workers consequently demanded a 10 per cent increase in wages. Reasonable men of all parties, both inside the Government and in Opposition, realized that with this huge increase a balanced Budget was impossible, and the Radical Left took up the agitation in informing the small agriculturists and the middle class that such heavy increases would undoubtedly mean higher taxation. At the same time the Radicals urged the lower classes of Civil servants to protest against the disproportion in the ratio of their salary increases with those of the higher grades. A fierce struggle ensued which plunged the country into a storm of excitement, the opposition against the unsound financial proposals in the bill being led by Dr. Schacht, the *Reichsbank* President, and budget experts of the political parties, among them Heinrich Brüning, the leading authority of the Centre Party on economics and finance.

In this struggle Hindenburg took no direct part, but his personal opinions were strongly coloured by the views of Dr. Meissner, who symbolized, *par excellence,* the senior Civil servant. Gradually the opposition became weaker. The senior bureaucracy bought off the Left Parties by promising them large increases in social insurance allocations and wages, and Schacht, fearful lest he should "get in wrong" with the *Reichswehr* and the President, withdrew his opposition, leaving Brüning to carry on the fight alone. In the end the bill was passed; despite the strong protests of Parker Gilbert, the only victory which the opposition were able to achieve was the insertion of a clause designed to bring about ultimate economies; for the next five years every third vacancy in the Civil Service should not be filled.

As if this crisis had not been sufficiently severe, an even more acute issue opened over the Confessional Schools Bill. With the greatest difficulty it passed a first and second reading, but in committee the fight resolved itself into a direct struggle between the German People's Party and the Centre, and in the end Stresemann torpedoed the bill. The Marx Cabinet was split to its foundations, and its prestige was so badly impaired that the new elections, which were due in July 1928, had to be held in May, a full two months before the statutory limit to the life of Parliament.

In the electoral campaign which followed, nothing was so remarkable as the transparent casuistry and the pathetic ineptitude of the Nationalists, the party with which Hindenburg's name was still associated. One of the major tragedies of the Weimar System was the complete failure of the great Conservative body to realize either its national obligations or its political opportunities. Its logical mission was to achieve the national awakening of young Germany (which was later accomplished by Adolf Hitler in his own peculiar style), and at the outset, if properly led, it could have succeeded. Instead, it confided its leadership to Alfred Hugenberg, the newspaper and film magnate, and allowed him to juggle with the party funds to such an extent that he very soon had them completely under his own control. So firm a grip did Hugenberg attain on the party that those who disagreed with him had no choice but to resign. That they did resign is to the credit of such men as Count Westarp and Treviranus, but they were too late to be able to build up a real conservative movement. The Nationalist Party, which could have done so much to bridge the gulf between the new Germany and the old, betrayed its trust and its traditions. Under Hugenberg it deliberately put political before national considerations, and went so far as to contemplate with equanimity a national collapse which might bring it political advantage. Finally, it surrendered abjectly to Hitler on his own terms, and reaped the well-merited reward of all time-servers.

Hugenberg's tactics during the election of 1928 were characteristic of his whole career. Anxious to profit both from the national popularity of the President and from the failure of the Government which the President had put into power, the Nationalists adopted two conflicting slogans: "Every Vote cast for the Nationalists is a Vote for Hindenburg" was used on some occasions, and "Vote for the Nationalists if you are discontented" on others. Finally, when they realized the fact that the tide was turning against them and that the only alternative to a Socialist Government was a Cabinet appointed by Hindenburg, they exhorted the electors, by means of placards and handbills, to "Extend the Power of the President."

Their efforts were in vain. When the country went to the polls on May 20, 1928, it was found that, with the exception of the Economic Party, all groups had lost heavily to the Socialists and Communists, who between them had 40 per cent of the whole. The Centre Party representation fell to its lowest level at any time during the Republic; the Nationalists lost a fifth of their supporters, and moreover serious differences of opinion arose between themselves. Not only had they lost to the Social Democrats but to new parties, whilst at the same time the National Socialist followers of Adolf Hitler were only returned to the *Reichstag* with twelve seats.

The effect of the elections upon the household of the President was almost one of panic. At a dinner-party given to a number of Party Leaders a few days after the results had been declared, Meissner declared that Hindenburg would be only too pleased to have a Government of the great Coalition, his sole conditions being that Stresemann should be retained at the Foreign Office and Gröner at the Ministry of Defence. In reality, the President's advisers favoured a much greater swing to the Left than had ever been contemplated even under Ebert. Greater moderation, however, prevailed, and a Government was eventually formed by the Social Democrat leader, Hermann Müller, including both Stresemann and Gröner, and based on the support of the Socialists, Democrats, and Centre, with the German and Bavarian People's Parties adopting an attitude of benevolent neutrality. In the phrase of Stresemann, it was a Government of the Grand Coalition *in possee* but not *in esse*.

Whilst the Müller Government was struggling at home with the problem of balancing the budget, and abroad with that of reparation payments, the Nationalists endeavoured to recover some of their shattered prestige. As usual, they took refuge behind the personality of Hindenburg. Hugenberg, allying himself with the *Stahlhelm*, who were at that time in need of political exercise and a new slogan, developed his agitation for granting dictatorial powers to the President, and throughout the remainder of the year busied himself with the preparations for a popular referendum on: "Hindenburg *versus* the Democratic State."

The issue was made entirely without Hindenburg's approval or support. At this time he was still opposed either to dictatorial power or to presidial government. But he did nothing to dissociate himself from the agitation. He remained the honorary president of the *Stahlhelm* and confined himself to sharp criticism of Hugenberg in private. The strictures, however, were passed on by Schleicher to the rebellious younger members of the Nationalist Party in such a way as to give them the impression that they would be doing the President's pleasure if they ousted Hugenberg from the leadership of the party.

The plans of Hugenberg for a referendum proved a complete failure, though the Right wing of the German People's Party was sufficiently won over to the idea to make a vague movement in the *Reichstag* for an extension of the presidential powers. Hugenberg was a sufficiently astute politician to know when he had picked a loser. Without compunction he abandoned the campaign and turned his attention to other, more troubled, waters in which he could fish with greater advantage.

The winter of 1928–29 was particularly hard. All Europe shivered, and in Germany the numbers of the unemployed increased heavily, bringing social unrest and political complications. Distress spread alike in town and country, and in both there grew up a discontent with the ineptitude of the *Reichstag* and the meanderings of the mentally ossified political parties. Gone were the days of comparative contentment which had followed Hindenburg's eightieth birthday. He was back in the maelstrom of political crises, and his own personality was beginning to be obscured by the intrigues which emanated from his household and shrouded and befogged his natural shrewdness. Schleicher and Oskar were working in close harmony with Meissner; they were clever enough not to attempt to supplant the Secretary of State, but rather to enlist his aid in influencing the President in the desired direction. They were not yet prepared to throw in their lot with the Nationalists, but with them Hugenberg's agitation for an increase in the President's powers had not fallen upon barren soil.

With the New Year (1929) Stresemann, supported by Müller, Schacht, and Parker Gilbert, pushed forward his negotiations for the termination of the Dawes Plan and a final settlement of reparations. The first conversations had taken place during the summer of 1928 in the Bank of England, when both the Governor and Professor Sprague had urged Schacht to abandon his policy of revision, but in vain. Many members in all parties who were experts in finance and economics implored the Chancellor not to pursue this line of action, as the whole financial policy of Germany since 1925 had been based upon the supposition that the machinery of the Dawes Plan would stop automatically as soon as the so-called *Grosser Besserungschein* should come into force in the late autumn of 1928.[1] It was their intention that, without talking about the necessity of revision, Germany's futile efforts to carry on under this additional burden should prove that the breakdown of the Dawes Plan was inevitable.

Stresemann, however, persisted. His struggle with his rapidly deteriorating health was reaching its final phase, and before his eyes still shone the dream of a delivered Rhineland. He carried the Chancellor with him and pushed on his negotiations as rapidly as possible. In February 1929 the Young Committee met, and in June its report was ready for signature. Again opposition arose in Germany. The sum which might be deducted each year by the New Plan from the total annuities of the Dawes Plan was very small, and would, it was declared, bring little relief to Germany. Strong pressure was brought to bear upon the President, both by the Right and the Left, not to authorize the acceptance of the Plan, but Schacht asserted that in case of refusal he could not be responsible for the financial situation of Germany. Stresemann and Schacht won the day; on June 7 the New Plan was signed in Paris and its contents became known to the world.

There can be no question that the provisions of the Young Plan brought certain advantages to Germany not contained in the Dawes Plan, amongst them the fact that a "final" solution had been found for the whole problem of reparation payments. In many respects it was a spectacular success for the Policy of Fulfilment, but there were men in Germany at that time who would have preferred a national disaster to a victory for Stresemann.

Among these was Hugenberg, who seized upon the provisions of the Young Plan as a God-given opportunity to attack the Re-

---

[1] Under the prosperity index devised in accordance with the Dawes Plan, the full annuity payment of 2½ milliards was only reached in the financial year 1928–29, at which time the portion to be contributed from the Budget was more than doubled, representing, in fact, exactly half the annuity.

publican system and the policy of *Erfüllung*. Even before the plans for the Hague Conference, which was to give legal form to the Plan, had been completed, he had set about mobilizing his old allies and adding to them new forces. The full blast of his press and film propaganda, the combined might of the Nationalists, the Pan-German League, and the *Stahlhelm*, were thrown into the fight against the Young Plan, and in the frenzy of his zeal Hugenberg condescended to seek the support of Hitler and the National Socialists.

Without regard for this storm gathering at home, Stresemann proceeded to the conference at the Hague in the month of August. His contempt for Hugenberg's mud-slinging was such that he might well have used Guizot's famous taunt: "You may pile up your abuse as high as you like, it will never reach the height of my disdain." At the Hague he wrestled heroically with death, while grasping at the realization of his ideal. So often during those seven years of his foreign policy had he dreamed of a liberated Rhineland, and ever the vision had vanished before his waking eyes. Now with his own strength at its final ebb, he could not face the possibility of another disappointment. To gain the evacuation of the Second and Third zones he made concessions which a man in full possession of his health and strength might have hesitated to make. He agreed to certain amendments in the Young Plan which added considerably to the future burdens of Germany, and accepted in principle the treaty with Poland whereby Germany renounced her claims to former German property in that country. The sacrifices were heavy, but Stresemann achieved his ideal in the Rhineland Evacuation Agreement of August 29, 1929.

Yet while Stresemann fought thus desperately at the Hague, the internal political situation of Germany became daily more unsatisfactory. For weeks on end the machinery of government was practically at a standstill. The ill-health of the Chancellor

necessitated his long and frequent absences from Berlin, while
Stresemann, with three other Ministers, was at the Hague. A
rump Cabinet, presided over by Gröner as Minister of Defence,
endeavoured to cope with the business of Government but without conspicuous success, and as a result the emasculated *Reichs-
kabinet* became the butt of many a joke at the café tables and
cabaret performances.

It was at this period that Schleicher's direct contact with party
politics and State affairs began. Gröner, unused and in many
ways unsuited to the position of acting Chancellor, leaned more
and more for support upon his brilliant young assistant, on
whom he depended for the preparation of his Cabinet statements
and routine business. Soon it became necessary for Schleicher
to join the Secretaries of State of the President and the Chancellor at Cabinet meetings. He became conversant with all secrets
of State, and Gröner used him frequently to act as go-between in
negotiation with Party Leaders. The situation appealed strongly
to Schleicher's inherent tendency to intrigue and to the sense of
pleasure which he felt in the exercise of power. Once in possession of this new toy, he could not be restrained in his use of it.
He saw himself as the secret arbiter of German destinies and
seized the opportunity to embark upon a course of personal negotiations which led him on to those later intrigues of colossal
and fateful dimensions.

For the moment he was justifiably and deeply anxious as to the
political situation, which, were it to be prolonged much further,
would bring the authority of the Government into such ridicule
that it could never recover. In company with many others he desired a speedy rectification of the position, and he added his voice
to those who were urging a policy of change upon the President.

Hindenburg had by this time repented of his panic-stricken
rush towards the Left after the 1928 elections and was beginning to drift again towards the Right and Centre. But he was

deeply disappointed with the whole trend of politics since the signing of the Young Plan, and openly declared his regret at ever having given his consent to it. He began to prepare for a reshuffle of the Cabinet which should result in the disappearance of Hermann Müller, Stresemann, and several other Ministers, and of Schacht from the *Reichsbank*.

Both Schleicher and Gröner were agreed that the new Chancellor must enjoy the confidence of the *Reichswehr* and they were united in their choice of their candidate. Heinrich Brüning stood out pre-eminently as the man who should take the helm of the ship of State at this stormy period. He possessed two vital qualifications for the position; he was a sound and acknowledged authority on economics and finance, and, both by personal contacts and through his friendship with Willisen, he had earned the high regard of the army, to whom he had been of considerable service in the Budget difficulties of 1928–29.

Particular importance was attached by Schleicher to the necessity for close and friendly relations between the prospective Chancellor and the *Reichswehr* because he was premeditating drastic action to remedy the ills of the State; action which must, in the final resort, depend for its success upon the full collaboration between the Government and the army. The country was faced with a serious political crisis, and to meet it the President and his advisers, amongst them Schleicher, were prepared to follow the example already set by Ebert, Luther, and Marx on a previous and similar occasion. They proposed to make use of Article 48 of the Constitution [1] to bring the economic life of the

[1] The text of Article 48 of the Weimar Constitution ran as follows:
"If any State does not perform the duties imposed upon it by the Constitution or by national laws, the President of the Reich may hold it to the performance thereof by force of arms.
"If public safety and order in the German Commonwealth is materially disturbed or endangered, the President of the Reich may take the necessary measures to restore public safety and order, and, if necessary, to intervene by force of arms. To this end he may temporarily suspend, in whole or in part, the fundamental rights established in Articles 114, 115, 117, 118, 123, 124, and 153.

country out of chaos, and if necessary to amend the Constitution in such a way that the many prevalent ills and errors might be obviated in the future. The drastic decrees which were envisaged might easily result in grave political repercussions, and for this reason it was essential to have a Chancellor in whom the *Reichswehr* had complete confidence.

But Brüning, when approached tentatively by Schleicher, was not enamoured of the prospect. He was primarily opposed to any change of Government before the evacuation of the Rhineland had been accomplished, and was frankly astounded at the use of Article 48 which was proposed. Such a proposal disclosed to him a lack of foresight and appreciation of the gravity of the situation among the President's advisers. The action which they were prepared to take would necessitate the application of Article 48, not for six months, as they optimistically envisaged, but possibly for two or three years. The existing *Reichstag*, Brüning knew well, would be unquestionably opposed to such a policy and would refuse the two-thirds majority necessary to legalize many of the actions which it was proposed to take; only by the very greatest care and preparation could this opposition be overcome, and the necessary parliamentary support assured.

All these objections Brüning voiced to Schleicher, but the General remained undaunted. The legal position he said had been fully examined by the Law Officers, and they were at complete variance with Brüning's views. To convince him of this, Schleicher promised to send him a copy of the legal opinion. When the document duly arrived, to Brüning's surprise he found

---

"The President of the Reich must immediately inform the National Assembly of all measures adopted by authority of Paragraphs 1 or 2 of this Article. These measures shall be revoked at the demand of the National Assembly.

"If there is danger from delay, the State Cabinet may for its own territory take provisional measures as specified in Paragraph 2. These measures shall be revoked at the demand of the President of the Reich or of the National Assembly.

"The details will be regulated by a national law."

that it confirmed on all points the objections which he had raised with Schleicher, and was, in fact, completely contrary to the General's views. Brüning's first thought was that Schleicher had given the opinion, without reading it, to one of his staff officers to make *a précis*, for his intelligence was too great for him to have made such a mistake. Subsequently, however, he learned that the views of Oskar von Hindenburg and of the President's friends coincided on all points with Schleicher's. This was enough to convince Brüning that, without the knowledge of the President and in direct opposition to the expressed opinion of the legal authorities, Schleicher was preparing the ground for a military dictatorship. The mystery is still unsolved as to why he sent to Brüning a document which must manifestly have confirmed the other's opposition.

This incident is characteristic of the atmosphere which surrounded Hindenburg at this time. He was beset by problems of State to which neither he nor his immediate advisers were qualified or capable of finding solutions. Every week seemed to bring some fresh factor in the bewilderment of an old gentleman of eighty who longed more and more for the peace of retirement and whose one consolation seemed to be that only three more years of office separated him from it.

Upon Hindenburg, in this despondent frame of mind, burst the storm of national reaction. Hugenberg's agitation against the Young Plan took the form of a popular referendum to bring before the *Reichstag* a "Bill against the Enslavement of the German People," whereby the acceptance of the Plan was declared to be an act of treachery and those Ministers of the *Reich* who were responsible for its acceptance were declared guilty of high treason. To be brought into Parliament this preposterous document required more than 10 per cent of the votes of the electorate and the campaign was carried on with an almost fiendish fanaticism. The attacks on Stresemann were more bitter than at the time of Locarno, yet in his greatness he ignored them.

The very frenzy of the Nationalists defeated their aims, and the only people to benefit by the campaign were their very doubtful allies, the National Socialists. The money so liberally provided by Hugenberg for propaganda was used by Hitler for the equipment and expansion of his Storm Troops, and the payment of the campaign expenses was left to the Nationalists. When the vote was taken on November 3, the necessary percentage was gained by the fractional figure of 10·02; but the principal figure against whom the bill had been directed had passed beyond the range of insult and intrigue. Early on the morning of October 3 Gustav Stresemann had died.

Defeat with ignominy awaited the bill in the *Reichstag*; defeat that was the more significant in that twenty-two Nationalists, led by Schiele and Treviranus, absented themselves. Treviranus left the party, to be followed six months later by other members, including Schiele and Count Westarp, the parliamentary leader. Nothing, however, could check effectively Hugenberg's fantastic and childish fulminations.

Far more dangerous was the accession of Dr. Schacht to the opponents of the Young Plan. Having signed the original text in Paris and incurred much odium thereby amongst his former friends, Schacht seized upon the concessions made by Stresemann at the Hague to repudiate his signature and to campaign openly both against the amended pact and the financial policy of the Müller Government as a whole. His attacks, not entirely unwarranted, brought about the resignation of the Finance Minister, Hilferding, and precipitated a crisis which once more threw the household of the President into panic.

No longer was there thought or talk of military dictatorship, and in the second week of December 1929, the President's intermediaries were actually negotiating with Hugenberg for the formation of a Nationalist government. Hermann Müller, without whose knowledge the offer had been made, told the Party Leaders of it as soon as he received the news, and confessed that he did not believe he could command a vote of confidence before the Hague Conference reassembled in January.

But Hugenberg refused the offer. He wished to figure in history as the man who saved his country from the abyss, and from his point of view Germany was not yet sufficiently far over the edge. Complete collapse was apparently necessary before the Nationalists would come to the rescue, and this collapse they set themselves with gusto to precipitate. Müller, however, scraped through with a vote of confidence greater than he had any cause to expect, and in January 1930 he and Julius Curtius, the successor of Stresemann in the Foreign Office, formally accepted the amended Young Plan at the Hague.

If the campaign against its acceptance had been bitter, the efforts made to prevent ratification of the Young Plan attained a pitch of vitriolic invective unequalled even in German politics. This time it was not against the Chancellor or the Foreign Minister that the attacks were directed, but against the person of the President himself, with whom the final decision lay. Again Hugenberg and his Nationalists entered the fight with all the fierceness of fanatics, but in vain. Step by step the bills of ratification were fought through the *Reichstag,* and then the full pressure of propaganda was brought to bear on Hindenburg.

Under this ordeal the Marshal bore up very well. Despite the threats and entreaties of his Nationalist friends, he took his stand steadfastly upon the Constitution. A few months before the Weimar Republic had celebrated its tenth anniversary with solemn thanksgiving and to mark the occasion a new three-mark piece had been issued, bearing the head of Hindenburg on one side and his hand upraised in reaffirmation of his oath to the Constitution on the other. Now in the hour of trial he remained,

at least outwardly, faithful to his oath; his Government had negotiated an international agreement, the *Reichstag* had ratified
it, and it was the duty of the President to place his signature
upon the bills of ratification. Whatever his personal inclinations
may have been, his constitutional course was clear. He made it
known that he would sign the bills.

The storm of invective became a tornado. Those who only a
short while ago had cried "More power to the President," now
execrated this same man as a traitor and a coward. "The suicidal attitude of a misguided portion of our nation is only paral-
leled in our history by that of the President," howled one Nationalist daily. "He has today forfeited the unlimited confidence
originally reposed in him by every genuinely patriotic German." "Respect has given way to hatred. No merit is so great
that guilt cannot wipe it out," cried the *Deutsche Zeitung.* "It is
henceforth to be war to the knife, a war in which there can be
no retreat." Communists and National Socialists joined hands in
vilifying the old Marshal, alleging that he had been bought by
the French or the profiteers or the Marxists, and Goebbels asked
jeeringly in the *Angriff:* "Is Hindenburg still alive?" That all
sense of decency had been abandoned is shown by the remark of
old General Litzmann, who had commanded a division under
Hindenburg on the Eastern Front: "Unfortunately we have no
secret *Vehmgericht* to render these signers harmless." Hindenburg was now threatened with that same death which had come
to Erzberger and to Rathenau.

But these wild insults were easier for him to bear than the
genuine and sincere reproaches of a body of young Nationalist
undergraduates, who appealed to him in the name of the "dead
of Langemarck" and of the young volunteers who had gone to
their deaths in Flanders in 1914. Hindenburg, who had left the
attacks of the politicians unanswered, replied to these boys with
sad restraint, yet firmly: "The memory of the young volunteers

who sacrificed their lives for the Fatherland, imposed upon their generation and yours the special duty of making sacrifices in order to procure the liberation of German territory."

Drinking deeply of the cup of sorrow and humiliation, Hindenburg held fast upon his course. He had known what it was in war and in peace to be the idol of his people, and he was now tasting the bitter wine of repudiation. His old world had rejected him and it was little comfort to him that the press of the Left and Centre hailed him as the saviour of the republic; their praise could not assuage the pain of parting from all that he had reverenced throughout a long life. Yet he kept on. The bills of ratification were signed on March 13, 1930, and on the same day he issued a manifesto to the German people which, though in no sense an apologia, was yet an explanation of his conduct:

After a thorough and conscientious examination of the Young Plan laws, I have with a heavy but resolute heart put my signature to the Agreement. Having listened to all the arguments for and against the Plan, and having carefully considered both points of view, I have come to the conclusion that, in spite of the heavy burden which the new Plan will lay upon Germany's shoulders for many years to come, and in spite of the serious objections which may be raised against some of its provisions, the Young Plan represents, in comparison with the Dawes Plan, an improvement and a relief, and a step forward economically and politically along the hard path of Germany's re-establishment and liberation. In view of my responsibility for Germany and Germany's future, I could not consent to a rejection, since the consequences of such an action would be incalculable for German commerce and finance, and would lead to serious crises, exposing our country to considerable dangers.

I am fully aware of the fact that mere acceptance of the Young Plan does not free us from all anxiety for the future; nevertheless, I confidently believe that the course upon which we have now embarked and which brings to German Occupied Territory its longed-for freedom, and to us all hope for further progress, will prove the right one.

Many letters have begged me, no doubt with well-meant intention,

not to besmirch my name—the name of a former great soldier—in the
eyes of history, by placing it beneath these laws. To this I reply: I
have spent my life in the great school of devotion to duty—the Old
Army—and there I learnt to do my duty towards my country without
any regard for my personal feelings. Therefore, any consideration of
self had to be put aside when I made this decision, and any thought
of relieving myself of this responsibility by a referendum or by my
resignation could not be entertained.

If it had been hoped to disarm or silence criticism by this
manifesto, which no doubt represented the true feelings of Hindenburg, such hopes were doomed to disappointment. Though
they, the critics, had failed to achieve the rejection of the Young
Plan, they could still at least vilify the President. The appeal
with which the manifesto ended for a sinking of political feuds
and quarrels in the common interest of the *Reich* fell upon deaf
ears, and the reply of the Nationalists and of Hindenburg's old
comrades-in-arms was made by Ludendorff a few days later:

Field-Marshal von Hindenburg has forfeited the right to wear the
field-grey uniform of the army and to be buried in it. Herr Paul von
Hindenburg has destroyed the very thing he fought for as Field-Marshal.

· 8 ·

The Young Plan crisis marked a vital turning-point in Hindenburg's political career. The Right, his own people, had rejected him, and to them he had become a renegade, whose crime
was only to be expiated years later in the "national resurgence"
of 1933. To the Left, however, the President appeared in a new
light: no longer was he the potential MacMahon of Germany,
but the champion of the Constitution and the saviour of the
Republic. The words of welcome, "Hindenburg belongs to the
German nation," with which Grzesinski had acclaimed him in

1918, took on a new meaning, for it did seem now that the Marshal stood for Germany and not for his own caste and party.

But before the ratification of the Young Plan bills was secured it was evident that both the President and the country were faced with as severe an economic crisis as had been known since the dark days of the Ruhr and the inflation. In three months' time, that is to say by March or April 1930, the Treasury would no longer be able to pay the obtaining rates of insurance to the unemployed, and either the contribution of the men themselves must be increased or the payments diminished. Those responsible for the payments, the higher Civil servants of the Ministries of Finance and Labour, were at their wits' end, and, as usual in such emergencies, they turned to the *Reichswehr*. The assistance of Gröner and, by the same token, of Schleicher, was implored in persuading the Cabinet to make the necessary economic and financial reforms, the necessity for which had long been emphasized in the reports of the Agent-General for Reparation Payments. To the army the bureaucrats admitted that, if in a few months' time it should prove impossible to continue the full legal scale of unemployment payments, there would be such serious civil disturbances that the military authorities would have to take control. To the *Reichswehr* this threat meant the realization of their greatest dread during all the years after the Revolution—that they should be forced to fire on the workers. National Socialists they had scattered in Munich, Communists they had suppressed in Saxony and Thuringia, but the acid test would only come when the young soldiers were ordered to fire upon the ordinary decent working man in arms against a Government which had contracted to pay him unemployment insurance and had failed in its promises.

Urged on by this fear, the *Reichswehr* brought pressure to bear once more upon the President to change the Government. This too presented difficulties. Who should replace Müller? The hopes of the President for a government of the Right, or even for a coalition of the Right and Centre, had been shattered by implacable opposition of Hugenberg to the Young Plan. In the last personal effort which the President had made with the Nationalist leader he had offered a number of far-reaching concessions, even promising the constitutional reforms necessary to fulfil the most vital of Hugenberg's demands, the increase of the power of the President at the expense of the *Reichstag*. All that he asked in return was the formation of a Cabinet of the Right and a modification of Hugenberg's attitude towards the Young Plan.

Hugenberg's reply had been that he would relentlessly oppose the Plan and all connected with it, and the President, who had long set his heart on having a National Cabinet in power when he participated in the liberation ceremonies in the Rhineland, was so wounded and mortified that he determined, and proclaimed the fact to his friends, that under no circumstances during his lifetime should Hugenberg ever be asked again to form a Cabinet.

Schleicher and Gröner now repeated his claims for Brüning as Chancellor. The fears that they had expressed a little earlier had now been revived and had grown even stronger. They were even more convinced that Germany needed a strong government; they meant a government which would work with them and through which they could work. Though the march of events had prevented their earlier plans from materializing they had not abandoned them, and they were still confident that Brüning was the man of the hour.

Heinrich Brüning was at that time forty-four years old, a young man if judged either from the standards of German political leaders or world statesmen. His career had been rapid, and he had been early marked out for office. Of a very sensitive nature, he was at once a romantic and a paladin, a dreamer of dreams and a man of courage. A devout Catholic, he came of a middle-class Westphalian family, and, as a delicate, shy and brilliant young man, he was about to complete his doctor's thesis at the University of Bonn when the outbreak of the war destroyed the sheltered life which till then had been his. The glamour of war appealed to him; the paladin and the romantic in him merged into one and sent him unhesitatingly to volunteer. To his dismay he was rejected for defective eyesight, and returned disheartened to complete his thesis. The subject of his choice had been the comparative study of private and State ownership of railways, and the thesis disclosed a remarkable knowledge of the British railway system. A brilliant degree in economics was his reward, but still he hankered for the opportunity to fight for the Fatherland. He volunteered again. The inroads of war upon the man power of Germany had made the medical authorities less particular and Brüning was accepted. It was May 1915 and he was then twenty-nine.

His first sojourn at the front was brief. He was wounded almost immediately and invalided home. His cure completed, he trained for a commission, specializing as a machine-gunner, and returned to the front line as a lieutenant in time to take part in the great battles of '16 and '17, in the offensive of March 1918, and in the bitter retreat of the same year. Brüning was a good soldier and a capable officer. Whether as adjutant or in active command, he displayed a natural ability and cool courage which belied his student appearance. His machine-gun squadron achieved a notoriety and fame wherever it was engaged, and was cited on more than one occasion for "unparalleled heroism"; Brüning himself received the Iron Cross (First Class). In the last phases of the struggle he was constantly in action, his company forming part of the famous "Winterfeldt Group"— a group of units picked for their fighting qualities and their endurance—and with them he participated in the actions around

Aix-la-Chapelle and Herbesthal, his squadron remaining loyal amid the surrounding hordes of mutineers. What his men thought of him may be gauged by the fact that on the formation of Soldiers' Councils, on the orders of G.H.Q., he was unanimously elected as his squadron's representative.

His war experiences had wrought a great change in Brüning. Much of the romanticism of youth had been burned out of his soul and in its place there was a certain mysticism of comradeship. He had learned to command men, and to earn their respect and loyalty; and he himself had come to know the spiritual satisfaction of following a leader in whom he had confidence. Military discipline in its finest sense appealed to him and he carried out of the war an abiding devotion to duty and public service.

In the chaos of the revolution he gradually developed for himself a political credo. His religion and his upbringing influenced his decisions, and he found himself inclined to the life of a civilian rather than that of a member of the Free Corps. Though an honest republican, there was enough of the "realist-romantic" left in Brüning, as well as his Catholic beliefs, to make him regret the disappearance of the monarchy, with its wealth of traditions and its welding force of unity. To the end he remained—and still remains—a conservative and a monarchist at heart.

Brüning's interest lay in politics and social work. Chance threw him in the path of Stegerwald, the leader of the Catholic Trade Unions and at that time Prussian Minister for Social Welfare. Brüning became secretary to the Minister and a member of the Centre Party; he also became an expert on trade-union affairs. His genius for organization found full scope, and was used with great effect at the critical period of the Ruhr Occupation. With headquarters just outside the "frontier," Brüning forged and wielded the weapon of passive resistance with such excellent results that the machinery of occupation was paralyzed and such advantages as accrued were rendered sterile. In the election of 1924 he entered the *Reichstag* on the Centre Party list in Silesia, and at once achieved a reputation as an expert in economics and finance. His speeches in the Budget debates commanded respect and admiration even from his bitterest opponents, for it was obvious that this tall, slight figure, with the thin lips and nose, the receding hair and clear, blue eyes twinkling through gold-rimmed spectacles, knew what he was talking about. He soon came under Schleicher's notice, and his relations with the *Reichswehr*, established and maintained through his friendship with Willisen, grew rapidly cordial. His personal efforts, both with the *Reichstag* and the army, facilitated the passage of the military budget of 1928–29, and when in December 1929 he became leader of the parliamentary group of the Centre Party, Schleicher hesitated no longer.

His first overtures to Brüning had been unfortunate, and should have implanted in Brüning's mind a greater mistrust than was the case, but the General soon returned to the attack and at Christmas 1929 he again approached Brüning with a view to the Chancellorship. At a dinner-party at Willisen's, Meissner, Schleicher, Treviranus, and Gröner all urged Brüning to prepare himself to become Chancellor in a few weeks' time. Brüning protested. It would be a mistake, he said, to have any change of government before the evacuation of the Rhineland had been completed. Then, if a change was really necessary, the President, in accordance with parliamentary procedure, should ask Hugenberg, as leader of the opposition, to form a government which should make the far-reaching reforms. The President, Meissner answered, had repeatedly sought to persuade the Nationalists to take a share in the responsibility of government by joining or forming a Cabinet, but all his efforts had been in vain, and, if one thing was certain, it was that the

President would have nothing more to do with Hugenberg. In that case, Brüning said, the case for not precipitating a Cabinet crisis was even stronger than he had thought. It would in fact be a leap in the dark. They redoubled their persuasions, but Brüning remained adamant. At last, when the discussion had become a little heated, Schleicher rose from the table and said heavily, "I am afraid I shall have to take office myself."

He did not long entertain this idea, but set about preparing Hindenburg's mind for the idea of Brüning as Chancellor. The Marshal was not enamoured of the idea of having another Catholic about him—he had all the Prussian Lutheran's intolerant distrust of Popery. But he liked what he heard of Brüning's war record. Here at last was a man who could talk his language and to whose sense of discipline and military ardour he could appeal on occasion. By the time Schleicher, with the assistance of Oskar, Meissner, and Gröner, had finished, Hindenburg was enthusiastic about his new Chancellor-designate, and could scarcely wait to get rid of Hermann Müller.

But Brüning was not won over easily. He was loyal to Hermann Müller, whose personal friend he was, and he knew well how desperately Müller was fighting to bring his party to its senses, and to force them to adopt the necessary reforms. In order to give the Chancellor both a breathing-space and additional support, Brüning persuaded the Centre Party to announce its decision only to support the ratification of the Young Plan if at the same time the more urgent of the financial reforms were adopted by the *Reichstag*. By this means, Brüning also hoped to bar the way to the adventurous ideas of Schleicher in the application of Article 48.

In the meantime Schleicher had not been idle, and when in the New Year Brüning paid his formal visit to the President on his election as parliamentary leader of his party, he found a mind already well disposed towards him. The interview, which normally was of the briefest nature, and had never been known to exceed a quarter of an hour, became more and more prolonged.

Save at formal gatherings and public ceremonies the two had never met, and now they sat alone in that great workroom which overlooked the garden. They made a strange contrast. Eighty-three faced forty-four; the gigantic military bulk of the President confronted the slight, stooping figure of the statesman; the Field-Marshal looked into the eyes of the company commander. Brüning was deeply moved. Here before him was that great figure which had been an object of veneration to every German soldier. He was surprised at how little the Marshal showed his age. His eyes were clear and blue, and his skin as smooth and ruddy as a child's. He looked, as he sat behind the great work-table with the sunlight of early spring shining on him through the windows, a grand and lonely figure. Brüning was touched by his evident sincerity; both his admiration and his affection were aroused.

They talked of the war days, and the Marshal spoke with high praise of the Winterfeldt Group. The years seemed to slip away and it was only as if two soldiers were comparing their experiences. Hindenburg began to think of Brüning less as a Catholic Party Leader and more as an ex-officer. The basis of a strange comradeship was gradually forming.

From the war they passed to politics and Hindenburg gave full expression to his disgust and disappointment. Suddenly he began to weep, those facile tears of old age, and with that historic gesture which had begun, and ended, so many of his relationships, he clasped Brüning's hand in both his own: "So many have forsaken me; give me your word that now, at the end of my life, you will not desert me." The Centre Party, said Brüning, would always support him as long as he remained loyal to the Constitution, and he told the President of the decision of the party linking the ratification of the Young Plan with financial reforms. Urgently Brüning appealed to Hindenburg to retain Müller in office until after the evacuation of the Rhineland.

The President approved the line of policy and concluded the interview even more well pleased than before with the man whom he was now determined to have for Chancellor.

But Brüning was only able to keep his followers true to the policy of their resolution for less than a month. The Centre Party, both in committee and in the *Reichstag*, showed signs of wavering and uncertainty, and their parliamentary leader could never be sure that they would not "run out" at the last moment. In financial circles there arose a grave anxiety that a new crisis would develop comparable to that which followed the publication of the Young Plan in 1929, and the bankers were bringing considerable pressure to bear, both upon the President and the other political parties, to induce the Centre to abandon its policy of linking the Young Plan with financial reforms, and to accept the Plan without pressing for the latter. At the urgent request of the Chancellor, however, the Centre Party leaders refused to abandon their course and they would have continued thus adamant had it not been for the introduction of a new factor.

The bitter attacks of Hindenburg's old friends and comrades had affected him very deeply, and, while he keenly resented their strictures, he was at the same time anxious to propitiate his critics. In his old mind he sought to find a way whereby he could preserve the support of the Left with regard to the Young Plan and at the same time regain his popularity, not so much with the political forces of Hugenberg as with his fellow estate-owners of East Prussia. He therefore made it a condition of his support for the Plan that three hundred million marks should be set aside from the saving which the Plan would effect for the *Osthilfe* fund, established some months earlier for the assistance of great estate-owners. Hermann Müller had been forced to accept this condition and had written a formal letter to the President signifying his consent. This letter had appeared in the press.

It now occurred to the *Landbund* and to the President that if discussions on financial reforms were initiated in the *Reichstag* the true state of the national finances would become public and the parties of the Left and Centre might well refuse to vote additional sums for the *Osthilfe* when the money was more urgently needed for unemployment insurance payments. There were not sufficient funds for both enterprises, and the fact that the President had already exacted the promise of three hundred million marks for his fellow landlords might easily cause irreparable damage to his authority and personal prestige.

At all costs, then, the demand for financial reforms must be postponed and in the last days of February 1930 Hindenburg sent post-haste for Brüning. The Centre Party, declared the President, must abandon its demand for simultaneous action and must support the ratification of the Young Plan without conditions. If they refused to do this Hindenburg would resign the presidency—again those "pistol-at-the-head" tactics with which Ludendorff had so often terrorized the Emperor and the Imperial Government—if, on the other hand, they agreed, he would give his solemn word that at a later date he would use his whole influence, even to the extent of applying Article 48, to effect the necessary financial reforms.

In face of this demand Müller and Brüning had, like Wilhelm II on similar occasions, no choice but to accept the inevitable. The Centre Party withdrew its demands and set about the discovery of a further formula of compromise which should unite a majority in favour of ratification while still retaining some vestige of hope for dealing sanely with the acute gravity of the economic and financial situation.

Gradually, as the month of March 1930 drew to its close, the compromise took form and one by one the political parties in support of the Government accepted it. There remained only the Social Democrats, the Chancellor's own party, and on their acceptance or rejection the situation hung.

Müller was now in a position of great weakness, for rumours were already spreading through Berlin, zealously fostered by interested parties, that the President had withdrawn his support from the Chancellor and that, even if the compromise were formally adopted, a change of Government was necessary. More and more frequently Brüning's name came to be circulated as Müller's successor and this proved a source of embarrassment and annoyance to both, who, to a far greater degree than any other Party Leaders, were genuinely and harmoniously striving in the interests of the country.

Within his own party Müller was also faced with a crisis, a crisis strangely analogous to that which confronted Mr. Ramsay MacDonald's Labour Government a year later. At the fateful party meeting on March 27 an event occurred unique in the history of the German Socialist Party. There were present for the first time not only the members of the Social Democratic Parliamentary Party, but also the leader of the Trade Unions, and between them—as between the British Labour Party and the T.U.C. in 1931—there was a great gulf fixed; for the latter were obstinately opposed to any financial reforms which necessitated cuts in unemployment insurance or wages.

Undermined from without by the rumour emanating from the Palace, and from within by the opposition of the Trade Unions, Müller's position became untenable. By a large majority the meeting rejected the compromise and, fully aware of the historical importance of the decision, the Chancellor summoned an emergency Cabinet meeting. He declared his intention of requesting the President to make use of Article 48 to save the country from financial chaos. The answer came immediately; without a moment's hesitation, Meissner, who represented the President at all Cabinet meetings, replied that the President was not prepared to invest the present Government with the emergency powers entailed in Article 48. The implication was clear; the sword of Damocles had fallen, and that same evening the Cabinet resigned.

On March 28 Heinrich Brüning was summoned to the Palace. It was his third interview with the President in three months and he had learnt something—though not enough—of Hindenburg's tactics. He was not therefore altogether surprised when the old gentleman made his familiar manœuvre and proclaimed his intention of resigning the Presidency if Brüning would not become Chancellor. Faced with this alternative and deeply concerned for the well-being of his country, Brüning accepted, but on conditions. He must be allowed to form a Cabinet above party alignments and he must have the unqualified support of the President, for he expected that the economic and financial crisis would continue for at least three or four years.

"Yes, yes," said the old Marshal eagerly, "you shall be my last Chancellor and I will never give you up, but you must make those fellows in the *Reichstag* come to heel."

The tragedy of Brüning is the tragedy of Weimar. He wished to do so much, he was allowed to accomplish so little. He was fated to be the undertaker rather than the physician. In his desire to carry on the Policy of Fulfilment he was no less eager than Rathenau and Stresemann, yet it was his rôle to initiate the policy of repudiation. There was no greater believer in German parliamentary institutions than he, yet under the irresistible pressure of events it was he who struck the first blow at their foundation. None desired more passionately the welfare and happiness of the German people, yet he became known as the "Hunger Chancellor," and was forced to impose upon them the most crushing of burdens. It would have been hard to find a greater German patriot, yet he was hounded from office and from his country for "lack of patriotism." He played the game according to the rules and failed, but to his less scrupulous successors was conceded all that he had sought to achieve and more. One fundamental error Brüning committed at the outset. He trusted Hindenburg.

But in the early days of his administration his position was very strong. The *Camarilla* and the *Reichswehr* were his allies and the President was his enthusiastic supporter, agreeing wholeheartedly with the remark of Oldenburg-Januschau, that "Brüning is the best Chancellor since Bismarck." Fortified by this encouragement, the Chancellor followed a course of daring and courage. When the *Reichstag* refused to vote the financial and economic measures with which the Government sought to oppose the rising tide of crisis, Hindenburg and Brüning brought Article 48 of the Constitution into play, enacting the measures by decree, and when the *Reichstag* refused by eight votes to give the necessary two-thirds majority, it was dissolved.

It was significant that in the General Election which followed in September 1930, almost every party went to the polls with "treaty revision" in its programme; but it was still more significant that the party which made "treaty revision" the most salient factor of its policy, was returned as the second largest in the *Reichstag*. The failure of the Allies to implement the disarmament pledges given in the Treaty of Versailles, the increased burden of the Young Plan payments, the heavy taxation, and the economic crisis all contributed to a state of popular discontent which was welcome grist to Hitler's mill. With promises for all, a bitter attack upon the Government, and a clamour for repudiation of all foreign commitments, the *Führer* attracted many malcontents to his banner. From the meagre 800,000 votes which he had polled two years before, he now achieved nearly six and a half millions, and his parliamentary following swelled from 12 to 108.

Brüning was now faced with the prospect of a race against time. He realized fully that the National Socialist advance had only begun. He never under-estimated either the force or the dangers of this new phenomenon in the political life of Germany. His Government must show results or perish, and with it would perish the Weimar Republic. The economic crisis, which enveloped the world in a blanket of depression and undermined confidence in governments all over the world, had its most deadly effects in Germany, and increased the task of the Chancellor a hundredfold. Foreign governments, themselves suffering heavily, were unwilling even to consider the easing of Germany's burdens, and turned a deaf ear to Brüning's warnings. Each country was suffering too greatly from introspection to take any interest in the troubles of its neighbours, even to make a common effort for their mutual salvation.

But Brüning did not relax his efforts. None had a more profound realization than he of the heavy sacrifices made by the German people, and of the popularity which he would attain for himself and his administration by some spectacular alleviation of them. But he resisted the temptation, renouncing easy palliatives for the sake of achieving greater aims. Deliberately sacrificing his own popularity, he made use of the supreme power with which the President had bested him, to dole out to the German people the bitter medicine which they had so long refused to take voluntarily. In normal times such treatment might well have proved efficacious, but in the crisis which then gripped Germany in a vice, it could but fend off final disaster. The tremendous sacrifices which Brüning called upon his country to make, could only have been justified in their eyes by some great achievement in foreign affairs. The inferiority com-

plex which had embittered German politics since the Treaty of
Versailles could only be removed by a spectacular success, the
cancellation of reparations or the partial rearmament of Germany. This the Chancellor knew, and for this he laboured in
vain. All Germany now realized that the Policy of Fulfilment
was barren of success and there arose a low rumbling in favour
of Repudiation.

When the ghastly summer of 1931—during which the Chancellor toured Europe in a vain attempt to awaken understanding of the catastrophe with which Europe was faced in Germany
—had shaded into autumn, the Brüning Government had become
the most unpopular ever known in Germany. All that it had
gained, and the personal impression which Brüning had made
abroad—the temporary cessation of reparations through the
Hoover Plan, the gradual realization abroad that a choice must
be made between the public and private debts, and the more
determined attitude at Geneva in the matter of disarmament—
was lost in the growing discontent at home. The "Hunger Chancellor" had cut deep into the life of the country and was preparing
to cut deeper. His decrees only were ratified by a majority
of the *Reichstag*, because the support of the Social Democrats
could be secured by threats of a dictatorship of the Right.
Hindenburg watched with dismay the growing antagonism to
Brüning. Like most Prussians he knew his Bible and was heard
to mutter one day at Neudeck, "I am distressed for thee, my
brother Jonathan."

The enemies of Brüning and of Weimar, for the Chancellor
had become the symbol of the System, gathered to indict him
and to demand his dismissal. At Harzburg in Brunswick, on
October 11, Hugenberg and Hitler, Seldte and Schacht, in all
the bravery of uniforms and the dignity of frock-coats, and
surrounded by the hosts of the *Stahlhelm* and the Brown Army,
concluded a solemn bond and covenant declaring war upon the

Governments of Brüning in the *Reich* and of Otto Braun, the Socialist Prime Minister who had controlled Prussia since 1921. It was the last effort of Hugenberg to keep the leadership of the National Opposition in his own hands, and even from its inception it was a failure, for Hitler, having taken the salute of his own Brown legions, left the meeting before the march-past of the *Stahlhelm,* and from that moment it was Hitler and not Hugenberg who gave orders to the Harzburg Opposition during its brief existence.

Why, indeed, should it be otherwise? The National Socialists were now the largest single party in the country and their power and popularity were increasing steadily. Elections in Brunswick, in Oldenburg, and in Hessen showed the rapid growth of the polling strength, and by the close of the year the party was to have a registered membership not far short of a million. Hitler had little to gain from an alliance with Hugenberg save that of using him as a means of attaining power, and the advantage of dipping into the treasury of the Nationalist Party. He had openly proclaimed his intention of following Mussolini's example of beginning with a coalition government, and if the Nationalists were ignorant of the fate which subsequently overtook these early allies of the Duce, *tant pis pour eux.*

All this was not lost upon Schleicher; he was quick to realize that the glittering attractions of the National Socialist Party and not the gruelling sacrifices of the Brüning Government were what the German people would welcome, and he sought for some means to split the party and thereby deprive it of much of its chance of success. In any case, he felt, this great force of national resurgence must not go unchecked.

To Schleicher may well have occurred the historical parallel of the days before the War of Liberation, when the idealistic patriotism of national resurrection engendered by the *Tugenbund* had been "captured" and controlled by the genius of

Scharnhorst and Gneisenau. The Prussian General Staff had forged from it a weapon which had overthrown Napoleon and led on step by step to Sadowa and Sedan and to . . . But there the vision paled. Nevertheless, the fatal mistake would not be made this time, and it was clearly the mission of the *Reichswehr*, and, in particular, of Schleicher, to canalize this great force of awakening youth into channels where it could do most good to Germany, to the army, and to Schleicher. Hitler's potential power must be nipped in the bud and every means must be used to bring him within Schleicher's influence. Thus the *feld-graue Eminenz* of the *Reichswehr* planned and plotted, and from that day, in the autumn of 1931, began his early contacts with Röhm, Chief of Staff of the Brown Army; contacts which remained unbroken until that summer day when both were murdered.

Nor was Brüning unappreciative of the situation. He was fully aware that his policy of personal and national immolation had resulted, through no fault of his, if not in actual failure, at least in earning him a degree of unpopularity almost unparalleled in German history. Yet in this the lonely Chancellor wrapped himself, as it were in a cloak, and wearily planned anew for the salvation of his country.

Two opportunities, he knew, were about to present themselves; the report of the committee of experts at Basle appointed to enquire into the financial and economic position of Germany should give him the chance to make public declaration that the country could no longer pay reparations, and the opening of the Disarmament Conference in the coming year would give the signatories of the Treaty of Versailles a last opportunity to make good their promises to Germany. With reparations gone and a formula either for the disarmament of the Allies or the rearmament of Germany, much of the Nazi thunder would have been stolen, and it might then be possible to take them into the

Government and to give them a taste of responsibility. It was the last chance for Europe and for Germany.

But a more immediate problem for the Chancellor which had overshadowed the policy since 1930 was that of the Presidency. In March of the following year Hindenburg's term of office would end. Could Brüning persuade him to stand again? Should he do so? Was the old Marshal physically capable of taking on another term? Was there anyone else who could rally the nation in opposition to the Nazis, who would certainly contend the election? These were the questions which Brüning pondered in the ascetic monasticism with which he surrounded himself.

Hindenburg's condition at the time was on the whole very satisfactory. At eighty-four he was a very remarkable old man; in excellent physical health, he ate and drank enormously, and slept well and long. His brain, if caught at the right moment, was clear and perceptive, and his shrewd common sense had not deserted him. A visitor to Berlin well remembers seeing him one brilliant morning in October 1931. Some military ceremony was taking place and a guard of honour awaited the President's arrival. A large closed car drew up, an orderly opened the door, and out jumped two smart young staff officers. Then a pause, and slowly, very slowly, there emerged, backwards and bare-headed, an enormous figure. Again a pause, though shorter this time, while one of the young officers extracted from the interior of the car a *Pickelhaube,* which was ceremoniously placed upon the great square head with its hair *en brosse.* Then the figure turned about and one had the momentary impression of a gigantic clockwork doll waiting for the spring to be released which galvanized it into movement. His eye caught the motionless line of soldiery. At once the absent glance changed—the spring had been released—and, one hand grasping his baton and the other resting on his sword hilt, Hindenburg moved stiffly and erect towards the guard of honour. The episode has always seemed to the writer symbolical of the Marshal's whole career. The moment of suspension, while the mind was in a plastic state awaiting an impression, and then, once received, the immediate and vigorous action in the direction in which service and duty had pointed.

Such then was Hindenburg towards the close of his first presidency. After deep consideration, and consultation with his colleagues, Brüning reached the inevitable conclusion that the Marshal must stand again. Some of his friends urged him to offer himself for election, but he refused with complete finality. He knew well enough that, his own unpopularity apart, the man who could beat Hitler at the polls must have more glamour and appeal than he could muster. It would take a Field-Marshal to beat the corporal.

But Brüning was aiming beyond the mere re-election of Hindenburg and the perpetuation of the Weimar System. He was thinking of Germany and was fearful of what a Nazi victory might mean for her. The re-election of Hindenburg would but postpone such a victory, for it was hardly to be expected that he could survive a further seven years of office, and to Hindenburg, Hitler was the logical successor. To Brüning's conservative-democrat spirit the implications of a National Socialist régime were abhorrent, and to save Germany from such a fate he was prepared to take bold and radical measures. Long hours of contemplation had convinced him that one course, and one course only, could prevent Hitler from ultimately obtaining supreme power—the restoration of the monarchy.

This then became the final aim of Brüning's strategy, and in his plan a rôle of vital importance must be played by Hindenburg. The Chancellor discounted at the outset any possibility of recalling the Kaiser to the throne; such a move would require a long period of preparation, and at the moment time was the essence of the contract. For the same reason the accession of the

Crown Prince was impossible. Above all there must be no revolution, the republican régime must give way to the monarchical quite smoothly by prearranged stages and with the approval of the majority of the people concerned.

In secret talks with influential members of the *Reichstag* of different Parties, Brüning had derived sufficient encouragement to approach the question not only as an ideal but as a practical proposition, and the details began to take shape in his mind. The primary condition was that Hindenburg should be re-elected, thus inflicting an initial defeat on the Nazi Party. But once this was achieved, there were still a number of obstacles to be overcome. There must be a definite end to reparations—that is to say, the rendering *de jure* of the *de facto* situation which had obtained since the Hoover Moratorium of the previous July —and a successful *démarche* must be made at the Disarmament Conference. Brüning's instinct as an economist led him to believe that an amelioration of the situation in Germany might be looked for in the coming February (1932)—a premonition which proved true—and so he hoped that, by a combination of diplomatic successes abroad and an improved situation at home, he might both give the Nazis a set-back and sufficiently influence Parliament in his favour to make his next step possible.

This was to secure a two-thirds majority in the *Reichstag* and the *Reichsrat* to declare Hindenburg *Reichsverweser* (Regent) for his lifetime, at the end of which one of the sons of the Crown Prince should succeed to the throne.

The initiative for this move would come from one of the parties immediately to the Right or Left of the Centre so that no taint of Vatican influence should prejudice the issue, and the prospects of success were not unhopeful. With the realization that the only alternative was a National Socialist dictatorship, some of the leaders of the Left whom Brüning had consulted were already reluctantly agreeable, and it would be virtually impossible for Hugenberg to oppose a programme which aimed ultimately at the restoration of the monarchy. With the support of the Nationalists a two-thirds majority was assured, and if the Nazis opposed the measure Brüning was prepared to give them battle, being confident that on such an issue the conservative element of Hitler's supporters—officers of the Old Army, East Prussian landlords, former governmental officials, and the like —who had joined the National Socialist Party out of despair or as the only means of realizing their political ambitions, would desert the *Hackenkreuz* and revert to their old fealty.

Such was the bold plan conceived by Brüning to save Germany from Nazi dominance, but its essential premise was the re-election of Hindenburg to the presidency. Little opposition to this was expected from the old gentleman, for Brüning counted on his welcoming a chance of laying the spectre of Spa for ever. The restoration of the monarchy would be a fitting close to his career, and it was hoped and believed that he would seize the opportunity presented.

Early in November 1931 the Chancellor broached the subject to the Marshal and was astonished to find that he was not interested in the proposal. "I am the trustee of the Emperor," he declared, "and can never give my consent to anyone succeeding to the throne save the Emperor himself." Quite evidently Hindenburg preferred to die without seeing a restoration of the monarchy rather than betray his trusteeship for the Kaiser. It was the old story of "Henri V" and the Tricolour over again. He seemed to wish to drop the subject altogether, but Brüning persisted.

A restoration could only achieve stability, he explained, with the consent of the workers. The Social Democrats and the Trade Unions would never consent to the return of Wilhelm II or of the Crown Prince; they might, however, be persuaded to support Hindenburg as Regent for one of the sons of the Crown Prince.

The restored monarchy could never be that of 1870, or even that which the vague reforms of Max of Baden had sought to create in 1918. It must be a constitutional monarchy on the British model, based on the consent of the people and operating through a system of checks and balances.

Hindenburg was scandalized at such an idea. A monarchy on the English model was no monarchy at all, and he would be no party to such an emasculation of the royal prerogative. So moved was he that he betrayed the fact that he too had dreamed dreams. The monarchy which he would wish to see re-established in Germany was not indeed that of 1870, but a complete reversion to the warrior state of Prussia as it existed before 1848.

In vain Brüning impressed upon him that these were illusions, and assured him that in the plan which he, the Chancellor, had outlined was the sole hope of restoration. Hindenburg was lost in his own visions and would not listen. Abruptly he closed the audience.

"Though I spoke with the tongues of men and of angels," Brüning said later, "I could have made no impression on him."

But this was not quite true. Some tiny modicum of what had been said had remained in Hindenburg's mind and had created an itch of conscience. A few days later he sent for Brüning.

It was November 11, a day of humiliation to Germany, the thirteenth anniversary of the bitter morning on which Hindenburg had advised acceptance of the Armistice terms. Brüning found him sitting at the window, staring out into the grey winter sky, his huge bulk silhouetted against the light. For a while after the Chancellor had been announced, Hindenburg continued to sit motionless. Then he turned heavily in his chair and greeted his visitor. He seemed bowed down with years and memories; a lonely, pitiable figure.

"I do not wish to go through the trials of an election for the

second time. In the campaign they will reproach me all over
again with the events of November 1918. It will be worse this
time."

He paused and then, without introduction, plunged into an
unwonted torrent of self-justification.

"I meant well by His Majesty. There have been other occasions in history when monarchs have left their thrones and were
recalled by their peoples when times had changed. I thought it
would be like that when His Majesty went to Holland. I still
believe his abdication was inevitable, and his flight too. The
front was not holding, the troops were mutinying and, as an
old Prussian officer, I had no choice but to protect the person of
my King."

Brüning had been through those November days as a company machine-gun officer. He had experiences gained personally
and not from headquarters' reports, and he felt it his duty to
defend the army, as he knew it, from the general charge of mutiny. Moreover, he had been at Herbesthal from whence came
the reports which finally decided the Marshal that the Kaiser
must fly.

"With all respect," he said, "I hold a different opinion to
Your Excellency. At Herbesthal, for instance, everything was
Red when we occupied the station, but we had order restored in
a very short time. If our messages had been received at G.H.Q.
as we had sent them out the Emperor might not have been in-
duced to leave. The mistake was made in the telegraph office
at Spa."

He added that he had deposed to this effect before Gröner's
Court of Honour in 1922, and that his evidence had influenced
the verdict. But Hindenburg had no recollection of this.

"You may be right about Herbesthal," he said, "but I am
certain of one thing, the Second Division of Guards behind you
was no longer loyal."

"They could have been made loyal in twenty-four hours," said Brüning earnestly. "We never believed in their defection." But Hindenburg would have no more of his pet established theories challenged. The case which he had built up to convince himself was too flimsy to permit of searching cross-examination. He grew petulant.

"No, no, no," he cried, shaking his head energetically. "I know you are wrong. They were all wrong. I knew already in February 1918 that the war was lost, but I was willing to let Ludendorff have his fling."

He relapsed into rumbling silence, and the Chancellor left him to his memories and his conscience.

But Brüning did not lose heart, though he might well have been excused for doing so. He was fighting on so many fronts now; the opposition of the Nazis was becoming daily fiercer, and so many factors were desperately important for his success. Moreover, he was unable to give the people any alleviation of their sufferings. On the contrary, he was compelled to add to their burdens. The Fourth Major Emergency Decree, in which, on December 8, he promulgated the legislation considered necessary to meet the situation, he himself described in a national broadcast as cutting deeper into the established notions of legal right and sanctity than any since "times of great antiquity," and the Committee of Experts, then in session at Basle, declared it to be "without parallel in modern legislation."

Throughout these days of ordeal Brüning was sustained and encouraged by the magnificent spirit of loyalty and encouragement which animated his Cabinet. A reconstruction had been necessary in September 1931; Curtius had been forced to leave the Foreign Office after the unfortunate affair of the Austro-German *Zollunion*, and Wirth had resigned the Portfolio of the Interior on account of the antipathy of the President. In reality, however, this had strengthened rather than weakened the Government.

Brüning had taken the Foreign Office himself and Gröner had combined the Home Office with the Ministry of Defence—a very useful combination in such times of civil tension. In loyal old Gröner, his former chief Stegerwald, and his devoted friends, Treviranus and Dietrich, Brüning had a team at least faithful, able, and dependable, a group of men without political ambition and with few political ideas in common, save their admiration for the Chancellor and their determination to do their utmost for the good of the country. Brüning was spared those disastrous Cabinet intrigues which had destroyed so many former Weimar cabinets, and the loyalty of his colleagues was a vastly important factor in the courageous battle which he fought for two years against increasing odds and under the most difficult conditions. That he survived the forces of intrigue so long was a great political achievement and not merely as an act of strength and legerdemain.

At the close of 1931—the *annus terribilis* of Germany and of Europe—the Chancellor's principal task was to get Hindenburg's consent to stand again for President. Whether the larger plan of the restored monarchy were pursued or not, it was absolutely necessary that the Marshal should be re-elected, for the alternative was already casting its shadow darkly across the path. Yet Hindenburg was himself so undesirous of continuing longer in the thankless drudgery of office that he presented one of the gravest barriers to his own re-election.

Again it was the call of duty which broke down the Marshal's objections to a further term of office. The Chancellor, the Prime Minister of Prussia, his own intimate friends, all urged him to remain, partly because they trembled at the thought of the alternative and partly because of the weight which his personal prestige carried abroad. For the Foreign Powers, though they would do little to help Germany, had come to look upon the Hindenburg-Brüning combination as a permanent factor of stability, and were but dimly aware of the intrigues which seethed beneath the surface.

Personal vanity may also have played a part in influencing Hindenburg to stand for re-election. Should he, a Field-Marshal, and one of the largest of East Prussian land-owners, make room for a former corporal who was not even a German-born citizen and who, if indeed he decided to contest the election, would have to acquire citizenship by some legal quibble? Besides, he had met the fellow and he had not cared for him at all. Brüning had arranged that Hitler should be formally presented to the President, and the impression produced upon Hindenburg by the *Führer's* frenzied eloquence had been far from favourable, while Hitler had been equally disillusioned by the meeting!

As early as September 1931, shortly before the formation of the Harzburg Front, Brüning had approached both Hugenberg and Hitler with the object of securing their support for Hindenburg's re-election. He was prepared at this time even to resign from office, after the cancellation of reparations had been accomplished, and to make way for a Chancellor more acceptable to the parties of the Right, if by so doing he could ensure the maintenance of Hindenburg in the presidency. At the same time he had a shrewd suspicion that if nothing tangible came of the offer to the leaders of the Right it would at least serve to embarrass them and to render less formidable the combination of forces which they were preparing. It happened exactly as Brüning had foreseen. Both Hitler and Hugenberg refused to pledge themselves in support of the President's re-election, but neither wished to take the responsibility for their refusal. Each blamed his inability to co-operate upon the other, and relations between them became so strained that Brüning was able to regard with comparative equanimity the façade of unity which was later developed at Harzburg.

Now, however, new tactics had to be employed. The political

and economic condition of the country made it desirable that, if at all possible, the *Sturm und Drang* of an election campaign should be avoided. In addition it was hoped that some means might be found to spare the old Marshal the strain and obloquy which would inevitably accompany such a contest. In face of these exigencies it was agreed between the President and the Chancellor that the latter should endeavour to reach an agreement with the parties in the *Reichstag* for a Constitutional two-thirds majority prolonging the presidential term of office.

In decision of the President to continue in office, Brüning had gained his first point. But there must have been many moments when he was tempted to wonder whether it was all worth fighting for or not. The edifice itself was so rotten and worm-eaten. Oskar von Hindenburg, his appetite as landlord only whetted by what was already his, approached certain members of the Cabinet for their assistance in acquiring part of an estate adjoining Neudeck, in such a way that they did not even care to submit the proposal to the Chancellor for consideration, and, as a result, Oskar joined the ranks of his enemies.

Was he really fighting for this sort of thing? Brüning asked himself, and ever the tormenting answer came back, how much worse was the alternative.

With the New Year of 1932 the Chancellor made the opening moves in his last campaign. The publication on Christmas Eve 1931 of the Report of the Special Advisory Committee had shown to the world that continued reparation payments by Germany were both impossible and undesirable, and Brüning seized the opportunity to declare on January 9, that, at the forthcoming conference at Lausanne, the German delegation would press for the complete cancellation of reparation payments.

Two days earlier (January 7) he had begun his negotiations with the Party Leaders for two-thirds majority of the *Reichstag* for prolonging the President's term of office, and for this the

Communists could be excluded from the calculations. Of the support of the parties of the Left, Brüning could be certain, but he needed the votes of the Nazis and the Nationalists. At the suggestion of the Chancellor, Hitler was invited to a conference with Brüning, Gröner and, incidentally, Schleicher, at the Ministry of the Interior, the Government Department directly responsible for constitutional reforms and amendments. This was the first occasion on which Schleicher had met the *Führer*, who had hitherto refused to see him. Hitler now came with the Chief of Staff of his Storm Troops, Ernst Röhm, whose homosexual practices were notorious throughout Germany, and in this unsavoury company Brüning appealed for the support of the Nazi Party.

Further conversations took place on January 10 and then Hitler withdrew to discuss the latter in party conclave. Schleicher had counted upon Röhm to support the proposals of the Government and to swing the meeting in favour of acceptance; he was under the impression that Röhm was entirely in agreement with him. But the Storm Troop Chief of Staff found it more politic to urge rejection upon the *Führer*. In the fierce discussions which followed, Röhm resolutely opposed all thought of acceptance, and so demolished the arguments of Gregor Strasser, the man who had "organized" Berlin for Hitler and who now advocated a temporary truce with the Government, that the party meeting adopted a policy of rejection by a large majority.

In the meantime Hugenberg had also been consulted by Brüning and had given an ambiguous answer just as Hitler had done two days before. Each Party Leader was afraid of the decision of the other. Negotiations between the Nationalists and National Socialists began. Only negative agreement was reached for repudiating the re-election of Hindenburg by a two-thirds majority in the *Reichstag*. On January 12 the two leaders made their formal replies to the Government's proposal. Hugenberg, in a letter to the Chancellor, declared bluntly that he could not support the Prolongation Bill in the *Reichstag* because it would be a manifestation of confidence by the Nationalists in the Chancellor. This was very far from being the case, wrote Hugenberg, and he reproached Brüning for tolerating in the *Reich* and in Prussia governments behind which there was no majority. He added that the position of Germany abroad would be strengthened by the resignation of the Brüning Cabinet, which had shown itself unable to impress on the world in an authoritative manner the changed will of the German people. In conclusion, Hugenberg, whose party had done more than any other to identify Hindenburg with their own interests, protested against the manner in which the personality of the President had been "dragged into party and parliamentary discussions which do not do justice to the constitutional position and high esteem which the *Reichspräsident* enjoys among his people."

Hitler, on the other hand, addressed himself directly to Hindenburg and carefully avoided any vilification of the Government. To the surprise of all he took his stand on the Constitution and explained in great length and detail his juridical scruples at the parliamentary prolongation of the President's term of office, when it was clearly stated in the Constitution that he must be elected (or re-elected) by popular vote. But while rejecting the idea of a parliamentary solution of the question, the *Führer's* letter did not convey a blunt refusal of the proposal of re-election, and the impression was left with many who read it that the Nazis would not oppose the Marshal in a popular referendum.

But Hitler, after a few days, was apparently afraid of losing followers to the Nationalists if he did not take a stronger position against the Government. Therefore, on January 16 he addressed a memorandum to the Chancellor which was not behind Hugenberg in invective. Prolongation of the President's term of office by the *Reichstag*, he wrote, would be but a mockery, because the *Reichstag* as elected in 1930 no longer represented the German people. The plain duty of the Cabinet was to resign at once and to hold new elections, and the *Führer* reiterated his slogan that "The System," which had reduced Germany to insolvency and impotence, must vanish.

This refusal of the Right to support Hindenburg's re-election by parliamentary methods greatly annoyed the Old Gentleman. His pride and anger were aroused and his last reluctance to contest an election was demolished. He agreed to fight but in his tired old brain there was resentment against the man who, he considered, had forced him into so doing, and this was not Hitler but Brüning. Upon this spirit of resentment certain of his advisers played. Brüning had mishandled the whole thing, they told Hindenburg; he had been tactless and he alone was responsible for forcing the Marshal into an open fight against his old supporters of 1925. Little by little there developed a definite sense of dislike in Hindenburg's mind, and Brüning, "the best Chancellor since Bismarck," the Brother Jonathan for whom Hindenburg had been distressed, was changing his rôle to that of David as against the Marshal's Saul.

But at this moment, when there were those among the President's advisers who would have jettisoned Brüning, he received assistance from an altogether unexpected quarter. Schleicher had been furious with Röhm for not having carried out his instructions at the National Socialist Party meeting and had for the time severed relations with him. To Schleicher it was essential that Hindenburg should be re-elected as soon, and with the least to-do, as possible. The one man who could achieve this was Brüning, and it was no part of Schleicher's plan that the Chancellor should fall before the re-election had been accomplished. Once this had been done, Schleicher had schemes of a grandiose nature. The *Reichstag* must be dissolved and no new elections must be held for a considerable period of time. In the interval the

President, secure in his new term of office, must rule by decree and with the support of the *Reichswehr*.

In Brüning Schleicher saw an obstacle to his ultimate plans. He had outlined them to the Chancellor in the autumn of 1931, and it was partly Brüning's refusal to consider them that had driven Schleicher, after the formation of the *Harzburg Front*, to coquette with the Nazis. After the re-election of Hindenburg, therefore, Brüning must go, but in the meantime his retention in office was essential, and Schleicher, therefore, joined Gröner in defending the Chancellor before Hindenburg. Their efforts were successful and Brüning remained.

Schleicher prided himself on his political astuteness; he was seen about a great deal in Berlin at this time, in restaurants and cabarets, always the centre of an admiring group chiefly composed of ladies. One evening a group of English and American friends were dining at the Königin Restaurant on the Kurfürstendamm when Schleicher's party arrived at the next table. The General was resplendent in uniform and in excellent form. The dance band stopped with the abruptness of syncopation, and Schleicher, whose voice had been raised to be heard by his friends above the music, was overheard declaiming, "What Germany needs to-day is a strong man," and he tapped himself significantly upon the breast.

And yet, while Kurt von Schleicher was congratulating himself on his cunning, Joseph Goebbels was writing in his diary: "To put the thing in a nutshell, Gröner must go—followed by Brüning and Schleicher, otherwise we shall never attain full power." The astute General was himself a dupe.

Nor was he, indeed, in such an impregnable position with the President. No one in his position or with his career could be without enemies, and these were numbered both among the Nazis and among the East Prussian aristocrats who knew that Schleicher had always favoured the policy of settling small-

PRESIDENT VON HINDENBURG—1929

holders in the East and had opposed the grants of the *Osthilfe* to the estate-owners. It so happened that a few weeks later, in early February 1932, two intrigues against Schleicher, one by the Nazis and the other by Oskar Hindenburg at the instigation of his East Prussian friends, coincided. The *Camarilla* were no longer in blissful harmony and their jealousies were frequently finding expression in thus fighting and jostling to poison the mind of the President one against the other. With the agility of a practised intriguer, Schleicher at once abandoned his well-known views on small-holdings in East Prussia, and, in an effort to retain the President's favour, began to criticize the scheme which Brüning had in mind for the expropriation of certain of the bankrupt estates.

This *volte face* was more even than Hindenburg could stand. His head reeled with the gyrations on the political trapeze, and on his giddiness followed nausea. To Brüning he declared that he had had enough of Schleicher and his intrigues, and that he had made up his mind to send him away. It was now Brüning's turn to save Schleicher—so fantastic a situation can scarcely be conceived—and, realizing that the General's dismissal at this moment would please the Nazis more than anything else, he pleaded with the President.

There were Generals in the *Reichswehr* more friendly to the Nazis than Schleicher and it was the hope of the Party to replace him by one of these military allies, whose business it would be in his turn to get rid of Gröner. If this were accomplished Hindenburg would be lost before the election was held, and for this reason Brüning pled for Schleicher. At the moment neither could afford to let the other go.

But Brüning having learnt from preceding negotiations proposed to the President that he should give the direction of the discussions for his re-election by a plebiscite into the hands of Meissner and Schleicher. He informed the President of his wish that both should have the power to offer the National Socialists and Nationalists his resignation as Chancellor if they could succeed in winning over the two Parties to the re-election of Hindenburg. Schleicher accepted the task with enthusiasm. Schleicher eagerly accepted Brüning's offer, but neither party would negotiate with him or with Meissner, but both found means of informing the President that had they been discussing the matter with Brüning and not with the "Gentlemen of the President," the result might have been different.

Amidst this atmosphere of Byzantine intrigue, Brüning fought on undaunted, though with more than a strong suspicion that he was being betrayed by Schleicher and Oskar von Hindenburg, and fully conscious that the President's confidence in him was wavering.

There had been some talk of the Crown Prince being put forward as the candidate of the united parties of the Right, but a stern parental admonition from Doorn had put an end to all thought of it. The Chancellor took the opportunity of the Kaiser's veto to urge for the last time upon Hindenburg his plans for the restoration of the monarchy. "Let me go to the Crown Prince," he pleaded, "and beg him not to take any part in the election save in your interest and let me explain to him that the House of Hohenzollern, like others, must make sacrifices for the monarchy. I may not be able to convince him at once, but at least I can show him the line which might be followed with success. Then I will come back and report to you and your son."

The mention of Oskar was important. Hindenburg at once became agitated and annoyed. "My son is meddling in politics too much already," he said. "I like to decide things myself." Then said Brüning, "Will you not give me authority to press on with my foreign policy and with the restoration of the monarchy? I give you my word that as soon as it has reached the point when the transition from the republic to the monarchy is assured, I will resign and then you can form a Cabinet entirely from the Parties of the Right."

But Hindenburg would not grasp his opportunity. The man was too old, and he was still dreaming of the ancient glories of Prussia. He gave an evasive answer, saying only that he hoped the Crown Prince would not oppose him, and with this crumb of comfort Brüning had to be content. His conversation with the Crown Prince brought him little satisfaction. He had promised his vote to Hitler, Wilhelm said, and Brüning was backing the wrong horse if he put his faith in Hindenburg. "He betrayed my father and he betrayed Ludendorff. When the time comes he will betray you too."

Another shock awaited the unhappy Chancellor. In his preparations for the contest he discovered that the expenses of Hindenburg's election campaign of 1925 were still unpaid, and so little faith had the printers in the word of the President that they demanded cash payment in advance for all orders for propaganda literature. Again the bitter reflection, was it all worth while?

The German presidential election of 1932 must surely be unique in the annals of such political contests, if only on the grounds of contrariness. All traditional affinities were swept aside in this amazing struggle. Behind Hindenburg, the Protestant Prussian monarchist, stood the embattled forces of the Catholic Centre, Social Democracy, the Trade Unions, and the Jews, while to the standard of Hitler, the Catholic Austrian quasi-socialist who had only recently become a German citizen, were rallied the upper classes of the Protestant North, the German Crown Prince, the great industrialists of the Ruhr and the Rhineland, and the conservative agrarians. Hugenberg put up an independent Nationalist candidate in Colonel Düsterberg, the Second Leader of the *Stahlhelm,* and the Communist Party was represented by the other veteran of the 1925 election, Ernst Thälmann.

The campaign was far more bitter than before. On the floor of the *Reichstag* Hindenburg was branded by Goebbels as "the candidate of the party of the deserters," an accusation for which he was expelled and which called forth from Gröner, then a very sick man, a spirited defence of his chief. The *Deutsche Zeitung,* which had championed the Marshal in 1925 and attacked him in 1930, now spat venom in utter and complete contempt. "The present issue at the polls is whether internationalist traitors and pacifist swine, with the approval of Hindenburg, are to bring about the final ruin of Germany." The nobles openly declared that "they had had enough of the old traitor," and Hitler, flying hither and thither over the country, heaped insult and invective upon his opponent.

Beyond his declaration of candidature Hindenburg himself took no part in the campaign, but his one statement was a fighting speech and remarkably virile for a man of his age. Meissner had excelled himself.

In full consciousness of my great responsibility [listening thousands at every radio in the country heard the booming voice declare], I have resolved to offer myself for re-election. As the request does not come from any party but from the broad masses of the nation, I feel it my duty to accept. . . . Not one of my critics can deny that I am inspired with the most ardent love of my country, and with the strongest possible will that Germany shall be free. . . . If I am defeated, I shall at least not have incurred the reproach that of my own accord I deserted my post in an hour of crisis. . . . I ask for no votes from those who do not wish to vote for me.

The full burden of the campaign fell upon Brüning, and he rose to the emergency with magnificent courage. For the first time it was discovered that he was an orator, and that magnetism and personal charm which had impressed so many at close quarters was now communicated to the vast audiences which thronged his meetings. Without resort to the tactics of the circus parade and the ballyhoo practised by the National Socialists, he was able to hold his hearers spellbound, and to command their respect and their confidence. Unsparingly he flogged his weary spirit forward and his gallant struggle, carried on single-handed against the vitriolic assaults of his opponents, is among the epic achievements of modern politics.

The country went to the polls on March 13, and the world waited breathlessly for the result. It was the first of five General Elections in nine months, on the outcome of each of which the fate of Germany seemed to hang. But the long-drawn struggle was by no means ended yet. The final figures, made known on the following day, were as follows:

Hindenburg	.	.	.	18,661,736
Hitler	.	.	.	11,338,571
Thälmann	.	.	.	4,982,079
Düsterberg	.	.	.	2,557,876

A sigh of relief arose throughout Europe, especially when it became known that the S.A. and S.S. (*Sturmabteilungen*, Storm troops, and *Schutzstaffeln*, guards) had been secretly mobilized for a *coup de main* should Hitler have headed the poll. But the battle was only half won. The figures showed that the large mass of the people had voted for Hindenburg and that Hitler had no further chance; yet though the Marshal had achieved a majority of seven million votes over his principal opponent, it missed (by 0.4 per cent of the poll) the absolute majority essential for election. A second ballot was necessary, and though the result was a foregone conclusion, the renewed campaign was an excuse for further bitterness, more invective, and an increase of those bloody clashes between armed partizans of the Left and Right which had come to be a recognized factor in German political life.

The Nationalists, whose humiliation at the polls had been devastating, withdrew their candidate, and exhorted their previous supporters to vote for Hitler, whom only a week before they had been defaming with ecstatic energy. The contest resolved itself into a straight fight between Hindenburg and Hitler, for Thälmann remained, as ever, negligible.

The result of the second ballot, held on April 10, allowed the German nation not only to sigh with relief but to breathe again freely. The Marshal's victory was handsome and complete; he had a clear majority of 53 per cent.

Hindenburg	.	. .	19,359,642
Hitler		. . .	13,417,460
Thälmann		. . .	3,706,388

The Nationalist vote had gone almost equally to the two chief contestants, and a million Communist votes had vanished altogether, many of them belonging to that floating vote which swung with disconcerting instability between the extreme Right and Left. The election had clearly demonstrated, however, that whatever else Germany needed, it did not need to be saved from a Red Peril, and the lie direct was thus given to the chief of Hitler's pretensions, which, even as early as this, he was actively prosecuting.

But the two ballots showed more important facts even than this. The forces of the Right had claimed that Brüning's majorities in the *Reichstag* were not representative of the feelings of the country. Yet this was clearly disproved by the presidential voting, which disclosed that in seven years the strength of the Right had severely diminished. In the first ballot of 1932 Hindenburg polled four million votes, and in the second, five million votes more than in the decisive ballot of 1925. In that year Hindenburg had achieved 14,655,000, and in 1932 the united votes of Hitler and Düsterberg realized only 13,900,000. The forces of the united Right had lost some seven hundred thousand votes. Hindenburg was once again President, re-elected by the votes of those very parties which seven years before had so vehemently opposed him. In 1932 he had as clear a mandate as in 1925. Then it had been the destruction of Weimar and the restoration of the monarchy, now it was the safeguarding of the Constitution and the rights and liberties of his fellow citizens. After his first election he had grievously disappointed his supporters, and after his second, the betrayal of those who had voted for him was more complete and more terrible. In each case the excuse was the same —the welfare of Germany. The welfare of Germany had demanded in 1925 the abandonment of the Nationalist Party and the support of the Policy of Fulfilment, and in 1932 it demanded the sacrifice of Brüning and the adoption of the Policy of Repudiation. In both cases the President was confident in the belief that his pledges were not dishonoured and that his oath had been kept. "His honour rooted in dishonour stood, and faith unfaithful kept him falsely true."

The real victim of the election was Heinrich Brüning; he who had fought and struggled with even more than his usual energy and a strength almost superhuman, was to reap the reward of all those who had served the Marshal long and faithfully. The gratitude of the House of Hindenburg was becoming as notorious as that of the House of Habsburg had been, and Brüning was to meet the fate of Benedek, but as a reward for victory, not failure.

The first signs of disfavour came almost at once. In accordance with established custom the Chancellor came to present the congratulations of the Cabinet to the elected President and to go through the formality of offering their resignations.

"I had been expecting your resignation," was Hindenburg's

cold reply. "You may issue a statement that I have asked you to remain temporarily in office. I may consider the appointment of a government of the Right."

Brüning was not astonished, having already been informed three days before as to what would happen. By the early morning, of course, the President had changed his mind and sent word to the Chancellor that he declined even to talk about the formal resignation. Two hours later the President, under the influence of Oskar and Schleicher, had changed his mind a second time, and in the meantime the Chancellor had informed Mr. Stimson, who was waiting in Geneva, that he would be prepared to meet him there at the end of the week. Brüning could not go there with a temporary mandate, and he therefore implored the President, not on behalf of his Cabinet but in the interest of the country and of Hindenburg's own good name, to reconsider. It was unthinkable that on the morrow of his re-election by the votes of the Left that he should appoint a government of the Right.

Faced with these arguments Hindenburg gave in, and the *communiqué* read that the Cabinet had offered their resignations to the President, who had refused to accept them. But another nail had been driven into Brüning's coffin.

And now Schleicher began preparing his *coup de grâce*. Brüning had exhausted his period of usefulness, and as Müller had gone, so must he go. Schleicher began his campaign on general lines. To the President he conveyed the impression that Brüning's tactics had exposed Hindenburg to unnecessary humiliations and had identified the spirit of Tannenberg and the Hindenburg Legend with the abhorrent doctrines of Social Democracy. He had made the Old Man cheap in the eyes of the people. And then Brüning was no fellow to handle these Nazis. A Strong Man was needed for that. It was time the *Reichstag* was closed down.

Meanwhile, to the Nazis, with whom he kept in touch through

Röhm—they were now reconciled—Schleicher preached patience. Brüning's days were numbered, he assured them; only a few weeks more and then there would be a real Government in Germany. Let them but be patient a little longer.

There were some among the Nazis, however, who trusted Brüning and would have made an agreement. Of these was Gregor Strasser, ever a thorn in the side of the *Führer*, for his pessimistic views and his longing for compromise. Discussions between Brüning and the Nazis were going on through the help of intermediaries for a solution regarding the new Government in Prussia. Brüning, following the wish of his own Party, offered a Coalition Government in Prussia on the condition that the Nazis should have no influence whatsoever upon the Prussian policy. These offers were debated in conclave and Strasser made an eloquent appeal in their support. He was answered by Röhm with such vehemence and such an uncanny insight into the insecure position of the Government, that Strasser was defeated. As the meeting closed, Strasser, in passing Röhm's place at the table, noticed that he had left his notes behind, and, on looking closer, saw that they were written on the notepaper of the Ministry of Defence. . . .

Schleicher dealt the Government the most severe blow it had yet suffered four days after the second ballot for the Presidency. Because of the mobilization of the S.A. and S.S. on the night of March 12/13, and in view of the generally subversive nature of all their activities, the Ministers of Interior of a number of the Federal States insisted upon seeing Gröner in his capacity of *Reichsminister* of Interior. At the moment the Chancellor was touring the country as the chief supporter of Hindenburg, but on his return to Berlin on polling day (Sunday, April 10) Gröner informed him that, on the recommendation of Schleicher, he had promised his insistent Federal colleagues to ask the President to issue a decree suppressing the private army of the Nazis' throughout the *Reich*, as, under similar circumstances, the militant wing of the Communist Party, the Red Fighting Front, had been prohibited some years before. Schleicher was called into personal conference and astounded his superiors by suddenly asking that an ultimatum should be sent to Hitler on the issue of the S.A. and S.S. All present opposed such an idea as being ridiculous. If the position was really sufficiently serious to warrant the suppression of the Brown Army it must be done, but there must be no negotiation on the subject with Hitler. In deference to these views Schleicher withdrew his suggestion. Hindenburg was convinced by Gröner and Brüning that the authority of the *Reich* Government was at stake and on these grounds he signed the Decree.

The views of the Army regarding the Storm Troops had been clearly stated by Gröner, Hammerstein and Schleicher. It had been Röhm's dream that the Brown Army should one day be absorbed, as it stood, into the *Reichswehr*, and to this idea the military leaders were unalterably opposed. Let the Storm Troopers come in as recruits by all means, and they would get all the amateur soldiering knocked out of them in barracks, but under no circumstances must they be admitted as a corporate body.[1] The army as a whole, therefore, welcomed the suppression of the Brown Legions, and with this view Schleicher had expressed his agreement.

But now on April 11, the day after Hindenburg's election, Schleicher began to use the affair of the suppression of the Storm Troops as an additional lever with which to destroy the foundation of the Brüning cabinet. He completely reversed his position

[1] Hitler himself was as opposed to such a step as were the *Reichswehr*, but for different reasons. The S.A. were *his* army and he had no intention of allowing them to be contaminated with the *Reichswehr* spirit unless and until he also controlled the *Reichswehr*. It was Röhm who had originated the idea of incorporation, and between Röhm and Hitler the relation of the S.A. to the army was always a source of disagreement, a disagreement which only ended on June 30, 1934, when one of the disputants ceased to take an interest in the argument.

and confidentially informed the commander of the seven military districts of the *Reich* that in the pending issue he dissented from his chief, Gröner, and no sooner had the Decree been made public and the inevitable agitation begun, than he proceeded to undermine the position of Brüning and Gröner with the President. While Brüning was in Geneva, by the dexterous arguments of which he was a master, Schleicher persuaded Hindenburg to the view that he had been made a fool. It was just another of Brüning's errors of judgment. These Storm Troops were not nearly as dangerous as they had been made to appear. But since the mistake had been made, the Government must be fair to all. The prohibition must be extended to the private army of the Socialists, the *Reichsbanner*, a most insidious institution contaminating the youth of the working class with Marxist principles. So argued Schleicher, but cunningly made no mention of the *Stahlhelm*, of which, notwithstanding all that had passed, Hindenburg was still an honorary president.

The President had quite forgotten that, on the day after his election, Brüning had suggested two alternatives: the suppressing either of all militant Party organizations or only of those of the Nazi Party. He was trying to make it clear to the President that a prohibition of the *Reichsbanner* would not be possible without a prohibition of the *Stahlhelm*. Hindenburg did not realize this alternative when he was approached by Schleicher in the absence of the Chancellor. He had been getting a little tired of Brüning anyway, and was disagreeably aware that he owed his re-election in very great measure to the personal efforts of the Chancellor. He disliked being under an obligation to anybody, and it seemed that Brüning had been behaving very oddly of late—all this talk of expropriation in East Prussia. It wasn't healthy. A change really ought to be made. Someone who could keep these Nazi fellows in order. And Gröner too; he was a sick man and ought to retire.

But Hindenburg's natural shrewdness prompted him to ask for evidence of the activities of the *Reichsbanner* and an interval ensued while the "evidence" was "produced" by the press department of the Ministry of Defence and printed in the newspapers of the Right. The cuttings were then brought to Hindenburg, who accepted their authenticity, and in accordance with Schleicher's suggestion he sent a letter to Gröner—which Schleicher arranged should be in the hands of the press as soon as, or even before, it had reached its proper recipient—calling his attention to the activities of the *Reichsbanner*, and exhorting him to keep a watchful eye on the treasonable and obscure activities of this organization.

Gröner was not deceived. Though he did not connect his friend and protégé Schleicher with the affair, he did detect the base ring of falseness in the "evidence" produced. He caused enquiries to be made and, though he could not pin down the guilt, he discovered enough to justify carrying the matter to the President. With arguments advanced with an obstinacy as relentless as a pile-driver, he succeeded in convincing Hindenburg that the whole premise of his letter had been faulty, that nothing treasonable could be proved against the *Reichsbanner*, and that the allegation was baseless.

Hindenburg agreed reluctantly and testily, but it was impossible to withdraw his letter, and his annoyance at being put in the wrong by Gröner only deepened his dislike for the General. The position therefore remained unaltered, save that Gröner's personal position with the President had been greatly weakened. But there was one other important result. In the Prussian General Election campaign, which was then in full swing, the Nazis made great play with the President's letter in order to demonstrate the partiality of the Government to the Marxists, and to this tactical move must be attributed a success at the polls which changed the situation altogether four weeks after the presidential elections.

From this moment Schleicher gave himself up to the undoing of Brüning. A continual stream of complaints poured into the Palace, and these, through the willing agency of Meissner and Oskar, found their way to the presidential table. From Hindenburg's fellow estate-owners in East Elbia, with no thought of gratitude for the large sums which, through the *Osthilfe,* they had received from the Müller and Brüning Governments and had squandered, came querulous enquiries about a rumoured programme of expropriation of bankrupt estates and the settling on them of small-holders. Former friends and enemies in the ranks of the Nationalists assured the Marshal that all breaches between him and his natural allies would be sealed once he had got rid of that scheming internationalist Brüning. Owners of property and many investors, frightened by Hitler's programme of abolition of interest, wrote anxiously to ask why, if the Brüning Government could not handle the Nazis, the President did not appoint one that could. Among the complaints and protests came those of certain of the former ruling monarchs of Germany, and these weighed with Hindenburg perhaps more heavily than any of the others. The wishes of kings must be obeyed.

It was true that the Nazi menace was growing rapidly. The suppression of the Storm Troops after the publication of the President's letter had had the unfortunate effect of making them appear martyrs, and this was particularly unwelcome in view of the fact that, on April 24 (1932), elections were to be held in Prussia, Bavaria, Württemberg, Anhalt, and Hamburg, in all an area amounting to four-fifths of the *Reich,* and the results being therefore almost tantamount to those of a General Election. And the results were indeed alarming for the electors of Hindenburg and for all those who were not blind to the signs and portents which the Nazis themselves had so lavishly displayed as to what they would do when they came to power. It can never be said of Hitler, or of his followers, that they gave no warning. Their programme was widely distributed for all to read and make of it what they could. But more definitely still were the declarations of the *Führer* of the type and method of government which he would set up. "Heads shall roll," he had declared, and had promised his followers "a night of long knives." Those who voted so overwhelmingly for Hitler in 1932 and 1933, and who but a few years later would willingly have recalled their votes, have only themselves to blame.

The elections of April 24 resulted in a series of victories for the Nazis. In Bavaria they increased their representation by 34, securing 43 seats in the new Diet, while in Württemberg, Anhalt, and Hamburg they made enormous advances. In Prussia they increased the number of their seats from 9 to 162, their gains being mostly at the expense of the parties of the Right, including those splinter-parties which had supported Brüning's policy.

It was the last warning to Germany and to Europe: to Germany, that each successive election might see an increase in National Socialist power; to Europe, that unless some definite indication were given of intention to fulfil the disarmament pledges of the Treaty of Versailles, a new Germany would take its own steps to rectify and redress the unequal position thus created.

Brüning staked all on his ability to achieve a spectacular success in foreign policy. The opportunity at Lausanne for which he had hoped had eluded him, for the Reparations Conference had been postponed till July. But there remained Geneva, where the statesmen of the world were gathered at the Disarmament Conference. True, the results of that body's deliberations had been distressingly meagre, but now only a bold stroke could succeed. Although the Nazis were in the ascendant, they had nowhere achieved an absolute majority. They were as yet neither strong enough nor sufficiently well organized to take over the government of the country. They were still malleable, capable of being controlled, and if Brüning could secure some specific agreement that when the Disarmament Conference was finally drawn up it would definitely be substituted for the inequalities of the Treaty of Versailles—if he could take back this achievement to Berlin, to be followed by the cancellation of reparations in July, then he might realize his long-cherished plan of bringing the Nazis into the Cabinet on his own terms and making them share the responsibilities of government.

But this approach at Geneva was only the forerunner of a far more ambitious plan of treaty revision which had been in Brüning's mind. He was convinced that the world was ripe for the promulgation of a plan of revision so eminently reasonable that it must of itself command success. The primary difficulty had been to find a sponsor for the plan and after making a survey of the statesmen of Europe, Brüning had failed to find among them one who could give a lead in the economic stabilization of Europe. He therefore turned to the one remaining figure of outstanding and compelling dignity, the *roi-chevalier*, Albert of Belgium, and through the agency of friends, Brüning placed before His Majesty a composite programme of treaty revision which envisaged the following adjustments: The immediate return of the Saar Territory to Germany with compensation to France, and a complementary agreement between the French and German industrialists; the final reparation payment by Germany of a lump sum of two milliard marks; an international loan to be made to Germany of two milliard marks, on which payment of interest and amortization would begin immediately; a settlement of the Corridor question, with compensation to Poland in the matter of railway transit, and free zones in the ports of Danzig and Gdynia similar to that enjoyed by Czechoslovakia in the port of Hamburg; a political truce for ten years; the encouragement of common enterprise between French and German industry; and an agreement for international co-operation in a system of European electrification.

It was Brüning's desire that an international conference to consider these points should be held in Belgium, under the immediate patronage of King Albert himself, and private negotiations between His Majesty and the Chancellor had reached a most satisfactory point by the middle of April 1932. Thus with high hopes and, with them, doubting fears, the German Chancellor left the capital to make his last and most gallant effort.

Though Schleicher never allowed the Chancellor's presence in Berlin in any way to interfere with the course of his intrigues, he seized upon the moment of Brüning's absence to redouble his energies. The President left for Neudeck as was his custom at the end of April, and it was seen to that he was surrounded by his fellow landed proprietors, all breathing suspicion and dislike of Brüning and the projected land reforms which he wished to bring into force.

In the meantime Schleicher busied himself in Berlin. Some time before he had brought to Hindenburg the man whom he had selected for the next Chancellor, and the President had been very much *épris* with him. Now the General was engaged in securing the support of the Nazis for his plans. With Röhm and with the young Count Helldorf, the leader of the Storm Troops in Berlin, he held almost daily conferences—supplemented by occasional meetings with Hitler—and outlined to them something of what was in his mind. The proposal was that Brüning should be dismissed and that the President should appoint a Cabinet of his own friends. The prohibition of the S.A. and S.S. would be at once repealed and the *Reichstag* dissolved, and in the ensuing election the Nazis would be given a free hand. In return the National Socialists agreed to "tolerate" the new Government for four years and to give it their parliamentary support. What Schleicher imagined he was really going to do with the Nazis eventually, nobody has ever quite succeeded in discovering. Whether he intended honestly to make an alliance with them, or to bring about their fall and finally their destruction by refined diplomacy, may not have been quite clear even to the General himself. He was for the first time in his career being too clever even for himself, and he had become inextricably entangled in the web of his own intrigue. For the Nazis took greedily what he offered them, yet gave nothing in return.

Meanwhile, in Geneva, Brüning was on the edge of achieving great things. Having learnt from experience that the pivotal power of Central Europe was Czechoslovakia, he had approached Dr. Benes with a proposal that their two countries should give a lead by announcing that they were agreed upon a cut in their mutual import tariffs of 15 per cent in the first and 10 per cent in the second year, with the intention that the agreement should be extended to the other Danubian States. Brüning sincerely hoped that at some future date this agreement might be adhered to by all European States, for it was his chief anxiety to keep Great Britain within the economic orbit of Europe and to prevent that drift of policy which later found expression in the Ottawa Agreements. Brüning was anxious to avoid the formation of isolated and possibly antagonistic groupings, which he regarded as fatal to the economic recovery of the world, and the proposals which he made to Benes, and which were sympathetically received, were intended to be the basis not only of a Central European, nor even of a Continental *Zollunion*, but of a wider agreement.

Brüning's greatest success, however, was with his peers in the matter of the equality of armaments. On April 26 conversations took place between him and Ramsay MacDonald, Stimson, Norman Davis, and, subsequently, Dino Grandi, at the close of which Brüning had won their unanimous agreement to his formula. In return for an undertaking by Germany that her armaments would not be increased for five years, or until the second Disarmament Conference, she should be permitted to reduce the twelve-year period of service in the *Reichswehr* to five years; to organize a militia, with eight to twelve months' training for 100,000 new men yearly; and to have freedom from the restrictions imposed by the treaty on the purchases and manufacture of war material. Germany should be granted the right to possess all weapons of offence, but would agree to the abolition of all, or any of them, if all other Powers agreed to do the same; alternatively, Germany would be satisfied with "samples" of these weapons. In addition, it was accepted that this new agreement should replace, as far as Germany was concerned, Part V of the Treaty of Versailles.

A formula had therefore been found which satisfied four out of the five Powers, and Mr. Stimson turned delightedly to Mr. Norman Davis, asking him to telephone this good news to M. Tardieu, then in the midst of a General Election campaign, and to beg him to hasten back to Geneva.

In later years Brüning was wont to say that at this moment he had been but a hundred yards off the finish, and it is tragic to think that, on this spring day of 1932, Europe was within an ace of reaching an agreement which would have changed the course of history; and yet it was not to be, for just as the thirsty travellers pressed forward to the shimmering oasis, it vanished in a mirage. Even at this distance Schleicher's power could be felt. Two evenings before, he had met the French Ambassador at the house of a common friend, and had there tendered the advice not to negotiate with Brüning, whose fall was already virtually accomplished, and whose successor, whom he named, would be more amenable to deal with. There followed telephone conversations between Berlin, Paris, and Geneva and, as a result, M. Tardieu made more of an attack of laryngitis than he might otherwise have done, regretfully refusing the urgent invitation of Mr. Norman Davis to return to Geneva.

Nor was there anyone at Geneva, save Brüning, who appreciated the stark tragedy of the position. To send the Chancellor back to Berlin empty-handed was to sign his political death-warrant and to play unreservedly into the hands of Hitler. Yet the statesmen of Europe adopted this course with calm equanimity and were astonished at the results. Within two years they would have made any sacrifice to have again before them the Brüning formula in all its fairness and restraint, for what they had refused to Brüning's wisdom, they were to concede a hundred-fold to Hitler's blackmail. Never was Europe so barren of statesmanship as at this moment.

His visions shattered and his hopes in ashes, Brüning returned wearily to Berlin on May 1, to find an atmosphere fetid with the breath of intrigue. He reported to Hindenburg on the fate of the Geneva negotiations and found the President distinctly cool towards him. Yet within an hour the obvious sincerity of the Chancellor had wrought a change in Hindenburg's attitude; he grew warmer and friendlier, complimented Brüning on all he had done, sympathized with him in the lack of result, and took leave of him, clasping his hand between his own. Later, walking with Meissner in the garden of the Palace, Hindenburg said, "Brüning has really done wonderfully well; we must keep on with him to the end."

Schleicher also received the Chancellor with fair and honeyed words. The reason was not far to seek. The *Reichstag* was about to convene on May 9, and before it was a Finance Bill of great importance, providing credits which, once voted, would make any Government secure for a year. Brüning alone could obtain the passage of this bill, and hence the *coup de grâce* must be postponed.

The Finance Bill was safely piloted through stormy waters

and was followed by the rejection of a motion of no confidence in the Government. Then with dramatic swiftness Schleicher dropped the mask and began to pull the strings of his puppets. Hindenburg's attitude change once more—the old weather-cock was veering from point to point in these fatal days—and he warned Brüning on May 12, one hour after his victory in the *Reichstag*, that he would send for the Party Leaders to confer on the composition of a new Cabinet. At the same moment, in the *Reichstag*, the Nationalist deputies, taking their cue from Hindenburg's letter of April 16, urged fiercely upon Gröner the suppression of the *Reichsbanner*. Gröner was a sick man, his voice was failing, yet in a speech full of courage and determination, delivered in the teeth of continued interruption, he refused to take action against an organization which he believed to be neither dangerous nor subversive.

The sequel was swift and dramatic. As Gröner concluded his speech and sank exhausted into his chair, Schleicher and Hammerstein appeared beside him on the ministerial bench, and with cold brutality informed him that he no longer enjoyed the confidence of the *Reichswehr* and must resign immediately.[1] Gröner was thunderstruck. He had cherished Schleicher as a son and had purposed resigning the Ministry of Defence to him in the near future. Overwhelmed by such desertion and treachery, he appealed to Hindenburg, but, as he might have known, the Marshal "could do nothing for him." It was the inevitable sequel to Spa and to Kolberg, and to Gröner had come the fate of Ludendorff, of Wilhelm II, and of others. Yet in his hour of bitter humiliation, there came a crumb of consolation. By devious means there came to him a remark which the Kaiser had made to a

---

[1] Not till years later did Hammerstein and the seven district commanders who had been consulted by telephone, realize that Schleicher had duped them and lied in his representation of the case against Gröner. Many of them subsequently sought him out in his retirement and explained sadly that, had they been fully and accurately informed of the facts, they would never have thus deserted him.

member of his suite in Doorn: "Tell Gröner he has my full sympathy; I always expected that this would happen." Wilhelm II had not forgotten Spa, but he knew now where the responsibility lay.

A week after Gröner's fall Brüning sent for Schleicher, and gave himself the satisfaction of telling the General frankly what he thought of him. He also told him that, having undermined the confidence of the army in Gröner, he must take over the Defence Ministry himself.

"I will," Schleicher replied, "but not in your Government." In the Chancellor's library, that same room in which Bismarck had planned the greatness of the German Empire, they talked for hours, each unwilling to break off the battle; Brüning because he had long desired to speak his mind to this man, Schleicher because he hated to leave the field to Brüning. They made a strange contrast, these two, who had fought through the war, and wore each the Iron Cross, First Class. Brüning the scholar-paladin, with the light of honest anger shining in his eyes, and Schleicher, the dandy officer, who could not meet the stern gaze of the other.

At last, as the light of a new day struggled through the curtained windows, Brüning brought the conversation to a close on a note of prophecy. Schleicher was leaning against a bookcase, his face pale and haggard, sweating slightly; Brüning stood in front of him.

"The difference between us as soldiers," he said, "was that I fought in the line and you served on the Staff. In the line, with the machine-gun corps, we learned to control our nerves and to hold our fire sometimes till the enemy were almost on us. At the end of the war it was G.H.Q., not the army, that lost its head in a panic. *We* would have fought on, it was *you* who threw up your hands. And when the time comes, you, General von Schleicher, will give up your battle before it is lost and you will become caught in your own intrigues."

At that moment, standing upon the threshold of his own defeat, Brüning appeared to have been gifted with the power of second sight, for within six months Schleicher had risen to the highest office and fallen therefrom, and in two years he had been murdered, a victim of his own scheming.

With the resignation of Gröner on May 12, the life of the Brüning Cabinet began to ebb swiftly away. Nor did Schleicher give it breathing-space to nurse its wounds. Lest the Chancellor should exercise his influence on the President, Hindenburg was again hurried off to Neudeck. Before the President left Berlin Brüning informed him in detail of the negotiations then in process between the Centre Party and the Nazis for the formation of a government in Prussia. The great anxiety of all was that while the National Socialists should receive a taste of the burden of government, they should not gain control of the Prussian police force, and to obviate any danger of this, Brüning had prepared a decree whereby the police of all the Federal States, with the exception of Bavaria, Württemberg and Baden, should be placed under the *Reich* Ministry of Interior. It was his further plan to unite the premiership of Prussia with the office of the Chancellor, as had been the case under Bismarck, but he did not yet consider the moment ripe for this step.

To these suggestions Hindenburg listened with a certain interest but with little enthusiasm. Even with these safeguards he declined definitely to give the Nazis power in Prussia, believing on the advice of Schleicher that they might be prepared to tolerate a new Government in the *Reich* and in Prussia without participating in it on the condition that the Storm Troopers should be reinstated. In vain the Chancellor tried to persuade Hindenburg that Hitler could never accept such a solution, which would mean political suicide for him. The President set aside this argument with a single sentence: "I will have their word of honour." He closed the conversation by saying that he needed time to consider these points, and, regardless of the fact that every day was of vital importance to the plans of his Chancellor, he gave him strict orders that no further decrees were to be promulgated and no changes made in either the *Reich* or Prussian Cabinets till his return.

The air of Berlin hummed with rumour and intrigue, one paper gave a list of the conspirators against the Government, which even included the private secretary of the Chancellor, who had previously been an officer of Schleicher's. The General was in continual touch with the Nazis—Goebbels's diary, which, though unreliable generally as a chronicle, may be trusted in this respect, shows that throughout the month the leaders of the party were in constant communication with Schleicher and other "gentlemen of the President's circle"—and by the fourth week of May not only the date of the Chancellor's dismissal was known to them but also the composition of the new Cabinet. Brüning himself heard of it at a reception given in honour of the eldest son of Ibn Saud, when he was told that the French Ambassador had blandly asked a journalist when Herr von Papen would take office.

Through this veil of darkness there shone one slender ray of hope for Brüning. Tardieu had fallen in the General Election of May 8 and there was just the chance that his successor, Herriot, might prove more receptive of the proposals which the Chancellor had put forward at Geneva. Brüning knew that Mr. Gibson, the American Minister at Brussels, was keeping in close touch with the situation, and might prevail on the new French Government to reopen negotiations on this basis. Fortified by this slight hope, he continued his preparations for the Lausanne Conference, now only six weeks away, and at the same time took further steps to safeguard the economic life of Germany.

Among the new measures which the Chancellor was now about to bring forward were the final steps to re-adjust the Budget of the Municipalities and the Social Insurance institutions. It was considered to be the last step on the road of deflation which was forced upon Germany by the large withdrawal of foreign short-term capital. As stocks were liquidated and as since February the orders on the books of the large industrial firms had increased, the Chancellor thought that the time was ripe to start with a moderate credit expansion, and to finance by that means new employment. Two special measures were considered as most urgent: the reconstruction of roads and the breaking-up of bankrupt estates in the Eastern Provinces. This was the celebrated plan for the expropriation, with generous compensation, of certain bankrupt estates and the settlement thereon of small holders, or their use for afforestation. Despite the protests and threats of the *Landbund*, Brüning had persisted with his measure as being essential to the whole agricultural situation in Germany, and he now included it in the batch of decrees which Meissner was to take to Neudeck for the President's consideration.

In the calmer atmosphere of his estate Hindenburg had again swung around to the side of his Chancellor, and when Meissner returned to Berlin he was able to tell Brüning that the President had provisionally consented to sign the decrees. Brüning thought of going to Neudeck to talk over the whole situation with the Old Man, but Meissner dissuaded him, pointing out that Hindenburg would now be prepared to sign the Decrees. The President would be returning to the Palace in a couple of days, he said, and it would be better if the Chancellor waited till then to see him. He himself was not going back to Neudeck. Brüning agreed, and to this day it is uncertain whether Meissner was honest in his advice. Was he keeping Brüning from the President in order that further influence, unfavourable to the Chancellor, might be brought to bear on him, or was he for the moment satisfied that Brüning's interests were better served by awaiting the Old Gentleman's arrival in Berlin? Here lies one of the impenetrable mysteries with which this period of German history is beset, but whatever the answer, the sequel was significant.

Whether Meissner told Schleicher of the change in Hindenburg's attitude, or whether the conversation with Brüning was reported to the General by one of the spies which he maintained in the Chancellor's office, is for practical purposes immaterial. The important fact was that Schleicher that night (May 26) left secretly for Neudeck to wind the President up once more for the final overthrow of the Chancellor. History was repeating itself ironically. Just twelve years before, in the summer of 1916, Ludendorff and Hoffmann had administered a last "gingering-up" to Hindenburg before that final journey to Pless, which was to end in the fall of Falkenhayn; so now Schleicher worked on the Marshal's feelings and briefed him for the interview which was to mark the fall of Brüning. The scene and the supernumerary actors had changed; only the central figure remained, outlasting all of them, gigantic and, seemingly, immortal.

Yet between this secret visit to Neudeck and the final sequel three days later there occurred another event which, almost incomprehensible in nature, enhances the enigma of Kurt von Schleicher. The General was not entirely certain of the success of his mission to the President. He had found Hindenburg better disposed towards Brüning than he had feared, and though the Old Gentleman had listened to Schleicher's arguments and had appeared to agree with them, Schleicher was uncertain as to how far the President had become convinced of the necessity of dismissing the Chancellor. He knew very well—who better?—how changeable was the mind of Hindenburg, and he was by no means sure what the state of that mind would be when Hindenburg returned to Berlin, nor how it would be affected after a conversation with Brüning.

Scarcely had Schleicher reached the capital on May 28, therefore, when he made certain advances to Brüning for a reconciliation. It was the old story of changing his coat when he thought his position was endangered. He was no friend of the Nazis and no friend of Brüning's, but he feared that if Brüning should regain the confidence of the President his own position would be appreciably weakened. But this time things had gone too far, and Brüning, though he had always pitied Schleicher rather than hated him, could not agree to forgive and forget. He knew well enough that the General would change his coat again on the slightest provocation and with as little warning or hesitation.

To Schleicher's emissary he replied, therefore, that if the General could discover a way to start again the negotiations between the Centre and the Nazis in Prussia, which by his intrigues with Röhm he had so flagrantly destroyed, the Chancellor would receive him, but he must have Schleicher's answer by the evening. By this means Brüning had avoided a trap and placed Schleicher on the defensive, for the General was too astute not to realize that by his own actions he had rendered all hope of resuming negotiations in Prussia impossible. Rebuffed and furious, Schleicher then devoted his whole energy to maintaining Hindenburg's mind and soul in opposition to his Chancellor.

On May 28 Schleicher and Meissner were not at all sure about the definite decision of the President. Meissner went to see the Chancellor and asked him if he was prepared to stay in office on condition that the President would guarantee him that the Nationalist and National Socialist Parties would tolerate him. Brüning was not sure if this offer was not a further trap for him. He replied that toleration of a Government by the National Socialists was in his eyes not a realistic proposition. He had no intention of changing the Government in the *Reich* but he was prepared to have coalition Ministeries in the Federal States to find out if the Nazis really were prepared to share responsibility, on condition that nowhere should they have the police in their hands. Meissner made it clear that the President wanted Brüning to drop nearly all the Members of his Cabinet and this the Chancellor refused to do.

On the morning of Sunday, May 29, Brüning was summoned to the presence. It would, he knew, be the final game of the rubber, that long dreary contest in which he had given all his strength ungrudgingly only to meet defeat at the end. He was not, however, in view of Meissner's message, prepared for the coolness of his reception. Hindenburg barely acknowledged his greeting. The Old Gentleman seemed disconcerted and ill at ease, as he always was when playing a part. He cut short Brüning's opening sentence, and, putting on his spectacles, began to speak from a sheaf of notes which shook in his old hands.

The two confronted each other, as they had so often done before during those two fateful years; President and Chancellor, Field-Marshal and machine-gun officer, eighty-five and forty-seven. Generations and traditions separated them, and they moved in different worlds, each speaking a language the other could not understand. Yet with a strange veneration Brüning had trusted and admired Hindenburg, and Hindenburg had once showed confidence in Brüning. Now all that was over and Brüning was to follow the road over which Wilhelm II, Ludendorff, Hoffmann, and Gröner had passed before him.

The Marshal began to read a series of set statements which had evidently been jotted down as headings and notes for a more formal address.

"You have Bolshevik Ministers in your Government and they persuade you to make this Bolshevik policy," he began. The reference was to Stegerwald.

The Chancellor started to reply, but Hindenburg cut short his explanation. He went on rasping out his staccato statements.

"The Government has not been authorized by me to promulgate any new decrees."

Again Brüning sought to answer, but again he was swept aside. After the next remark, however, he waited and allowed Hindenburg's allegations to pass unchallenged. When the Marshal had got to the end of his brief, Brüning again began a defence of his policy and, for nearly an hour, they argued back and forth. At the close, Brüning asked a direct question. "Do you wish me to resign?" The Old Gentleman would not give a direct answer. "It is against my conscience to keep a Cabinet which is so unpopular; it must go as soon as possible. But you must remain as Foreign Minister in a new government, as Stresemann did. That is your duty."

The parallel was an unfair one. Stresemann had never been asked to abandon his friends and to keep office himself. He had never attained in internal affairs the same predominance as Brüning. Had it been a question of merely maintaining a continuity of foreign policy, Brüning might have remained, but to have done so under the given circumstances would have been to betray his colleagues. The suggestion, which was undoubtedly Hindenburg's own, was typical of him, for in thus following the path of "duty" himself he could have hushed his conscience in the clash of loyalties. That Brüning rejected it, and with anger, was equally characteristic; his friends came first with him and his conception of loyalty was altogether different.

"I, too, have a conscience," he retorted to the President, "and it forbids me, at a moment when the State is in peril, to change my mind every day." And with that he took his leave, a Chancellor *ad interim*.

The Cabinet met to decide its course of action, which, after the interview with the President, could only be resignation. Dawn was already far advanced when Brüning retired to rest, yet by half-past 8 he was again at his writing-table. The day was perfect—a May morning of blue and gold, a day on which things should have not an end but a beginning. Sixteen years before on a May evening, shrouded in mist, the fleets of Britain and Germany had grappled at Jutland and the issue had been acclaimed a victory by both. In honour of this engagement the guard at the President's Palace was mounted by naval ratings for the week of the anniversary, and at this noon of May 30, 1932, they would take over from the *Reichswehr*. The thought crossed Brüning's mind as he sat at his table, but his attention was instantly diverted by the voice of his secretary. The American Ambassador, it appeared, wished to see him immediately upon urgent business. By 9 o'clock the Ambassador was with him and Fate had dealt Brüning a further ironic blow.

That for which he had dreamed and planned was at last within his grasp and now he was powerless to seize it. For the news which the Ambassador brought was none other than that France had reconsidered her view on disarmament. Hugh Gibson had met Herriot at Lyons and had there persuaded him that the proposals, which Brüning had made at Geneva and which Tardieu had refused to discuss, presented in reality a sound and honest basis of negotiation. He had written as much to the Ambassador, who had come at once to Brüning, in view, as he said, of the internal and external importance of the news to the Chancellor. For the purport of Mr. Gibson's message was: "Persuade Brüning to return to Geneva as soon as possible, for there is every prospect of his speedy success there."

Here is one of the great "ifs" of history. Had Mr. Gibson's news arrived but twenty-four hours earlier, the destiny of Europe, and of Germany, might well have been changed, and the name of Brüning might have been numbered amongst those great ones who succeeded, instead of among those who went down fighting. Now, however, he could only thank the Ambassador for his swift action and communicate the news to the permanent head of the Foreign Office.

But hardly had the Ambassador taken his leave when the purport of his visit was known to Meissner and Schleicher. The latter's spies were everywhere and the Chancellor's own room was not free from their surveillance. The *Camarilla*, who knew the President as well or even better than the Chancellor, at once took action to prevent Brüning from using this new information to win once more the confidence of Hindenburg. A sudden telephone message informed the Chancellor that his audience had been postponed from 10.30 to 11.55—and at noon it was the Marshal's habit to inspect the *Skaggerakgarde*.

The last scales fell from Brüning's eyes and he saw at last the whole truth. He was to be dismissed without a hearing and he prepared to accept his fate with dignity. With head held high and erect as if on parade, perhaps again, in his imagination, wearing field-grey, he stood before the Marshal at the appointed hour. Hindenburg spoke no word of compunction or gratitude; he mumbled his sentences, and spoke again of duty and honour and his conscience. But now it was Brüning who cut him short.

"I too have my name and my honour, Herr *Reichspräsident*, and I give you the resignation of my Cabinet."

As Hindenburg began to reply, an aide-de-camp entered, from without came the blare of trumpets of the *Skaggerakwache*, and the tramp of their feet sounded in the court below. The Old Man grasped his stick and started for the door; as he passed Brüning without a glance, he muttered, "Now I can have a Cabinet of my friends."

And the man who had been "the best Chancellor since Bismarck" walked out into the sunlight of the garden with the sound of the trumpets in his ears.[1]

· 9 ·

Franz von Papen. This was the name which, for weeks past, Schleicher had been whispering into the ears of his fellow conspirators. To the President, to the *Herrenklub*, to the *Landbund*, to the Nationalists, to the Nazis, and to the French Ambassador, Schleicher had commended Papen as the man whom Germany most needed at this moment, by which he meant the man who would best do his, Schleicher's, bidding, for the General fancied himself as a maker and breaker of Chancellors.

Fifty-three years old at the time, Franz von Papen had already been a figure, if a notorious one, in international affairs. As military attaché at Washington he had been expelled in 1916, with his naval colleague, Captain Boy-Ed, for activities of sabotage in American munitions works and other abuses of diplomatic privileges. Deported to Germany, Papen made the error of believing that his personal safe-conduct also covered his luggage. The ship on which he was travelling was stopped and searched by a British warship, and amongst his correspondence was discovered the full proof of his guilt, and the details of his work with Secret Service agents in America and the counterfoils of the cheques with which they had been paid. All this material was made public in a White Paper, but additions to the collection

---

[1] Having had practically no rest for a week, Brüning went immediately to bed and slept for nearly twenty-four hours on end. When he awoke it was to find a further ironic repetition of history. As in 1917, the Supreme Command had offered the Embassy at Constantinople to the fallen Bethmann Hollweg, so now the new Government requested Brüning to become Ambassador in London. In each case the refusal was the same, and because of his unwillingness to be removed from the political sphere, the Foreign Office allowed a rumour to reach the press that Brüning was suffering from a nervous breakdown. This was completely untrue. The author was with the ex-Chancellor within a week of his dismissal and was particularly struck by his good health and spirits.

were thoughtfully contributed by Papen himself. Arrived back in Germany, he wrote to friends treating the matter lightly, as the British could not know of certain other contacts, which he named; this letter in turn fell into hands for which it was not meant.

It may be justifiably argued that such a background was scarcely a qualification to take over control of the destinies of Germany at a moment of acute tension. But Papen's American achievements were practically unknown to his own countrymen, who learnt of them with interest and surprise when published by the press of the world on his appointment as Chancellor.

In Germany Papen was known as a member of the Westphalian Catholic nobility, who by marriage had acquired large industrial interests in the Saar Territory. Primarily, however, his claim to fame was as a gentleman rider, and a prominent member of the *Herrenreiter-verband* and of the *Union-Klub*. In truth he was an excellent and fearless horseman, but with an unfortunate inclination to rush his fences, a tendency which he carried into his political life. As a member of the Centre Party he had been elected to the Prussian *Landtag*, but had failed to earn the confidence of his colleagues to any marked degree. At one moment there was a proposal to put him on the list for election to the *Reichstag*, but this met with unyielding opposition from the veteran leader of the party.

"But why do you object so strongly to Herr von Papen?" his supporters asked.

"I am too old to have to give reasons," was the reply, "but I will not have him in the *Reichstag*."

Witty, excellent company, and of very considerable personal charm, Papen was a well-known favourite in the social world and in such political circles as the *Herrenklub* of Berlin, and it was here that Schleicher picked him as his nominee to succeed Brüning. In making his choice he had a number of factors in mind. Papen was a member of the Centre and played a certain part in the direction of the party journal, *Germania*. By replacing one Centrist Chancellor by another, it was Schleicher's plan to split the party and thereby destroy it as a political factor. In addition, through his wife's interests in the Saar, Papen had many intimate contacts with the French and was an ardent exponent of the idea of a Franco-German industrial rapprochement and a military alliance against the Soviet Union. Here lay a reason for Schleicher's advice to the French Ambassador that Brüning's successor would prove more amenable to French policy.

This, then, was the Man of Shadows whom Schleicher brought to Hindenburg in exchange for the great personality of Heinrich Brüning, and the President accepted him without demur. Well might Brüning reflect bitterly that "Hindenburg thinks no more of taking on a new Chancellor than of changing his chief of staff." But to the President himself he was more subtle. On the occasion of his formal call of resignation some days later, he told the Marshal he was delighted to see him in such good health as he would need all his strength for the trials that were ahead of him.

One of the more extraordinary episodes of Hindenburg's long life is his relation with Papen, for of the seven Chancellors who served him there is no doubt that none so enjoyed his confidence as did this strange little man. With the volatility of a bird, the sublime confidence of the amateur, and the ineffable valour of ignorance, "Franzchen" won the heart of the Old Man, where Müller, Marx, and Brüning had failed, and retained his affection to the end. Indeed, Papen owes his life to Hindenburg.

Their first contact had been fortunate. Hindenburg recollected —or it was recalled to him by his "official remembrancer"— the telegram which Papen had sent him on his first election in 1925, and he was attracted by the fact that, in contrast to Brüning, Papen had for years endeavoured to break the connection

of the Centre Party with the Left and to build up a Catholic Conservative movement. Hindenburg was pleased with the personal
charm of Papen. Here was another sort of soldier, not the cold
realistic view of the machine-gun officer, but the debonair gaiety
of the cavalry captain. Papen made the Old Gentleman laugh,
he took him back to his own young days as a subaltern. Moreover he flattered him, as Brüning had never done, and traded on
the natural patronizing affection of the very old for the no longer
young.

The Marshal entered almost enthusiastically into this new
experiment in government and set about picking his Cabinet
with a reawakened zest. The Chancellor invited nearly all the
members of the Brüning Cabinet, whose resignation two days
earlier the President had urged, to join his new Cabinet. He received unanimous refusals, thereupon the President forced civil
servants to accept seats in the cabinet. To one he appealed on
his knightly oath as a Württemberg nobleman, to another on his
oath as a Prussian officer, while in the case of a third, a competent Civil servant who doubted his ability to assume Cabinet
responsibilities, the President gave six hours in which to decide
whether he would accept promotion or dismissal. As a result,
on June 1 the new Presidential Government was announced to
an astonished world. Within six weeks of his re-election by over
nineteen million votes of the Left and Centre, Hindenburg appointed a Cabinet of which seven Ministers were of the nobility
with definitely Right affiliations, and in which, for the first time
since 1918, there was no representative of organized labour. To
such an extremity had the path of duty led him.

The new Government in which Schleicher, as Minister of
Defence, was the dominant force, had no support in the *Reichstag* apart from the Nationalist Party, for the Centre had remained solidly loyal to Brüning and had unanimously expelled
Papen from its midst. The Chancellor depended upon the good-

will of the President, the armed forces of the State, and the unreliable backing of the National Socialists, who were prepared to "tolerate" the new régime in return for the promise of the raising of the ban on the S.A. and S.S., and of new elections in which they justifiably expected to make great gains. It was with this promise of toleration, which Schleicher and Meissner had extracted from Hitler, that Schleicher had made such play in persuading Hindenburg to appoint the new Government. Brüning had failed either to control, placate, or destroy the Nazi Party; Schleicher and Papen, the General had promised Hindenburg, would certainly achieve either the first or the last, but to do either it was necessary to use the middle course.

From Hitler's point of view the plan was eminently satisfactory. He received much and gave little in return, for he regarded the whole affair merely as a means whereby his Trojan Horse might gain admission within the walls. Once this was accomplished, Hitler would unhesitatingly break the pledges given to his allies. Had either Papen or Schleicher taken the trouble to study that illuminating work, *Mein Kampf*, they would have found therein, set out for all to read, the *Führer's* thesis that "The Strong Man is strongest when alone," and had they read further they might well have hesitated before trusting the word of a political leader who so frankly stated that "no really great achievement has ever been affected by coalitions, but has been due to the triumph of one individual man . . . the national state, therefore, will only be created by the adamantine willpower of a single movement, *after* that movement has won through, having defeated all others."

Hindenburg, however, was delighted with the new turn of events. He now moved once more among those whom once he had called his friends but who subsequently had reviled him. The former generals and officials of the old régime now flocked to the Palace, and the President again became the venerable and respected head of the Nationalists. No wonder his affection went out toward the Chancellor who had effected this reconciliation. Papen had indeed become the "white-headed boy" of the Palace. Nevertheless, he was shrewd enough to doubt the capability of the new Chancellor. On the very day of the latter's nomination, he told a visitor: "Now at least I have a Cabinet of my friends, but I am afraid it will not function under this Chancellor."

The President saw clearly that the Chancellor had singularly little following in the country, and no previous government had showed itself to be so bankrupt of original ideas as this "Cabinet of Barons." Its entire foreign policy was inherited from its predecessor, Papen reaping the reward that should have been Brüning's; while at home he could do no more than put into force the decrees found ready drafted in the pigeon-holes of Brüning's writing-table. The only original contribution made by the Papen Government itself was the singular lack of adroitness with which the measures were executed.

From the first there was little pretence of toleration by the Nazis. Their relations with the Government became strained almost at once, when the withdrawal of the prohibition of the S.A. and S.S. was delayed for a fortnight after the change of régime. Both Papen and Schleicher were taken seriously to task by Hitler for this delay, and were warned that resentment against the Government and discontent were rising in the ranks of the Party. Nor was this criticism allayed by Papen's personal success at Lausanne, where, as a result of Brüning's diplomacy, he achieved the cancellation of reparations, except for the nominal payment of three milliard marks. The extreme elements in the Nazi Party took advantage of this opportunity to make a fierce attack on the Government. At a mass meeting of over a hundred thousand on July 9, in front of the Berlin Schloss, Count Helldorf declared that the confidence which many Germans had given to the Papen Government had been misplaced.

"Revealing incomprehensible weakness, Herr von Papen has approved proposals which we liberty-loving Germans never endorsed"; and Goebbels added that the National Socialist Party did not consider itself bound by the Lausanne Agreement, since Papen had no authority to sign it.

Disturbed at this attitude on the part of those who he had been assured would support him loyally, Papen took measures calculated both to appease the Nazis and to demonstrate his own independence of spirit. On July 28 the German Government made a protest—all too well justified, alas—against the disregard of the Disarmament Conference for German aspirations for equality, and threatened to withdraw from the Conference altogether if more consideration were not given to German aims, a threat which was made good two months later. It was hoped that this step would increase the prestige of the Government both at home and abroad, where Papen had failed signally to win that confidence which Herriot had been prepared to give to Brüning.

Papen's second manœuvre was intended to please the Nazis and at the same time to steal their anti-Marxist thunder. Since the Prussian elections of April 24, in which the Left had lost heavily to the Nazis, the Socialist Cabinet of Braun and Severing had continued to discharge the functions of government pending the formation of a further coalition. For though the National Socialists were the largest party in the Diet, they had no clear majority and only by allying themselves with the Centre could they form a government. For months abortive negotiations had taken place and in the meantime the Socialist ministers acted *ad interim*, confining themselves to the maintenance and conduct of routine business. To overthrow the Braun Government, thought Papen, would serve a number of useful ends. It would please the President, who, since the formation of the new Cabinet had turned his back upon his electors of three months before; it would placate the Nazis, who could scarcely oppose any assault upon Marxism, and it would, at the same time, take the wind from their sails; more important than all, however, it would place the control of the Prussian police, one of the most efficient forces in the world, in the hands of the Government of the *Reich*.

Among the draft decrees and proposals which Papen had inherited from his predecessor was one which outlined a form of government in Prussia, whereby the office of Prime Minister was vested in the Chancellor of the *Reich*. Braun himself had offered to resign the Prussian Premiership to Brüning, if such an identification of offices would prove an added bulwark against National Socialism, and though the Chancellor had then refused, he had prepared a plan by which the Nazis might one day be given a share of responsibility, but only with the police and the premiership safely in the hands of the *Reich*.

It was this plan that Papen now found and put into force, regardless either of its significance or its original intention. There resulted, on July 20, the Rape of Prussia, and one of the dreams of old Oldenburg-Januschau came true. From the earliest beginnings of parliamentary government in Germany, that veteran had declared that the *Reichstag* must never get so strong that it could not be turned out by a captain and twenty soldiers. He had now lived to see the whole government of Prussia evicted by a lieutenant and ten policemen.

Papen, Schleicher, and Meissner brought to Hindenburg the news that Braun's Government was conducting affairs without parliamentary authority and was particularly tolerant of the activities of the Communist Party in Prussia. It was therefore proposed to dismiss them summarily, if necessary evicting them by force, and to replace them by a cabinet of officials presided over by Papen himself as Prime Minister and *Reichskommissar*, with Dr. Franz Bracht, the Bürgermeister of Essen, as his deputy.

Hindenburg forgot that the man against whom this coup was

being directed, Otto Braun, had pleaded with him to remain President, and, with Brüning, had worked feverishly for his re-election. He did not concern himself with the legality of the proposed action. He was becoming obsessed with a loathing of the word Marxist, loosely used by his entourage to describe anyone from a rabid Communist to an innocuous pacifist, and he disliked the feeling of obligation. He owed his re-election to the efforts of Brüning and Braun, and to the votes of the Centre and the Socialists. Brüning had gone, Braun must go, and Prussia, Hindenburg's Prussia, must be purged of the Socialist taint which had held to it for the past twelve years.

The presidential agreement was therefore gladly given to the plans of Papen and Schleicher. Martial law was proclaimed throughout the military district of the Mark, the Socialist Ministers were dismissed, and those of them and their officials who refused to leave were placed under arrest. Among them was the Berlin Prefect of Police, that same Grzesinski who, at Cassel in November 1918, had welcomed the defeated Marshal with the words: "Hindenburg is fulfilling his duty to-day in a manner which endears him to us as never before. Hindenburg belongs to the German nation. . . ." The Marshal was still doing his duty, but somehow it had all got a little mixed.

Within a week practically every outspoken Republican in the upper ranks of the Prussian Administration had been peremptorily turned out of office and replaced by a man of the Right. Even former officials, who had lost their position in 1920 through complicity in the Kapp *putsch*, were reinstated in office. The Weimar Constitution, which Hindenburg had twice sworn to defend, was rocking upon its foundations, and the blows that assailed it were struck with his authority and consent. He was now firmly convinced that only by Presidial Government, apart from and above the *Reichstag*, could Germany be saved. It was his duty, his friends never ceased to tell him, to rescue Germany from the Marxist danger which threatened to undermine her moral life, and if the existing Constitution could not protect Germany, then another must be devised. Papen sought to allay the fears of the purists by promising that any reforms would only be applied in a legal manner, but the real intention of the group surrounding the President was voiced again by that incorrigible octogenarian diehard, Oldenburg-Januschau, who, having, with the revival of oligarchy, taken on a new lease of life, declared publicly that he and his friends would "brand the German people with a new Constitution that would take away its sight and hearing."

To many it came as a surprise that the forces of Social Democracy had not shown greater fight in defence of their principles, and particularly in the case of Prussia. Here again the hand of Schleicher is to be found. He had always been on good terms with the Trade Union leaders and had looked upon their organizations as the reservoirs of man-power on which almost unlimited draughts could be made. But like most of the General's friends they suffered from his duplicity. Schleicher, when the Papen Government took office, assured the Trade Union leaders that he was in no way planning to bring the National Socialists into power. All that he proposed to give them was the right to reorganize the S.A. and S.S. Nothing more. Indeed, said Schleicher, he was far more the friend of the Trade Unions than of the Nazis. His real aim, he declared, was to get rid of the *Reichstag* and to replace it by a form of corporative parliament, based largely upon the Trade Unions. It was no longer possible to save the political parties, which were doomed through their own ineptitude, but their place must be taken by the great guilds of organized labour, in whose hands the constitutional powers of Parliament must lie.

With these promises and visions Schleicher was able to split the forces of the Left, for whereas the Social Democrat Party

frankly disbelieved him and set about putting their militant organization, the *Reichsbanner,* on a fighting basis, the Trade
Union leaders were beguiled by his words. The spell even lasted
after the Rape of Prussia. The Social Democrats were prepared
to call a general strike immediately, to meet force with force, but
the Trade Union leaders, still trusting blindly in the word of
Schleicher, prevailed upon their members to wait for the promised millennium.

Despite all his efforts to woo his "tolerant" allies, Papen
failed signally to win them. In the course of the campaign
which preceded the General Election of July 31, the Nazis assailed the Government with as much enthusiasm as did the Socialists, the Communists, and the Centre, and "Down with the
Cabinet of Barons" became an election slogan common to all
parties save the Nationalists.

One member of the Government alone escaped the insults of
the Nazis. General von Schleicher was notably omitted from
all attacks on his ministerial colleagues. Though Hitler de-
spised Papen and had broken his troth with him, he still had a
use for the man who, as Minister of Defence, controlled the
military power of Germany and who had overthrown Brüning
and Gröner for the sake of the Brown Army. The *Führer* had
ambitions for the future which he intended that Schleicher
should help him to fulfil.

At the close of a campaign in which violence of every kind
was more prevalent than at any time since 1918—in the street
fighting in Altona on July 17, for example, twelve Nazis and
Communists were killed—the result of the polls was a stalemate. The National Socialists, though they increased the number of their deputies from 107 to 230, two-fifths of the whole
house, were not able to add very greatly to the number of votes
which Hitler had polled in the second presidential ballot,
whereas the Communists, who captured 89 seats, becoming the

third largest party in the *Reichstag,* increased their poll by nearly two millions. Yet the result was outstandingly a defeat for the Papen Government. The Nationalists and the German People's Party, the only groups upon which it could unhesitatingly depend for support, could muster only forty-four deputies between them; whereas the Nazis, in alliance with the 75 deputies of the Centre—if such support should be forthcoming —could command an absolute majority and decide the fate of any parliamentary government. On the other hand, Hitler's success gave him the claim that, even in defiance of the Constitution and against the law, the President should appoint him to the Government and retain him in it.

It was this line that the *Führer* proposed to take. A few days after the elections he had a rendezvous with Schleicher at the barracks of Fürstenberg and there outlined to him the terms of an offer to be made to the President; for himself Hitler demanded the Chancellorship and for his followers the premiership of Prussia, the *Reich* and Prussian Ministries of Interior and the Ministry of Justice. Schleicher would remain Minister of Defence, and there was some talk of the Vice-Chancellorship. The name of Papen was not mentioned in the shadow Cabinet.

Hitler was so well satisfied with his conversation with Schleicher that he seriously suggested that a memorial tablet should be let in to the wall of the house in which they had talked: "Here the memorable conference between Adolf Hitler and General von Schleicher took place." In less than two years' time he had accepted the responsibility for Schleicher's murder.

In the delighted conviction that only a few days now separated him from the Chancellorship, Hitler departed for Munich, leaving Schleicher to make good his promises with Hindenburg and Papen. Here the General found unexpected but unyielding opposition. The President, as in all previous years, refused to have a National Socialist in the Government and

Papen had not the slightest intention of resigning in Hitler's favour. Quite unperturbed by the result of the elections, he was preparing to enjoy the sweets of office and to meet, without a programme or a plan, a *Reichstag* almost wholly hostile to him. Moreover, the President was now completely captivated by the Chancellor. His charm outshone even that of Schleicher, and Hindenburg had no thought of exchanging this delightful companion for the wild eccentricities of Adolf Hitler. The Marshal was deeply interested in the movement of national awakening, and in more than one aspect sympathized with its ideals, but he regarded its leader, whom, at this time, he usually referred to as "the Bohemian Corporal," as a strange and inexplicable phenomenon whose personality he frankly and unrestrainedly disliked. The one formal interview which had been arranged between the two men had left in Hindenburg's mind no vestige of confidence in, or approval for, Hitler, and Papen, the latest of the Old Gentleman's "Jonathans," was for the moment secure.

Far from agreeing with Schleicher's tentative suggestions, Hindenburg was deeply displeased at the attacks made upon Papen during the election, and it had not escaped his notice that Schleicher had gone unscathed through the campaign. He proposed to see the curious political fellow again and tell him what he thought of him.

To Hitler in Munich, therefore, there came a telegram summoning him to Berlin to an interview with the President on August 13, 1932. It could mean but one thing. Schleicher had carried out his plans, Papen was about to resign, and he, Adolf Hitler, former corporal and house-painter, would become Chancellor of the German *Reich*. The united command of the hundred thousand *Reichswehr* and of his own half million Brown legionaries would be his; the control of Germany was within his grasp.

So Hitler came to Berlin and took up his quarters at the Hotel Kaiserhof in the Wilhelmsplatz, a stone's-throw from the Chancellery and the President's Palace. With high hopes he went to a preliminary conversation with Papen and here he met the first douche of disillusionment. For Papen, secure in Hindenburg's favour, had no intention of resigning and told the Nazi leader so quite plainly. He offered Hitler the position of Vice-Chancellor for himself, and that of Prussian Minister of the Interior, which carried with it control of the police, for one of his lieutenants.

Hitler was staggered. Papen had, then, not resigned and Hindenburg was not about to make him Chancellor. The Nazis were being fobbed off with offers of secondary positions. Hitler suddenly discovered that he was insulted. His hysterical disposition got the better of him. He began to speak; the sentences became a speech, the speech an oration, and Hitler's voice rose to the shrill key of the fanatic. He stormed at Papen, demanding for himself as the idol of over thirteen million voters that same degree of power which had been granted to Mussolini after the March on Rome. Here arose a misunderstanding. To Papen, whose knowledge of contemporary Italian history was scanty in the extreme, the simile of the March on Rome conveyed the demand for the supreme power of dictatorship. Hitler, however, who had studied the rise of the Fascist Dictator with great care, knew well that in Mussolini's first Cabinet his followers were in a minority, but held the key positions. He was also aware that in a comparatively short space of time the Duce's original allies had disappeared from the scene.

The torrent of the *Führer's* rhetoric continued unchecked. The *Reichstag* must enact an Enabling Bill giving his Government full power. If such a Bill were rejected, the *Reichstag* must be dissolved. Hitler passed on to what he would do with this unlimited power once he had got it.

"I consider it my duty to mow down the Marxists," he declared, and demanded that the S.A. should be given "three clear days."

Like old von Kahr in 1923, the highly civilized and kind-hearted Papen was horror-struck at the bloodthirsty sadism of Hitler's demands. He realized that with a man who can only talk and will not listen, it is impossible to argue. The business of putting Hitler in his place must be left to Hindenburg. He therefore suggested that further discussion was useless, and that Hitler should put his views before the President that afternoon. He refused to become the *Führer's* emissary. Hitler must try himself to convince the Marshal.

In a cold fury, Hitler drove to luncheon with Goebbels and Göring at the former's house in the Reichskanzlerplatz. Papen had betrayed him; he was beset with traitors and plots, and snares were about his feet. Frick and Röhm joined the party, and together they anxiously discussed the situation. At three o'clock there came a telephone call from the Chancellery. The voice of Erwin Planck, who had been in turn staff officer to Schleicher, private secretary to Brüning, and was now Secretary of State to the *Reichskanzlei*, stated that the President would receive Hitler in an hour's time. "Has a decision been arrived at already?" Goebbels asked. "If so, there is no point in the *Führer's* coming." "The President wishes to see him first," Planck replied.

A vague hope arose that perhaps Hindenburg had refused to support Papen. Perhaps after all Hitler would be Chancellor before nightfall. With Wilhelm Frick and the pervert Röhm, Hitler drove to the President's Palace. If he had really entertained any illusions since Planck's telephone call, they were instantly dispelled. He was confronted by a very angry Old Gentleman, with a face of granite and a barking voice, who shot a look of loathing and contempt at Röhm, and did not offer them chairs. Like a good strategist Hindenburg took the offensive and got his word in first. He outlined for Hitler's benefit the programme which he and the Chancellor proposed to put into force. Would Hitler co-operate? Angrily and abruptly Hitler answered that he had already given his views to Herr von Papen. He would co-operate with the Government only as Chancellor. Hindenburg, who had adopted Papen's interpretation of the Mussolini parallel, now understood Hitler to be repeating his demand for dictatorship. "So you want the supreme power?" he asked. But Hitler remained unexpectedly silent. He was emotionally and physically exhausted with rage and disappointment.

Having fought his opponent to a standstill, Hindenburg proceeded to demolish him with an admonition of great severity. He refused Hitler's demands definitely and explicitly, for he could not, he said, reconcile it with his conscience and his duty to hand over the government of the country to the exclusive control of the National Socialist Party, which would wield this power one-sidedly. He regretted that Hitler did not see his way to keeping the promises of toleration and co-operation which he had made to the Government; and, in conclusion, he recommended him to exercise a greater chivalry in his future campaigns.

With this dressing-down the Old Gentleman closed the interview, which had lasted only fifteen minutes, and as the Nazis left the room, he turned to Meissner, still with the ring of anger in his voice, saying, "That man for a Chancellor? I'll make him a postmaster, and he can lick the stamps with my head on them."

Now it was no longer a case of election hostilities but of open war between the party and the Government, and in their attacks the President was included, for Hitler was bitterly offended by the way in which Hindenburg had outmanœuvred him and then lectured him like a naughty schoolboy. The *Führer* turned to the Centre with a proposal for a coalition cabinet with himself as Chancellor. Hoping to strike a chord of sympathy in Brüning, in view of his treatment by Hindenburg, Hitler suggested that a motion, jointly sponsored by their two parties, should be forced through the *Reichstag,* deposing the President and providing for a new election. But though Brüning had little cause for personal loyalty to Hindenburg, he was no Byzantine, and he rejected out of hand so dramatic a means of revenge. For a while the negotiations dragged on with the Nazis on the subject of the coalition, but in the end no real basis of agreement could be found.

The singularly unlovely building in the Königsplatz which housed the German Parliament for half a century had seen few more curious episodes than that session of the *Reichstag* which opened on September 9 and closed three days later. By the rules of procedure the oldest member, regardless of party, presided at the first meeting at which the President was elected for the session, and the Communists had taken advantage of this to stage a demonstration. Among their candidates at the election they had included, for this purpose alone, the name of Clara Zetkin, the eighty-four-year-old revolutionary, and had elected her *in absentia.* This remarkable old lady, who had lived for a considerable time in Moscow, made the journey to Berlin and insisted upon exercising her privilege to preside. There she sat in the Speaker's chair, a grey, wizened little figure, staring down at a House of which two-fifths wore the brown uniform of her inveterate opponents. Beside her stood Torgler, the Communist parliamentary leader, stooping every now and then to prompt her in the long discourse in defence of Marxism which quavered out in her weak old voice.

Whether in deference to the old lady's courage or whether held by the hopeless incongruity of the whole proceeding, the

House gave Frau Zetkin an almost uninterrupted hearing, and only when she had been lifted like a bundle from the platform and conveyed carefully away, did the *Reichstag* resume its usual appearance of a beer-garden. Amid tumult and uproar Göring was elected to the Chair.

All Berlin was agog on the day of the first plenary meeting on September 12. It had been agreed among the Party Leaders, none of whom wanted a new election, and between them and the President of the *Reichstag*, that the House should hear the declaration of the Government and then adjourn for a week in order to give the Government a chance of negotiating for a majority—it was known that, some days before, Hindenburg had signed a draft decree of dissolution which Papen could use in case of emergency. Thus for the first time in history the death-warrant of a Parliament had been signed before it had met. Papen was perfectly prepared to go on having elections indefinitely in the hope of wearing down the opposition. This was a short-sighted policy, for though the Nazis would in all probability be the losers, such contests would undoubtedly hinder the gradual economic recovery which had just begun, and, in addition, would cause a general lack of confidence and a sense of insecurity both at home and abroad.

But besides Papen's decree there was known to be a further surprise development. The Communists, the one group which might be expected to benefit by a continued state of political uncertainty, intended to move a vote of censure on the Government as an amendment to the Order of the Day. All other parties were united in considering this a mischievous proceeding, and it was agreed between them that the Nationalists should oppose it formally, the objection of a single member being sufficient to prevent an amendment of the Order of the Day without due notice.

With all these rumours in the air the galleries of the House were packed at an early hour. In the diplomatic loge ambassadors and ministers were crowded together, and the press gallery buzzed with conjecture. All expected drama, but few were prepared for the farce which followed.

The Ministers filed on to their bench and the great bulk of Göring appeared in the President's chair. The crack of his gavel called the House to order with a start, and they proceeded to the business of the day. Serene and smiling Papen sat back in his chair, with all the appearance of having something up his sleeve. He felt in complete command of the situation. Torgler, the Communist leader, rose and proposed his motion. The House sat waiting for the Nationalist objection. There was a dead silence, an anti-climax. Hugenberg sat motionless in his place. To save the situation Frick, the Nazi leader, sprang to his feet and asked for a half-hour's delay, and in a buzz of excitement the House adjourned.

Hurried discussions took place in the Committee-rooms and corridors, and it was discovered that at the last moment the Nationalists had double-crossed their colleagues. Papen had decided to dissolve the *Reichstag*, and it was in agreement with him that Hugenberg, without warning his fellow Party Leaders, had raised no objection to the Communist motion. Indignation seethed and hostility to the Government reached fever-pitch.

Meantime, the Cabinet was also meeting in the building. Papen called for the Red Portfolio in which the decree of dissolution was traditionally conveyed to the *Reichstag*. Again an anti-climax and consternation; it was nowhere to be found. Once more Herr von Papen had left his papers behind! In an agony of apprehension Planck's car fled back through the Brandenburger Tor and up the Wilhelmstrasse to retrieve the lost decree. With a few moments to spare the Chancellor affixed his signature beneath that of the President. They were saved!

As the House reassembled, the atmosphere of impending drama was intensified. Again the Cabinet filed into their places with Papen bringing up the rear and waving the Red Portfolio with its precious contents at the diplomatic loge. No sooner had Göring called the House to order than the Chancellor demanded the word. But Göring chose to ignore him and announced that the vote on the Communist motion of censure would be taken. The voting began, and pandemonium broke loose. Papen remained standing; Göring continued to ignore him. White with anger, the Chancellor handed the Red Portfolio to Planck, who laid it on the President's desk, whence it slipped to the ground. Then without further ado, Papen and his Cabinet left the chamber. The voting continued and the Government was declared to have been censured by 513 to 32. In the uproar which followed the vote, the Nationalists left the House; no one knew what to do next, and, having declared the Government overthrown, Göring adjourned the sitting.

It was in fact a very doubtful service that the *Reichstag* President had done his leader. The events of August 13, to which Papen had given great publicity, had done little to enhance the prestige of the *Führer* or of the party in the eyes of the electors, and the scene in the *Reichstag*, however detrimental it may have been to parliamentary institutions, had in no way redounded to the credit of the Nazis. Moreover, the funds of the party were dangerously low, and the usual sources of supply, such as the great industrialists and certain individuals abroad, had not had their confidence strengthened by the Potempa affair, in which a Communist workman was brutally done to death by five Nazis, with whom Hitler had publicly proclaimed blood-brotherhood.

But if Hitler had little to hope from a new General Election, the Papen Government, in so far as gaining a parliamentary majority was concerned, had nothing to hope at all. The Chancellor, despite his tactical victories over Hitler, had done nothing to recommend himself or his Government to the electorate. To be sure, he had the confidence of the President, but the former electors of Hindenburg, whether in 1925 or 1932, had grown wary of this doubtful honour. His success at Lausanne had been discounted in advance, as merely rendering permanent a situation which had really existed since the Hoover Moratorium of 1931, and his gesture in withdrawing from the Disarmament Conference had been received with apathy.

On the other hand the high-handed policy of the Government in regard to Prussia and the *Reichstag* had awakened very grave misgivings in many quarters. The champions of parliamentary government and of the sanctity of the Constitution found themselves strangely allied with the protagonists of State rights, who feared that a fate similar to that of Prussia awaited their States; and indeed the Government had planned a structural reform whereby all but the three Southern States would be merged into the *Reich*, thus strengthening still further the Central authority.

In the face of this growing opposition from all sides the Papen Government sailed blithely into the November General Election with the slogan, "Support our ideas or we shall continue to govern alone until you do"; and the long-suffering electorate, which was now being appealed to for the fifth time within a twelvemonth, proceeded unhesitatingly to reject them. For the elections of November 9 showed that the vast majority of the German people were opposed to the Hindenburg-Papen model of presidial government. They had demonstrated their dislike for it in July, and they re-emphasized their dislike in November, when 90 per cent of the votes were cast against the Government.

For the Nazis, too, the elections were disastrous. From thirteen millions their poll fell to eleven—the figure of the first presidential ballot—and their seats in the House decreased from 230 to 197. On the other hand their deadly rivals, the Communists, profited by this defection to the tune of a million votes, bringing up the number of their deputies to a round hundred. But the atmosphere of tragicomedy which surrounded this period of German politics was enhanced by the Gilbertian situation, which found Nazis and Communists attacking one another on the hustings, murdering one another in the streets, yet uniting to support a strike which paralyzed Berlin's transport services on the eve of the polls.

Nor did the streak of ill-luck for the Nazis end with the General Election. During the ensuing weeks they consistently lost votes at the local elections. Sunday after Sunday saw a steady falling-off, and it was apparent that if a further General Election were forced upon the country, their seats in the *Reichstag* would fall below a hundred and fifty. The fainter hearts in the party began to urge upon the Leader the need for compromise. Let him accept the Vice-Chancellorship, they said, otherwise they would never attain office, and it speaks well for both Hitler's courage and political wisdom that he withstood the counsel of these weaker brethren and stuck to his guns.

The election had one other important result. The continued political stalemate convinced Schleicher that in Papen he had backed the wrong horse, that this man was not capable of dealing with the National Socialists, and that new tactics must be adopted. The General was also very displeased at the way in which Papen had replaced him in Hindenburg's confidence and favour, and he began to turn against his former comrade in conspiracy the machinery of that very Palace *Camarilla* which had brought him into power and which had compassed the fall of Müller, of Gröner, and of Brüning.

Papen, however, perturbed neither by the gravity of the situation which had resulted from the November elections nor by the findings of the Supreme Court that at least one part of the Presidential Decree of July, authorizing the Rape of Prussia, was against the Constitution, was perfectly prepared for further elections, even though they should plunge the country into civil war. His Cabinet colleagues were already in considerable anxiety as to where their volatile leader was taking them, and there was considerable speculation among them as to whether he knew himself. They therefore joined with Schleicher in urging him to offer his resignation to the President, in order that Hindenburg might consult the Party Leaders in an effort to find a way out of the deadlock.

Papen fell in with this suggestion more readily than had been expected. He himself suggested to Hindenburg that the Cabinet should resign and be retained *ad interim,* and that Hitler should be sent for to form a government which could command a parliamentary majority. Assured that the *Führer* would fail in this task, Papen saw himself restored to office with a new mandate either for further elections or any other form of government which might seem feasible.

The Chancellor accordingly resigned on November 17 and Hitler arrived at the Kaiserhof with a flourish of trumpets and a numerous staff. Two days later, cheered by enormous crowds —the Party always admirably organized the spontaneity of its demonstrations—he drove to the Palace. There was no repetition of the humiliating episode of August 13. Hindenburg received the leader with courtesy and there were chairs for everybody. On this occasion, Hitler had had the good sense to leave Röhm behind and the conversation, which lasted for an hour— the limit which the Old Gentleman's age would now permit —passed off quietly and with dignity.

But it was not a pleasant interview for Hitler. His position was far weaker than in the summer, at which time he had thirteen millions behind him and the possibility of an alliance with the Centre. Now, with his following decreased by two millions and a *Reichstag* in which no combination was possible, he was on the horns of a dilemma. Hindenburg did not spare him. He offered him these alternatives: either to accept the Vice-Chancellorship under Papen, as had been offered in August, or to become Chancellor in a government which could command a majority in the *Reichstag*.

Faced with the choice of two impossibilities, Hitler sought to prevaricate. He returned to the Kaiserhof, and during the next few days an exchange of letters passed between him and the President which indicated all too clearly the unbridgeable gulf which lay between them. Hitler refused the terms of August 13 out of hand and repeated the demand for the Chancellorship, indicating that in such a position he would like to enjoy the "special confidence" of the President. To this Hindenburg replied: "You know that I prefer a presidial Cabinet, one that is conducted not by a Party Leader but by a man who is above Party, and that is the kind of man in whom I should have special confidence. You have announced that you will only place your movement at the disposal of a Cabinet presided over by yourself as the Party Leader. If I agree to this plan, I must request that such a Cabinet should have a majority in the *Reichstag*. . . ."

The meaning of the letter was clear. Hitler was not the sort of man in whom Hindenburg would repose his "special confidence." He re-emphasized this view in a later letter: "I cannot give a leader of a party my Presidial power, because such a Cabinet is bound to develop into a party dictatorship and increase the state of tension prevailing among the German people. I cannot take the responsibility for this before my oath and my conscience." Fine words these, and worthy of a Father of his People, yet within two months Hindenburg had forgotten them.

By the end of November Hitler had admitted defeat and had retired in a passion to Munich. Papen had now achieved his aim and expected Hindenburg to re-confirm him in his office. But he had reckoned without Schleicher. The General had hoped, it is believed quite genuinely, that the negotiations with Hitler would come to some definite issue, and in his subtle way he had done his best to sound out the possibility of a majority in the *Reichstag*, but most of the parties had suffered at one time or another from Schleicher's intrigues and they were no longer willing to play with him. His tortuous plottings had at last brought Schleicher to the inevitable point at which he had no alternative but to put his own head into the noose he had so frequently tied for others. Power without responsibility had been his ambition, and well would it have been for him if he had remained the mystery man of the *Reichswehr*. His first mistake had been to accept Cabinet office with its share of responsibility of government, and now he had no choice but to accept the full burden of the Chancellorship. He had intrigued himself into a position out of which there was no escape.

But Papen had first to be disposed of. Schleicher adopted a line similar to that which he had used in the case of Gröner. He told Hindenburg that the Papen Government no longer enjoyed the confidence or support of the army. That which had been untrue in the case of Gröner was true of Papen. The *Reichswehr* would go anywhere and do anything at the command of the Marshal, their Commander-in-Chief, but they would not obey Herr von Papen. Hindenburg grew alarmed. Anything which touched the loyalty of the *Reichswehr* affected him deeply. Yet he loved Papen like a son and a brother, and Oskar was as fond of the Chancellor as his father. Hindenburg resented the grain of suspicion which Schleicher had implanted in his mind regarding Papen. He had not minded parting with Brüning very much, but Papen was a different person. Through

Meissner the Old Gentleman sounded the views of other political leaders, and in almost every case the answer was the same: Papen must go and Schleicher must be Chancellor. This comparative unanimity with regard to the General was not dictated by any great respect for his political ability, but a general agreement that the gravity of the situation demanded a man who could unite the policy of the Cabinet with that of the *Reichswehr*. One man alone could do this, Kurt von Schleicher, and it was believed the only government against which he would not intrigue was one in which he held both the Chancellorship and the Ministry of Defence.

Hindenburg became bewildered, and not without reason. Schleicher had in turn nominated Müller, Brüning, and Papen as the saviours of the country, and had ultimately engineered the dismissal of all of them. Having built up the confidence of the Old Gentleman in each of his protégés, he next began to undermine it. The effect upon the President was, not unnaturally, to make him suspicious of everyone, and now particularly of Schleicher himself. The Old Gentleman liked Papen more than any other of his Chancellors; he had given him his special confidence. He was prepared to back him with the full weight of the presidential influence and authority, and now everyone told him that Papen must go, and that it was his duty to appoint Schleicher. It was all very upsetting and disagreeable for an Old Gentleman of eighty-five. Still, if it was his duty . . .

Even more striking was the success of Papen with Oskar von Hindenburg, who had been Schleicher's intimate since they were subalterns in the *Dritte Garde*, and his fellow conspirator intermittently for over eight years. Now, when under pressure of advice, his father seemed ready to dispense reluctantly with Papen, Oskar defended his new friend vigorously, and urged Hindenburg to continue his support of the Chancellor as everything would shortly be all right. Oskar had been reading a book, a romantic biography of the great Bismarck, by Beumelburg, and the highly indigestible mental pabulum which he had absorbed seems to have stimulated his never latent vanity. To his distorted imagination appeared a vision of Papen as a second Iron Chancellor, with himself in an important rôle, and under this delusion he planned with Papen a scheme which Bismarck would have considered an insult to his intelligence.

At a Cabinet meeting early in December 1932, from which Schleicher was conspicuously absent, Papen airily announced his intention of dissolving, if necessary by military force, not only the *Reichstag* itself, but the Trade Unions, and all political parties and associations which were in opposition to the Government. The Chancellor told his colleagues that on the previous day he had discussed the matter in detail with the executive officers of the Ministry of Defence and that they had played a "war game" (*Kriegspiel*), which showed that the thing could be accomplished "quite easily."

The Cabinet were, in effect, being asked to become a party to a violation of the Constitution so wholesale that civil war must almost certainly result therefrom, and the subsequent creation of a new State based upon the bayonets of the *Reichswehr* and the support of a party with about 10 per cent of the electorate behind it. Reactionary though the Cabinet of Barons might be, they were quite unprepared for such drastic measures. The absence of the Minister of Defence from a discussion of such vital military operations made them suspicious, and the volatility of the Chancellor had not increased their confidence in him.

They determined to play safe and, while showing great interest in Papen's suggestion, they asked that the officer with whom the war-game had been played, and who would be in charge of the operations, should give his own opinion to the

Cabinet. When that gentleman appeared, he gave, perhaps not entirely to the surprise of the Cabinet, an opinion so contrary to that of the Chancellor that it amounted to a flat denial. It was no longer possible, he said, for the army and the police to subdue the Nazis by force, without the united forces of the Trade Unions, the Social Democrats, and the Centre, and it was implied that in any case the army would not march for Herr von Papen.

It is impossible to say whether the Chancellor had sought deliberately to mislead his colleagues or whether he had honestly misunderstood the issue of the war-game played in the Ministry of Defence, but whatever the motive, the result was the same. The Cabinet as one man declared that Papen must give their collective resignation to the President, and, they insisted furthermore, lest he should again "misunderstand the issue," that two of their number should accompany him when he did so. Their opinion of Papen was clearly shown by their almost unanimous decision to continue in office under Schleicher.

But the Old Gentleman was deeply grieved at parting with his "Fränzchen." Unable to refuse the resignation of the whole Cabinet, in appointing Schleicher he made no effort to hide the fact that the new government would not enjoy his confidence to the same degree as had its predecessor. Rarely had a Chancellor been appointed with such cold hostility and never had one retired with such manifestations of affection from the President. To Schleicher, Hindenburg refused the decree of dissolution; to Papen he sent his photograph inscribed *"Ich hat' einen Kameraden."*

And now Schleicher himself experienced those torments he had often inflicted upon others: insecurity of high office, the wavering loyalty of the President, the machinations of the Palace *Camarilla.* To him came the realization that in the seat of supreme power he was far more isolated than in that little room overlooking the Landwehr Canal which had been the scene of his early intrigues and triumphs. The rats knew how near his ship was to sinking. His agents deserted him; the marionettes no longer responded to his touch. Though he was in command of all the armed forces of the State, he knew they could avail him nothing, and his mentality, attuned to intrigue rather than to leadership, was barren of constructive statesmanship. To his amazement he found that no policy was possible save that of Brüning, and what was left of that policy he espoused, even that hated measure of *Agrarbolshevism,* the decree expropriating the bankrupt estates of East Prussia, on which the former Chancellor had been brought down. Never had nemesis been more complete.

One factor alone was in his favour; the *Reichstag,* in which he could only count upon the eleven votes of the German People's Party, was unwilling to risk a further crisis, and agreed to adojurn after the formal election of its officers, until early in the New Year. Schleicher was granted a month's reprieve from certain overthrow, and with this breathing-space he had to be content. Yet even this brief interval might have been sufficient if he had used it profitably for negotiations. But Schleicher seemed paralyzed and, beyond tentative discussions with trade-union leaders and amateur politicians, he did nothing.

Meantime the net was drawn around him. Within a week of his appointment, the first feelers had been put out for an alliance between the Nationalists and the Nazis. Werner von Alvensleben, a member of the *Herrenklub* which had assisted in bringing Papen into power, and Joachim von Ribbentropp, a wine merchant, who later was to be Hitler's Ambassador-at-Large, were zealous in this work, and their efforts were greatly aided by the support of the powerful East Prussian *Landbund,* once more mobilized to oppose the revived scheme of expropriation. Meetings with Papen and Hugenberg and with Nazi leaders followed, and of these Oskar von Hindenburg, if not his father, was cognizant and was favourable to them. The President confined his opposition to Schleicher to a hostile coolness which increased as the weeks went by.

This concentration of his enemies galvanized the Chancellor into action, and to meet it he threatened to publish the report of the *Reichstag* enquiry into the *Ostpreussenhilfe* loans of 1927–28 with which the estates of East Prussia had been kept alive. The investigation had disclosed scandals of which the stench reeked to heaven and of which the mud splashed even to the steps of the Palace itself. Here indeed was a Pandora's box which, opened, poured forth a flood of loathly, crawling things. There stood disclosed the example of a landowner, bankrupt through his own ineptitude, whose estates had been "reconstructed" three times, and, after a fourth break-down, had been ceded, under the *Ostpreussenhilfe*, to a daughter who was still a minor. There were absentee landlords who, with the money loaned to them by the Government to reconstruct their estates, had bought motor cars and driven to the Riviera, while banks and tradesmen, who had trustfully given them credit, remained unpaid. There were those also, in the inexorable report of the Government investigator, who had squandered the public money on "wine and women," yet had received more public money since their names had been for centuries coupled with their estates.

This first *Ostpreussenhilfe* had been advertised as the means of saving the farmer. But the reconstruction of farms had assisted primarily the fortunes of estate owners and only the smallest percentage of the money reached the real peasants. The scandal affected not only the average landowner, it struck at the titled leaders of the *Landbund;* none was spared.

By the threat of these disclosures Schleicher hoped to cow the Junkers and bring them to heel; he thought to spin one of his usual intrigues and did not realize that he was sawing off the branch on which he was sitting. At one stroke he had destroyed the union of two forces from which he might have received support. For two hundred years the army and the Junker had been inseparably bound together by a bond of common interest. Schleicher had broken the bond. In entering upon this battle with the Junker he underestimated the strength of the economic and political vested interests which he was attacking, and he was too superficial to sense the power of tradition which hundreds of years had centred in one caste.

Representatives of thirteen thousand Junker families rallied to the defence of their prerogatives. They surrounded the President and clamoured for Schleicher's dismissal. The Palace teemed like an ant-heap which has been stirred with a stick. The house of the *Reichslandbund* became the centre of intrigue against the Chancellor.

With extraordinary obstinacy Schleicher refused to believe in the progress of the movement against him, even though he was informed that the crucial meeting between Papen and Hitler was shortly to take place. At the parties which he attended during the Christmas and New Year festivities, he declared himself to be quite secure. He had, he said, the President's confidence and support, and Herr von Papen had given him his promise not to intrigue against the Government; he had even expressed his willingness to accept a diplomatic post abroad. So Schleicher pursued his paralytic policy.

In the meantime Papen was essaying to play the *deus ex machina*. The motives which actuated him during these days will doubtless always remain obscure. Certainly his colossal vanity, which made his continued disappearance from the public eye intolerable to him, played an important part, for the itch of ambition had been greatly excited during his six months as Chancellor. Certainly, too, there was the lust to revenge himself on Schleicher. Yet it is almost inconceivable that these two factors could so far warp Papen's judgment that he could forget all that he knew of Hitler and his proclaimed policies. In August he had been shocked and disquieted by the *Führer's* demand for three clear days on the streets for the S.A., and, even his short memory could not have let slip the ghastly prophecy that "Heads shall roll." One hesitates to believe that, at this moment, when Papen held his hands for Hitler to vault into the saddle, he knowingly gave his consent to a policy of murder and torture.

In all fairness to Papen it must be believed that he was not yet undeceived as to his ability to make a captive of Hitler, to harness the Nazis to his own chariot, and to unite them in a great alliance with the Junker and heavy industry. Nor was this dream entirely impossible of realization. The National Socialist Party after the November election was bankrupt in every sense of the word. There was not even enough money to pay the salaries of Hitler's body-guard, of which Röhm, single-handed, quelled a mutiny and foiled an attempt upon the *Führer's* life. Funds the party must have, and if Papen could supply them he had a right to make his own terms. Thus he who, when he had been Chancellor, had threatened the great industrialists for subsidizing the Nazis, now negotiated with them to meet the party's overwhelming deficit. A greater politician might have succeeded; as it was, Papen, far from harnessing the Nazis, was riveting upon his own wrists the fetters which should bind him captive to their chariot wheels.

The historic interview between Papen and Hitler took place at Cologne on January 8, 1933, at the house of the great banker Baron von Schroeder, and here the basis of a working agreement was laid. Nothing was put in writing, but it was agreed that, in return for the Chancellorship and the funding of the enormous debts of the Nazi Party, Hitler would give his word

ADOLF HITLER

that he would not infringe the Constitution in any respect. For Papen this undertaking was of the greatest importance, for only by this fiction could he reconcile the President to the idea of Hitler as Chancellor.

His oath to the Constitution, his conscience, and his duty were Hindenburg's lodestar. In August and in November he had been unable to reconcile them with the appointment of Hitler; now, two months later, on the unsubstantiated word of Hitler himself, the trustworthiness of which Hindenburg had had every reason to doubt, he was beguiled by Papen into acquiescence. Anxious to have his "Fränzchen" with him again, to be rid of the now abhorrent Schleicher, and to be quit of the importunings of his fellow landed proprietors of East Prussia, Hindenburg turned with relief to Papen's proposals as a means whereby peace and security at home might be achieved. But again his "horse sense," his *Bauernshlauheit*, did not entirely desert him. He did not give his full consent at once, but only sufficient of his blessing to encourage Papen to proceed a little further.

The news of the Cologne meeting and its upshot struck Schleicher like a thunderbolt. To the end he had persisted in disbelieving the information given him. He had counted so much on the impossibility of an alliance between the Nationalists and the Nazis, and he could not credit the fact that, after the scenes which had attended the interviews of August and November, Papen and Hitler could come to terms. But the incredible had happened and Schleicher fulfilled the prophecy which Brüning had made to him as the dawn crept through the windows of that very library in which he now sat in the Chancellor's chair. Behind his façade of assurance, Schleicher was in a panic. Instead of planning calmly how to outwit his enemies, he indulged in the most fantastic negotiations which could bring him no possible strength either inside or outside the

Reichstag. Brüning had been right in his discernment; the nerves of the machine-gun officer were better than those of the staff captain.

The Party Leaders, none of whom desired a further political crisis, were ready to agree to a further postponement of the *Reichstag* until late in January. Schleicher refused their offer, saying that he had the assurance of the President that full power should be his in the event of an adverse vote. In this Schleicher had allowed himself to be misled by the guileful promise of Oskar, that he was sure the President would grant him full power if he asked for it. The truth was that the negotiations between Papen and Hitler had progressed slowly but steadily, and it was necessary to give the Chancellor a temporary assurance till it was time to administer the *coup de grâce.* Schleicher's experience as a conspirator and his knowledge of the Hindenburgs, *père et fils,* should have warned him that their promises to Chancellors were notoriously brittle. That he believed Oskar, notwithstanding their recent quarrel, is evidence in itself of his bewildered state of mind. How often had he himself conveyed a similar assurance to Chancellors about to fall!

For what reason did Schleicher thus refuse the offer of support from the Party Leaders? It was his last avenue of escape from certain disaster and he deliberately refused to make use of it. Was he ill? Had all sense of balance left him? Or was it that his work for eighteen years in military and political intelligence made him profoundly distrustful of anybody, and particularly of those whom he had wronged? The answer is surely in the last reason. Schleicher could not conceive of doing such a thing himself and, with the conscience of Cain, he could not imagine that anyone whom he had wronged could give him sincere advice. Brüning had taken the lead in persuading the other Party Leaders to give the Chancellor a respite, but such was Schleicher's sense of guilt that he would rather resign than owe a victory in the *Reichstag* to Brüning's support.

Having rejected the offer of a further breathing space he embarked on a series of negotiations, incongruous and contradictory. He offered Gregor Strasser the Vice-Chancellorship in a vain endeavour to split the Nazi Party, with the result that Hitler "disciplined" his erring lieutenant and stripped him of his party offices, though he had been amongst the oldest members of the movement. In desperation Schleicher sent for Leipart, the Trades Union leader, and proposed to him a general strike supported by the army. But though this plan found favour among the younger officers of the *Reichswehr*, who dreamed of re-establishing the old Prussian Warrior State on the foundation of the labouring class, the Trades Unions would have none of it.

Reports of the progress of his enemies now beat in upon the distracted Chancellor. Hitler was again at the Kaiserhof, and this time with victory assured. Papen went regularly to the Palace, and the attacks on the Chancellor in the Nationalist and Nazi press became daily more venomous. As a last resort Schleicher sent Hammerstein, the G.O.C. of the *Reichswehr*, to Hindenburg to impress upon him the dangers of a régime such as that proposed by Papen. The Marshal refused to discuss the political situation and coldly criticized the conduct of the recent army manœuvres.

At last Schleicher realized his fate, the fate that he had meted out to so many before him. On January 28 he went to the President to ask for a dissolution of the *Reichstag* if he met with a vote of no confidence. In the presidential study, through which in the past seven years a procession of Schleicher's victims had passed, the General faced his Commander-in-Chief and sometime friend. With all the eloquence at his command he besought Hindenburg not to give Hitler the power he had so long withheld. He did not plead for himself; indeed Schleicher in his defeat showed greatness, he only asked that this policy, which could only end in disaster, should not be followed.

It was useless; with that curt cruelty which Gröner and Brüning had known so well, the Marshal cut him short. "Thank you, General, for what you have done for the country, and now let us see *'Wie der Hase weiter läuft.'* "

The long career was ended, and in the depths of his humiliation Schleicher turned to the greatest of his victims. In his cloistered retreat, where he lay on a sick-bed, Brüning received the penitent. "Your dismissal was a hard one," said Schleicher, "but, believe me, it was pleasant compared to mine."

With that same lack of emotion which usually characterized his parting from a Chancellor, Hindenburg firmly placed the Schleicher episode behind him and turned resolutely to the business in hand, the negotiations with Hitler. The Marshal was frankly delighted to have Papen back at his side, partly because of his congenial company and partly because he relieved Hindenburg of the trials and, above all, of the responsibilities of negotiation. For in this situation, as in all previous critical moments of his life, Hindenburg ran true to form. He shirked the ultimate responsibility. He knew that the decisions which must be taken within the next forty-eight hours were of the most vital importance to Germany. Instinctively he realized that an end to the Weimar System had come and that the country of which he was the head was on the threshold of tremendous happenings, the final issue of which could not be seen. It might be that Papen's plans would succeed; it might be that they would meet with ghastly failure. In any case Hindenburg's instinct was to protect himself against the future. He named Papen his deputy, with the task of "clearing up the political situation within the framework of the Constitution and in agreement with the *Reichstag*."

Papen, whatever else he lacked, was fully alive to the eccentricities and weaknesses of the President, and particularly those which had placed him in his present position of arbiter. The inherent dislike of Hindenburg for shouldering the final responsibility was a trump card in Papen's hand which he kept back until he could use it to its fullest advantage. He was not even decided in his own mind whether he would make Hitler Chancellor or not, and in his first effort at Cabinet-making, which occurred on the afternoon of Schleicher's dismissal, he gave himself the leadership of the Government and the key positions to members of the former Cabinet, leaving only minor Ministries to his allies. Hitler, however, never abandoned his fundamental demands: the Chancellorship for himself, the control of the Prussian police, the passage of an Enabling Act, and, if necessary, new elections. He refused to consider anything else and reminded Papen of their pact at Cologne.

With considerable reluctance the President, late on the night of Saturday, January 28, authorized Hitler to form a Cabinet and the following morning was spent in bickering and argument. The air seemed heavy with the presage of great events; rumour followed rumour. The city was restless, and armed police patrolled the streets. Now the Palace would make a concession, now the Kaiserhof, till shortly before noon Papen made his final offer. Hitler should have the Chancellorship and the *Reich* and Prussian Ministries of Interior for his party; Papen himself would be Vice-Chancellor and *Reichskommissar* for Prussia; and Hugenberg, as representative of the Right and of heavy industry, the Minister of Agriculture and Economic Affairs in the *Reich* and in Prussia; the Ministries of Foreign Affairs and Finance were to remain in the hands of their present holders, Neurath and Schwerin von Krosigk, and General (now Field-Marshal) Baron von Blomberg was to be the new Minister of Defence.

Though this proposal went far to meet the demands of the Nazis, it omitted all mention of an Enabling Bill and of the right to dissolve the *Reichstag*, and while it gave the party control of the whole police force of Prussia, it necessitated their agreement with Hugenberg's economic theories of *autarchie*. After consideration the offer was refused. Once more Papen began to play with the idea of assuming the Chancellorship, and by the evening had almost succeeded in forming a Cabinet when again dramatic events changed the course of history. It became known that Schleicher, who still remained in office as acting Chancellor, had summoned by telegram all the Trade-Union leaders throughout the country to an immediate conference in the Ministry of Defence.

While the Palace debated as to whether this was a prelude to a general strike, Werner von Alvensleben came hot-foot from a dinner-party with even more disturbing tidings. There had been present General von Bredow, Schleicher's closest friend and colleague, beside himself with grief and anger at the curt dismissal of his chief. Without restraint he had cursed the House of Hindenburg for its perfidy and cried in the fury of his rage, that Schleicher *should*—or *would*—summon the Potsdam garrison and restrain the Old Gentleman (but this was not what Bredow actually called him) by force from committing the monstrous crime of giving the supreme power to Hitler; he added that Papen, Oskar, and the *Führer* himself should be confined in the fortress of Lötzen.

Though it is virtually impossible that this plan could have been anything but the figment of Bredow's rage-drunk mind, for the Potsdam garrison would never have changed their loyalty from Hindenburg to Schleicher, the news which young Alvensleben brought to the Palace and which soon spread to the Kaiserhof, threw both camps, already in a state of nervous tension, into complete panic. The need for an immediate agreement was obvious and both sides prepared to make concessions. Hitler accepted the offer of the morning on condition that Göring should become a Minister without Portfolio in the *Reich* Cabinet, giving the party three votes instead of two. But the greatest obstacle was the Enabling Bill.

It was now that Papen used his trump card. He knew well how weary Hindenburg had become of government by decree, which laid upon him the responsibility of all *Notverordnungen.* The Enabling Bill, passed by a two-thirds majority of the *Reichstag,* would relieve him of this burden. From Hitler was extracted the verbal undertaking that he would not make use of the extraordinary powers accorded him in any point to which the President objected, and, further, to liberate the President from all responsibility, it was suggested that Papen should exercise this power of veto in his name. But in order to secure a parliamentary majority for such legislation fresh elections were necessary—and the Nazis were determined that, with the machinery of government in their hands, the result should be satisfactory—and thus it came about that the decree of dissolution which had been denied to Schleicher was granted to Hitler.

Under the blandishments of Papen, Hindenburg was turned once more along a fresh path of duty. The new Government, it was urged upon him, would wipe out for ever the stain of November 1918. He was reminded of his own words, written under the shadow of defeat: "The old German spirit will descend upon us again, though it may be that we shall first have to go through the purifying fires of passion and suffering." How nobly he had written, they told him, and how truly. The days of the refining fire were over and the new dawn of an awakened Germany was about to break. He who in his person united whole generations, had outlived the wandering in the wilderness to bring his people into the promised land. Germany, once arraigned as the criminal of Europe, would again be a power in the councils of the world, and the traditions of the German army would take on a fresh lustre and a new brightness.

All these things were told to Hindenburg and he was fain to believe them. And did not Papen perhaps whisper something else into the Old Gentleman's ear? The Spectre of Spa had grown appreciably dimmer in these later years and it seemed at times as if it had been altogether exorcized. But now it grew again in strange new guise. With the powers of the Right united and in the saddle, with Hitler, though Chancellor, yet securely the prisoner of the Nationalists, it might at last be possible to do that which in his heart of hearts Hindenburg had long believed it his duty to do; to restore the monarchy and recall his "Most Gracious Kaiser, King and Lord" to his throne. He himself had written that "from the tempestuous seas of our national life will once more emerge that rock—the Imperial German House"; now perhaps he might himself make good his words.

The blandishments of Papen, the insistent importunings of Oskar, the guileful counsel of Meissner, had their effect. Convinced, as always, that the path of duty stretched straight before him, Hindenburg signified his consent. The ardour of the Nazis would be curbed by giving them the responsibility of government; Papen would exercise the presidential veto to prevent any violation of the Constitution; responsibility of government was once and for all removed from his shoulders and the injustices of November 1918 would for ever be wiped out. Without a tremor, apparently without a thought for the nineteen million voters of the Left who had re-elected him, the Jews, the Catholics, and the Socialists whom the National Socialist Party had declared to be its enemies, Hindenburg gave his assent, and on the morning of January 30, 1933, the Third *Reich* came into being. "How gloriously," writes Göring in a transport of triumph, "had the aged Field-Marshal been used as an instrument in the hand of God."

Berlin was in a ferment. The Brown Legions were aggressively triumphant, the *Stahlhelm* looked with satisfaction to the inclusion of their leader in the Cabinet, the Communists breathed defiance, albeit disconcertedly, and the hopes of the Trade Unions and of Social Democracy turned with pathetic trust towards the Palace, where lived the man their votes had re-elected to power.

The day passed in feverish excitement. The Cabinet was sworn early in the morning in circumstances of great confusion. Seldte, the *Stahlhelm* chief, could not be found, and ultimately arrived to find a wild search in progress for someone to take his place as Minister of Labour. Two other Ministers came to the Palace under the impression that they were joining Papen's Government. Everything was in a turmoil.

But by noon Germany began to know who was master in the new Government and by evening the triumph of National Socialists was complete. A gigantic torchlight procession passed endlessly along the Wilhelmstrasse, and from the open window of the Chancellery Hitler leaned far out to receive the acclamations of his followers. Further down the street, behind windows closed to protect him from the damp night air, Hindenburg too watched the throng. Thousands of cheering Germans marched beneath him, but they were acclaiming another.

There is a story—*se non è vero, è ben trovato*—of Hindenburg at this moment. The events of the day had undoubtedly excited him; he had received many compliments, the burden of which had been that for a second time he had saved Germany. The Hindenburg Legend had suddenly blazed up again in a white-heat of enthusiasm, and his old mind went back to past glories as he watched the marching thousands. The Brown Shirts passed at a shambling pace, to be followed by the field-grey ranks of the *Stahlhelm*, moving with a precision born of discipline. The old Marshal watched them from his window as in a dream, and those behind him saw him beckon over his shoulder. "Ludendorff," the old voice said, with a return to its harsh barking, "how well your men are marching, and what a lot of prisoners they've taken!"

When the great torchlight procession had passed cheering through the Brandenburger Tor into the night, leaving behind it streets filled with mafficking partizans, there was no prouder man in Germany than Franz von Papen. How splendidly it had all come out in the end and how well his plans had carried. Schleicher had paid the penalty for his treachery at last, and Hitler at last, too, was a hostage in the camp of the Nationalists. The *Osthilfe* scandals had been suppressed, and all at the cost of three portfolios. Why, with himself governing Prussia, with Hugenberg and the Nationalists and the great industrialists, with Seldte and the *Stahlhelm*, all in the Government, the position was as safe as could be. "We can always outvote them in Cabinet," he gaily assured one who later questioned the security of his position.

Alas for his vanity, his complacency, and his dreams. In a few weeks, when the new elections had given the Nazis a vote of seventeen millions, Papen found himself deprived of the government of Prussia; Goebbels, Hess, and Röhm entered the Cabinet; Hugenberg was obstructed at every turn and eventually dismissed with ignominy; Seldte cringed to the crack of the Nazi whip and the *Stahlhelm* mounted the swastika. Hitler, who at first had been content to be received by the President in the presence of the Vice-Chancellor, intimated his intention of going alone to the Palace. Papen's better feelings and natural good-nature were revolted by the bestialities of the Brown Ter-

ror, which for months after the elections cast a pall of fear over
Germany and sent a shudder of horror throughout the civilized
world. Too late did he awake to a realization of the true state
of things which he had created, to find himself playing the rôle
of hostage for which he had cast Hitler.

But on the first night of triumph, all this was distant and
unthought of; the glow of achievement warmed Papen's soul
and the warmth of congratulation was like wine to him. His
new colleagues pressed his hand in gratitude that might well be
heart-felt; his old friends praised his tact and wisdom. This was
his hour, and the cheers were music to his ears.

Above the cheering multitudes and the songs of triumph
Hindenburg slept, and in his sleep he dreamed that he was
dead. In awe he came before the gates and faced the Great Ex-
aminer:

"Your name?"

"Paul von Beneckendorf und von Hindenburg, General
Field-Marshal and President of the German Reich."

"What have you done in life?"

"I think, Sir, that I have done my duty."

"But have you kept your Oath?"

And in the effort to find an answer to this question Hindenburg, with relief, awoke.

They were still cheering. . . .

· 10 ·

For every man and woman who paraded through the streets
of Berlin in triumph on the last nights of January 1933, there
were those who sat at home in fear and anxiety. The supporters
of what had now become the opposition, the Socialists, the Trade
Unionists, the Catholics, the Jews, and many an honest patriotic
German without specific party affiliations, looked on in appre-

hension at this new dawn which was breaking over Germany. They had read the warnings of the Nazi leaders as to what would happen when they, the Party, came to power, the fierce threats of Hitler, the bloodthirsty promises of Göring, the lurid articles which had flowed from Goebbels's facile pen; and they waited, their eyes turned hopefully towards the Palace.

Moving amongst one's friends in Germany at this time was to receive a startling revelation of the touching faith which so many still reposed in Hindenburg. The Legend—so soon to be recognized as a Myth—was never stronger than at this moment of ordeal, when those who had re-elected him not a year before turned to him for justice and protection with a pathetic confidence. Everywhere the same phrase was heard, "It's all right so long as the Old Gentleman's there." No Father of his People had so genuinely enjoyed the trust of his electors as did Hindenburg at this moment.

And it is certain that the Old Gentleman had no conception of how terribly he had betrayed his trusteeship. He had only accepted Hitler on the condition that the Constitution should be respected and law and order maintained. He had undoubtedly done his duty as it had been indicated to him. Besides, Hitler did not appear to be as obnoxious as he had at first believed. The *Führer* had acquired a certain tact and subtlety since August and November of the previous year. He had behaved in Hindenburg's presence with a becoming modesty and had made no difficulties about recognizing Papen as the President's deputy. Moreover, he had adhered closely to the letter of his bond. On the day after his appointment as Chancellor he had made at least a pretence of negotiations with the Centre for a working majority in the existing *Reichstag*, and it was only after these conversations had broken down—as indeed they were bound to do—that he had made use of the decree of dissolution. In declaring for the new election Hitler had made a speech calculated both to please the President and proclaim a deathless war upon the System. His *leit-motiv* had been "Because of November 1918," and it had been a masterpiece: "Fourteen years have passed since the day, when, blinded by promises from within and without, the German people lost honour and freedom. Fourteen years of Marxism has ruined the country; one year of Bolshevism would destroy it. In this hour of anxiety the venerable leader of the World War has called upon the men of the National Parties and associations once more, as formerly at the front, to fight for the salvation of the *Reich*."

That was the kind of language Hindenburg liked to hear. This fellow Hitler, if kept properly in check, might prove a very useful asset to Germany.

There were already growing signs that Hitler and his lieutenants had no intention of being kept in check. While the Chancellor kept within the letter of his agreement, Göring was quietly making himself secure in Prussia. The election campaign was proving a fierce and bitter one. The Communists were fighting for their lives. The Chancellor had given his word that law and order must be maintained, and as a result picked men of the Storm Troops were enrolled as auxiliary police and armed with rifles and side arms. This did not, however, prevent fifty-one opponents of the Government, by no means all of them Communists, from being killed during the campaign, and a far larger number, including Stegerwald, Brüning's former chief and Minister, and other opposition leaders, from being badly beaten and man-handled. Party meetings of the Social Democrats and Centre were broken up by S.A. men while the auxiliaries looked on and the regular police were nowhere to be seen, and at Kaiserlautern Brüning's speech to his followers was punctuated by bursts of rifle fire from the street fighting outside.

And yet as the campaign proceeded it became evident that, with all the machinery for propaganda and terrorization in their hands, and despite their attempts by posters and in speeches to identify the person of the President with their cause, the Hitler Government was not, in all probability, going to achieve the necessary majority to control the *Reichstag*. The election, it seemed, would result in the usual stalemate. The incalculable factor of the floating vote could not be sufficiently reckoned on to go the right way, and it became increasingly obvious that nothing short of a bombshell would stampede them in the required direction.

As if in obedience to the needs of the Party, the bombshell duly burst. On February 24 a police raid on the headquarters of the Communist Party at the Karl Liebknechthaus "disclosed" plans for an armed uprising accompanied by incendiarism and the poisoning of the water supply of Berlin. Three days later the *Reichstag* building sympathetically caught fire.

There are few now, whether inside or outside Germany, who harbour illusions regarding the responsibility for this action. The Leipzig Trial proved nothing save the guilt of the half-witted van der Lubbe,—which no one had ever doubted since he was caught red-handed,—and the moral superiority of Dimitroff over Göring. Few political trials have been a greater disappointment to the prosecution. Yet by executing the unfortunate Dutchman the Nazis satisfactorily disposed of the only man who, on their own findings, could ever have been expected to supply evidence as to the origin of the fire. But the onus of responsibility is of little comparative importance with the result. The *Reichstag* Fire provided the Nazis, whether by intent or by good fortune, with the very factor for victory which had been lacking. Not only could they suppress the Communist Party as a whole and thereby make certain of a majority in the new Parliament, but they used this sinister phenomenon to woo, albeit somewhat fiercely, the floating vote.

They did both with great effect. With astounding celerity for a Government so completely taken by surprise, the necessary steps were taken for public security, and Hindenburg, who had congratulated himself that with this new Government he would at last be released from the responsibility of signing decrees, found that his signature must be put to one which suspended the most important fundamental rights of the Constitution: those same rights which he had twice sworn to defend.

In their masterly handling of the emergency the Nazi members of the Cabinet gave their Nationalist colleagues a taste of what they must expect in future. The objections which the conservative element raised were swept aside and it was intimated to the objectors that they would hold their tongues if they knew what was good for them. So great was the tension during the last week before the election that it was seriously feared that the Chancellor, who had ordered a concentration of the S.A. in Berlin, might seize the person of the President; in a panic Papen mobilized the *Stahlhelm* and even considered carrying off Hindenburg for greater security to the military depôt at Döberitz. The differences were composed, however, and in a fine show of comradeship the Nationalists and the Nazis made their final appeals to the electorate on the eve of the poll.

The elections of March 5 showed that the Nazis had added nearly six million votes to their total in November. They achieved a poll of over seventeen and a quarter millions with 288 seats; their allies the Nationalists had retained the fifty-two seats they had held in the previous *Reichstag,* and together the Government parties controlled 340 seats in a house of 647, or just over 52 per cent. With all the odds in their favour, therefore, and after employing every electoral artifice, they had only succeeded in convincing a bare majority of the electorate. With the exception of the Communists, who had laboured under considerable difficulties and had lost 20 seats, the parties of the opposition had stood the test remarkably well. The Social Democrats had only lost one seat and the Centre had gained three. But the floating vote had gone overwhelmingly to the Nazis and, still within the letter of his undertaking, Hitler had gained his parliamentary majority.

Immediately the change was felt. Simultaneously with the declaration of the poll, *coups de main* had taken place in Bavaria, Hamburg, and elsewhere, as a result of which the existing governments were evicted and Nazi commissioners installed. At the same time the police forces of Saxony, Baden, and Württemberg were placed under the control of the *Reich* Ministry of Interior, and, as a final declaration of independence, Hitler insisted upon dispensing with Papen's presence at his interviews with Hindenburg.

Now, too, the S.A. were given their freedom on the streets and the Brown Terror was released from whatever restraint still remained. Personal grudges were paid off in blood and the natural brutality of exuberant youth found a bloody outlet in assaulting men and women whose only crime had been that they believed in a different political creed. Socialists, Jews, Communists, and pacifists, in fact anyone who could be embraced by the elastic opprobrium of "Marxist," were herded into lorries and transported to those concentration camps where, as Frick, now *Reich* Minister of Interior, put it, "Marxists are trained to become useful members of society once more."

Nor was this persecution confined to the rank and file of the opposition. Men who had held with dignity high offices of state were subjected to shameful indignities or forced to hide from searching parties of brown-shirted hooligans. Löbe, who had been President of the *Reichstag* for more than twelve years, and who had once praised Hindenburg for his loyalty to the Constitution, was arrested and placed in a concentration camp, and the Marshal's erstwhile "Brother Jonathan," Heinrich Brüning, was hunted from house to house, not daring to sleep two nights beneath the same roof.

At last the men and women who had placed their trust in Hindenburg as a protector of their civil liberties realized the futility of their faith. They had seen his head on election posters silhouetted in profile with those of Papen and Hitler, but they had not known how wholly he had deserted them. The love and confidence which they had given him was now replaced by hatred and bitterness, and in many a prison camp his name was execrated and reviled.

The mood, as ever in Berlin, found its ventilation in stories.

"Have you heard," a man would ask his friend, glancing over his shoulder to make sure he was not overheard, for such stories were a penal offence, "Hindenburg was at the Oranienburg Concentration Camp yesterday?"

"Oh? Why?"

"He wanted to visit some of his electors."

"That's nothing," his friend would answer. "They say the Old Man signs anything now. The other day Meissner left his sandwich bag on the table and when he came back the President had signed it."

In effect, Hindenburg knew very little of what was going on. He had been assured that the provisions of the decree which he had signed on February 28 would be used only in accordance with the demands of national safety, and he had swallowed, hook, line, and sinker, the story of a Communist plot. That the powers which he had thus conferred upon the Government were being shamefully abused he was completely ignorant, and it was the rôle of his intimate advisers to keep him in this blissful state.

Yet that hypersensitive conscience which had so often in earlier days prohibited his taking certain action, could not have passed over in complete silence his decrees abolishing the colours of the Weimar Republic, both as the national flag and from the military standard of the *Reich*, nor his proclamation that in so doing he was "glad to give visible expression to the increased

affinity of the fighting forces with resurgent national forces of
the German people." As Commander-in-Chief of an army whose
loyalty to him never wavered until his death, he could, had he
been so minded, have held the military forces of the *Reich* aloof
from the Revolution and thereby preserved the non-political nature of the army.

Those who surrounded him knew well how to touch the Old
Gentleman's sensibilities. Hitler was anxious to establish the link
between the Revolution and the military glories of ancient Prussia, and what better means could there be than a dedicatory service, before the opening of the new *Reichstag,* in the Garrison
Church of Potsdam above the Tomb of Frederick the Great?

It was an affair of glittering splendour, that scene on March
21. The *Reichswehr* stood in long lines of silent immobility and
for the last time the Brown Army and the *Stahlhelm* paraded as
allies. All the great military figures were there, and some of
lesser greatness. Mackensen and the Crown Prince, both in the
magnificent uniform of the Death's Head Hussars; Seeckt, the
creator of the modern *Reichswehr;* the heads of the army and
navy, Hammerstein and Raeder, and many other figures emerg-
ing from retirement, in ancient uniforms that started at the
seams, and *Pickelhauben* that perched precariously on heads
that had changed their contours. The Cabinet was in civilian
dress, save for Blomberg in field-grey. Lastly, there came the
President, Field-Marshal Paul von Hindenburg, gigantic, and
seemingly unmoved.

Yet he was moved. Deep memories stirred within him; the
day in 1866 when he had first stood at the tomb of Prussia's·
greatest king, a young lieutenant of the Guards but recently returned in victory; that second pilgrimage of Wilhelm I after the
triumphs over France—then, too, he had been there, a lusty
young subaltern; and now after more than half a century he was
again in this same shrine with Germany perhaps on the threshold

of future glories. These pictures must have recalled themselves as the service proceeded, and those sitting close to Hindenburg saw tears on his cheeks.

The procedure had been designed to associate the Marshal firmly and for ever with the new order, and both his speech and that of the Chancellor had been prepared with this in mind. By honouring him as Germany's veteran leader of the World War, it was hoped to obliterate his unfortunate connection for the past eight years with the Weimar System. Hindenburg, who had been the hero of German arms, must be established as the symbol of the National Revolution.

The speech of the President was of particular interest since it laid upon him alone the responsibility for the formation of the new "Government of National Alliance," and closed with a stern injunction to the *Reichstag* that they were expected "to stand behind the Government and do everything possible to support it in its difficult work."

Hitler's oration, on the other hand, was one in glorification of the Marshal, and a justification of the principles which he cherished. The event was one which appealed to the romantic mysticism of the Chancellor's southern temperament, and his voice shook as he spoke:

Neither the Kaiser, nor the Government, nor the people willed the war. But the decline of the Nation, the general collapse, compelled a weak generation, against its own better judgment and against its most sacred convictions, to accept the assertion of our war-guilt. . . . By a unique upheaval, national honour has been restored in a few weeks, and, thanks to your understanding, *Herr General-Feldmarschall*, the marriage has been consummated between the symbols of the old greatness and the new strength. We pay you homage. A protective Providence places you above the new forces of our nation.

Deeply moved by his own eloquence, Hitler crossed the dais and, with an obeisance of humility, grasped the old Marshal's hand. Magnesium flared; cameras clicked; and there was perpetuated a scene which Joseph Goebbels, the Reinhardt of the Revolution, was to exploit so fully in the weeks to come. The Field-Marshal and the Corporal, the old Germany and the New, united by a hand-clasp of comradeship—it was to be a theme and an event which no German was to be allowed to forget and which was to be implanted in the mind of every German child.

When the *Reichstag* adjourned to its new quarters in the Kroll Opera House, it had but one item of business, to commit harakiri by passing the Enabling Bill. Hitler was anxious to make this event a great mass-suicide of the political parties, and to that end had been at some pains to negotiate with the party leaders in order that the Bill might be passed by as large a majority as possible. A Government majority was, of course, assured, and it was taken for granted that those Communist Deputies who had so far escaped arrest, would not attend the sitting. But the Social Democrats would vote against the Bill and it was therefore to the Centre that Hitler addressed himself.

In view of the fact that the Bill would be passed anyway, even in the face of a united opposition, the Centre Party leaders devoted themselves to an attempt to save what they could of the constitutional privileges. The Bill transferred the power of legislation from the *Reichstag* to the Government and empowered them even to change the Constitution if they thought fit. Though it was specifically stated that the rights of the President of the Republic should remain untouched, this provision was virtually nullified by vesting in the Chancellor the President's principal prerogative, that of ratifying legislation, in order, it was explained, "to relieve the President of unnecessary work."

It was upon this last item of the Bill that the leaders of the Centre took their stand. Would not the Chancellor respect the President's prerogatives of veto? Hitler replied that he had given his promise, that he would promulgate extreme legislation only after consultation with the President, and he could assure them that he would never disregard the President's wishes. Brüning and Kaas, with a previous knowledge of this kind of negotiation, demanded a written confirmation of this promise before the Centre Party voted for the Bill, and to this the Chancellor agreed. A letter should reach Kaas before the final vote.

On the morning of the fatal session in the Kroll Opera House on March 23, no letter had arrived and Kaas again applied to Hitler. There was no need for anxiety, the Chancellor replied; he had already signed the letter, but it also required the counter-signature of Dr. Frick, the Minister for the Interior; it would arrive in time. The opening of session came; still no letter. Kaas approached Frick. The Minister was all apologies; he was so overtaxed with work that he had had no time to sign all the papers which had been brought to him. But the letter was in his portfolio; he would give it his earliest attention. Brüning advised that unless the letter had arrived before the vote was taken, the Centre should oppose the Bill, but the final decision lay with Kaas as head of the party.

Hitler introduced the Bill to the *Reichstag* in a speech remarkable for its moderation and lack of colour. A more fiery oration had been expected and had, indeed, been prepared, but at the last moment the counsel of the Foreign Office had been heeded and the original text toned down. As the Chancellor sat down, Göring, from the presidential chair, called peremptorily upon the leader of the Social Democrats. There was a moment's deathly silence, and from outside could be heard the ghastly chant of the Storm Troopers who packed the streets: "Give us the Bill or else fire and murder." It was the voice of the New Germany. With a tremendous effort Otto Wels rose from his place and, as if on leaden feet, mounted to the rostrum. Then with squared shoulders he faced the House and, in a voice which did not shake, gave the decision of his party. It was an uncompromising and courageous rejection. The great Socialist Party of Germany, which had defied Bismarck and Wilhelm II, would not betray its traditions and its honour. The Government might take their lives, it could not destroy their souls.

Amid the subdued cheers of his followers and the infuriated yells of the Nazis, Wels returned to his place, and Hitler, pale and shaking with rage, was on his feet, brushing aside Papen's restraining hand. To the obvious dismay of the Vice-Chancellor, the *Führer* gave to the House all that had been expurgated from his opening speech, and more. Wels may have signed the death-warrant of his party but in doing so he had provoked that display of uncontrolled passion which the saner members of the Government, zealous for the good reception of the new order in Europe, had been so anxious to avoid. But the House was frenzied by Hitler's rhetoric. Again and again they rose at him and only physical and emotional exhaustion brought him to a close. When the tumult had subsided, Göring called Kaas to the tribune.

The moment of crisis had come but the letter had not arrived. Was the prelate still so naïve that he believed in Nazi promises or were his nerves a little shaken by the Chancellor's outburst and the grim incantations from without? Whatever the cause, Kaas showed less courage than the Socialist leader. He recorded the vote of the Centre in favour of the Bill and thereby condemned his party in the eyes of many of his faith.

In a roar of excitement the vote was taken, and in a sudden hush Göring declared the figures. For the Government 441; against 91. The Bill was law; Hindenburg signed it, and the parliamentary institutions of Germany were in their grave.

But though the promised letter from Hitler never arrived, the Centre Party leaders did after all receive a written confirmation of the Chancellor's promise to the President. Three days after the vote in the *Reichstag*, Hindenburg sent a personal assurance in explicit terms:

> I am glad to be able to confirm [he wrote] that the Chancellor has assured me that even without constitutional compulsion, he will not use the power conferred on him by the Enabling Act without having first consulted me. By this means I shall always endeavour to secure our intimate co-operation and to fulfil my Oath "to do justice to all men."
>
> VON HINDENBURG[1]

Here then was the one remaining check upon Hitler's power, a gentleman's agreement to consult the President, and it may be asked why did Hindenburg not more energetically defend his Oath? The answer is obvious. A weary Old Gentleman of eighty-six, of rigid mind and slow reasoning, anxious to avoid responsibility and surrounded by a pack of watch-dogs, is no match for a virile young politician of forty-four, free as the air and with no inhibiting political scruples. The agreement has the appearance of the most sardonic hypocrisy. Had Hindenburg been younger and not so completely under control, it is doubtful whether Hitler would have ever entered into such an understanding. But as things were it imposed no check on him at all, for, with the signing of the Enabling Bill, the President simply faded from the picture and from the public mind. A new hero had arisen, Adolf Hitler, and with traditional fickleness they shouted for him. Only in the concentration camps Hindenburg's name was remembered, and with bitterness.

The Old Gentleman spent more and more of his time in the seclusion of Neudeck. It had been enlarged now by the addition

---

[1] *Ich kann Ihnen nur bestätigen, dass der Herr Reichskanzler mir seine Bereitwilligkeit erklärt hat, auch ohne formale verfassungsrechtliche Bindung die auf Grund des Ermächtigungsgesetzes zur ergreifenden Massnahmen nur nach vorherigem Benehman mit mir zu treffen. Ich werde hierbei stets bestrebt sein, enge Zusammenarbeit zu wahren und getreu meinem Eide „Gerechtigkeit gegen jedermann üben."*

VON HINDENBURG

of Oskar's "Naboth's vineyard," which a grateful New Germany had presented to him, and soon it was to be called "the smallest concentration camp." Both here and in the Palace at Berlin the tragedy of 1918 was being re-enacted. Ludendorff had surrounded the Marshal at Spa with those who breathed "the will to Victory," and now the President was studiously "protected" from all critics of the new régime. He could not know the truth, for Papen would not yet admit, even to himself, how far his schemes had miscarried, and it was the business of his advisors to keep Hindenburg in ignorance.

Thus the Old Gentleman could not know that within six months of Hitler's coming to power his foreign policy had very nearly provoked drastic action on the part of the Powers and that he had only withdrawn at the last moment in face of grave warnings from Great Britain and America. He could not know that all over the country the Nationalists were being ousted from the governments and their places taken by Nazis; that frequent clashes occurred between the *Stahlhelm* and the Storm Troops, and that in many places the Steel Helmets had been suppressed. He could not know that in camps and cellars throughout Germany thousands of his countrymen were herded like animals and beaten, in many cases for no better reason than that they had voted for him. These things were hidden from him, and his only visitors assured him that all was well. The stories of atrocities were entirely false, they said, and in giving Hitler the power to regenerate Germany he had performed the crowning act of his career.

From time to time there may have been—there must have been —some doubts in Hindenburg's mind as to whether he had done the right thing. Certainly he must have been surprised that many of his old friends and comrades no longer came to see him; for there were many great Germans, and friends of Germany from abroad, who tried to acquaint him of the true state of the country, but who failed to pass that watchful Cerberus, the Secretary of State. But Hindenburg was very old and very tired; he enjoyed the quiet peace of his seclusion and became more easily receptive to reassuring blandishments.

Every now and then he would emerge from his retirement. Race meetings delighted him, and he attended the German Derby at Hamburg and the "Hindenburg Cup" at Grünewald. The crowds still cheered him, but not with the frenzy that they reserved for Hitler. The Hindenburg legend was a little passé now. The national pilgrimage to Tannenberg in August was the occasion for a fresh burst of compliments from the Chancellor and further affirmation of Hindenburg's unswerving fidelity to his "Kaiser, King and Lord"; and in October he was haled forth in some bewilderment to summon the German people, incongruously enough, to subscribe to Hitler's policy of peace in withdrawing from the Disarmament Conference and from the League of Nations.

Did he, one wonders, have no twinges of that so sensitive conscience? Was there no memory of that fight, in which he had supported Stresemann so staunchly, to bring Germany to Locarno and Geneva? Or had all recollection of those years of struggle passed, and was he waiting in patience, but by now a little anxiously, for the day when a regenerated Germany should recall her Kaiser?

From time to time distinguished visitors from abroad, eminently "safe" politically, were allowed through the blockade, and among these on one occasion was a famous British general on a "good-will" mission. Because it was desired to do him honour, for he was very distinguished, an aide-de-camp from the *Reichswehr* was attached with instructions to take him round Potsdam and bring him back to tea at the Palace. This task accomplished, the Marshal began in his usual way to cross-examine his visitor.

"What did you think of Potsdam, General?"

"Well, sir, I confess it impressed me with the difference between the Hohenzollerns and ourselves," was the reply.

"Really, why?"

"In my country it is a point of tradition with our families
that generation after generation lives in the same house, but so
far as I can see, each Hohenzollern built a house for himself."

"Oh," said Hindenburg heavily, "that's very interesting; nobody ever told me that before."

While Hindenburg thus passed his latter days in peace and
seclusion, the new Germany which he had helped to create was
rapidly approaching a period of acute crisis. In the space of a
year Adolf Hitler had succeeded in crushing or terrorizing into
submission all forms of opposition to the new régime, but he had
failed signally to allay the rivalries within his own party and had
apparently gone contemptuously out of his way to antagonize his
late allies, the Nationalists. With the appointment of Darré to
succeed Hugenberg as Minister of Agriculture, and of Hess,
Röhm, and Kerrl as Ministers without portfolio, the Nazis now
had a majority in the Cabinet, and the remaining Nationalist
members had become no more than figure-heads.

But the figure-heads talked, and—with the exception of Seldte,
who seemed to welcome insult with an almost masochistic lust—
talked loudly. They charged that the terms of the coalition of
January 1933 had been broken, forgetting Hitler's declared em-
ulation of Mussolini's tactics. And, in addition, they were very
frightened. The Movement had swung far too rapidly to the Left
for their liking or comfort, and already Goebbels was talking
with distressing frequency of a second and more radical Revolution to follow closely upon Hindenburg's death, an event which,
all knew, could not long be delayed. If, therefore, the Nationalists were to regain some of their ground there was no time to

be lost, for once Hindenburg had passed finally from the scene, all feared that radicalism would be rampant and unchecked.

The friction between the two Government parties grew steadily and culminated in a series of incidents during the first six months of 1934. On the anniversary of the Kaiser's birthday in January the monarchist organizations were wont to hold a dinner, an annual gathering of officers of the old army and former Court officials purely sentimental in character and without political significance. Goebbels had frequently referred to this "hot-bed of reaction" in scathing terms, and on January 26, 1934, the dinner was raided by riotous Storm Troopers, who broke up the tables, insulted the guests, and so humiliated the presiding officer, the veteran General von Horn, that he died of a stroke two days later. In April high *Stahlhelm* leaders were arrested in Stettin and sent to a concentration camp, and, in June, Seldte's car, with Seldte in it, was stoned by S.A. men at Magdeburg.

At last Papen's eyes were opened to the enormity of his error. His own vanity had been wounded at the manner in which Göring had ousted him from the government of Prussia, and he was frankly alarmed, like Frankenstein of old, at the way in which this monster of his creation had thrown off all control. He had been revolted by the brutalities of the Terror, but was lulled by the age-old sophism that an omelette cannot be made without breaking eggs. Now, however, he awoke to a full realization of the degree to which the German mind had been imprisoned and all free speech and criticism stifled. Appalled, he raised the matter in Cabinet and was rebuffed by Goebbels, and when he carried his protest to the Chancellor himself, Hitler was evasive and unhelpful. Now really roused, Papen took counsel with the group of young men which had grown up around him, Jung, Bose, Tchirchsky, and others, and to a man they urged him to seek the support of the President for a public protest, if necessary supported by the authority of the *Reichswehr*.

But the rising antagonism of the Nationalists was among the least of Hitler's troubles at the moment. The inner state of his own party was a far more pressing problem. A bitter rivalry divided Göring and Goebbels; and depravity and corruption were rampant. The erotic orgies of Röhm in Berlin and of Heines in Breslau were common knowledge, as was the fact that the greater part of the proceeds of the *Winter Hilfe*—a fund for the benefit of the unemployed collected from house to house and door to door, accompanied too frequently by threats and menaces—went into the pockets of the Storm Troop leaders to defray the expenses of the luxurious establishments which many of them had set up. To many Germans who had voted in genuine enthusiasm and confidence for Hitler in 1933, this record of a Government which had seized supreme power with the proclaimed intention of rooting out corruption and setting up a rigid economy, came as a terrible disillusionment: while from foreign countries, and notably from England, representatives of the highest authorities of Church and State, not unfavourable to the National Socialist movement, urged upon Hitler the necessity of setting his house in order and cleaning up his party by legal methods.

More pressing even than this, however, was the problem of the Storm Troops themselves. The old dispute with Röhm, which had flared up in 1926 and again in 1930, was now at white heat, for with the withdrawal from the Disarmament Conference and the subsequent avowed policy of rearmament, Röhm had the most pleasing visions of a *Reichswehr* enlarged by the incorporation of many of his legions, with the remainder standing behind it in a brown phalanx of trained reserves. He considered himself and his Storm Troops indispensable to the progress and consolidation of the Revolution, and the rank and file of his followers represented, far more genuinely than did the casuistical Goebbels, the Left Wing radical tendencies of the party.

And they too were dissatisfied. For if the Nationalists were alarmed at the progress of the Revolution towards the Left, these men, who from their youth in the party had imbibed its pre-revolutionary propaganda, regarded it as not having gone far enough. Indeed, they were sadly disillusioned. They had been promised the return of the Polish Corridor and they had seen a ten-year pact of non-aggression with Poland; they had been promised National Socialism "in our time," and they had seen the great industrialists and landowners become still more strongly entrenched; and finally, they had been promised honour and glory as the soldiers of the Revolution, and they were threatened with disbandment.

For, faced with an unruly body of Prætorians two and a half million strong and under an erratic chief, and a Europe uniting against him, Hitler was seeking to improve his position by sacrificing the one to the other. The efforts made by the British Government during the spring of 1934 to find a disarmament formula between the French and German theses, and thereby to bring Germany back to Geneva, presented the Chancellor with a golden opportunity for disembarrassing himself of the Brown Army, which had now become both a threat and an incubus, and at the same time of gaining credit with the Powers. When, therefore, that peripatetic statesman, Mr. Anthony Eden, visited Berlin in February, 1934, he was met by Hitler with an offer of a reduction of the S.A. by two-thirds and the institution of a system of supervision which should verify that the remainder should neither possess any arms nor receive any military instruction or take part in field exercises. This offer was repeated to the British Government in April.

But German diplomacy, by its indomitable stupidity, defeated its own ends. All hope for its success was lost with the peremptory closing of the negotiations by the French Government in answer to the publication of the German military budget, showing a very extensive increase in the appropriations.

The news of the offer and the rumours of large reductions in
their numbers to follow the annual period of leave in July caused
great discontent in the ranks of the S.A., which found voice
through Röhm in the Cabinet. Here, however, Hitler had the firm
support of Blomberg, the *Reichswehr* Minister, and of Göring,
who, since he had been made a general, had espoused the well-
known doctrines of the army regarding the S.A., and would, in
any case, have opposed practically any views advanced by
Röhm. The Chancellor was also assured of the loyalty of the
S.S., a force now some two hundred thousand strong, whose contempt for the S.A. was reminiscent of the scorn evinced by the
Guard for the Line in the old army.

The dissensions within the party and the general feeling of
crisis in the air had a further unexpected result. General von
Schleicher, recovered from his chagrin yet nursing a desire for
revenge, emerged from his retirement to pursue his life's delight
of fishing in troubled waters. His passion for intrigue was on
him once more, but he had failed to realize that what was merely
treachery before the establishment of the Totalitarian State was
now regarded as high treason, and that he no longer controlled
the secret forces of espionage. He began again to indulge his
flair for shadow Cabinet-making, and before long it was reported
that he had re-established his old contacts with Röhm. In return
for the Vice-Chancellorship under Hitler, it was rumoured, he
would agree to the appointment of Röhm as Minister of Defence
and the partial amalgamation of the Brown Army with the
Reichswehr. It was also rumoured that Papen, Göring, and Neurath were to be excluded from the Government and that Brüning
was to be offered the Foreign Ministry. How irresponsible and
unreliable these conversations were may be judged by the fact
that no communication passed between Schleicher and Brüning,
and that if the latter's name was included in the "Shadow Cabinet," it was without his consent or knowledge. In so far as

Schleicher was concerned, the affair was little more than one of building castles in Spain, for he no longer had access to the President, and was discredited and without influence.

But in the hands of Göring and Himmler, the chief of the S.S. and the *Gestapo* (Secret Police), the story took on gigantic proportions. It became a plot, a conspiracy to murder, an incipient counter-revolution to be fought with its own weapons. A drastic "purge" of the party was planned, which should include within its scope all the enemies of the régime, both past and present, to the Right and to the Left. Lists of those to be executed were prepared and a certain bargaining went on whereby the friends of one were removed from the list of another in return for reciprocal treatment. The date was fixed for June 16, and at the end of May both Brüning and Schleicher received warnings that they were among the condemned. Brüning left the country, but Schleicher, regarding the affair as a passing storm which would soon blow over, merely went into retreat on the shores of the Starnbergersee.

Suddenly there was a new development. For a long time Hitler had courted Mussolini in an attempt to enlist his aid against France, but the campaign of terror and interference which the Nazis persisted in carrying on in Austria had so far proved a stumbling-block. Now it appeared that it was possible for the two dictators to meet for the first time and discuss their common problems face to face; the rendezvous suggested was Venice, and the date the 15th and 16th of June. Plans for the purge were hastily postponed and the *Führer* departed to meet the man from whom so many of his ideas had been derived.

In the meantime, Papen had not been idle. He had been the guest of the President at Neudeck, and had there disclosed to Hindenburg sufficient of the true state of affairs in Germany to upset the Old Gentleman very thoroughly. There was, Papen said, no question of supplanting Hitler, but steps must be taken to curb the power of such people as Goebbels, whose radical opportunism was a danger to all. It was a national reproach, and one that the European countries did not hesitate to level against Germany, that a gag should be put upon free speech and constructive criticism. Such had never been the object of the movement of national resurgence as he had visualized it, or as he had explained it to Hindenburg, and he felt that as one of those chiefly responsible for bringing the new régime into power, it was his duty to utter a protest. He proposed, with Hindenburg's approval, to make an important speech shortly, which might have very severe repercussions. Should this be so, he asked for the President's support.

Whether Papen explained in detail to Hindenburg exactly what was the nature of the support he desired—which was in effect the President's authority to suppress the Goebbels policy if necessary with the assistance of the *Reichswehr*—or how much was understood by the Old Gentleman, to whom the whole thing had come as a shock of disillusionment, it is impossible to say, but certainly Papen left Neudeck with the impression that whatever the result of his protest might be, he was assured of Hindenburg's loyal support and assistance. Being Papen, he said so in the diplomatic circles in which he moved, and his listeners waited breathlessly for the approaching day.

It was before the University of Marburg, on Sunday June 17, that Papen made his now historic appeal. The speech, itself a composite work, owing most to the Hebrew genius of Edgar Jung, was a masterpiece in style and content. Throughout it had the hall-mark of greatness:

My personal obligation to Adolf Hitler and his work [said Papen] is so great that it would be a mortal sin for me, as a man and a statesman, not to say what must be said at this decisive stage of the German Revolution. . . . We know full well that there are rumours and whisperings in dark corners, but they evaporate when brought out into the light of day. A free press ought to exist to inform the Government with open and manly statements where corruption has made its nest, when bad mistakes have been made, where the wrong men are in the wrong place, and where the spirit of the German Revolution has been sinned against. . . . If the official organs of public opinion do not throw sufficient light on the mysterious darkness which at present hides the spirit of the German people, then a statesman must step in and call a spade a spade. Such a step should prove that the Government is strong enough to bear reasonable criticism, which, as the old maxim says, only weaklings and fools cannot bear. . . .

Any talk about a second wave which will complete the Revolution has no meaning. Whoever plays with such thoughts must not hide from himself that a third wave can easily follow a second one; that he who threatens the guillotine comes the sooner under its knife. No race can afford constant uprisings by the lower classes if it wishes to have a place in history. . . . In the long run no propaganda and no organization, however good, can by itself maintain confidence. A sense of trust and willingness to serve can only be fostered by taking the people into confidence and not by working up high feelings, especially among youth, nor by threats against sections of the people who are helpless. The people know that heavy sacrifices are expected of them. They will make them and follow the Leader with implicit faith if they are allowed to have a voice in council and action; if every word of criticism is not at once interpreted as of evil intent; and if patriots in despair are not branded as enemies of the State.

The courageous tone of the speech, as well as the thinly veiled attack upon Goebbels, met with welcome favour throughout the world, and it is difficult to describe the joy with which it was received in Germany. It was as if a load had suddenly been lifted from the German soul. The sense of relief could almost be felt in the air. Papen had put into words what thousands upon thousands of his countrymen had locked up in their hearts for fear of the awful penalties of speech. He had given fresh hope to those who had almost gone under in the depths of their despair. Could it mean that a new era of toleration was really about to dawn?

But in the little town of Gera there was tumult and affright. Here were assembled the party chiefs to hear Hitler's account of his conversation with the Duce, and to them news and rumour came hot upon each other's heels. Papen, it was said, had raised the standard of counter-revolution at Marburg and had behind him not only the President but the *Reichswehr*. Momentary panic ensued. The leaders anxiously discussed to which foreign countries they could escape and whether, under the exchange restriction which they themselves had imposed, they could get funds out of Germany.

Saner counsels, however, prevailed, and it was decided to meet the crisis and fight. The first suggestion, to arrest Papen, was vetoed on the advice of Goebbels, who proposed that no measures should be taken against the Vice-Chancellor personally, lest he become a martyr, but that every means should be employed to prevent the speech from becoming public. It had not been broadcast, but gramophone records had been made of it, and the order was at once given for their destruction. The edition of the *Frankfurter-Zeitung* in which the text appeared was suppressed; the pamphlet edition printed at the press of Papen's own paper, *Germania,* was seized—but not before a number of people, including the writer, had secured copies—and it was even proposed to close the frontiers to prevent the speech from leaving the country. The *Baseler Nachrichten* had, however, smuggled out a press copy, and though its issue was banned in Germany, it was soon in circulation everywhere. The Radical press at once let loose a flood of invective, both in articles and caricature, with pointed references to "effete aristocrats," "top-hatted noblemen," and "cavalry captains"; while Goebbels demanded in the *Angriff:* "Is it not time that this nest of stink-pots was cleaned out?"

Papen's protest could not thus lightly be set aside. He had received letters of congratulation from the Crown Prince, from

Seldte, and from a number of moderate Nazi leaders. Despite all Goebbels's efforts the gist, at least, of the speech had become generally known and public enthusiasm was growing daily. On June 24, at Hamburg, on the occasion of the German Derby, the Vice-Chancellor received a huge ovation. The crowd forsook the Nazi salutation of "Heil," and reverted to the old "Hurrah"— for Papen and for Marburg. Goebbels was also present and was hissed. In the President's box (Papen was acting as Hindenburg's deputy) the two shook hands for the benefit of press photographers. A bitter moment for them both.

But from Neudeck there came only a telegram of congratulation. And as the days slipped past, and Hindenburg made no further sign, the Nazi leaders began to regain their courage and Papen knew that his *coup* had misfired. Did Hindenburg betray him? He he ever really understood the full meaning of what Papen had told him in the June sunlight as they sat on the terrace at Neudeck? It was difficult at eighty-six suddenly to reverse his ideas and to be told that what he had been led to believe for the last eighteen months, those months so blessedly free from trouble and responsibility, had been false. Papen will never know just what had happened. He had seen the President for the last time in life.

During the week which followed in Berlin the atmosphere seemed charged with an ever-increasing tensity, and as one golden June day gave place to another, the presage of impending tragedy grew stronger. Rumour was rife. It was known that Ribbentropp had repeated in Paris the offer which Hitler had made to Eden regarding the S.A., and the whisper went forth that, after the Storm Troops had gone on leave in July, very few of them would return. A conference of these leaders was summoned at Munich for the end of the week. Behind the scenes Göring and Himmler were feverishly pushing forward the plans which had been postponed from June 16, and were working on

Hitler's nerves—always the *Führer's* weak point—to ensure his support and participation.

All unsuspecting of their own danger, the several characters in the drama pursued their way. Papen was unconcerned as ever. He had had a long interview with Hitler in the course of which he had tendered his resignation from the Cabinet. This the Chancellor had refused, but added ominously that while he personally agreed with much of what had been said at Marburg, he regarded the manner of saying it as a breach of faith. Though Papen knew that attempts were now being made in Berlin to explain away the President's telegram of congratulation, he persisted in regarding the incident as closed, an attitude in which he was imitated by most of his group. Only Edgar Jung sensed the coming danger, but, though he went into hiding, he could not be persuaded to fly the country at once.

I met him in a secluded part of one of the many wooded districts surrounding Berlin one afternoon of that momentous week, and he was then convinced that nothing could save him. He was entirely calm and fatalistic, but he spoke with the freedom of a man who has nothing before him and therefore nothing to lose, and he told me many things. Later two others of the Marburg circle talked with me, and I, still strongly under the influence of Jung's certainty of death, was amazed at their lack of anxiety. Though they hinted at the fate of others, "Protective Detention" was the worst that they envisaged for themselves. Within forty-eight hours one of them, together with Jung and others of my friends, was dead.

The blow fell suddenly, and without warning. In the early hours of the morning of Saturday, June 30, Hitler at the head of a party of S.S. raided a villa at Wiesee, in the neighbourhood of Munich, and there discovered Röhm and Heines under circumstances which definitely precluded any idea of an immediately premeditated *putsch*. Heines and his Storm Trooper paramour were despatched out of hand, but for a long hour Hitler strove with the man who had been his closest friend for sixteen years, the only one among his followers with whom he was on terms of "thee" and "thou," and finally gave instructions that a revolver was to be left in his cell. That Röhm disdained the way of suicide and bravely faced a firing squad in his own cellar, is to be counted in his favour and is a strange ending to his notorious and nefarious career.

These acts of justice done, the *Führer* turned over the further work of execution to Major Buchs, the head of the "Disciplinary Section" of the S.S., who dealt faithfully with many enemies of the régime in Bavaria. The memory of the Party was a long one, and among those murdered was the seventy-eight-year-old von Kahr, who had scotched the Bürgerbrau *putsch* of 1923. Though few tears need be shed over such men as Röhm and Heines, there was nothing in their career which precluded them from the privilege of fair trial, which might or might not in due course have brought them to the gallows, but if they lacked justice, how much more so did such leaders of the S.A. as Hans Peter von Heydebreck and Hans von Falkenhausen, nephew of the war-time General? These men, the best type of officer which the Old Army produced, had served Hitler loyally from early days but had criticized the brutality which had attended the Revolution. They too died on June 30, with many others whose only crime was that they had placed too strong a faith in the promises of their leader.

Meantime in Berlin, Göring, having first assured himself of the success of the Munich operations, launched his own attack, flinging his net far to right and left. Papen, placed under arrest in his own house, faced for hours the prospect of immediate death until imperative instructions from Hitler placed his life out of danger. That strange quirk of loyalty in the *Führer's* character forbade the death of the man who had placed him in power. But this protection did not extend to his staff. In the office of the Vice-Chancellor, Bose, his first adjutant, was shot down in his room and the remainder of the group placed under arrest, with the exception of Jung, who had been executed earlier in the morning.

Schleicher, who had returned to Berlin when the 16th of June had passed uneventfully, was murdered with his wife, as they were awaiting the return of his stepdaughter to luncheon, and it was left for this sixteen-year-old child to find their bodies riddled on the floor. Schleicher's closest friend, General von Bredow, was also shot. Treviranus, who, most characteristically, had disregarded all warnings, evaded the raiding party which called at his house, slipped away in his own car, and arrived, after a series of hairbreadth escapes, in England.

Towards evening those who had not been shot in their own homes were brought to Lichtefelde Barracks, the former cadet school of the Old Army, where a series of perfunctory courts-martial were held with but one sentence. Here died the handsome young Karl Ernst, who had risen rapidly from bell captain in the Hotel am Knie to be supreme commander of Storm Troops in the district of Berlin-Brandenburg. Arrested in Bremen as he was about to leave for Madeira, he was brought handcuffed by air to Berlin, protesting his loyalty to the Leader, who but a few weeks before had been present at his wedding. Ernst faced his death with the cry "Heil, Hitler" on his lips.

All through the nights of Saturday, Sunday, and Monday the executions went on, the bursts of firing from the execution squads of S.S. men, among whom were the sons of some of the most distinguished men in Germany, being plainly heard in the still air. In other parts of the country similar scenes were enacted, and among the victims was Gregor Strasser, the man who had once organized Berlin for Hitler, but whose sin was that he had negotiated with Brüning and with Schleicher. At the same time wholesale arrests were made on all sides, and Hitler issued an hysterical Order of the Day, protesting his ignorance of Röhm's private life and proclaiming his desire to make the S.A. an organization to which German mothers could confide their sons with perfect peace of mind!

The full toll of that ghastly week-end can never be known, but it is certain that it exceeded the figure of seventy-seven which Hitler later admitted in his *Reichstag* speech of July 13, when he informed a bewildered Germany, and a shocked and incredulous world, that he had saved the country from a national peril of a gruesome nature. Men left their homes on that Saturday morning never to return, and to this day their relatives do not know when or where they died. One woman received the first news of her husband's murder when his ashes were sent to her through the post by the Secret Police. Others have never received a notification.

For three days the *Reichswehr* held aloof, keeping the ring, but on the Tuesday (July 2) they indicated that the slaughter must stop. Their humanitarian feelings had not, however, been roused before it was certain that all their rivals in the high command of the Brown Army had been "liquidated." That they tolerated this political gangsterism even for three days is a blot upon the escutcheon of the German army which it will find difficult to erase, but a darker stain was the fact that it was the *Reichswehr* Minister, Colonel-General (now Field-Marshal) von Blomberg, who conveyed the congratulations of the Cabinet to the Chancellor.

How much news of the ghastly week-end penetrated to Neudeck? Very little, it is to be believed, and that in a suitably prepared form. It is certain that the murder of Schleicher and the arrest of Papen were kept from Hindenburg, and it is probable that only the story of the S.A. conspiracy was told to him. But the world, already nauseated by the events of June 30, was shocked to hear that the President of the Republic had warmly congratulated Hitler upon his exploits:

From the reports placed before me [Hindenburg telegraphed to his Chancellor on July 2] I learn that you, by your determined action and your brave personal intervention, have nipped treason in the bud. You have saved the German nation from serious danger. For this I express to you my most profound thanks and sincere appreciation.

Did Hindenburg authorize the telegram or was it merely sent in his name by some of those zealous officials who "protected" him so efficiently? Let us believe that the latter was the case, as it may well have been, for it is a fearful thing to find Hindenburg, in the last weeks of his life, openly condoning murder even in the name of justice.

Slowly the smoke cleared and Germany began to resume its normal course. But the country was stunned and the hand of the Secret Police was heavy on it. Arrests were still made constantly, and many who could no longer bear the strain of constant fear, tried to leave the country. Some were successful, others were turned back at the frontier, others again effected escapes by various means. A former member of the British House of Commons earned for himself the reputation of a Scarlet Pimpernel for the successful rescues which he twice achieved.

Scarcely had Europe begun to recover from the effects of June 30, when it was once more revolted by a second crime. The Austrian Chancellor, the gallant little Dollfuss, whose struggle against foreign terrorism and interference had earned him general admiration, was cold-bloodedly and brutally murdered on July 25 by Austrian Nazi gunmen, who allowed him to bleed to death without the service of a doctor or a priest.

In the political welter which followed, a solution was presented to the problem of what should be done with Papen. With that extraordinary preservation which attends him, Papen had survived the events of June 30, which had claimed the lives of

LOYAL SUPPORT.

JUNE 30TH, 1934

Reprinted by the special permission of the Proprietors of Punch

two of his friends and endangered his own and those of many of his circle. He had refused to attend further sessions of the Cabinet but he had not resigned the Vice-Chancellorship. In justice to him, it must be said that the possibilities of resignation under a dictatorship are strictly limited, and Lenin's famous telegram to Krassin may be recalled: "Soviet representatives are not allowed to resign; if they are unsatisfactory we dismiss them." Clearly, however, Papen's life was under a constant threat if he remained either in the Government or in Germany; Göring would have shot him on June 30, and Goebbels had not forgotten the strictures of Marburg. Hitler did not desire his death, and here he was at one with the President.

It had reached Hindenburg's ears that Papen had been in danger, and, as he felt his strength failing, he laid upon Hitler the solemn charge of his protection. Nothing must happen to "Fränzchen." To the end he was true to this one friend of his bosom, and in his relations with Papen there was none of that marked lack of loyalty which had marred his parting from Ludendorff, from Gröner, and from Brüning. This act of protection was to be the last occasion on which he exercised his waning authority.

The Chancellor agreed and searched his mind for a solution. It came from an unexpected quarter.

The assassins of Dollfuss had claimed the right of negotiation with the German Minister in Vienna, thereby incriminating him in their guilt. The unfortunate Dr. Rieth, who had been appointed by Brüning, is believed to have had no previous knowledge of the plot, but he was recalled and dismissed, a victim of circumstances. To Papen was awarded the position of Minister of "Peace and Goodwill," as the *Führer's* personal representative, and in Vienna in comparative safety, he awaited the further caprice of Fate.[1]

---

[1] With that indefatigable energy which has characterized his whole career, Papen laboured unceasingly to further the policy of bringing Austria within the

Hindenburg's long life was drawing to an end. He had been
weakening all spring and summer, and the disconcerting affairs
revealed to him first by Papen and then by the Government had
worried him exceedingly. In the last week of July he began to
fail fast and the first bulletins betokening the end were issued
on the 31st. There was nothing dramatic in his passing; it was
just that of any other very tired and fundamentally pious old
gentleman. Though he had in his last days moments of deep
regret and contrition, he was consoled by the confident belief that
for seventy years he had done his duty as he had seen it, or as
others had indicated it to him. Now he was quite quietly dying.

On the afternoon of August 1 he called the great doctor Sauerbruch to his bedside:

"You have always told me the whole truth and you will do so
now," he said. "Is Friend Hein [Matthias Claudius's euphemism
for Death] in the Schloss and waiting?"

"No, *Herr Feldmarschall*, but he is walking round the house."

Hindenburg was silent for a moment.

"Thank you, Sauerbruch, I wanted to know; and now I will
confer with the Lord a little."

He kept the doctor by him while he fumbled with the leaves
of his Bible. Sauerbruch wanted to give him more light, but the
Marshal stopped him.

"Leave the curtain as it is," he said; "I have known by heart
for a long time what I want to read."

In a soft whispering voice, very unlike his normal military
gruffness, he read for a while; then laying down the book, he
called to the doctor again.

political orbit of Germany. For two years his efforts met with a signal lack of
success, but, in the European welter following the Italian victory in Ethiopia,
Fate again smiled on him. His ambitions were realized in the Austro-German
Treaty of Reconciliation signed in July 1936, by which Austria proclaimed herself a German state. The success of his policy has restored Papen's political fortunes to a great extent and such is his remarkable political resilience that more
may well be heard of this strange figure in German history.

"It is all right, Sauerbruch, now tell Friend Hein he can come in."

Early on the morning of August 2, just twenty years after the declaration of the World War which had called Hindenburg from obscurity to fame, the blue-and-white Prussian standard above the Castle of Neudeck was lowered to half-mast. After seventy years of service, the Marshal had laid down his last command.

EPILOGUE

✠

EVEN in death, it seemed, Hindenburg followed the path of service, for he could have rendered no greater boon to Hitler than by dying at this moment. The events of June 30 and the assassination of Dollfuss had gravely impaired the Chancellor's position at home, and had deprived him of all support abroad. The illusion which Hitler had sought to create of a Germany standing firm and united behind her *Führer* had been shattered, and within the *Reich* itself he had dangerously imperilled his connections with the proletariat and with the lower middle class from which the popular support of his party had been originally so largely drawn. To the disaffected elements of the Socialists, Communists, Jews, Catholics, and Protestants, he had now added many disgruntled Storm Troopers and disillusioned Nationalists, and for the time being he was dependent upon the support of the S.S., the *Gestapo,* and the *Reichswehr.* Germany had temporarily been handed over to the tender mercies of Göring and Himmler; the S.S. had become the new Prætorian guard. So greatly had the prestige of the Revolution been damaged that it seemed doubtful whether Hitler could recast the spell over the German people.

It was at this moment that Hindenburg died, presenting Hitler with complete and indisputable control of power, and with a providential opportunity for concentrating the full force of propaganda upon the country. Within an hour of the Marshal's death, it was announced that the office of President would be merged with that of the Chancellor, and Hitler became the head of the State and Supreme Commander-in-Chief of the armed forces of the *Reich*. On the same day he received the oath of allegiance from the *Reichswehr,* and set about his preparations for a national referendum which should be the ratification by the people of this new régime.

Thus the funeral of Hindenburg at Tannenburg on August 6, a pageant of military solemnity and splendour, had the dual nature of a last tribute to a great soldier and a clever move in an election campaign. In the orations much stress was laid upon the trust which the old Field-Marshal had reposed in the young Corporal, and there was a strong implication that Hitler had now acceded to power in apostolic succession to Hindenburg. The tradition must be maintained; the torch carried on.

But the world was waiting for something else. Concurrently with Hindenburg's death there were rumours of a political testament of great importance. The document, it was said, had been drawn up not long before and contained certain injunctions to Hitler, laying upon him obligations, grave and explicit. As the date of the funeral approached, the rumours increased in number and irresponsibility, but the Ministry of Propaganda issued a formal denial that any will or testament of a political nature existed. Public interest in the question subsided and was transferred to the feverish efforts of the party to secure an overwhelming personal vote of confidence in the *Führer* at the referendum on August 19.

Few political organizations are so acutely efficient as the National Socialist Party. On August 15, four days before the country went to the polls, a statement was issued from Hitler's country estate at Obersalzberg. The missing document had been "found" and brought to the *Reichsführer* by Herr von Papen, on behalf of Colonel von Hindenburg. It was to be published at the special request of Herr Hitler.

The document, which was calculated to carry much weight with any who had not yet decided to cast a vote of approval on August 19, implicitly bequeathed the destiny of Germany to Hitler. Explicitly it reaffirmed Hindenburg's faith in an Imperial Germany, and by inference it made his successors the trustee of the principle of monarchy. It laid particular emphasis on the importance of the *Reichswehr* as the guardian of tradition in the transitional period now over and in the German State of to-day and to-morrow.

To the German Nation and to its Chancellor, my testament.

In 1919 I wrote in my message to the German Nation: "We were at the end! Like Siegfried under the cunning javelin of the furious Hagen, our exhausted front collapsed. In vain had we endeavoured to drink new life from the perennial spring of native strength. It was our task now, to save the remaining strength of our army for the later reconstruction of the Fatherland. The present was lost. There remained now only hope—and the future!

"I understand the idea of escape from the world, which obsessed many officers, in view of the collapse of all that was dear and true to them. The desire to know nothing more of a world where seething passions obscured the vital qualities of our nation so that they could no longer be recognized, is humanly conceivable. And yet—but I must express it frankly, just as I think! Comrades of the once grand, proud German army! Can you speak of losing heart? Think of the men who more than a hundred years ago created for us a new Fatherland. Their religion was their faith in themselves and in the sanctity of their cause. They created the new Fatherland, basing it not on freak doctrinaire theories foreign to our nature, but building it up on the foundations of the free development of the framework and of the principles of our own common weal! When it is able, Germany will go along this way again.

"I have the firm conviction that now, as in those times, the links with our great rich past will be preserved, and, where they have been broken, will be restored. The old German spirit will again assert itself triumphantly, though only after thorough purgings in the fires of suffering and passion.

"Our opponents knew the strength of this spirit; they admired and hated it in times of peace; they were astonished at it and feared it on the battlefields of the Great War. They sought to explain our strength to their peoples by using the empty word 'Organization.' They passed over in silence the spirit which lived and moved behind the veil of this word. But in and with this spirit we will again courageously construct.

"Germany, the focus-point of so many of the inexhaustible values of human civilization and culture, will not go under so long as it retains faith in its great historical world mission. I have the sure confidence that the depth and strength of thought of the best in our Fatherland will succeed in blending new ideas with the precious treasures of former times and from them will forge in concert, lasting values for the welfare of our Fatherland.

"This is the unshakable conviction with which I leave the bloody battlefield on international warfare. I have seen the heroic agony of my Fatherland and never, never will believe that it was its death agony.

"For the present our entire former constitution lies buried under the flood-tide raised by the storm of wild political passions and resounding phrases which has apparently destroyed all sacred traditions. But this flood-tide will subside. Then, from the eternally agitated sea of human life, will again emerge that rock to which the hope of our fathers clung, that rock upon which, nearly half a century ago, the future of our Fatherland was, by our strength, confidently founded— the German Empire! When the national idea, the national consciousness, has again been raised, then, out of the Great War—on which no nation can look back with such legitimate pride and with such clear conscience as we—as well as out of the bitter severity of the present days, precious moral fruits will ripen for us. The blood of all those who have fallen in the faith of the greatness of the Fatherland, will not then have flowed in vain. In this assurance I lay down my pen and rely firmly on you—the Youth of Germany."

I wrote these words in the darkest hours and in the conviction that

I was fast approaching the close of a life spent in the service of the Fatherland. Fate disposed otherwise for me. In the spring of 1925 a new chapter of my life was opened. Again I was wanted to co-operate in the destiny of my nation. Only my firm confidence in Germany's inexhaustible resources gave me the courage to accept the office of *Reichspräsident*. This firm belief lent me also the moral strength to fulfil unswervingly the duties of that difficult position.

The last chapter of my life has been for me, at the same time, the most difficult. Many have not understood me in these troublous times and have not comprehended that my only anxiety was to lead the distracted and discouraged German nation back to self-conscious unity.

I began and conducted the duties of my office in the consciousness that a preparatory period of complete renunciation was necessary in domestic and international politics. From the Easter message of the year 1925—in which I exhorted the nation to the fear of God, to social justice, to internal peace and political sanity—onwards, I have not become tired of cultivating the inward unity of our nation and the self-consciousness of its best qualities. Moreover, I was conscious that the political constitution and form of government which were provided for the nation in the hour of its greatest distress and greatest weakness, did not correspond with the requirements and characteristics of our people. The time must arrive when this knowledge would become general. It therefore seemed my duty to rescue the country from the morass of external oppression and degradation, internal distress and self-disruption, without jeopardizing its existence, before this hour struck.

The guardian of the State, the *Reichswehr*, must be the symbol and firm support for this superstructure. On the *Reichswehr*, as a firm foundation, must rest the old Prussian virtues of self-realized dutifulness, of simplicity, and comradeship. The German *Reichswehr* had, after the collapse, cultivated the continuation of the high traditions of the old army in typical style. Always and at all times the *Reichswehr* must remain the pattern of State conduct, so that, unbiased by any internal political development, its lofty mission for the defence of the country may be put to good account.

When I shall have returned to my comrades above, with whom I have fought on so many battlefields for the honour and glory of the nation, then I shall call to the younger generation:

"Show yourselves worthy of your ancestors, and never forget, if you would secure the peace and well-being of your native country, that you must be prepared to give up everything for its peace and honour. Never forget that your deeds will one day become Tradition."

The thanks of the Field-Marshal of the World War and its Commander-in-Chief are due to all the men who have accomplished the construction and organization of the *Reichswehr*.

Internationally the German nation had to wander through a Gethsemane. A frightful treaty weighed heavily upon it, and in its increasingly evil effects threatened to bring about the collapse of our nation. For a long time the surrounding world did not understand that Germany must live, not only for its own sake, but also for the sake of Europe and as the standard-bearer of Western culture. Only step by step, without awaking an overwhelming resistance, were the fetters which surrounded us to be loosened. If many of my comrades at that time did not understand the difficulties that beset our path, history will certainly judge rightly, how severe, but also how necessary in the interests of the maintenance of German existence, was many a State act signed by me.

In unison with the growing internal recovery and strengthening of the German nation, a progressive and—God willing—a generous contribution towards the solution of all troublesome European questions, could be striven after and obtained, on the basis of its own national honour and dignity. I am thankful to Providence that, in the evening of my life, I have been allowed to see this hour of the nation's renewal of strength. I thank all those who, by unselfish devotion to the Fatherland, have co-operated with me in the reconstruction of Germany. My Chancellor, Adolf Hitler, and his movement have together led the German nation above all professional and class distinctions, to internal unity—a decided step of historical importance. I know that much remains to be done, and I desire with my whole heart that the act of reconciliation which embraces the entire German Fatherland may be the forerunner of the act of national exaltation and national co-operation.

I depart from my German people in the full hope that what I longed for in the year 1919, and which was coming slowly to fruition in January 1933, may mature to the complete fulfilment and perfection of the historical mission of our nation.

In this firm belief in the future of the Fatherland, I close my eyes in peace.

VON HINDENBURG

BERLIN, *May 11th,* 1934

There did not lack those who at once proclaimed the will a forgery, adducing in support of their contention the differences of literary style in the text and the fact that it was only produced on the eve of the referendum. There were those who said that the original text of the will had been mutilated, that certain passages had been added and certain excisions made. It was darkly hinted that a true copy, containing an abject apology from Hindenburg for having failed to restore the monarchy, had been smuggled out of Germany and was now in the hands of the Kaiser at Doorn; and another version of the same story declared that, in a covering letter to the Emperor, Hindenburg had stated that before he appointed Hitler Chancellor, he had received a definite promise that the monarchy would be restored. One Austrian paper even went so far as to say that the Kaiser was making use of his copy of the will in his financial negotiations with the *Reich.*

Amid this jungle of rumour and conjecture it is impossible to define the truth with any clarity. But from such evidence as has been produced and as a result of such researches as it has been possible to make, the writer has formed certain personal beliefs. To him it seems that the will, as published on August 15, is genuine. That it was kept back until its publication could prove of definite advantage in the referendum campaign is very probable, but there seems to be no reason so far produced for believing it a forgery.

The question of difference in style may be dismissed when one considers the composite authorship of Hindenburg's memoirs in 1919 and the fact that the Marshal was surrounded by a totally different circle in 1934. It is probable that the will also was of composite origin. Just as General von Mertz and another collab-

orated in the writing of the memoirs, so may Hindenburg's intimates have assisted him in drawing up his testament. It would
be very strange if they had not.

The date, too, is of importance. The will was signed by Hindenburg at Berlin in May 1934, before he left the Palace for
Neudeck for the last time. At that moment he had no reason to
be anything but satisfied with the results of his handiwork on
January 30, 1933. So far as he knew everything was progressing
swimmingly, and great care had been taken that he should continue to believe so. The disclosures made to him, first by Papen
and later by Hitler, only occurred after his arrival in Neudeck,
when it would have been difficult to prepare a new testament
even had he thought of doing so. The text as it stands has all the
hall-marks of that satisfaction which may well be credited to Hindenburg at the moment.

Of all the stories regarding suppressed codicils and covering
letters, most may be discounted as fiction and propaganda. That
which seems least fantastic is that a second document did accompany the testament and in it Hindenburg conveyed paternal injunctions to his successor. It is said that these were three in
number: to keep the *Reichswehr* above politics; to re-introduce
conscription; and to restore the monarchy. The first of these Hitler, despite outward appearances, has so far succeeded in doing;
the second he has done also. Time alone will show whether the
third injunction will be fulfilled and the Spectre of Spa be laid
for ever.

INDEX

484

peals to Kaiser, 50-52; proposed as Dictator, 53-54; conference at Posen, 57; dominated by associates, 60; 50th anniversary of entry into army, 62; refuses troop transfers from Eastern Front, 63-65; commands Eastern Front, 67-68; supported by Kaiser, 68-69; renewed conflict with Falkenhayn, 70-72; appointed Chief of General Staff of Army in Field, 72-74; problems of High Command, 75-81; "The Wooden Titan," 77-78, 93, 178; exercises Supreme War Command for the Central Powers, 80; disinclination for politics, 81; and Polish Kingdom, 84-86; and unrestricted submarine warfare, 86-92, 171; veneration for, 94-95; on Western Front, 96, 98; forces out Bethmann Hollweg, 99-104; approves Michaelis, 106; dictatorship by, 107-110; dominated by Ludendorff, 60, 63, 83-84, 110, 134-135; attitude toward Papal Peace Note, 112-114; opinion of Austrians, 122; annexationist policy, 123-131; Western offensive of March 1918, 131; memorandum to Kaiser, 137-139; demands dismissal of Valentini, 139-140; controls internal government, 141-142; on Western Front, 143-160; asks armistice, 161-169, 174; letter stating causes of German collapse, 166-167; views on peace conditions, 170, 172-177; offers resignation, 177-179; part played in Kaiser's abdication, 183-184, 186-187, 189-195, 198-205, 238; persuades Erzburger to lead Armistice Commission, 188-189; allegiance to Republic, 205-214; on Eastern Front, 1919, 214-215; avoids treaty responsibility, 218, 220; conflict of loyalties, 220-221; farewell proclamation, 222; homecoming, 223-225; memoirs, *Out of My Life*, 19, 226-228, 477-478; "War Criminal," 229-230; before Committee of Investigation, 231-238; in retirement, 242-244, 246; political agitation against, 247-248; asks Ludendorff to withdraw as Hitler candidate, 253; candidate for President, 256-264; divided loyal-

ties, 260; elected President (1925), 265-266; President, 267-352; dismisses Müller, 345; re-elected, and second term, 351-470; dismisses Gröner, 384; dismisses Brüning, 391-394; dismisses Schleicher, 430; meeting with Hitler, 408-410, 417-418; accepts Hitler as Chancellor, 425-426, 428-437; will of, 473-477

Hindenburg, Frau von, 16, 77, 224, 239-240, 441

Hindenburg, Oskar, vii, 277, 366-367, 450; intrigues with Schleicher, 295, 297, 300, 323, 329, 340, 372, 377; Neudeck and, 311-313, 360, 448; turns against Schleicher, 365, 427; his contacts with Papen, 419-421; and Nazis, 424-427, 432, 434

Hindenburg, Major Paul von, shot, viii, 4

Hindenburg, cruiser, 77, 225

Hindenburg Legend, ix, 7, 31, 33-34, 39, 44-46, 60, 76-77, 80, 94-95, 148, 159, 176, 210, 221-222, 280, 291, 372, 435, 438, 451

"Hindenburg Line" (*Siegfried Stellung*), 92-93, 95-97, 159

"Hindenburg Loans," 303-304

Hintze, Admiral von, 155-156, 158, 162, 182, 189-190, 192-193, 195, 198, 200-202, 204n, 240n

Hitler, Adolf, vii, 205, 228, 233, 242, 246, 253, 267, 283, 290-291, 320-321, 325, 330, 346, 348-350, 352-354, 359-363, 374, 377-378, 380, 383, 386, 398-399, 414-415; candidate for President, 367-371; is refused Chancellorship, 406-410, 417-418; becomes Chancellor, 426-437; foreign policy, 450, 455; executions, 461-467; régime, 435-478; head of State, 471-472; publishes Hindenburg's will, 473-477; *Mein Kampf*, 399

HLH, 35, 37, 42-76, 130, 136-137

Hoffmann, Lieutenant-Colonel, 11-12, 15-16, 25, 28, 35-36, 50, 52, 57-59, 71, 76, 86, 96, 172, 177, 182, 227, 243, 292, 294, 316, 389, 391; account of Samsonov and Rennenkampf, 19-21; credit for Tannenberg, 23, 26-29; diary, 40-41; proposed counter-offen-